"In this timely book, Birchall and Knight provide a much needed and nuanced account of Covid conspiracy theories. Combining both distant and close reading, they show what is new and what isn't, and make a compelling argument that these conspiracy theories are often rooted in legitimate concerns and social anxieties."

Michael Butter, *Professor of American Studies, University of Tübingen, Germany*

"This essential and timely book by two leading scholars simultaneously provides a wonderful synthesis of scholarship on conspiracy theory and an insightful and informed account of the theories surrounding Covid. It's a necessary corrective to simplistic assumptions about popular belief and disbelief and will remain relevant for decades."

Mark Fenster, *University of Florida, USA*

"A careful, nuanced overview of the way conspiracy theories help make—and unmake—the world we share, and how Covid-19 conspiracy theories have seamlessly become part of broader, much older narratives about power and control, freedom and paranoia."

Anna Merlan, *Author of* Republic of Lies: American Conspiracy Theorists and Their Surprising Rise to Power

CONSPIRACY THEORIES IN THE TIME OF COVID-19

Conspiracy Theories in the Time of Covid-19 provides a wide-ranging analysis of the emergence and development of conspiracy theories during the Covid-19 pandemic, with a focus on the US and the UK.

The book combines digital methods analysis of large datasets assembled from social media with politically and culturally contextualised close readings informed by cultural studies. In contrast to other studies which often have an alarmist take on the "infodemic," it places Covid-19 conspiracy theories in a longer historical perspective. It also argues against the tendency to view conspiracy theories as merely evidence of a fringe or pathological way of thinking. Instead, the starting assumption is that conspiracy theories, including Covid-19 conspiracy theories, often reflect genuine and legitimate concerns, even if their factual claims are wide of the mark. The authors examine the nature and origins of the conspiracy theories that have emerged; the identity and rationale of those drawn to Covid-19 conspiracism; how these conspiracy theories fit within the wider political, economic and technological landscape of the online information environment; and proposed interventions from social media platforms and regulatory agencies.

This book will appeal to anyone interested in conspiracy theories, misinformation, culture wars, social media and contemporary society.

Clare Birchall is Professor of Contemporary Culture at King's College London, UK. She is the author of *Knowledge Goes Pop: From Conspiracy Theory to Gossip*, *Shareveillance: The Dangers of Openly Sharing and Covertly Collecting Data*, and *Radical Secrecy: The Ends of Transparency in Datafied America*.

Peter Knight is Professor of American Studies at the University of Manchester, UK. He is the author of *Conspiracy Culture*, *The Kennedy Assassination*, and *Reading the Market*, and is co-author of *Invested*. He is the editor of *Conspiracy Nation* and *Conspiracy Theories in American History*, and the co-editor of *The Routledge Handbook of Conspiracy Theories*.

Conspiracy Theories
Series Editors: Peter Knight, *University of Manchester,* and
Michael Butter, *University of Tübingen.*

Conspiracy theories have a long history and exist in all modern societies. However, their visibility and significance are increasing today. Conspiracy theories can no longer be simply dismissed as the product of a pathological mind-set located on the political margins.

This series provides a nuanced and scholarly approach to this most contentious of subjects. It draws on a range of disciplinary perspectives including political science, sociology, history, media and cultural studies, area studies and behavioural sciences. Issues covered include the psychology of conspiracy theories, changes in conspiratorial thinking over time, the role of the Internet, regional and political variations and the social and political impact of conspiracy theories.

The series will include edited collections, single-authored monographs and short-form books.

Plots: Literary Form and Conspiracy Culture
Edited by Ben Carver, Dana Craciun and Todor Hristov

Thinking Critically About the Kennedy Assassination
Debunking the Myths and Conspiracy Theories
Michel Jacques Gagné

Conspiracy Theories in the Time of Covid-19
Clare Birchall and Peter Knight

Jews and Muslims in the White Supremacist Conspiratorial Imagination
Ron Hirschbein and Amin Asfari

Religious Dimensions of Conspiracy Theories
Comparing and Connecting Old and New Trends
Edited by Francesco Piraino, Marco Pasi and Egil Asprem

CONSPIRACY THEORIES IN THE TIME OF COVID-19

Clare Birchall and Peter Knight

Routledge
Taylor & Francis Group

LONDON AND NEW YORK

Cover image: © Getty Images

First published 2023
by Routledge
4 Park Square, Milton Park, Abingdon, Oxon OX14 4RN

and by Routledge
605 Third Avenue, New York, NY 10158

Routledge is an imprint of the Taylor & Francis Group, an informa business

© 2023 Clare Birchall and Peter Knight

British Library Cataloguing-in-Publication Data
A catalogue record for this book is available from the British Library

Library of Congress Cataloging-in-Publication Data
A catalog record has been requested for this book

ISBN: 978-1-032-32512-5 (hbk)
ISBN: 978-1-032-32499-9 (pbk)
ISBN: 978-1-003-31543-8 (ebk)

DOI: 10.4324/9781003315438

Typeset in Bembo
by Deanta Global Publishing Services, Chennai, India

CONTENTS

FIGURES

ACKNOWLEDGEMENTS

Although this book was written by the two of us, it is the result of a large conspiracy of fellow researchers. The underpinning research was supported by the Arts and Humanities Research Council as part of the UK Research and Innovation Covid-19 scheme, with the project "Infodemic: Combatting Covid-19 Conspiracy Theories" (grant number AH/V008706/1). We are very grateful for the time and resources provided by the grant and the wider support provided by the AHRC and the Pandemic and Beyond team at the University of Exeter. The Infodemic project involved collaboration with Liliana Bounegru and Jonathan Gray at King's College London; Emillie de Keulenaar, Marc Tuters and Fabio Votta at the University of Amsterdam; and Gabriele Colombo and Michele Mauri of DensityDesign Lab at Politecnico di Milano. Our research also drew on the energy and insights of the teams of stellar students involved in the data sprints organised by the Digital Methods Initiative at UvA and the Department of Digital Humanities at KCL, as well as our own classes at KCL and Manchester. We benefitted immensely from the commitment of our research assistants Sean O'Brien, James Woods and Cornelia Sheppard Dawson. Emily Harless provided impeccable assistance in compiling the final manuscript. The Infodemic project also involved a very fruitful collaboration with three external partners—Sense about Science, the Institute of Education and First Draft—and we are particularly indebted to the work of Tracey Brown, Alex Clegg, Nita Pillai and Josh Gascoyne (Sense about Science); Jeremy Hayward (Institute of Education); and Tommy Shane (First Draft).

Other researchers working on related projects generously shared ideas, datasets and papers with us, including Michael Butter, Chloe Colliver, Rod Dacombe, Daniël de Zeeuw, Rachel Gibson, Daniel Jurg, Andrew Kehoe, Ivan Kisjes, Alex Krosodomski Jones, Jo Fox, Sybille Lammes, Daniela Mahl, Eleni Maragkou, Boris Noordenbos, Ciaran O'Connor, Stijn Peeters, Jason Reifler, Mike Schäfer,

Colin Strong, Timothy Tangherlini and Jing Zeng. Thanks also to feedback from audiences at the presentations we've given at Policy@Manchester; the Institute for Government; Ecole Pratique des Hautes Etudes, Université PSL, Paris; Modern and Contemporary Cluster, Leiden University Centre for Arts in Society (LUCAS); Carl-Schurz-Haus, University of Freiburg; History & Policy, Institute of Historical Research; Ipsos-Mori; DialoguePerspectives (Leo Baeck Foundation); Spui25/University of Amsterdam; the UK Health Security Agency; the Conspiracy Games and Counter Games podcast; the Digital Methods Institute at University of Amsterdam; the International Communications Association Annual Conference; and the Institute for Philosophy at Bochum University. At Routledge, Craig Fowlie and Hannah Rich went above and beyond to see this book speedily into print. We are grateful to the University of Nebraska Press for allowing us to reuse portions of chapters 6 and 7 which appeared in an earlier form in Clare Birchall, "The Paranoid Style for Sale: Conspiracy Entrepreneurs, Marketplace Bots, and Surveillance Capitalism," *symplokē* 29, no. 1-2 (2021): 97-122.

Our respective departments and host organisations have also provided the intellectual environment and institutional support that made the completion of this book possible: the Department of English, KCL (C.B.); and the Department of English, American Studies and Creative Writing, University of Manchester, Leiden University Centre for Arts in Society, and the Netherlands Institute for Advanced Studies, which provided the perfect conditions for completing the book (P.K.). Finally, we are indebted to our families and friends who have patiently tolerated the time we have spent examining Covid-19 conspiracy theories, even while the pandemic swirled around us.

INTRODUCTION

Pandemic, Plandemic, Infodemic

In May 2020—just a few months into the Covid-19 pandemic—an online documentary about the disease went viral around the world. Within a week of its release, *Plandemic: The Hidden Agenda Behind Covid-19* had been viewed more than eight million times on YouTube, Facebook, Twitter and Instagram, and it was liked, commented or shared 2.5 million times on Facebook alone (Frenkel, Decker, and Alba 2021). Anticipating that it would be deplatformed, the makers and promoters of the film created a coordinated campaign of downloading and amplification on social media to ensure that it spread far and wide (Nazar and Pieters 2021). Even after it was removed by most of the mainstream social media platforms, it continued to circulate (Bellemare, Nicholson, and Ho 2020). In addition to its dedicated website, it appeared in closed groups on WhatsApp; dark platforms such as BitChute (where it racked up another 900,000 viewings) and BANNED.video, an offshoot of Infowars (another 800,000); as well as via clips on TikTok (Andrews 2020; Callison and Slobodian 2021; Cook et al. 2020; DFRLab, Kharazian, and Knight 2020). The 26-minute film makes a dizzying number of conspiracy theory claims: Bill Gates is using the pandemic in order to push vaccines; Big Pharma promotes unnecessary vaccines merely to make money; SARS-CoV-2 was created in the Fort Detrick and Wuhan labs; hydroxychloroquine is an effective treatment for Covid, and its use is being suppressed by the pharmaceutical industry to protect profits; having been vaccinated with the flu vaccine *increases* your chance of catching Covid; the number of Covid deaths in the pandemic is being exaggerated both to enrich hospitals and to mislead people; and wearing a mask gives you Covid, because it "literally activates your own virus." The film suggests that the pandemic was planned, and ultimately there is a vast medical conspiracy whose aim is to reduce individual liberty. (The hashtag "plandemic" was already circulating on Twitter, before the film chose it as a catchy title and it went viral (Kearney, Chiang, and Massey 2020)).

DOI: 10.4324/9781003315438-1

Although the *Plandemic* video gained considerable attention, it was just one of countless conspiracy stories about the Covid-19 pandemic that circulated widely on social media and which were subsequently reported in legacy media. The film spoke to a loyal following who sought alternative explanations for how the pandemic had started and who was to blame. But others found the viral spread of conspiracist misinformation about the disease on social media deeply alarming. While some conspiracy theories (such as the idea that the moon landings were a hoax or the earth is flat) have tended to be dismissed (or celebrated) as either merely harmless entertainment or the refuge of a fringe group of tinfoil-hat-wearing cranks, the conspiracist narratives that have circulated during the pandemic cannot be discounted so easily. Conspiracy talk is increasingly prominent in the public sphere and can be heard coming from figures that occupy a range of positions on the legitimacy spectrum (see Lewis 2021). A terrifying event of global proportions with profound consequences, the pandemic has coincided with the full flourishing of social media and its attendant "context collapse" through ease of sharing, as well as highly visible forms of populist distrust of expert knowledge, democratic institutions and the mainstream media—even if, as some studies have shown, the level of trust in science has increased on average in some countries (Mede and Schäfer 2021). This particular convergence of a global health, economic and political challenge, the technological and communicative affordances of social media, an epistemic crisis and populist distrust certainly looks like the perfect conditions for the rise of conspiracy theories. Some theories focus on the origins of the virus, especially the idea that it was the result of a bioweapon programme or the result of a covered-up lab leak; some concentrate on the supposed real mode of transmission (e.g., 5G or chemtrails); some fixate on imagined revelations of government or scientific cover-up concerning the progress and treatment of the disease (e.g., exaggerated numbers of dead, or dangers of vaccines); and some speculate on the imagined ultimate purpose behind the conspiracy (control of the masses, genocide or profit). Many conspiracy claims merge elements from all these theories.

The viral spread of conspiracy allegations in films such as *Plandemic* raises a number of important questions. One cluster of questions concerns the nature and origins of the conspiracy theories that have emerged. How popular are conspiracy interpretations of events? Which conspiracy rumours have gained most engagement and traction, and how have they mutated over the course of the pandemic? Where do these conspiracy theories come from? Are the conspiracy theories that have arisen completely new, or do they have longer histories? How do they compare with conspiracy theories in previous pandemics? How do conspiracy memes and narratives mutate as they spread from the margins to mainstream? A second set of questions considers the identity and rationale of those drawn to Covid-19 conspiracy theories. Who would believe in such seemingly far-fetched accusations? What does it mean to believe in a conspiracy theory, and what counts as a conspiracy theory anyway? Which clusters, communities and groups have been most significant? Are conspiracy theories the result of grassroots activism, or are they promoted from the top down by celebrities, politicians and other "superspreaders"? What role do online and offline community spaces and forms of activism play? Are Covid-19 conspiracy theories associated more with right-wing extremism or the alternative health movement? A third avenue of inquiry addresses how these conspiracy theories fit within the wider political, economic and technological landscape of the online information environment. How do the conspiracy theories that have emerged fit with the wider social and political climate in the UK and the US (the focus of this book)? What is the relationship between conspiracy theories and other related kinds of misinformation? Who creates conspiracy theory content, how does it spread and who consumes it? What role does monetisation play? Are social media platforms largely to blame for the mushrooming of conspiracy theories, misinformation and fake news? Which forms of social media and legacy media are the most significant vectors for the spread of conspiracism? Does each platform create its own distinctive conspiracy theory subcultures? And a final set of questions deals with proposed interventions. How have the social media companies and regulatory bodies responded? What can and should be done to combat Covid-19 conspiracy theories?

Although further research will be needed to answer some of these questions in detail (not least because the pandemic is still evolving), this book provides a provisional attempt to make sense of conspiracy in the time of Covid-19. During the pandemic, many researchers have addressed the prominence of conspiracy theories and other forms of mis- and disinformation, from academic disciplines such as cultural studies, sociology, political science, social psychology and data analytics, as well as think tanks and research organisations specialising in the online environment, including ISD Global, Graphika, First Draft and Hope Not Hate. While we have learned a great deal from the raft of empirical reports and research papers published on conspiracy theories during the pandemic, our approach in this book takes a somewhat different line to much of that research. In our view, that data-driven work often takes an overly alarmist position on the seemingly unstoppable spread of conspiracist mis- and disinformation (especially in the digital sphere). Although researchers have found considerable evidence of the correlation (if not exactly the causal connection) between conspiracy beliefs and harmful medical behaviours during the pandemic (e.g., Cuthbertson 2020; Freeman et al. 2020a; Imhoff and Lamberty 2020; Romer and Jamieson 2020; van Prooijen et al. 2021), at times the research still starts from the implicit assumption that conspiracy theories are a bizarre and fringe cognitive trait, even if psychologists have in recent years come to recognise that conspiracy thinking is comparatively normal (Butter and Knight 2016, 2020). In contrast, we start from a position that we are all, to some degree, "conspiracy theorists." We all entertain some unfounded, speculative narratives and fears about the way power and politics operate. Critical theory shares with conspiracy theories a reliance on what Paul Ricoeur termed the "hermeneutics of suspicion" (Sedgwick 2003; Ricoeur 2008; Felski 2015; Beckman 2022). In this book (as in our previous work) we have tried to avoid diagnosing or pathologising those who believe in conspiracy theories or engage in conspiracy talk, even as we reject—at the literal, factual level—the often far-fetched claims made in those conspiracist allegations. Indulging in what Noortje Marres calls the "politics of demarcation" (2018, 429) risks not giving adequate thought to how we can, as Marres puts it, "develop new strategies to secure a central role for knowledge in public life" (425). It also distracts us from examining the underlying causes of a turn to conspiracy thinking, especially in the midst of a global medical emergency. However, the pandemic, and the racially charged, politically polarised "culture wars" which have shaped its trajectory, have produced a more troubling edge to conspiracy narratives compared to those that entertained us in some previous eras. Those leaning to the right, that is, seem to have taken up much of the conspiracist air during Covid-19 (although, as we will show, recent conspiracism has also scrambled traditional vectors like right and left). Moreover, the stakes are that much higher during a pandemic in which the quality of information and knowledge can mean the difference between life and death.

Our starting assumption is that conspiracy theories, including Covid-19 conspiracy theories, often reflect genuine and legitimate concerns, even if their factual claims are wide of the mark or draw on troubling registers. The conspiracy theory that Covid-19 was created in a lab, for example, might point towards historical examples of states exercising power over their citizens' bodies, worries about the stockpiling and use of biological weapons, justifiable concerns about the lack of international oversight of biolab security or misgivings about controversial scientific activities such as gain-of-function research on potentially dangerous viruses. Likewise, 5G conspiracy theories might tap into the very real ways in which new technologies are enabling and legitimating invasive but quotidian forms of control and surveillance. And while any mention of a "cabal" or "global elite" can have disturbing antisemitic resonances, theories that fear such activity might also articulate suspicion of privilege and the myth of meritocracy, offering a Manichean narrative of class antagonism. As Alexander Galloway (developing Fredric Jameson's earlier remarks on conspiracy theories) puts it, "conspiracies are one of the few ways in which class and anti-capitalism—otherwise banned from mainline discourse—pierce through the ideological fog and imprint themselves directly on popular culture" (Galloway 2020). This is not to say the conspiracy theories are "right," but that they channel concerns about current and historical abuses of authority. Sometimes paranoia is a "rational"—if frustratingly misguided—response to uneven distributions of opportunity and power.

A Perfect Storm?

Many commentators have noted that the coronavirus pandemic seems to have produced a "perfect storm" of misinformation and conspiracy theories (Beaumont, Borger, and Boffey 2020; Doughton 2020; Schwalbe, Lehtimaki, and Gutierrez 2020). And we ourselves suggest something akin to this above.

But is this claim plausible? What is lost and what is gained in framing the pandemic in this way?

On one hand, the sceptical view sees disinformation and conspiracy theories as fairly constant over time, despite how they might seem in the midst of a global crisis. The political scientists Joseph Uscinski and Joseph Parent (2014) found that belief in conspiracy theories—as represented by letters to the editor in newspapers—has remained fairly constant throughout American history, with the only two significant surges of popular conspiracism occurring in the 1890s (with Populist attacks on big corporations) and the 1950s (with fears about communism). They argued that belief in conspiracy theories does not seem to have increased in any significant way with the coming of the internet, although their book was published in 2014, before the full flourishing of social media. Uscinski and others have even suggested that the internet should in theory curb the rise of conspiracy theories, because it makes easily and widely available the information needed for debunking the theories (Uscinski, Dewitt, and Atkinson 2018). Alternatively, the argument goes, conspiracy theories over time will tend to fade away online, because the "echo chamber" effect should mean that they remain confined within closed social groups, and do not spill out into the mainstream. The cultural historian Michael Butter (2020) who has examined conspiracy theories in a longer historical context notes that they might not be any more influential than in the past, even if they are now more visible. The reason for Butter's observation is that before the twentieth century interpreting historical events as the result of a conspiracy was a legitimate—even sophisticated—way of understanding the world. But as conspiracy theories came to be stigmatised as a form of knowledge (roughly after the rejection of McCarthyism in the US at the tail end of the 1950s), they became less influential in terms of mainstream politics, albeit more prominent in countercultural circles (Thalmann 2019).

There is a lot of sense in these warnings not to believe the hype that the internet has changed everything, which often underpin discussions about a supposedly unprecedented rise of conspiracism in the current pandemic. Conspiracy theories have a long and complex history in many societies, and there are no available metrics by which to easily compare whether conspiracism is more widespread or influential than in previous historical moments. Yet the coronavirus pandemic seems to have brought conspiracy theories to the forefront of public attention in a particularly striking way. At the very least, conspiracy theories are no longer quickly dismissed by academic researchers or media pundits as merely wacky, fringe beliefs of little consequence to society as a whole. (A handbook by Michael Butter and Peter Knight (2020) and an edited collection by Joseph Uscinski (see Butter and Knight 2018) demonstrate the vast range and rapidly expanding field of contemporary research on conspiracy theories.) Part of the reason is that the mainstream media has begun to take what is increasingly framed as the "problem" of online conspiracism seriously. We see this, for example, in the BBC's appointment of a specialist disinformation reporter, or the outpouring of newspaper and magazine articles during the pandemic on the dangers of conspiracy theories about Covid-19, or the many pieces giving advice on how to talk to loved ones who have gone down the rabbit hole of conspiracy belief, or the increasing focus on the responsibility of social media platforms to change their recommendation algorithms in order to stop fuelling conspiracism. These concerns have become increasingly common in recent years, although we need to remember there have been previous episodes of public anxiety about the spread of conspiracy theories—think, for example, of the alarm about the rise of white supremacist militias in the 1990s (Fenster 2008). Indeed, the popularisation of the very term "conspiracy theory" to describe a potentially harmful worldview can be traced to anxieties among sociologists in the 1950s and 1960s that the world was in danger of being again seduced by the kind of authoritarian populism that had led to the mass political hysteria and atrocities of the 1930s and 1940s (Thalmann 2019).

Although the prominence of conspiracy theories is not unprecedented, there are nevertheless good reasons to think that the coronavirus pandemic has created a perfect storm. It is the first truly global event that has taken place in the age of widespread social media. Previous epidemics, such as SARS and Ebola, were also accompanied by the viral spread of conspiracy theories online but were nowhere near as all-encompassing as the current pandemic. Likewise, the AIDS epidemic gave rise to a significant strand of conspiracy thinking that caused much harm (Nattrass 2013), but the theories spread more slowly, and less widely, and seldom in the full glare of public concern. Indeed, historians have shown how one of the main HIV/AIDS conspiracy theories—that the virus was a bioweapon created in a US Army lab—was initially spread as part of a Soviet and East German Cold War disinformation campaign (Selvage 2019, 71–123), with the first appearance of the narrative in a comparatively obscure pro-Soviet newspaper from India, and then painstakingly cultivated through a network of radio programs, journalists and pseudo-scientific studies. With the coronavirus pandemic, however, conspiracy theories have spread globally at great speed, even if they have also been adapted to fit local narratives.

If we go back further, we can find conspiracy theories routinely accompanying epidemics, and while they occurred without the communicative affordances of social media and the internet more broadly, they could often be found expressed in "legitimate" spheres prior to their stigmatisation in the 1950s (Thalmann 2019). As a precursor to fears that Covid-19 is some form of bioweapon, we might consider how lepers were accused of and persecuted for contaminating public water fountains and wells to target Christians in fourteenth-century France (Ginzberg 2017). And as a foretaste of the Sinophobic and subsequently antisemitic conspiracy theories circulating during the current pandemic, we could take into account how antisemitic rhetoric would rise in Europe during outbreaks of plague throughout history (Cooke 2009). Moreover, we can see contemporary pandemic-induced conspiracist fears as repeating another apparent "perfect storm": in vulnerable post-revolutionary 1790s America, an epidemic of yellow fever coincided with conspiracy theories about the Illuminati (Kaufman 2020).

Yellow fever epidemics recurred in the nineteenth-century Antebellum South and were also accompanied by conspiracy theories, but this time directly related to the disease. Disease denialism was rife in the 1850s, meaning that when the spread of yellow fever was not being blamed on "unacclimated" foreigners, it would be common to hear the argument that yellow fever was invented by abolitionists who were trying to undermine the "cotton kingdom." Such a vision expressed Southerners' fears of becoming a structural minority in the US (Olivarius 2021). Equally, during the influenza pandemic at the end of WW1, theories that it had been deliberately spread by Germany were commonplace. Crucially, such theories were to be found in respected outlets. On September 19, 1918, the *New York Times*, for example, quoted the head of the Health and Sanitation Section of the Emergency Fleet Corporation to have said, "It is quite possible that the epidemic was started by Huns sent ashore by boche submarine commanders" (see Givens 2020). We should also note, given the tense politics of vaccine mandates during Covid-19, the history of anti-vaccine discourse in the US. During the polio epidemic of the 1950s, the question of how best to roll out the vaccine became tied up with longstanding conservative pushback against compulsory national health insurance and public health, or what was dubbed "socialised medicine" (Lepore 2020). Recognising such historical precursors not only alerts us to the communicational contexts of any historical period, but also emphasises why Covid-19 conspiracy theories need to be seen as much in terms of continuity as rupture. If it is a "perfect storm," some of the elements in operation are not entirely new.

The pandemic has been marked by both a lack and a glut of information (Andrejevic 2013). On the one hand, and particularly in the early weeks and months when little was known about SARS-CoV-2, conspiracy theories and other forms of misinformation rushed in to fill the "data deficit" (Smith, Cubbon, and Wardle 2020) as many people around the world understandably sought to make sense of a deeply unnerving and rapidly evolving situation. On the other hand, the pandemic has also seen an overabundance of information, both accurate and unreliable. As we explore in more detail in chapter 2, at the outset of the pandemic the Director-General of the WHO warned about the dangers of an "infodemic" (Ghebreyesus 2020a), a torrent of conspiracy theories and other misinformation as dangerous as the virus itself. In addition to the well-meaning spread of misinformation and malicious spread of disinformation online, the information environment quickly became overloaded with scientific information, especially in the form of academic journal article pre-prints. Although a perfectly normal part of the regular process of peer review, during the pandemic these pre-prints—produced at a volume and velocity that is highly unusual—have often been picked up by journalists and social media influencers, quickly circulating provisional findings as major revelations to an audience often ill-equipped to interpret them. The flood of these sometimes contradictory reports has made conspiracy theories all the more appealing, because they cut through complex detail and offer a compelling, ready-made and overarching explanation.

Social media and other digital platforms as well as e-commerce sites have played a significant role in spreading conspiracist misinformation during the pandemic, and this is why our book places online conspiracism centre stage, even while we acknowledge that there has been plenty of communication and mobilisation beyond apps and screens. (However, we would also argue that because of smart phones and the internet of everything, there are few human endeavours we can unproblematically think of as offline today.) Some of the online conspiracist activity has been the result of bottom-up viral sharing, but a significant part has been led by influencers and those with a pre-existing network of followers, in some cases helped by an established network of right-wing funders—as appears to be the case with the *Plandemic* video, for example (Frenkel, Decker, and Alba 2020). However, we need to remember that social media is not the only way that mis- and disinformation spreads: research has shown that false narratives are still more likely to become dominant when they are promoted by politicians and celebrities (Benkler et al. 2020; Strong 2020), most often through more traditional forms of mass media such as television, with social media playing only a secondary role in amplification. Fox News can be as important as Facebook in spreading conspiracy theories and misinformation.

Leaving aside for the moment the question of whether social media is mainly to blame for the proliferation of conspiracy theories during the pandemic, we can point to other factors that have contributed to the perfect storm. The lack of transparency—at times wilfully misleading—on the part of the Chinese authorities (and, to a lesser extent, the WHO) meant that the outset of what was to become a global health crisis was shrouded in uncertainty and suspicion. This was not helped by President Trump's amplification of speculation that the CIA had intelligence that the virus was created in or escaped from the Wuhan Institute of Virology. (In chapter 3 we discuss the lab leak theory in more detail.) It is possible that the local or national authorities in China covered up their knowledge of the origins of the virus. While a report of an international panel of scientists convened by the WHO released in March 2021 concluded that a laboratory incident was "highly unlikely" (World Health Organisation 2020), President Biden instructed the US intelligence agencies to revisit the question in May 2021, but their report released in October 2021 was inconclusive (Barnes 2021). The lack of clear and transparent information in the crucial early weeks of the pandemic in 2020 meant that conspiracy theories inevitably flooded in to fill the data void. Health officials and politicians in both China and the West initially insisted that the outbreak was under control, and that it would not be as serious as the SARS epidemic in 2002–2004 that killed 773 people. Overconfident reassurances can quickly lead to an escalating distrust of all future pronouncements on the part of the authorities. The thinking goes: if they were so wrong about that, why should we trust them about anything else?

We also need to recognise that the virus itself led to an understandable sense of anxiety and, for some, perhaps paranoia. Even if the scales soon tipped back towards scepticism (discussions on social media about lockdown measures soon descended into a pile-on from those eager to trot out misleading and erroneous statistics about a disease that supposedly has a "99.9% survival rate"), in the early weeks of the epidemic many watched with increasing alarm as hospitals in Wuhan province and then northern Italy quickly became overwhelmed with the number of people requiring intensive care, just as the individual patients themselves had quickly been overwhelmed by a disease that leaves sufferers unable to breathe. The disease can be terrifying and, especially in the early days of the outbreak, confounded scientists trying to understand how it attacks the body's immune system. The response to the virus has also been frightening in many ways, leaving many people understandably afraid that their individual liberty has been curtailed and their livelihoods made precarious. The introduction of drastic lockdown measures has often confounded many people's common sense, especially in the early days of the pandemic when very few people personally knew anyone who was sick. Many have experienced a devastating sense of a loss of control over their lives, which, as psychologists have shown, is a common contributing factor in the turn to conspiracy theories (van Prooijen and Acker 2015). For conspiracy theorists, the public health measures introduced by many governments amounted to "confirmation" of all the warnings they had been making for years about the imminent institution of an oppressive regime of surveillance and curbs on individual freedom.

Although some of the conspiracy theories surrounding the coronavirus pandemic have been dismissed as crackpot, for the most part they speak to genuine questions and concerns. The policy choices involved in lockdowns and the rapid roll-out of a comparatively new and untested class of vaccines, for example, are cause for legitimate public debate. The problem with conspiracy theories, however, is that they make justifiable challenges to government decisions too easy to dismiss as irrational. Like many conspiracy theories, the ones surrounding the coronavirus pandemic often contain a kernel of truth, even if they go on to develop wildly exaggerated conclusions. As we explore in more detail in chapter 4, one of the most persistent and prominent conspiracy theories is the claim that Bill Gates is planning to use vaccinations to microchip and control the world's population (the details of the ultimate purpose of this evil plan tend to get a little hazy beyond this bare-bones summary). This notion might sound far-fetched—how can vaccines contain a microchip?!—but it has its roots in a genuine scientific project. The Gates Foundation asked researchers at Rice University in Texas to solve a problem often encountered by mass vaccination campaigns in developing nations, namely the difficulty of maintaining accurate records of immunisation among poor, rural (and sometimes nomadic) communities (McHugh et al. 2019). The solution proposed by the researchers was to deliver vaccines via a patch containing dissolvable microneedles that would leave a tiny readable, florescent trace beneath the skin that could be scanned by a mobile phone. This hi-tech solution to a problem that medical workers in the field commonly encounter has its own logistical and ethical dilemmas, but for those already convinced that globalist organisations are plotting to institute terrifying control of the world's population it rang alarm bells. Likewise, conspiracy theorists have latched onto accounts of pandemic preparedness exercises that took place before the outbreak of Covid-19, most notably Event 201, organised by Johns Hopkins Center for Health Security (in conjunction with the Gates Foundation and others) in October 2019. Although conspiracy theories regularly reinterpret coincidences as evidence of deliberate planning, the severity of the coronavirus pandemic has meant that these kinds of anticipatory events have been imbued with outsized significance. After all, the alternative situation is conceivably worse. What if scientists and health experts had never done any scenario-planning for the outbreak of a novel coronavirus, given that zoonotic transmission of diseases between species is becoming more common with the encroachment of humans on natural habitats, coupled with the increasing global interconnectedness enabled by mass air travel? (Less plausibly, conspiracy theorists also latched onto Dean Koontz's novel from 1981, *The Eyes of Darkness*, which contains some uncanny parallels with the current outbreak, including a passing reference to a viral bioweapon that is called, at least in the 1989 revised edition, Wuhan-400. Unlike the real-life SARS-CoV-2, the fictional virus has a mortality rate of 100%.)

To the casual observer, it can seem that the coronavirus pandemic has given spontaneous rise to a raft of new conspiracy theories—a veritable infodemic. But, as we will show in this book, the reality is that most of the building blocks of these conspiracy theories, and the communities that have promoted them, existed long before the outbreak of Covid-19. Conspiracy-minded fears about 5G and vaccines pre-date the pandemic, and they were adapted to fit the specific circumstances of the crisis (Bruns, Harrington, and Hurcombe 2020). Likewise, the pandemic has produced an intensification of existing trends within online conspiracism, rather than the explosion of a completely unprecedented fixation with conspiracy explanations in the digital realm. For example, as we show in chapter 6, prominent conspiracy theorists like Alex Jones already had a lucrative side-line in promoting snake-oil cures such as Miracle Mineral Solution and colloidal silver. Indeed, it appears that Jones only really began to make serious money from this conspiracy theory platform when he started selling these alternative health products. In a similar fashion, existing channels of disinformation (especially those promoting a pro-Kremlin agenda) have been of concern for a number of years. In effect, existing conspiracy theorists and promoters of misinformation have capitalised on the fear, information deficits and information overloads created by the pandemic to spread their ideas and their wares. Right-wing hate groups, for example, have taken advantage of the pandemic and the accompanying wave of interest in conspiracy narratives to recruit new followers to their cause (Colliver 2020; O'Connor 2021; Cendrovicz 2022). In this regard, the coronavirus crisis is less a perfect storm than a perfect opportunity for those who have long claimed to have worked out What Is Really Going On to reach new audiences.

As this book demonstrates, many conspiracy theorists have cynically jumped on the coronavirus bandwagon to promote their existing pet explanations to new recruits who are willing to entertain overarching narratives that promise to make sense of the global pandemic and the accompanying lockdown measures. In addition to conspiracy theories about globalist elites such as Bill Gates and George Soros supposedly planning mass control or even genocide (theories that are often antisemitic at heart), QAnon advocates have slotted the pandemic into their tale of an apocalyptic battle between the righteous patriots and the evil forces of the Deep State in cahoots with Satan-worshipping elitist paedophiles. The more the pandemic seems to be throwing society into chaos, the more QAnon supporters feel vindicated in their millenarian anticipation of a "Great Awakening" that will lead to the "Coming Storm" (Rothschild 2021). In a similar vein, conspiracy theorists have highlighted the idea of the Great Reset (a vaguely eco-themed road map of post-pandemic development goals outlined by the World Economic Forum in June 2020) as evidence that the pandemic had been planned all along by globalists as part of a sinister plot for depopulation—a conspiracy idea that itself has been around since the original Club of Rome think-tank discussions in the early 1970s of the perceived problem of planetary overpopulation. The coronavirus pandemic has necessitated a global response that inevitably involved globalist institutions such as the WHO (especially because of the lack of US leadership, not least with Trump's withdrawal of US funding from the organisation), at the same time as conjuring up understandable fears about "foreigners" as vectors of disease. Existing conspiracy-mongering about globalist institutions and invisible alien enemies has had much to feed on in the current crisis. Such conditions were only heightened by the US election in 2020 and Trump's "Stop the Steal" conspiracy campaign and the subsequent storming of the Capitol by his supporters on January 6, 2021. In short, the coronavirus pandemic has not caused a sudden, unanticipated rush of conspiracy theorising, but it has given an urgency and prominence to existing narratives that—in a process familiar to historians of conspiracy theories—have been adapted for new purposes.

It is becoming clear, however, that during the pandemic conspiracy thinking has spread considerably beyond existing conspiracy communities and channels. If the hope of some researchers was that conspiracy theories will tend to fade away on social media because they remain confined to restrictive echo chambers, the corona crisis has shown that conspiracy theories have gained far more visible mainstream attention, even if—as we explore in more detail in chapter 2—the percentage of committed believers is not significantly higher than pre-pandemic rates of conspiracy belief (Uscinski 2020). One reason is the simple fact that, with the widespread lockdowns, many people have had a lot of time on their hands. Without regular forms of in-person social interaction (that can tend to lessen the effects of online echo chambers), it has become more likely that people will spend time following threads online, which are at risk of turning ever more extreme in content. Especially in the early months of the pandemic, there were many anecdotal reports in the media of "ordinary" people coming across conspiracy theories and other forms of mis- and disinformation through neighbourhood WhatsApp and Facebook groups to an extent that had not happened before. More worryingly, the recommendation algorithms of platforms such as Facebook seem to have continued to nudge people towards more extreme pages and groups (Avaaz 2020a)—although other scholars dispute this (Lewis 2021). Of course, merely encountering a conspiracy narrative on social media does not mean that the recipient will inevitably believe it in any simple sense. But, as social psychology researchers have shown, repeatedly encountering false ideas—even when they are being debunked—makes it more likely that some people will end up believing them, or, at the very least, not discounting them (Fazio et al. 2015).

In the last couple of years, social media platforms—mainly in response to adverse publicity—have made some efforts to adjust their recommendation algorithms to dampen the promotion of harmful conspiracy theories (Faddoul et al. 2020). In response to mass shootings, some platforms (e.g., YouTube) had already begun in January 2019 to deplatform and/or demonetise some of the more extreme forms of conspiracism. The process of labelling and deplatforming potentially harmful materials, especially relating to health information, has quickened pace during the pandemic, along with the active promotion of medical information from authoritative sources. Although, as we discuss in more detail in the conclusion, the platforms have had some measure of success in these endeavours (at least according to the platforms' own reports), the viral proliferation of conspiracy theories and other forms of "problematic information" during the pandemic indicates that the issue is more pervasive than these optimistic reports suggest (Jack 2017). For example, although YouTube acted swiftly to deplatform the *Plandemic* video, it reappeared repeatedly on both YouTube and other less restrictive venues such as BitChute. Likewise, although YouTube made their recommendation algorithm less likely to promote conspiracist content, research has shown that people are coming to the content via direct links in Facebook posts, for example, rather than using the search or recommendation functions in YouTube.

One of the difficulties with social media research is the lack of transparency and independent verification by the platforms. Although researchers can use Facebook's own Crowdtangle tool to identify the most-engaged-with posts, there is no easy way to establish exactly what individual users encounter on their timelines. Crowdtangle has encountered staffing difficulties since 2021 and limited access to new researchers in January 2022 (Reuters 2022), seemingly in response to the negative publicity about the platform that research using the tool produced. Social media platforms have little to gain from opening their user data to the scrutiny of independent researchers of conspiracy theories. Even though during the pandemic the platforms went much further than before in content moderation and deplatforming, they still did not allow researchers unlimited and unrestricted access to their data. Because social media platforms are private companies which monetise the data they collect on users, there is much researchers cannot know about how conspiracy theories operate online. Some social media platforms make it possible for researchers to examine expression data (engagement such as retweeting or liking), but they do not grant access to impression data (who reads what, when) (see Pasquetto et al. 2020). As well as impression data, researchers of mis- and disinformation have called for randomised control trials, user demographics and other granular data. They have also called for private messaging apps to make aggregated, anonymised data available. In general, researchers want greater transparency and access as this is seen as "crucial to move research efforts from observational analyses to science- and data-driven policies" (Varol in Pasquetto et al. 2020).

What has made the information problem surrounding the pandemic far worse is the existing distrust of the mainstream media and scientific experts. A central component of recent conspiracy theories such as QAnon is not merely that there is a secret plot behind the contemporary events, but that the mainstream media is itself part of the cabal and needs to be actively rejected. The rise of populist political movements in the UK, the US and elsewhere in the last decade has been accompanied by a distrust of scientists, doctors and academics, driven in part by an understandable sense of resentment at the neglect of the working class by the governing technocratic elite (Frank 2020). Conspiracy theories often attract the cult of the amateur. They rely on ordinary people becoming convinced that their insights ("Do your own research!") are as valid as those of the experts, coupled with a naïve faith in the power of individual experience and visual observation ("Seeing is believing!") (see McKenzie-McHarg 2019). It is in this light that we can make some sense of episodes such as the #filmyourhospital craze accompanying the first lockdown (and subsequent lockdowns). People stuck at home and only able to access the world through online media became convinced that amateur video clips showing comparatively empty parking lots and hospital corridors gave the lie to the "official version" of events that spoke of intensive care units being overwhelmed. Many of the pieces of misinformation and conspiracy theories that spread virally in the early weeks of the pandemic on platforms such as WhatsApp shared similar narrative framing devices that emphasised the authentic, personal connection to the supposed revealed truth: "My cousin who is a nurse …"

Although trends such as the #filmyourhospital and "my cousin who is a nurse" narratives emphasised their rejection of authoritative sources of knowledge, one of the most significant reasons that conspiracy theories have proliferated in the pandemic—at least in the US—is the role of Trump as a superspreader of problematic information (Applebaum 2020). From the notion that the pandemic is a hoax to claims about the miracle curing properties of hydroxychloroquine and bleach, Trump fuelled the spread of conspiracism. Of course, Trump positioned himself as the mouthpiece of the ordinary citizen, often relying on circumlocutions such as "A lot of people are saying," as Russell Muirhead and Nancy L. Rosenblum point out (2019), to both avoid accountability and emphasise that he is in tune with the "truth" being revealed by lay people rather than experts such as Anthony Fauci, whom he repeatedly undermined. With an authoritarian populist promoter of false information such as Trump in charge, the pandemic could not have come at a worse time, with many of the president's supporters actively primed to discount both expert knowledge and the mainstream media, and willing to embrace an alternative reality in which the pandemic is a hoax and the election rigged.

Moreover, the increasing polarisation of politics (in both the US and the UK) has meant that a sizeable minority of people are willing to cling to dubious propaganda narratives because they bolster their firmly entrenched worldview and sense of identity (Benkler, Faris, and Roberts 2018). In this regard, polarising political events like Brexit, the Black Lives Matter protests and the US election have exacerbated the sense of people living in parallel realities, and conspiracy narratives have prominently accompanied all three. There are, of course, other political factors in the US and the UK that have made the pandemic worse than it might otherwise have been, from the inadequate and uneven provision of healthcare and welfare, to the incompetence, cronyism and corruption of the cabinet in the UK predicated on ideological commitment to the Brexit cause rather than talent. Coupled with the intensifying feedback loops of online echo chambers, the political atmosphere of extreme partisanship and failing infrastructure has made the so-called infodemic surrounding Covid-19 even more extreme.

Whilst the adaptation of existing conspiracy narratives to current events is not new, the coronavirus pandemic has produced a particularly pronounced convergence of different conspiracy communities. This has created a "conspiracy singularity" (Merlan 2020), a phenomenon which we examine in chapter 5. Divergent groups have rallied together under the broad banner of fears about the erosion of liberty and questioning of authority during the pandemic, including both evangelical, Trump-supporting, die-hard QAnon adherents and alt-right, antisemitic conspiracy theorists; both the New Age vaccine-hesitant and the more libertarian anti-vaxxers, along with those suspicious of Big Pharma; and both those quick to blame China for allegedly creating a bioweapon and those already convinced that new technologies like 5G are part of a concerted plot to turn humans into slaves. Their conflicting ideological positions and differing social backgrounds have created odd affiliations in the conspiracy milieu during the pandemic. As much as it has the potential to create echo chambers and filter bubbles, social media has also played a key role in bridging the gap between these various communities. It makes it easier to establish new connections and turn a loose collection of individually fringe beliefs into a sizeable minority who identify themselves as challenging received wisdom and the status quo. They find vindication in seeing themselves as part of a larger collective, even if they disagree with the specific content of some of the beliefs. Although (as we document in chapter 2) the results are often conflicted, a slew of opinion polls indicate that roughly a quarter of people in the US and the UK share conspiracy-infused beliefs about the virus and the public health response to it (Schaeffer 2020).

Conspiracy theories often emerge out of an existing, all-encompassing worldview, rather than a single piece of misinformation that can be easily corrected through fact-checking and debunking. They often provide an elaborate post-facto justification for a belief that advocates already hold or a behaviour they have already engaged in (for evidence of the post-facto nature of conspiracism, see van Prooijen et al. 2021). The pandemic itself "confirms" existing narrative about a massive plan to curb individual freedoms. Subsequent, unrelated events (such as the supposed rigging of the US presidential election in 2020) likewise provide "confirmation" for existing conspiracy theories, reinforcing the conviction that what we are witnessing is not an unfortunate mix of natural and manmade problems but a vast, concerted plan to remove our liberties. Most conspiracy thinking does not create brand-new theories, but instead assembles speculations out of existing narratives, images and fears. People who already view the world through the lens of a conspiracy theory quickly interpret current events as a part of that conspiracy. With QAnon and other conspiracy theories relying on an apocalyptic narrative that the world as we know it is in danger of imminent collapse, the imposition of severe restrictions on personal freedoms "proves" the prophecies about a "Coming Storm," while supposed revelations about election fraud in turn "prove" that Covid-19 is a "plandemic." Conversely, those who oppose lockdowns and mask-wearing can easily be drawn into the realm of conspiracy theories that then provide an all-encompassing justification for a stance that might otherwise seem merely selfish or ornery.

We need to be careful, then, not to utter dire warnings about the pandemic having created an unprecedented explosion of conspiracy thinking, especially on social media. But we can nevertheless recognise that there has been a coming together of various technological, political and social factors that have contributed to something resembling a perfect storm of conspiracy theory and misinformation.

Conspiracy Theories and Conspiracy Theorists

We use the terms "conspiracy theory" and "conspiracy theorist" in this book, but we recognise that they are highly contested terms that often raise more questions than they answer. There is now a substantial body of research on these terms exploring their historical precursors and etymological roots, the pejorative connotations they hold and the way they are mobilised in ideological and normative ways (Bratich 2008; Thalmann 2019). Even if there are good reasons to be cautious about using the terms, they are nonetheless widely used in both popular and academic writing. Conspiracy theories provide alternative explanations of significant happenings like wars, assassinations and plagues, and are usually presented in opposition to received wisdom. In some countries and regimes, however, they are the official version of events. Conspiracy theories usually start from visible effects in the present, and construct a story based on the conviction that someone deliberately planned to bring those events about. Conspiracy theories usually start from three fundamental assumptions: nothing is as it seems; nothing happens by accident; and everything is connected (Barkun 2013). Conspiracy theories insist that there are no accidents or coincidences in history. They ask, "who benefits?," and work backwards to identify the conspirators who must therefore have planned everything. If the coronavirus pandemic is likely to lead to some pharmaceutical companies making big profits by selling vaccines, for example, the logic is that they must have planned it in advance.

Conspiracy theorists tend to think of themselves as bravely going against received wisdom. Although believers in conspiracy theories usually see themselves as savvy and cynical, immune to the duplicity of the authorities and the mainstream media (unlike the rest of us "sheeple"), they are often oddly naïve in believing that there is a secret evil mastermind controlling everything. Conspiracy theories often (but not always) are populist in outlook, seeing history as a struggle between the innocent people and the corrupt elites, by-passing the usual structures of party politics. In general, they divide the world into a battle between good and evil, insiders and outsiders, Us vs Them, finding convenient scapegoats to blame for complex problems. In some cases, conspiracy theories serve to forge a sense of community: QAnon believers can resemble a cult at times, for example, and particular online conspiracy spaces can generate a powerful sense of being one of the enlightened few who are in-the-know. However, that sense of community and identity is constructed by blaming other groups for social ills. In more extreme versions, the conspirators are portrayed as evil and subhuman, who will stop at nothing to achieve their devilish plans. Conspiracy theories are thus frequently apocalyptic in tone, insisting urgently that the future of the nation or the liberty of the people hangs by a thread. Especially in the US context, they often draw on modes of "magical thinking" that are rooted in evangelical traditions of thought (Oliver and Wood 2018). As Michael Butter (2014) has demonstrated, conspiracy theories usually operate through a mixture of deflection (identifying genuine issues, but blame is deflected onto the wrong people) and distortion (latching onto the right group to blame, but the reasons are distorted).

Conspiracy theories operate as a distinct kind of knowledge, which are often closely related—but cannot be simply reduced—to misinformation (unwittingly false information), disinformation (knowingly false information) and fake news (false information produced to maximise clicks for profit). In their study of anti-vaccination discourse, for example, a report by First Draft found that conspiracy theory makes up only 29% of the vaccine hesitancy discourse in English-language online spaces, although it is 59% in French ones (Smith, Cubbon, and Wardle 2020). In a similar vein, Islam et al. (2020) found that in their dataset of "Covid-19 infodemic in 25 languages from 87 countries" 89% of the reports were classified as rumours, 7.8% were conspiracy theories and 3.5% involved cases of stigma. A team of researchers at Cornell University found that just under 3% of media coverage of Covid-19 mentioned misinformation and while almost half of this constituted what they classed as "misinformation/conspiracy based topics," the largest category of this subset was not a conspiracy theory at all, but talk about "miracle cures" (Evanega et al. 2020). Conspiracy theories might have attracted considerable media attention, but they usually make up a comparatively small part of misinformation, which in turn only forms a minor component of the overall mediascape. However, conspiracy theories may well have an outsize influence precisely because they provide a particularly appealing and intractable kind of misinformation.

Conspiracy theories are often accused of simplifying complex events. While it is true that they do tend to create simplistic overarching explanations, conspiracy theories often end up constructing phenomenally complicated accounts that are rich in detail. One reason is that they often start from the assumption that everything is connected: even seemingly unconnected events and people are all part of a fiendishly convoluted plot. Unlike scientific theories, conspiracy theories are usually unfalsifiable. If you try and debunk them by pointing to the lack of credible supporting evidence, the conspiracy theorist will often claim that the lack of evidence is proof in itself: the conspiracy is so all-powerful, the argument goes, that they have managed to cover up any trace of their existence. If people in the media, government or science seem to have evidence that undermines the theory, then they must be shills for the conspiracy. In this way, conspiracy theories become ever more elaborate, relentlessly incorporating any conflicting evidence into an ever-larger plot, even if the fundamental story arc is depressingly simplistic and repetitive. For this reason, it can be frustrating to argue against conspiracy theorists, but at times there is considerable ingenuity in providing an answer to any conceivable objection. Making the situation worse, conspiracy theorists often create a circular trail of reference: when you follow up their obsessive footnotes and links, you quite often find they refer to other conspiracy theorists, who in turn refer to others, and so on in a circle of citation that creates a veneer of credibility. What makes the situation more problematic now is that conspiracy theories often suggest that traditional sources and institutions of authoritative information—professional journalism, the law, the civil service, governing officials, science—are all part of the conspiracy. There is an increasing knee-jerk response to delegitimise all forms of expertise as corrupt and self-serving. In this situation, there is diminishing hope that appealing to facts and experts will cut any ice with a committed conspiracy theorist.

Arguing against conspiracy theorists is difficult not just because of the unfalsifiability of their views. It is also because, in many cases, their beliefs are expressions of a deeply held worldview. In the same way that people with a strong religious commitment often turn to theological arguments to help rationalise their emotional investment in their faith, so too do conspiracy theories serve to justify strong feelings of resentment and injustice. Although for many people flirting with conspiracy theories is no more than idle speculation or cynical provocation, for some committed believers a conspiracist mindset is tied up with their life history and sense of identity. Many QAnon and alt-right conspiracy believers, for example, talk about "red pilling," the moment when they came to feel that everything the mainstream media are telling them is a lie. Changing your mind about a conspiracy theory is therefore not simply a matter of revising your opinion about a set of disputed facts in the light of new evidence. It might mean unravelling your sense of who you are and how the world works.

Although conspiracy theories are woven into believers' worldview and sense of self, they are also increasingly positions to be adopted and discarded in a strategic, ironic or even nihilistic fashion. As we have noted in our previous work (Knight 2000), there has been a postmodern turn in conspiracy culture since at least the late 1960s, with conspiracy theories becoming the stuff of popular entertainment as much as serious politics. However, this postmodern turn to commodified, ludic and ironic forms of conspiracism has quickened pace in the last decade, most emblematically with the rise of QAnon. Conspiracy theories now increasingly operate in a gamified mode, treating the emerging revelations of the imagined conspiracy as a media spectacle that is both more real than the everyday world of fake appearances and yet at the same time entirely constructed, as if we are all living in *The Truman Show* or *The Matrix*. Along with "Do Your Own Research!" the repeated refrain of QAnon and other conspiracy theories during the pandemic has been "Buckle Up and Enjoy the Show!"

Big Data and Close Reading

In this book, we combine approaches from cultural studies and digital methods. Our aim has been to bring together the detailed perspective afforded by close reading with the bird's-eye view enabled by big data. Cultural studies has a lot to offer when it comes to making sense of the Covid-19 pandemic and the conspiracy theories and other forms of "problematic information" (Jack 2017) that have attended it. Cultural studies is inherently interdisciplinary. It draws on history, politics, economics; it encompasses attention to production and consumption, to institutions, media and discourses that shape realities and to those acts of meaning-making that we all engage in; it is a theoretical magpie, turning to concepts from all kinds of academic fields to make sense of culture understood as both "a whole way of life" and also as the signifying forms that circulate in a society (Williams 1958). However, much of the most prominent (if not necessarily the most influential) forms of conspiracism during the pandemic have emerged from the online environment, at least in the early stages of the pandemic before anti-lockdown movements mobilised for rallies. This new conspiracy climate cannot be divorced from the economy and ecology of digital media. To contextualise online conspiracy theories means looking at the online world in two ways. First, we need to consider the political economy and the business models of digital platforms: to take on board "platform capitalism" (Srnicek 2017), "surveillance capitalism" (Zuboff 2019) and the "ecology of attention" (Citton 2017). And second, we need to address the affordances for world-building, storytelling, networking and mobilising, but also scaremongering, amplifying and commodifying that are offered by different mainstream social media platforms as well as spaces characteristic of the deep vernacular web.

With this focus on cultural and digital politics, we are not seeking to apportion "blame" for Covid-19 conspiracy theories, an approach that would risk replicating the alarmist rhetoric that many journalists have adopted. Rather, this book offers an account that does justice to the complexity of the phenomena. We contextualise Covid-19 conspiracy theories not only in a history of conspiracy narratives, but also within the wider social, political, technological and economic conditions that have made conspiracy theorising a viable mode of interpretation and popular knowledge for so many during the pandemic. We consider what is thoroughly novel about Covid-19 conspiracy theories as well as what extends, repeats or draws on other conspiracy fantasies and alternative cosmologies.

The research for this book involved scholars from cultural studies and digital methods. Our aim was to combine the "telescopic" capabilities of data analytics with the "microscopic" lens of discourse analysis and digital ethnography (Kozinets 2019). In effect, we followed a "data hermeneutics" approach (Gerbaudo 2016; Romele, Severo, and Furia 2020) in order to engage with the interactive and multimedia nature of contemporary digital culture. Although "distant reading" methods of data analytics are increasingly employed in the social sciences, they often marginalise issues of cultural meaning and collective identity when analysing the dynamics of social media conversations (Tinati et al. 2014; Tufekci 2014). Conversely, traditional forms of close reading hermeneutics (Felski 2015) are unable to cope with the sheer volume and variety of social media. Moreover, without a digital ethnographic understanding of the community norms, cultural meanings and technological affordances of each platform, it can be hard to make sense of individual social media posts (Hine 2017; Kozinets 2019). In contrast, a data hermeneutics approach allows for targeted qualitative sampling procedures to create manageable social media datasets. These can then permit "close data reading" (Gerbaudo 2016) techniques that place individual social media texts within a framework of both ongoing online conversations and the wider discourses, narratives and worldviews which give conspiracy talk its meaning.

As soon as it became clear that the outbreak of a new disease in China would become a global pandemic, we began to collect datasets of conspiracy theories on social media relating to Covid-19, while also immersing ourselves in coronavirus-related conspiracy culture in other media (for more technical details on the datasets, see the Appendix). We confined the study to English-language materials, with a focus on the US and UK.[1] To produce manageable datasets for close reading, we used a variety of strategies, including top sampling (collecting the most-engaged-with posts, hashtags, keywords and/or posters per platform and/or group/channel on a particular topic); random sampling (taking a random slice through an assembled dataset to create a representative sample of a conversation or topic discussion); and zoom-in sampling (focusing on a particular point in an online conversation that is particularly significant, identified for example by a spike in engagement metrics). With help from our research assistants, we then conducted manual cleaning and coding of the datasets to remove false positives, identify significant recurring themes and group the data into categories. Using a seed list of hashtags and keywords, we created datasets of the most-engaged-with Covid-19 conspiracy theory content for each of the main platforms (Facebook,

YouTube, Instagram, Twitter and TikTok), divided into quarterly intervals from January 2020 to March 2021. We also conducted some separate investigations of other online spaces (e.g., the recommendation algorithm and comment function of Amazon), which are less often seen as hotbeds of conspiracism. The content was scraped mainly using existing tools such as 4CAT (developed by the Digital Methods Initiative at the University of Amsterdam), and the Crowdtangle tool provided by Facebook, as well as custom tools the team developed for gathering visual memes from Instagram, for example. In addition to close reading the top-performing posts in each quarter on each platform, we also zoomed in to individual channels, discussion threads and posts to get a richer sense of how these conversations emerge and develop in the online environments. We also used various social network analytical and visualisation tools to help make sense of trends and patterns in the datasets (which chapter 5 discusses in more detail). To augment our own data research, we also draw extensively on that conducted by others. In sum, our goal was to trace the development of conspiracy narratives and communities during the early phase of the pandemic, to understand the particular historical and political context out of which this conspiracy talk emerged and which it spoke back to and to identify the distinctive mechanisms and features of conspiracy in the time of Covid-19, drawing on our knowledge of the longer history of popular conspiracy culture.

The Hidden Agenda

Like an artist that returns to the same subject from different angles, this book visits and revisits Covid-19 conspiracy theories, covering new ground each time. It begins by addressing discursive frames before moving on to examine contextual political factors. It then offers an account of the different theories and their digital journeys followed by a list of some shared characteristics. The last third of the book examines questions concerning commodification before evaluating the various strategies that are advocated to curb conspiracy theories.

Because we believe that conspiracy theories are deeply tied to the historical moment in which they appear, that they are shaped by policies, institutions, discourses and political and economic forces, the first chapter offers a number of different threads and contexts that need to be taken into account when approaching contemporary conspiracy theories, including those that circulated during the Covid-19 pandemic. There has been a spate of radio documentaries and podcasts that look back to find events that "broke truth" (Lepore 2020), defined the parameters of the culture wars (Ronson 2021), and led to the storming of the US Capitol on January 6, 2021 (Gatehouse 2021). They offer convincing prehistories of post-truth. This chapter does not offer such confident narratives of influence or origins, but rather contextual factors that produced conditions ripe for distrust and disinformation to take hold when Covid-19 hit.

We look, therefore, at decades-long declining levels of trust in government, institutions and experts, not to berate individuals for losing that trust, but to ask what radical shifts must take place to produce institutions worthy of trust. We also chart the decimation of the welfare state which has made it easier for people to imagine the state as a shadowy operator that does not act in their best interests rather than a safety net for times of trouble. We consider the financial crisis of 2007–08 and rising income inequality to consider how feelings of grievance are no longer assuaged by the myth of meritocracy. This is closely tied to the rise of different kinds of populism and a turn to ethno-nationalism, as well as how these are mobilised within polarising culture wars. The current pandemic and its attendant conspiracy theories cannot be understood outside of a history of dis-information campaigns as well as the digital ecology through which they spread. Together these concerns foreground the necessity of thinking historically and contextually to understand Covid-19 conspiracism. If conspiracy theories are, in part at least, social symptoms, it is crucial to understand the conjuncture in all its historical, economic, political, cultural, discursive and technological aspects.

The second chapter considers two different ways in which Covid-19 conspir-acy theories have been framed as an issue of concern. This involves considering the metaphor of the "infodemic" that the WHO and others around the globe adopted to describe the mis- and disinformation that accompanied the pandemic and how that mis- and disinformation made the task of tackling the pandemic harder. We look not only at whether the mis- and disinformation circulat-ing was, in fact, comparable in scale to the pandemic in the way that the term "infodemic" might suggest, but also at whether this metaphor accurately cap-tures what is at stake. We ask whether viral metaphors in general are appropri-ate for thinking about how mis- and disinformation operates and question the suggestion that people are passive dupes unwittingly receiving a "virus." Such language, of course, has all kinds of implications when it comes to suggested remedies and interventions. For example, several initiatives have tried to "inoc-ulate" users against misinformation and disinformation, including conspiracy theories. Alongside this key framing metaphor, chapter 2 evaluates the many dif-ferent polls that have been conducted to demonstrate levels of belief in Covid-19 conspiracy theories. Polls might offer percentages as though they are raw data, but we unpack how such data are always already "cooked" in various ways. We argue that, in focusing on the question of belief, some polls miss what might be most important about Covid-19 conspiracy theories: that there is a proportion of the population that simply does not know whether something is true or not, but which is willing to entertain conspiracist explanations; that some people con-sider a conspiracy theory to be as plausible as any other explanation. We begin here to clear the way for the alternative frames we offer throughout this book.

If the first two chapters are interested in the events, tensions, materialities, technologies, histories and framing narratives that shape contemporary conspir-acism—the deep contexts and explanatory models that help us to understand the turn to and narrative tropes of conspiracy theories—chapters 3 and 4 tell a more recent story. Split across two chapters, we examine just over a year of Covid-19 conspiracy theories (beginning February 2020). Chapter 3 opens by detailing how a theory that Covid-19 was either leaked accidentally from a lab or developed as a bioweapon and deliberately released evolved over time. The chapter makes it clear that the claims were not only being made in online forums or on social media, but also by state actors within a tradition of Cold War disinformation campaigns and/or grandstanding. As the label "conspiracy theory" is never neutral, and verified knowledge about the pandemic is constantly shifting according to new scientific research or intelligence, the story we tell in these two chapters is complex. The "lab leak theory," first mooted in early 2020, for example, returns as a more legitimate or plausible explanation in 2021. We spend some time in chapter 3, then, exploring this case as a way to think through the definition of "conspiracy theory" and to insist that the line between conspiracy theory and plausible conjecture is not always clear, particularly when faced with a novel virus about which there is still much to learn.

Chapter 3 continues by looking at the conspiracist signalling of the Trump administration regarding Covid-19 and, subsequently, how the suggestion that Covid-19 was a hoax inflected the online expressions of his supporters through grassroots campaigns such as "#filmyourhospital." Crucial to any understanding of the trajectory of Covid-19 conspiracy theories is how the QAnon movement responded to and engaged with the pandemic. This is equally true of extremist groups who used Covid-19 conspiracy theories to recruit followers. Whereas chapter 3 largely considers theories that downplay the threat of Covid-19, fashioning it as some form of hoax orchestrated for international or domestic political advantage, the examples of conspiracy theory we look at in chapter 4 begin from the assumption that Covid-19 is dangerous and either the virus or the vaccine is being used by nefarious factions. We close chapter 4 by considering a number of "superconspiracy theories" that incorporate elements from conspiracy theories recounted in chapters 3 and 4 (Barkun 2013).

In chapter 5, we move away from this linear story to analyse what we consider to be the key characteristics of Covid-19 conspiracy theories. Some of these predate Covid-19, but what we see is an intensification of certain features or processes during the pandemic. Our intention is to build a picture of how conspiracy theory, understood as a distinct discourse, has operated and adapted during the crisis. What, if anything, is new about Covid-19 conspiracy theories? Some of these features concern the form and content of the conspiracy theories and some relate more to their social function. Looking at the former, for example, we consider how several conspiracy narratives have converged around the Covid story; how ready-made conspiracy narratives are assembled in a modular way; how pre-existing conspiracy narratives, like QAnon, incorporated Covid-19; and how superconspiracies that try to explain everything have become prominent. In terms of social function, we consider how we might read Covid-19 conspiracy theories symptomatically; how they are enmeshed in the contemporary information ecosystem, distributed across different nodes; and how some online Covid-19 theories have mobilised people to take real-world action. We also look at the appeal of Covid-19 conspiracy theories to ethnic minorities and women as well as the role that celebrities and superspreaders play in the proliferation of theories. In addition, we examine how various agitators and extremist groups have opportunistically used Covid-19 conspiracy theories to recruit new supporters and how lockdown protests have brought together unlikely bedfellows.

These features and contexts are an important part of the picture, but we also need to take into account how conspiracy theories are monetised today. In chapter 6, therefore, we turn to the methods that conspiracy entrepreneurs, such as Alex Jones, employ to convert conspiracism into cash. These include selling merchandise, setting up subscriptions to platforms, charging for public speaking and establishing crowdfunding sites. No account of this monetised sphere would be complete, however, without a consideration of online marketplaces and social media platforms and the ways that they themselves profit from Covid-19 conspiracy theories. We begin by looking at the appearance of conspiracist goods and comments on Amazon in this chapter but concentrate more fully on how the infrastructural design and exploitation of user data by social media platforms render conspiracism profitable in chapter 7.

This final chapter, then, looks at platform affordances that enable the rapid sharing of less than credible content as well as the amplification effect of algorithmic curation and how the latter supports, by Facebook's own admission, "divisiveness." Surveillance capitalism, understood as an economic model based on the extraction and monetisation of user data (Zuboff 2019), means that all engagement, including engagement around Covid-19 conspiracy theories on social media sites, is valuable to the host platforms. We adapt this formulation to posit "disinformation capitalism"—to map out the content-agnostic monetisation techniques that help platforms to retain user attention and accumulate their data. This chapter finishes, however, by considering what kinds of infrastructural-level challenges would be needed to interrupt disinformation capitalism and, moreover, what we might miss about the pleasures and rewards of online conspiracism, and digital sociality more generally, when we decry surveillance capitalism.

These pleasures and rewards—these affective investments and identity formations—play a large part in why existing strategies for combatting Covid-19 conspiracy theories might not work. In the conclusion, we argue that conspiracy theories are a sui generis category of mis- and disinformation and, as such, need to be treated differently. We evaluate fact-checking, deplatforming and digital literacy before pointing towards ten factors that our research has told us need to be taken into account when devising an intervention. These factors have informed the writing of this book: including understanding what conspiracism might offer to some people; taking into account the political, technological and historical context in which conspiracy theories arise and transform; and getting to grips with the aesthetic features of conspiracism understood as a dynamic and adaptive discourse. We end by questioning the efficacy of any quick technological fix and emphasise that structural changes are needed, in terms of both technological infrastructure and socio-political organisation.

Breathing Together

The Latin root of conspiracy is *conspirare*: to breathe together. It reminds us of the intimacy, trust and understanding necessary for an actual conspiratorial group to succeed. With a highly contagious, sometimes fatal, respiratory disease circulating in our communities, it is not only legally dubious to breathe together in ways that conspiracies necessitate, but can also be physically dangerous. Breathing together is the last thing anyone should do during a Covid-19 outbreak. Turning to acts of sharing conspiracy *theories* rather than plots to conspire, the internet in general and social media in particular have allowed people who might otherwise have remained lone, marginalised voices to find and breathe with (at least remotely) fellow sceptics of consensus reality. They use the language of likes, shares, retweets, posts, memes, videos, comments and blogs, giving oxygen to ideas that might, in pre-internet eras, have died out.

Under conditions that nobody could have wished for, Covid-19 produced an extraordinarily potent "stress test," a convergence of economic, health and political crises, for us to consider the astonishing hold conspiracy theories can have on the popular (and often populist) imagination.

Note

1 There continues to be a lack of big data research on the spread of conspiracist misinformation in languages other than English. There have been some comparative studies of the anti-vaccination narratives on social media in a number of European languages for example (Avaaz 2020a), but these are few and far between, and rarely include non-European case studies (Mahl, Schäfer, and Zeng 2022). The major social media platforms based in the US have put considerable effort into deplatforming potentially harmful anti-vaccination conspiracy theories in English, but they have failed to address the problem in other languages such as Arabic (O'Connor and Ayad 2021).

1

DEEP BACKGROUND

The Contexts of Conspiracy Theory

The pandemic seems to have created a particularly potent set of conditions for conspiracism to flourish. As we noted in the introduction, some commentators have declared it "a perfect storm" for conspiracy theories and theorists. Though there is some validity to this claim, it risks seeing the current situation as an unprecedented "infodemic," a view that contributes to a moral panic about a crisis of truth created by social media. Focusing only on the present conditions for a "perfect storm" also obscures the deeper currents, which feed into the epistemic and political moment, and lend themselves to conspiracist thinking. Indeed, it is important to situate the so-called infodemic that accompanied Covid-19 within other, slower crises that concern attacks on equality, social democracy, the welfare state, democratic institutions and expertise. It is also necessary to contextualise conspiracy theories within the wider ecology and economics of digital media to understand the relationship between forms of mediation and content.

Conspiracy theorising, albeit in different guises, is a historical constant. What we now term "conspiracy theory" (in English) has a long and varied history, from the political culture of ancient Greece and Rome (Roisman 2006; Pagán 2008) to the rise of antisemitism and state security fears in the Early Modern period (Zwierlein 2013), and from the countersubversive imagination in Europe and the US in the eighteenth and nineteenth centuries (Davis 1971; Boltanski 2014) to the rise of populist demagoguery and countercultural dissent in the twentieth century (Fenster 2008; Gray 2010; Olmsted 2008; Borenstein 2019). Nevertheless, conspiracy theories are shaped by the particular political, social, technological and epistemic moments in which they arise. They sometimes reflect and sometimes refract the anxieties of each era. In this chapter we will examine different historical forces that help to situate feelings of grievance,

DOI: 10.4324/9781003315438-2

disaffection and disenfranchisement, which in turn produce sympathy for populist movements and conspiracist explanations. It is important to note that there is nothing inevitable about this drift towards conspiracism; some of the same factors described in this chapter have given rise to feelings that have fuelled racial justice movements and protests attacking systemic and structural oppression during the pandemic, for example. Such contingency means that we are not listing a set of causally determining factors, but rather, analysing the context—the "deep background," as it were—that has shaped the parameters and possibilities of contemporary conspiracy theories.

Trust in Government, Institutions and Experts

Research demonstrates a general correlation between low levels of trust in government and a reliance on conspiracy thinking (see Smallpage et al. 2020, 273). This is important to note given that Pew Research (2019), for example, has found a steady decline in trust in government in the US since it began polling about this issue in 1958. In that first year, 73% of Americans said that they can trust the government in Washington to do what is right "just about always" or "most of the time." In 2019, the figure was just 17%. In a more finely tuned analysis, Edelman's "Twenty Years of Trust" Report (2020) looking at different developed countries identified a growing "trust gap" between a more trustful informed elite and a distrustful mass population.

While dwindling trust in government has been evident for some time, in recent years it has been reinforced—and exploited—by populist politicians and leaders who wish to distinguish themselves from the political milieu, government bureaucracy and expert advisors by aligning themselves with "the people." Think, for example, of Donald Trump's promises to "drain the swamp," Michael Gove's claim that "people in this country have had enough of experts," or Nigel Farage's assertion that the Brexit vote was a "victory for real people." As well as denouncing professional politicians and government agencies, contemporary populist politicians promote a general anti-intellectual, anti-legacy media, anti-NGO and anti-science stance until it is hard to see where trust should or could be placed. While trust, or at least loyalty, is placed in the very person who questions the trustworthiness of other politicians and institutions, populists like Trump might be merely "different elites who try to grab power with the help of a collective fantasy of political purity" (Müller 2016). However, cynical mobilisations of distrust should not lead us to infer that all lack of trust in government is wrong-headed. Thinkers such as Thomas Frank (2020), Will Davies (2019) and Michael Sandel (2020) all place the blame for anti-expertise populism at the door of liberals who have relied on a form of technocratic elitism that is sustained by the myth of meritocracy. Frank, who carefully delineates the original Populist movement in the US in the late nineteenth century as a multi-racial coalition of working people seeking economic democracy, calls Trump and others "faux populists." Declining trust might be understandable when we recognise the depth of what Frank calls "expert failure" in recent decades. He writes,

> I refer not merely to the opioid crisis, the bank bailouts, and the failure to prosecute any bankers after their last fraud-frenzy; but also to disastrous trade agreements, stupid wars, and deindustrialization … basically, to the whole grand policy vision of the last few decades, as it has been imagined by a tiny clique of norm-worshipping D.C. professionals and think-tankers.
>
> *(Frank 2020, 52)*

In the US, the need for trust between the people and experts goes back to the beginnings of the republic: "Ordinary people had to turn to some combination of elected officials and what would eventually be called 'experts' to supply, candidly and transparently, the preliminary factual truths that they needed to make well-reasoned judgments at the ballot box" (Rosenfeld 2018, 30). American democracy was never envisaged as a project that required voters to make arbitrary or baseless decisions in the dark. Rather, it acknowledged the necessity of translators, communication, outsourcing and representation from the beginning. Liberal democracies should, in theory, be able to tolerate this tension between "the supposed wisdom of the crowd and the need for information to be vetted and evaluated by a learned elite of trusted experts" (30).

Some research shows that declining trust in experts falls along partisan lines. A survey by YouGov (Smith 2017) in the UK found that supporters of the Conservative Party and UK Independence Party (UKIP), and those who voted to leave the European Union, are more likely to distrust experts from a range of professions. (It is also worth noting, given the discussion of poverty and income inequality below, that the research also found that working-class people have a lower level of trust than those in the middle classes.) Matt Wood (2019) observes a similar trend with respect to partisanship in the US, "as conservatives became increasingly distrustful of scientists compared to liberals in the late-2000s, with campaigns like the March for Science serving only to further polarise views."

The question of trust matters when it comes to conspiracy theories because a lack of faith in cultural, political, civic and scientific institutions and their representatives gives rise to scepticism about the evidence and information they put forth as well as the motives for doing so. Moreover, scepticism was amplified by the epistemic relativism of the Trump administration and its talk of "alternative facts." Indeed, the nature of evidence today is highly contested: many people—not just committed conspiracy theorists—now question what counts as evidence, how it has been gathered, how it can be used and whose vested interests it serves. Frank (2020) shows that early populist movements were keen for people to educate themselves and dig into economic data. Today, uncertainties about the nature of evidence encourage people to assemble their own rival archives of evidence from the deep recesses of the internet that exist beyond the verification performed by editors, academics and scientists. Indeed, such archives are valued precisely because they fall beyond the purview of such gatekeepers. In an era of information overload, more emphasis is placed on what you feel has an air of "truthiness," as talk show host Stephen Colbert put it, rather than what experts have verified to be true. Effectively, people are pushed into the market-place of ideas without the authoritative social institutions that could help with the need to make deliberative decisions (Gilbert 2020). In this context, it makes sense that the mantra of conspiracy theorists in the age of the internet is "Do your own research!"

As the work of Frank, Davies and Sandell indicates, we have to recognise that there may be good reasons why people lack trust in particular individuals and institutions, and the evidence they produce today. The question of whether con-spiracy theories are a sign of a crisis of trust can then be reframed to ask whether institutions are trustworthy. While there are non-state as well as state institutions in play here, we focus on the latter in the next section to address the ways in which the state might be seen to have let people down. We do so because such failures feed into contemporary conspiracist configurations of scepticism, albeit in distorted forms.

Demise of the Welfare State

One convincing if simple explanation for the prominence of conspiracy theories and a wider distrust of the state in post-war America is that all kinds of conspira-cies (including COINTELPRO, Watergate and Iran-Contra) were indeed com-mitted by government agencies throughout the twentieth century (see Olmsted 2008). Engaging in illegal or semi-legal covert activity is one way to lose the confidence of the public and increase suspicion of government conspiracy when such acts come to light. But we can also think about more quotidian and less newsworthy reasons for citizens to lose faith in the state.

In the UK and the US, notions of the scope of the state, its role in wider soci-ety and the social good have been systematically altered by the implementation of neoliberal policies since the 1970s. Margaret Thatcher famously remarked that "there is no such thing as society. There are individual men and women and there are families." If society is the plane on which inequalities and injustices can be seen and potentially rectified by state intervention, neoliberals felt it was much better to obfuscate that visibility and instead promote the idea that each person alone is responsible for their financial success or failure. Jeremy Gilbert (2020) suggests that the erosion of social welfare under these conditions has led to a disbelief in the possibility that public institutions could be supportive or even merely benign. In this case, he argues, the "Deep State" that features in many conspiracy theories is simply "the state as such under neoliberalism." In other words, while conspiracy theories fashion the Deep State as an evil force undermining the will of the people, the neoliberal state actually does its dirty work in plain sight (deflecting responsibility for inequality, privatising public goods, implementing regressive taxation, producing forms of labour precarity and deregulating capital). It would be a mistake to be too nostalgic about the actual welfare state—the state has never been a purely benevolent entity. Gilbert's point, rather, is about how people think and feel about the state under conditions of late capitalism. He sees this disbelief that the state can be anything other than conspiratorial as inevitable once its function has shifted from that which might be able to protect you from the worst excesses of free market capitalism to that which will expose you to them.

Instead of lamenting and protesting the loss of state support, some people become attracted to theories of a sinister, omnipotent Deep State. Neoliberal calls to individualism produce subjects who are hyper-suspicious of the state and the social in general. At the moment when the state is most decimated and ineffectual, conspiracy theorists imagine it as an omnipotent mechanism of conspiracy. It is possible that the appeal of a Deep State conspiracy theory like QAnon (which positioned the then head of state, Trump, as battling the Deep State) is that it provides a way out of such contradictions: it allows some forms of government interference to be experienced as good (the first wave of stimulus cheques issued by Trump, for example), while others are evidence of a vast, Satanic, Deep State plot.

The demise of the welfare state certainly leaves citizens exposed to the whims of the market. New global challenges in the 1970s, such as stagflation and oil crises, forced the UK's Labour government to look for alternatives to Keynesianism. It experimented with forms of hybrid Keynesianism, but these measures failed to improve the UK's financial situation. By the end of the 1970s, Britain was among the poorest of the OECD countries, having been ranked among the richest only 20 years before (Kus 2006, 506). The move away from Keynesianism and towards neoliberal policies was fully embraced by the Thatcher government of the 1980s as it implemented a monetarist approach to the economy, prioritising limits on inflation over full employment. Beyond the economy, Thatcher's vision sought to alter the very relationship between citizens and the state by firmly placing responsibility on citizens for their own welfare. The Conservatives justified welfare reform by claiming it would create incentives to work, produce self-sufficiency and assure more personal freedom. Despite the UK already in 1980 being one of the lowest-ranked European countries in terms of social security expenditure in relation to GDP, the Conservatives pushed through a series of budget cuts and reforms to the welfare state. For example, despite a 200% increase in the number of claimants of unemployment benefits between 1980 and 1987, spending on unemployment decreased by more than 50% over a period of 10 years (Kus 2006, 508).

The US picture is more complex because it never embraced a fully public welfare state, preferring instead corporate welfare capitalism, a mixed model of private and public forms of security (Brandes 1976). This is why many US citizens' healthcare insurance is provided by employers who then receive tax relief as an incentive. While local, less formalised welfare was on offer before federal-level programmes, it is notable that the US introduced social insurance programs much later than most European countries. Whereas unemployment insurance, for example, was introduced in the UK in 1911, the US did not implement it until 1935 (Lubove 1986). Equally, while the mixed public–private welfare model makes national comparisons complicated, the US lags behind welfare spending in most calculations.

As in the UK, it was the turn to neoliberalism (as both an economic and social project) that eroded welfare provision while at the same time casualising what forms of blue-collar labour had not been offshored within a globalised economy. Ronald Reagan implemented neoliberal monetary policies, tax cuts, deregulation and free trade (Harvey 2007). At the same time, he peddled the racist, inflammatory, stereotype of the "welfare queen"—typically depicted as an African American single mother living a glamourous life funded by the taxpayer. But it was not until Bill Clinton and his compromising strategy of triangulation in the face of a Republican-dominated Congress that welfare was fully reformed along neoliberal lines (Weissmann 2016).[1]

The financial crisis of 2007–8 pushed an additional 1.5 million American families into poverty, placing strain on the already inadequate welfare programme (Mencimer 2019). If we add to this the fact that because of increasing casualisation of the workforce in the US "the percentage of workers covered by health insurance and retirement benefits has decreased" in recent decades (Katz 2008), the welfare picture is bleak, and it is too soon to say what difference President Biden's more progressive policies will make. This is important when considering conspiracy theories not only because of the many ways in which the state fails citizens, thereby creating possibilities for figurations of the state (and beneficiaries of the system) as conspiratorial, but because research has found a correlation between conspiracy thinking and low levels of income and education (Smallpage et al. 2020, 266).[2]

After four decades of living under a mode of rationality that minimises or denies the role of the state in social justice, rectifying inequality, or providing a safety net, and a decade of austerity in the UK, the key message of which was that the state cannot afford the level of investment in social and health care and services that people need, the financial and social packages offered by many governments in Europe and North America as part of the response to the economic fallout of the pandemic were a revelation to many. It was a shock (and a relief) to discover that the state can provide support and care when required. In that moment, decisions concerning a lack of state support were revealed to be wholly political rather than inevitable or natural. (Something similar happened in the US in 2007–8 given the size of Obama's post-financial crash stimulus package, although the way in which the Federal Reserve shored up failing banks deepened the sense that there is an elite controlling events.) Neoliberalism has always appealed to "common-sense," insisting that "there is no alternative" to free markets, privatisation and individualism, to borrow Thatcher's slogan, even while simultaneously engaging in forms of intervention that prioritise corporate well-being over social welfare. As the state stepped up during the Covid-19 pandemic, providing support payments (in the US) and covering the wages of those being furloughed along with government grants (in the UK), some may have felt at best confused about previous messages concerning the limitations and capacity of the state, at worst suspicious about its reach. Any suspicions were fuelled by the fact that such support was accompanied by the necessity for people to make sacrifices concerning certain freedoms.

Income Inequality, the Financial Crash and Austerity

The picture we are sketching here points towards the material conditions and ideologies that might make it less possible to consider the state as a supportive or benign entity, and more possible to imagine it as susceptible to influence and operating with conspiratorial intent. Alongside the erosion of the welfare state, post-crash economic conditions might also have contributed to a sense that there are shadowy forces at work that benefit an elite and exploit ordinary people.

When we consider high levels of income inequality in the UK and US, it is easy to see why "elites" often become the target of conspiracy theorising. Since the 1980s, income inequality has remained high in the UK and has been steadily growing in the US.[3] As of May 2019, pay for non-college-educated men in the US had not risen for five decades, while for the first time in 100 years, mortality for less-educated white men and women in middle age had led to a fall in the average life expectancy (Partington 2019). Meanwhile, household incomes have increased faster for those in the top 5% than for those in the strata below since 1980, and between 1989 and 2016, the wealth gap between the richest and poorest families more than doubled (Menasce Horowitz, Igielnik, and Kochhar 2020). Such inequality falls along racial lines. In 2016, the median wealth of white households in the US ($171,000) was ten times the median wealth of black households ($17,100) (Kochhar and Cilluffo 2017). In the UK, the picture is not much better:

> the richest 1% … have seen the share of household income they receive almost triple in the last four decades, rising from 3% in the 1970s to about 8%. Average chief executive pay at FTSE 100 firms has risen to 145 times that of the average worker, from 47 times as recently as 1998.
>
> *(Partington 2019)*

Crucially, the Covid-19 crisis has increased the wealth divide in the UK with Black, Asian and Minority Ethnic (BAME) people hardest hit. Thirty-one percent of UK households have lost a quarter of their income, while those in more secure lines of work have managed to save money by not going on holiday or eating out, and those in the very highest earning brackets—with investments in a stock market that quickly rebounded and reached new heights—have done well during the pandemic (Collinson and Ambrose 2020). In the US, the number of Americans living in poverty rose by approximately six million (a jump from

9.3% to 11.1%) between June 2020 and September 2020 (see Han, Meyer and Sullivan 2020; COVID-19 Income and Poverty Dashboard), while the wealth of tech billionaires like Jeff Bezos and Mark Zuckerberg soared. Bezos's fortune increased by $80 billion during the first stages of the pandemic, for example (Cassidy 2020). In addition, Wall Street investment banks turned a tidy profit (Morgan Stanley made a profit of $2.7 billion between July and September 2020, a rise of 25% compared to 2019; and Goldman Sachs made a quarterly profit of $3.62 billion, almost twice the amount earned in the same quarter in the previous year) (Cassidy 2020).

The UK and the US responded to the financial crash of 2007–8 in different ways. Like much of the European Union, the UK pursued a project of austerity, cutting the budget for public services, education and welfare with the intention of reducing the budget deficit, liquidating the structural deficit and reducing the level of debt. The US implemented a more traditional path of Keynesian stimulus that enabled the US to regain its pre-crisis levels of GDP by 2011 (whereas the UK did not achieve this until 2014). But in terms of inequalities, the collapse of the housing market in 2008 meant that the property-dependent portfolios of middle-class American households fell while the portfolios of the wealthiest, geared towards a quickly rebounding stock market, increased (Kuhn, Schularick, and Steins 2018). Because the booming housing market had minimised the effect of wage stagnation, the collapse of the former arguably made the latter more apparent.

Robert Skidelsky (2018) argues that "the effects of failing to take precautions against a big collapse of economic activity and the botched and inegalitarian recovery measures implemented by most governments from 2010 onwards have left a damaging legacy of political resentment." And while the causes of populism exceed economic conditions, he finds the correlation between the economic crisis of 2007–8 and the rise of populism "too striking to be ignored." If economic instability is one factor that allows populism to enter mainstream discourse and politics, it also shapes the conspiracy imagination. While not all populist movements turn to conspiracy theories, many do and we can think of conspiracy theory itself as inherently populist in the way that it pits the people against the establishment (see Fenster 2008, 84).

Conspiracist Populism/Performative Authoritarianism

What exactly is the relationship between conspiracy theory and populism? "Populism cannot be reduced to its typical content (anti-intellectualism, for example, or mass mobilization by a charismatic leader) or its typical effects (scapegoating or conspiracy theorizing)" because content and effects are historically contingent, writes Mark Fenster (2008, 85–86). He advises that we should think of populism more as a process that can be mobilised by the left or right. Populism sometimes tries to disrupt these categories altogether—think of Marine Le Pen's comment in 2015, "Now the split isn't between the left and the right but between the globalists and the patriots." Populism arises in democracies, according to Fenster, when the gap between the public and its elected representatives constitutes a crisis and "a movement can plausibly offer some more direct or 'authentic' means of representation in the name of the people" (86). If populism serves as a necessary possibility of representative democracy—suturing the wound of representation when the distance between the people and elected politicians becomes too wide—conspiracy theory "as a mode of populist logic," is, therefore, "not foreign to democracy" (90). However, it has become increasingly clear in the twenty-first century that today's versions of populism and conspiracy theory alike "can play a destructive role by manipulating overly majoritarian, racist, or antidemocratic tendencies among the public" (90) and have played a part in undermining the ideals and institutions of liberal democracy (see also Muirhead and Rosenblum 2019).

Populist forces have been resurgent in Europe, the Nordic countries, South America, Asia and the US. While all cases display regional variation and national specificity, many capitalise on feelings of disenfranchisement, insecurity about social status, fear of demographic and cultural change and concerns about losing out to others. Populists deal in a Manichean world view, pitching evil elites against the virtuous people. "The people" is a notion built on exclusions, of course; it does not include all of those who stand for values contrary to the populist's vision. In Trumpist politics, for example, this included elites in general, but also scientists and other experts, legacy media, "woke snowflake millennials," "social justice warriors," ethnic minorities and undocumented immigrants. In this vein, during his presidential campaign of 2015, Trump made the claim that "the only important thing is the unification of the people, because the other people don't mean anything" (quoted in Müller 2017). The conviction of populists that they alone are "the expression of the one right and true majority" means that opposition is presented as "morally illegitimate," as Nadia Urbinati argues (2019, 120). This is important, she writes, because it lends itself to authoritarianism as "the leader feels authorized to act unilaterally" to disavow pluralism and the concept of a legitimate opposition (120).

While populist rhetoric does not always slide into conspiracy theory, and some argue that "conspiracy theorists usually constitute a significant minority within populist movements" (Bergmann and Butter 2020), it is clear that conspiracy theory offers tools and tactics that populists draw on. Equally, some studies have found that people with populist views are more likely to believe in conspiracy theories (Smith 2018), suggesting that there are sympathies between these ways of experiencing and framing the world. Eiríkur Bergmann and Michael Butter use the term "conspiracist populism" to indicate where and when the styles coincide. This formation requires us to pay attention to the ways in which it is performed—to consider the mode of delivery as well as the content (Moffitt 2016). This helps to understand the kind of performative authoritarianism that a figure like Trump employed. After protesters against racial injustice were forcibly removed from Portland streets into unmarked vans by officers dressed and armed for combat in the summer of 2020, Anne Applebaum (2020) commented that, unlike its twentieth century version, twenty-first century per-formative authoritarianism "does not require the creation of a total police state. Nor does it require complete control of information, or mass arrests. It can be carried out, instead, with a few media outlets and a few carefully targeted arrests." We need to combine several of the terms in play here to understand the particular mode of Trumpist politics and the role conspiratorial narratives played in it. To encompass the blend of rhetorical strategies and visual stunts, a figure like Trump is best described as a conspiracist-populist who operates as a performative-authoritarian.

In the UK, the campaign to leave the European Union was framed around the idea that the concerns of the EU government are remote from those of "real" British people. Again, we see populism given a foothold when the dis-tance between the representatives and those that are represented is seen to be too wide. More than this, membership of the EU was configured as being a bad deal for the British people because the "Brussels bureaucrats" were actively working against the interests of the British people (in a way that obscured the fact that elected British MEPs were part of that EU government). While the campaign for "Leave" was focused on amplifying concerns about immigra-tion and lamenting a perceived lack of sovereignty, Nigel Farage, of UKIP, also employed explicitly conspiracist ideas. Indeed, he appeared many times on Alex Jones's Infowars show, talking about "globalists" and a "New World Order." On these episodes, Farage repeated key conspiracy tropes: "Members of the annual Bilderberg gathering of political and business leaders were plotting a global gov-ernment; the banking and political systems are working 'hand in glove' in an attempt to disband nation states; 'globalists' are trying to engineer a world war as a means to introduce a worldwide government" and that "climate change is a 'scam' intended to push forward this transnational government" (see Mason 2019). During the pandemic, these existing conspiracy frameworks and populist calls-to-arms were quickly retooled for Covid-19. Anti-lockdown protests in the UK (and elsewhere) framed public health measures as a sinister plot to remove individual liberty, with a similar rallying cry to Brexit of needing to "take back control." At the same time, the pandemic was framed as a hoax, part of a vast, hidden agenda cooked up by globalist elites.

It is important to note that populism has also been mobilised on the left. More than this, Frank (2020) reminds us that the original Populist Party challenged the precepts of capitalism. However, Daniel Denvir argues that because the more recent leftist movements often labelled populist do not claim to exclusively rep-resent the one authentic people, the label is unjustified. In this light, Denvir continues, the political programmes of Bernie Sanders, Jeremy Corbyn, Syriza and Podemos might be better described as "plausible attempts to reinvent social democracy" (2020). Frank, too, balks at the false equivalences that commenta-tors drew between Sanders and Trump during 2016, which allowed populism to become a dirty word. It is true, however, that leftist movements like Occupy, and its demonising rhetoric about "greedy bankers" and "corrupt politicians," fed into a populist narrative that has been subsequently exploited by forces of the right.

During the pandemic, a turn to what Gideon Lasco and Nicole Curato (2019) call "medical populism" was evident. They explain this as "a political style based on performances of public health crises that pit 'the people' against 'the establishment.' While some health emergencies lead to technocratic responses that soothe anxieties of a panicked public, medical populism thrives by politicising, simplifying, and spectacularising complex public health issues" (1). While Lasco and Curato do not discuss conspiracy theories, we know how contemporary populism draws sustenance from and turns towards conspiracy thinking and their term offers a useful way to understand the dangers of populist and conspiracist framings of medical emergencies.

Ethnonationalism

While the original US Populist movement might have been multi-racial, contemporary right-wing populist forces more often licence forms of ethnonationalism. Ethnonationalism is an ideology that propagates and capitalises on myths of a homogenous culture and a common history. It seeks to protect an imagined community or cultural identity from dilution by other, seemingly incompatible, imagined communities or cultural identities. Ethnonationalism shapes policies as well as rhetoric: borders might be securitised, immigration policy tightened, and political or economic sovereignty might be enacted through a retreat from regional coalitions or international organisations and commitments.

Ethnonationalism is stoked by a feeling of what Roger Eatwell and Matthew Goodwin call relative deprivation: "a sense that the wider group, whether white Americans or native Brits, is being left behind relative to others in society, while culturally liberal politicians, media and celebrities devote far more attention and status to immigrants, ethnic minorities and other newcomers" (2018, 31). To illustrate this, they point out that 90% of Trump's core supporters believed that "discrimination against whites is a major problem in America" (31). And in the UK, 76% of Brexit supporters felt things had "got a lot worse for me compared to other people" (32). Ethnonationalism offers ethnically white communities a way of appropriating the language of discrimination by "obscuring power differentials by putting whiteness or European descent at the same level as minority identities" (Gambetti 2018). In these scenarios, people eschew establishment politicians and policies, seeing them as having been unable to prevent the perceived relative deprivation by giving up national sovereignty too easily and giving in to elitist ideals of multiculturalism.

Rather than focus on the way that globalised open markets have resulted in investment moving to the Global South to find cheap labour, right-wing populism capitalises on a fear of change in the dominant ethnic makeup of an area, of one culture being displaced by another. In some cases, this gets expressed in familiar conspiracist language. Consider Islamophobic conspiracy theories like "the great replacement theory" (Bergmann 2021). This phrase originated in France but has been adapted by figures elsewhere (including reactionary right broadcasters like Canadian YouTuber Lauren Southern and the New Zealand Christchurch killer in his manifesto). It warns of an explicit plot to displace historically ethnically white and Christian cultures through the influx of a different ethnicity, race or religion. Hari Kunzru (2020) explains how the idea has run its course through the right-wing media ecosystem and beyond: it "has made its way from the salons of the French far right into the chans, and out again to Fox News, informing the Trump administration's staging of the so-called border crisis (a term that is often enough repeated uncritically even by members of the so-called fake news media)."

As the following chapters document, race has indeed shaped the Covid-19 pandemic. Despite the ethnonationalist conspiracy rhetoric of victimhood, the disease has in fact disproportionately affected black and ethnic minority communities, most tellingly in the unequal rates of deaths and hospitalisations from the virus. These unequal health outcomes are the result of a complex, intersecting mix of factors that connect race and class, including the fact that those from minority communities are more likely to be engaged in "essential work" (low-paid, public-facing service work), take public transport and be unable to work safely at home; more likely to already have pre-existing health conditions and poor access to health care; and more likely to live in multi-generational households that do not easily permit isolation. Yet, as we will see, populists in both the US and the UK turned to ethnonationalist and xenophobic conspiracy narratives in their accounts of the emergence of the virus, coupled with calls for border closure and quarantine that were driven more by racist assumptions than evidence-based public health decisions.

Culture Wars and Polarisation

Nation states have long asked self-reflexive questions about national identity and values. Such questions can only be termed "culture wars" when there is little to no consensus about the answers—when disagreements are considered existential threats and become cause for deep grievance. Culture wars can be read as the transfiguration or displacement of purely economic and political issues. According to this interpretation, structural accounts of poverty, for example, are obscured by cultural narratives that distinguish between the "deserving" and "undeserving poor" (as the already mentioned "welfare queen" stereotype in the US, or the UK *Daily Mail*'s bid to catch benefit fraudsters in the UK attest to). However, this approach risks dismissing cultural concerns—disregarding them as false consciousness—when it is clear from the Brexit vote and working-class support of Trump that culture or values are often far more important than socioeconomic status to many. Working-class people might not, in any simple fashion, be "voting against their interests" if, as Alan Finlayson (2020) argues, "interests are multiple, material and ideal, and often contradictory." Rather than positioning culture as a displacement, it might well be the very terrain on which politics is fought.[4]

As a social as well as an economic programme, the neoliberalism embraced by Reagan in the 1980s also shaped cultural attitudes and the scope of debates concerning them. One of neoliberalism's original architects, Fredrich Hayek, emphasised the role of a traditional moral order that no state should interfere with. State-imposed social justice, in Hayek's view, has no place—it is merely the imposition of an artificial order that erroneously configures the state, rather than the individual, as the responsible unit. This means that redistributive interventions as well as what Hayek called the "social justice warrior," a pejorative term that has been picked up by the right today, can then be presented as unwelcome interruptions to a common-sense, natural order—as infringements on freedom (see Brown 2019).

In 1992, Pat Buchanan talked about "a war for the soul of America." He claimed that the election that year was about "whether the Judeo-Christian values and beliefs upon which this nation was built" would endure (quoted in Hartman 2019, 1). In the 1980s and 1990s, the culture wars focused on "abortion, affirmative action, art, censorship, evolution, family values, feminism, homosexuality, intelligence testing, media, multiculturalism, national history standards, pornography, school prayer, sex education, the Western canon" (Hartman 2019, 1). Some of these issues are still highly contested, albeit in slightly different manifestations. To update this list for the contemporary moment, we would need to remove some and add trans rights; climate change; gun ownership; undocumented immigrants; statuary of slave owners and other monuments; what constitutes sexual harassment; and now, also, responses to the pandemic, centring on social distancing, mask wearing and attitudes towards vaccination. Many of these concerns have flavoured Covid-19 conspiracy theories.

In the UK, the turn to Thatcherism instigated a war on "the loony left," which included unions, Ken Livingstone's left-wing Greater London Council, CND and movements for equal rights. The British culture wars of the 1980s were shot through with the attempts by the right wing to validate a traditional, monocultural morality (for example, through the implementation of the homophobic Clause 28), leveraging patriotism (especially with the Falklands War) and limiting definitions of British identity (by, for example, either doing nothing to tackle or actively supporting institutional racism).[5] Thanks to a series of liberal social reforms during the Labour government of 1997–2010, it became far less acceptable (in some spaces at least) to express racism and homophobia in public. Today's culture wars in the UK, however, offer prejudice new avenues for expression, focused as they are on immigration, Brexit, trans rights and the relationship of Britain to its history of Empire and/or slavery. Denigrations of the "loony left," reinvented today as an attack on "wokeness," focus on "political correctness," the funding of the BBC, the role and value of universities and the school curriculum.[6]

Only an acutely ahistorical view could claim that the US is more polarised than ever before given how divided the nation was during its civil war. With regard to the UK, some research suggests that a vociferous minority on social media make it seem more divided than in fact it is (More in Common 2020). However, as the finely balanced and hotly contested 2020 election in the US displayed, as well as the tight 2016 Brexit referendum in the UK, polarisation rather than consensus politics seems to be a lived reality in ways that have intensified in recent years and especially since the pandemic. Moreover, polarisation is today amplified by asymmetric media structures (Benkler, Faris, and Roberts 2018), partisan media outlets and social media in a way that rules out compromise or consensus. The other side is depicted not as mistaken, but as stupid and even evil. Polarised positions, further entrenched by vitriolic culture wars, can push some further to the extremes of political belief. This is important when studying Covid-19 conspiracy theories because, in comparison to moderates, extremists have been found to be more prone to conspiracy thinking (e.g., van Prooijen et al. 2015; Krouwel et al. 2017). Importantly, what we have seen during the pandemic is that conspiracist explanations become animated by existing polarised debates.

The "alt-right" and particular chan cultures and subreddits have amplified the culture wars by disparaging and goading its perceived enemies, calling refugees "rapefugees," ridiculing "social justice warriors" and even moderate conservatives, who they name "cuckservatives" (see Dafaure 2020). Such figures accuse progressives of "cultural Marxism"—of curtailing individual freedoms through aggressive forms of identity politics and plotting to destroy traditional ways of life and Western culture. Such attacks clearly respond to challenges to white privilege, patriarchy and racial capitalism. Within online subcultures like incels (self-identified involuntary celibate men who feel excluded from the sexual economy by women), particular contempt is reserved for women. Sentiments cultivated in fringe online spaces did not remain there for long: "Along with Reddit's r/The_Donald, 8chan and /pol/ became major drivers of far-right content into the mainstream media" (Kunzru 2020). In addition, Trump's loose alliance with figures of the "alt-right" and his refusal to condemn far right protesters also helped extreme conspiracist ideas enter mainstream discourse and visibility.

Both the image boards of the "deep vernacular web" (de Zeeuw and Tuters 2020) and social media from the surface web on which these far-right sentiments are aired are ill-suited to building consensus. The expression of far-right ideas is defended through an appropriation of the language of personal freedoms. This is where conspiracy theories come in, as they become a limit test for free speech in the current climate. When is a conspiracy theory about George Soros antisemitic hate speech? Is belief that Tom Hanks, as part of the cosmopolitan elite, is buying and ingesting adrenochrome harvested from children a cultural expression of difference or a libellous accusation? When does the right to express a conspiracy theory regarding mask wearing or vaccine taking impinge on another's right to good health or even life?

The polarising tendencies of the culture wars described in this section constitute the discursive context into which the pandemic arrived. Responses to Covid-19 in both the US and the UK quickly became politicised and consequently polarised. (Although, as we will see, the divisions were not always drawn along traditional left/right party lines, but rather what we term populist "coalitions of distrust.") Despite politicians in many countries trying to frame the pandemic as a time for national and international unity, the politicisation of the medical emergency happened so quickly and so thoroughly because the existing cultural wars machinery could so easily incorporate a new and seemingly unprecedented set of circumstances into its narrative explanations and calls to action.

We suggest that Covid-19 conspiracy theories present post-truth incarnations of the culture wars. They are offered as if to engage in a debate, but because they eschew consensus reality, there is not the necessary shared ground to begin an exchange. In this sense, conspiracy theories that purport that the pandemic is a hoax orchestrated by the liberal elite cannot and perhaps should not be debated in the real sense of that term. (This does not mean that such propositions should not be researched as cultural phenomena, but that they should not be framed as one half of a two-sided debate on a public platform.) "Debate" suggests that there are two legitimate interpretations of the same historical or scientific facts (just as the "war" of "culture wars" suggests a battle between forces using similar tactics and weapons). Bad-faith arguments based on false equivalences get cynically defended as relativism: as simply what someone happens to believe. Do all beliefs have a place in the public sphere? Just as culture wars seem to entrench positions, there can be no reconciliation or agreement at the level of logic and epistemology between many believers in conspiracy theories today and those that debunk them. To do so would require one side to completely acquiesce to the other side's worldview. This is, of course, how many feel about culture wars, which is why social media is so rife with practices of and incitements to "cancel" or "deplatform" those that people disagree with. The platforms themselves started to deplatform conspiracy theorists and peddlers of fake news during the pandemic—a move which, interpreted as censorship and suppression, inevitably stoked the conspiracist flames further.

Intensified Disinformation Campaigns

While most conspiracy theories we come across on social media and closed messaging groups are circulated by free actors, there is also a vast amount of state-sponsored disinformation to contend with. It is no secret that authoritarian states such as Russia, China, Turkey and Iran have been found to produce and/or amplify fake news or disinformation. It is helpful to think of disinformation as having taken over from Cold War–era propaganda. Whereas propaganda was intent on persuasion and ideological conversion, disinformation seems designed to confuse and disorient. Think, for example, of Russian interference in the lead-up to the 2016 US presidential campaign. Thanks to the Mueller investigation, we know that Russian troll farms developed a sophisticated network of social media accounts and groups designed to look like home-grown content. The Russian campaign suppressed support for Hillary Clinton and hardened Trump's base through conspiracist narratives and false claims. Such tactics became especially concerning during the Covid-19 crisis. In October 2020, *The Times* uncovered a Russian fake news campaign to cast doubt on the safety of the Oxford vaccine trials (Rana and O'Neil 2020) and reported a month later that Government Communications Headquarters (GCHQ) had begun an offensive cyber-operation to counteract anti-vaccination disinformation being spread by hostile states (Fisher and Smyth 2020).

Lest we think the phenomenon confined to authoritarian states, it is clear that forms of disinformation are also produced by politicians in liberal democracies. Trump's reliance on disinformation, most dangerously during the pandemic, offered numerous examples. The UK's Conservative government might have engaged in a scientifically robust public information campaign during the pandemic, but they had also previously engaged in disinformation tactics. For example, during a televised debate between Boris Johnson and Jeremy Corbyn during the 2019 election, the Conservative Party Twitter account changed its name to @FactcheckUK as it rebutted Corbyn's statements.

What this means is that the information ecosystem becomes increasingly confused and confusing, arguably causing people to retreat into factions, guided simply by which narrative appeals most or confirms their worldview. This reduces the chance of corrective, scientifically robust information reaching those who might benefit from it most, whether in the middle of a pandemic or not.

Digital Contexts

When considering the different contexts that shape conspiracy theorising in general today, and that shape Covid-19 conspiracy theories in particular, it would be remiss to ignore the design choices, platform affordances and business models of digital communication technologies. Given that platforms rely on extracting user data to sell advertising and services (an economic model that Shoshana Zuboff (2019) has called "surveillance capitalism"), provocative content that prompts a lot of user engagement can prove lucrative. This technological and economic paradigm is important for studying Covid-19 conspiracy theories because it means that engagement with conspiracy theories online generates a profit not only for conspiracy entrepreneurs (those people who produce conspiracy content and merchandise that we consider further in chapter 6), but for digital platforms also. It is true that social media platforms have developed policies about Covid-19 disinformation and have sought to deplatform particular purveyors of conspiracy content (Innes and Innes 2021). However, their business models require a certain amount of content agnosticism particularly in stages of consolidation, which is why newer platforms like

Gab and Parler have no such policies—Gab founder Andrew Torba actually welcomed QAnon (Jassa 2020). While we take a closer look at this issue in chapter 7, at this stage it is worth keeping in mind that it does not matter to social media platforms, if users are posting about cats or pandemic conspiracies as long as they engage with the platform and enable it to collect their data. Linking, liking and sharing are all important when attention (and the personal data that attention yields) is at a premium. Some commentators suggest that rendering fake news and disinformation unprofitable will help (Vorhaben 2022). This is no small feat. It involves challenging the very models of surveillance capitalism and internet advertising upon which digital platforms depend. Public and political pressure helps and has led to the current moderation policies about Covid-19 disinformation that go some way to mitigating harms.

Understanding Covid-19 conspiracy theories (and other conspiracy theories) today involves mapping the flow of information across the complex information ecology that allows more fringe ideas to feed mainstream platforms that are based on this data-harvesting business model. Daniël de Zeeuw and Marc Tuters (2020) have written about the flow of ideas between the deep vernacular web and mainstream social media. The former, they argue, is characterised by masks, the anti- and impersonal, the ephemeral and aleatory, the collective, and remains stranger-based whereas the latter is based around faces, the personal, the persistent and predictable, the individual, and is friend-oriented. Despite radically different cultural codes, relations, experiences and business models (the deep vernacular web does not rely on advertising revenue or data harvesting), ideas including conspiracy theories often emerge within the deep vernacular web and migrate to other platforms, shedding their original context and (often ironic) inflection. The anonymity upon which image boards like 4Chan and 8kun work facilitates the production of baseless theories that can then move—sometimes in diluted form, sometimes strengthened by "research" through links to other conspiracist web content—to spaces that require identification. As such ideas enter the monetised and monetisable spaces of the surface web, a cult of celebrity (for figures like Alex Jones or David Icke, for example) overtakes the allure of anonymity. As a result of deplatforming by mainstream social media during the pandemic, we have seen a migration of certain conspiracist groups to encrypted messaging apps like Signal and Telegram. The opacity of such spaces creates new challenges for those tasked with limiting the effects of disinformation and offers another stage of and site for the story of Covid-19 conspiracy theories that needs to be considered.

As this book is primarily concerned with conspiracy theories that are developed and that circulate in digital spaces, a consideration of how the business models, platform affordances and infrastructural design of the platforms shape conspiracy theorising is central, and we turn to this in chapter 7. A focus on the mediating qualities and political economy of certain technologies is always important for thinking about the circulation of knowledge but is even more critical when thinking about the information that circulated during various pandemic-induced lockdowns when so much of life, even more than usual, was confined to the virtual.

The contexts included here are not exhaustive by any means and we draw on others in this book. Moreover, these brief accounts necessarily simplify a complex story. Nevertheless, in articulating them together at this early stage, we hope to emphasise the importance of thinking contextually and historically for understanding Covid-19 conspiracy theories as a form of knowledge, a mode of politics and a symptom of cultural anxiety. Conspiracy theories must be understood as political, cultural and epistemic entities; as having both a long history and contemporary specificity; and as shaped by dominant modes of communication and mediation.

Notes

1 Later, with Clinton's approval, the Republicans implemented the Personal Responsibility and Work Opportunity Act. An integral part of this was the replacement of Aid to Families with Dependent Children (AFDC), created as part of the 1935 New Deal, with Temporary Assistance for Needy Families (TANF). TANF is a block-grant, the administration of which is devolved to states. Importantly, the value of the grant is fixed regardless of how many people are on the welfare rolls or how high the unemployment rate goes. Moreover, its value has been eroded over time by inflation.

2 However, we should be hesitant about overstating the connection between income and conspiracy theorising given the high proportion of conspiracy beliefs across income brackets today (Smallpage et al. 2020).

3 Both countries score highly on a sliding scale that uses the so-called Gini coefficient. The Gini coefficient is used by some economists to compare, as the Organisation for Economic Co-operation and Development (OECD) explains, "the cumulative proportions of the population against cumulative proportions of income they receive. It ranges between 0 in the case of perfect equality and 1 in the case of perfect inequality" (2020).

4 This is a proposition that undergirds the scholarly discipline of cultural studies.

5 This led to events such as the Day of Action organised because of institutional failures concerning a fire in New Cross in which a number of black teens perished and the uprisings in Brixton against police brutality (both in 1981).

6 Given that ideology presents that which is culturally produced as natural, the politically motivated as self-evident, it is wholly fitting that a self-appointed group of Conservative MPs have called themselves the "Common Sense Group." In the wake of Black Lives Matter protests in the summer of 2020, the group complained about museums that are reconsidering the legacy of historical figures and lobbied for tougher immigration policies.

2

INFODEMIC

Metaphor, Measurement and Moral Panic

During the pandemic, many commentators have remarked on the proliferation of misinformation, disinformation and conspiracy theories. This situation has been widely characterised as an infodemic. A piece in the *Financial Times*, for example, referred to an "'infodemic' of distorted analysis," which is "fuelling misleading information and a politicisation of prevention measures" (Jack and Dodd 2020). Likewise, both the *New York Times* and *The Lancet* headlined the word in their reports on the WHO's creation of a new information platform, as part of their collaboration with social media platforms to amplify accurate health information (Richtel 2020; Zarocostas 2020). Most observers agree that conspiracy theories have become widespread and influential during the pandemic, moving from the margins to the mainstream in a way that is, if not entirely unprecedented, nevertheless striking and disturbing. But is that assessment accurate? Has there been an increase in the volume and spread of conspiracy theories and other forms of misinformation, especially on social media? Does this flood of "alternative facts" constitute an "infodemic," and what is entailed by that instantly intelligible metaphor? Moreover, if we are indeed witnessing an infodemic, then do more people sincerely believe in the conspiracist narratives they come across, and do those beliefs affect their behaviour? Or are we instead dealing with a moral panic about the perceived pernicious influence of social media and the susceptibility of the masses to either accidentally or intentionally deceptive information? The first part of this chapter assesses the claim that the Covid-19 pandemic has been accompanied by an epidemic of misleading information, while the second part examines the welter of data from opinion polls on levels of belief in conspiracy theories about the pandemic. Although most commentators have taken for granted that there has been a viral explosion in the creation, communication and consumption of conspiracy theories during the pandemic, we want to show how this common-sense assumption has been constructed through metaphors and data that are potentially misleading.

DOI: 10.4324/9781003315438-3

Declaring an Infodemic

From early in the outbreak, medical officials warned about an epidemic of mis-information, which would make the task of tackling the spread of the virus much harder. In its Situation Report of February 2, 2020, the WHO warned that "the 2019-nCoV outbreak and response has been accompanied by a massive 'infodemic,'" which they defined as "an over-abundance of information—some accurate and some not—that makes it hard for people to find trustworthy sources and reliable guidance when they need it" (World Health Organization 2020). The report clarified that the WHO was combatting not merely an overabun-dance of information, but the rise of particular kinds of misinformation. "Due to the high demand for timely and trustworthy information about 2019-nCoV," it noted, "WHO technical risk communication and social media teams have been working closely to track and respond to myths and rumours." In a speech on February 15, WHO Director-General Tedros Adhanom Ghebreyesus made the point more forcefully. "We are not just fighting an epidemic," he explained. "We're fighting an infodemic. Fake news spreads faster and more easily than this virus, and is just as dangerous" (Ghebreyesus 2020a). The UN Secretary-General António Guterres offered a similar assessment, arguing that the spread of the Covid-19 pandemic "has also given rise to a second pandemic of misinforma-tion, from harmful health advice to wild conspiracy theories" (Guterres 2020).

The term "infodemic" quickly captured the attention of journalists, politi-cians and researchers (Simon and Camargo 2021). A report in April 2020 by the social media network analysis firm Graphika, for example, was titled "The Covid-19 'Infodemic': A Preliminary Analysis of the Online Conversation Surrounding the Coronavirus Pandemic" (Smith, McAweeny, and Ronzaud 2020). The "infodemic" label provided a compelling, short-hand expression that rightly emphasised that the problems caused by the Covid-19 pandemic were not only medical but also cultural and political, especially in the age of global social media. Even before they designated the outbreak of SARS-CoV-2 as a pandemic (with all the institutional health mechanisms triggered by such a declaration), the WHO understood that efforts to control the epidemic would need to focus on communication as much as containment. They worked quickly to secure agree-ments from the major search engines and social media platforms to implement measures to control the anticipated infodemic, in addition to establishing its own fact-checking "Mythbusters" campaign on its website (Richtel 2020). Despite its prescient warning about the likely dangers of politicised misinformation, in those vital early weeks the WHO itself engaged in misleading management and communication that was inevitably caught up in global politics. Presumably sen-sitive to the need to damp down the xenophobic tendency among some politi-cians and commentators in the Global North to blame China for the outbreak, the WHO delayed declaring a pandemic until March 11, 2020. In doing so, they compounded the problems created by the Chinese authorities who, contrary to international requirements, waited three weeks to report a "Public Health

Emergency of International Concern" to the WHO. Although the Chinese authorities in both Wuhan and Beijing were less than transparent, in those early weeks of the outbreak, the WHO also put out misleading information. Drawing on a bulletin from the Wuhan Health Commission, for example, a tweet from the official WHO account on January 14 announced that there was no danger of human-to-human transmission. But it omitted the qualification added by the Chinese authorities that the possibility could not be excluded (Gilsinan 2020). Even if we do not subscribe to President Trump's conspiracist claims that the WHO is controlled by the Chinese (a view which he used to justify removing US funding from the organisation), it is nevertheless possible to recognise that the WHO diagnosed the dangers of a potential "infodemic" of misinformation while also contributing to it.

Infodemics, Literal and Metaphorical

Although it only became widely used during the Covid-19 pandemic, the term "infodemic" was first coined in an article by David Rothkopf in the *Washington Post* during the SARS outbreak of 2003. Rothkopf argued that, as with other prominent events such as terrorist attacks, the fevered media response to the epidemic was out of proportion to the reality: "a few facts, mixed with fear, speculation and rumor, amplified and relayed swiftly worldwide by modern information technologies have affected national and international economies, politics and even security in ways that are utterly disproportionate with the root realities" (Rothkopf 2003). Rothkopf's neologism did not gain much traction at the time, but it struck a chord in the Covid-19 pandemic, in large part due to the WHO prominently championing the term early in the pandemic. Rothkopf's basic argument—that a cascade of misinformation makes a global health crisis harder to contain—remains valid, but he was wrong that disease outbreaks inevitably create moral panics that exaggerate the actual threat. While that might have been accurate in the case of SARS in 2003, if anything the initial media and political reaction (especially under the populist leadership of Trump in the US and Johnson in the UK) underestimated the seriousness of Covid-19.

It is often unclear whether commentators are using the term "infodemic" metaphorically or literally, and what implications follow from the use of the term. Most use it merely as a convenient shorthand to suggest parallels between the way the virus spreads and the way mis- and disinformation about the virus spread. In his original article, Rothkopf insisted that the similarities between infodemics and epidemics are remarkably close: "In virtually every respect they behave just like any other disease, with an epidemiology all their own, identifiable symptoms, well-known carriers, even straightforward cures." Some researchers, for example, focused on reconstructing the pathways of transmission of particular pieces of Covid-19 misinformation, such as the *Plandemic* documentary, which was shared on social media platforms 8 million times within its first week, with 2.5 million likes, shares and comments on Facebook alone (DFRLab 2020; Frenkel, Decker, and Alba 2020). Some studies have concentrated on the role that "superspreaders" have played in the infodemic (Avaaz 2020a). A study by a team of researchers at Cornell, for example, concluded that President Trump was by far the biggest driver of coronavirus misinformation (Frenkel 2021). In addition to considering the mechanisms of spread, other researchers, for instance, have looked into the possibility of "inoculation" against the threat of mis- and disinformation (van der Linden, Roozenbeek, and Compton 2020). This is meant as a metaphor, but it is a particularly appealing one because it suggests that, like actual vaccines, there might be a miracle cure to our current plight.

Although most of these studies rely on an implicit analogy between the virus and medical misinformation, some have taken the comparison more systematically and more literally. The idea of "infodemiology" as an emerging data-driven scientific field focused on epidemics of information has gained traction during the pandemic (Eysenbach 2009, 2020), with researchers, for instance, using the concepts and techniques of infodemiology to study the use of anti-Chinese stigmatising language online (Hu et al. 2020). Other researchers have started to explore possible correlations between the prevalence of low-credibility news and low vaccine take-up, with the Covaxxy Dashboard (created by Indiana University Observatory on Social Media), for example, providing an intriguing parallel set of maps with US states colour-coded according to twin measures of misinformation and vaccination adoption (Observatory on Social Media n.d.). Other researchers have taken the parallel more literally. One study starts from the premise that "models to forecast virus spreading … account for the behavioral response of the population with respect to public health interventions and the communication dynamics behind content consumption" (Cinelli et al. 2020). The researchers explain how they "model the spread of information with epidemic models, characterizing for each platform its basic reproduction number ($R0$), i.e. the average number of secondary cases (users that start posting about COVID-19) an 'infectious' individual (an individual already posting on COVID-19) will create."

Ligot et al. take the parallel between epidemiology and infodemiology even further, looking at the incubation period and spread over time of misinformation, trying to identify whether there is a similar time-lag between the initial emergence of a piece of misinformation and its subsequent transmission (Ligot et al. 2021). They then engage in a form of "contact tracing" of a particular set of misinformation URLs circulating on social media in order to identify both the "multiple carriers" (i.e., repeat offenders) and individual superspreaders of online misinformation. Next, they examine what they consider to be "mutations" in the cultural DNA of misinformation topics (from 5G and bioweapons, to anti-lockdown and anti-vaxx), which they characterise as equivalent to new strains of the virus adapting to new environments. Finally, their hope is that by identifying topic mutations in real time they will in the future be able to engage in inoculation against the infodemic by providing relevant counter messaging.

Where many commentators have used the infodemic metaphor without much reflection, Ligot et al. self-consciously adopt the analogy in order to see, in a spirit of pragmatism, what research insights it might generate. And their work indeed opens up some suggestive lines of inquiry, such as the idea of performing an equivalent of genome sequencing to see how particular narrative strands of conspiracy theories are recombined into new variants, all the while leaving tell-tale traces of their original form and content visible to the microscopic attention of cultural research. Although Ligot et al. are keen to emphasise the benefits of the comparison, they do not address its limitations, especially in terms of causal direction. In places they suggest that the same mechanisms might underpin both realms, making the idea of an "infodemic" more than a metaphor.

The infodemic metaphor has become widely adopted, and it does capture in a striking way some of the dangers of the spread of mis- and disinformation online. However, it is worth unpicking some of the implications of the metaphor (with its reliance on related ideas from virology, epidemiology and immunology) and the ways in which the comparison does not work. First of all, information does not literally spread like a virus at an individual level to create an epidemic in the social realm, and information inoculation cannot confer immunity. Cells have no conscious ability to resist infection by a bacterium or a virus, but people do have some choice in whether to accept and pass on a particular piece of online content, or, at the very least, it is not inevitable that an individual recipient of online mis- or disinformation will succumb to its truth-altering message. Discussions of the infodemic usually imply that social media is a particularly dangerous space of transmission, with viral memes—especially conspiracist ones—able to bypass a user's rational defence mechanisms. However, some recent research in behavioural psychology has suggested that often misinformation is spread not through malicious intention or being duped, but, rather, due to a simple lack of conscious attention (Pennycook et al. 2020, 2021). In contrast to both these positions, cultural studies research has shown that, compared to the traditional model of many-to-one broadcasting, the internet can enable more active and participatory forms of media engagement in realms such as conspiracy theorising—even if that more utopian model of Web 2.0 does not always hold true (Harambam 2020). Indeed, there is a long tradition of work in cultural and media studies that argues against the "hypodermic needle" theory of media influence (Bory et al. 2021). Even the metaphor of the viral transmission of memes is not new, with roots in discussions of crowd theory as contagion in the late nineteenth century (Mercier 2022). Writing in the 1990s, Douglas Rushkoff invoked the idea that ideas and images could circulate virally in the mediascape without the conscious control of manipulating producers of content, precisely to argue against familiar accounts of the entertainment industry as a conspiracy (Rushkoff 2010). But there are other possible explanations of how ideas spread that do not subscribe to either a conspiracy theory of sinister manipulation by media moguls or a technodeterminist account of viral transmission without conscious control. While some conspiracy entrepreneurs like Alex Jones and David Icke act as disinformation "superspreaders," for example, their community of followers are not merely passive recipients of their messages, for better or worse. Conspiracy theories are created and consumed in complex networks that cannot be reduced to either individual control or impersonal structures.

The analogy between viruses and information also falsely suggests that there is a single point of origin of the "disease" that can be clearly identified, allowing a targeted intervention in the form of an informational therapeutic treatment or vaccine. Although social psychologists have found evidence of the success of some forms of "inoculation" that build up "resistance" and even "immunity" (pre-bunking, media literacy training and so on) (Cook, Lewandowsky, and Ecker 2017; van der Linden, Roozenbeek, and Compton 2020), the effects tend to be comparatively short lived (Linden et al. 2021; Paynter et al. 2019). We now know that the Covid-19 disease is caused by the SARS-CoV-2 virus (with its many emerging variants), but the "disease" of misinformation does not have a clear causal counterpart. Moreover, in its need to maintain a clear boundary between accurate and mistaken information, research into the viral spread of conspiracy theories and misinformation online has to rely on an agreed classificatory system of low- vs. high-quality sources, sites and content. Sometimes this takes the form of a list of unreliable news websites maintained by organisations, such as NewsGuard, or a database of false claims identified by fact-checking groups, such as Full Fact or COVID19Misinformation.org. The infodemic metaphor suggests that the solution to the perceived problem will come from tracking, tracing and quarantining "diseased" pieces of information (Avaaz 2020a). Like other social media platforms during the pandemic, Facebook, for instance, has engaged in "performative transparency," proudly announcing, for example, that by March 2021 it had removed 12 million pieces of misinformation related to Covid-19 and vaccines (Rosen 2021). However, independent researchers are not able to verify such claims, undermining the idea that there is a clear and transparent distinction between harmful and harmless information—leaving aside the fact that, as studies have shown, a great deal of the deplatformed content still circulates online in other realms (Scott 2021). These taxonomic activities by think tanks, campaigning charities and the social media platforms themselves can be useful, although it is frustrating that we have to rely so heavily on a piecemeal network of under-funded voluntary organisations and non-transparent social media companies for this important work.

Nevertheless, the infodemic metaphor assumes that there is a clear-cut distinction between good information and bad information, and that our task is to identify and neutralise the threat from the latter. This boundary work of policing the division between good and bad information ironically confirms conspiracy theorists' populist suspicion that academic and research organisations serve as gatekeepers for hidden information. The notion that there is a binary division between healthy and unhealthy information also has much in common with the conspiracist mindset that sees the unfolding of history in Manichean terms, as an ultimate and apocalyptic struggle between good and evil. The characterisation of harmful misinformation as contaminating the body politic recalls the kind of Cold War paranoia that still structures much thinking in Russia and other authoritarian states, which view internal dissent as necessarily the result of clandestine Western influence.[1] Likewise, in the US and Europe, many commentators at first explained the spread of harmful information online during the coronavirus pandemic through the dominant paradigm—that had coalesced around the 2016 US presidential election—of disinformation as the product of foreign interference. However, the pandemic (along with the US elections of 2020) has made clear that the source of mis- and disinformation is just as likely to be home-grown.

With its implied analogies to viruses, epidemics and immunology, discussion of the Covid-19 "infodemic" relies on a host of medical metaphors in a way that has become normalised. The critical theorist Slavoj Žižek, for example, observed that "the ongoing spread of the coronavirus epidemic has also triggered a vast epidemic of ideological viruses which were lying dormant in our societies: fake news, paranoiac conspiracy theories, explosions of racism" (Žižek 2020, 39). But the notion of an "infodemic" is often combined with an array of other metaphors used to describe the spread of problematic information. Some are taken from the realm of espionage, propaganda and military discourse (with the language of infiltration, manipulation, disinformation, weaponisation and war, for example), leading to the seemingly self-evident conclusion that the problem is one for which we must be eternally vigilant and prepared to combat. At other times, metaphors from weather and other natural phenomena are invoked, with talk of floods, torrents and storms of misinformation and conspiracy theories. For example, Sylvie Briand, director of Infectious Hazards Management at WHO's Health Emergencies Programme, explained that "we know that every outbreak will be accompanied by a kind of *tsunami* of information" (emphasis added). The difference, Briand continued as she switched metaphors to the realms of audio equipment and medicine, is that "now with social media … this phenomenon is amplified, it goes faster and further, like the viruses that travel with people and go faster and further" (Zarocostas 2020). It is, of course, virtually impossible to avoid using figurative language. But some analogies are less problematic and more insightful than others. Instead of an analogy with disease infection, it might be more helpful to think in economic terms such as supply and demand, both in a literal and a metaphorical sense. We need to consider, for example, the ideological and emotional investment of those who consume conspiracy narratives as well as the financial and political incentives of those who produce them, not to mention the infrastructural logics of the platforms that host them and promote them via recommendation algorithms. After all, unless we address why people are drawn to conspiracy narratives—why they find a sense of identity and community in these stories—we will always be playing whack-a-mole. In all cases, though, it is vital that we think about the implications of the metaphors and analogies we use to identify and make sense of a phenomenon such as Covid-19 conspiracy theories.

Data Deficit or Infoglut?

Building on a Data and Society report on "data voids" (Boyd and Golebiewski 2019), First Draft (a non-profit dedicated to help journalists tackle misinformation) have theorised that in times of great uncertainty—such as the start of the Covid-19 pandemic—there are "high levels of demand for information about a topic, but credible information is in low supply" (Shane and Noel 2020). There is considerable evidence that conspiracy theories sometimes (but not always) fill these information voids, providing ready-made, compelling, overarching narratives that seem to explain everything (van Prooijen and Douglas 2017), for example the seeming mystery of why the label on bottles of Dettol—even before the pandemic—claimed to kill coronavirus. (The obvious answer is that SARS-CoV-2 is a *novel* coronavirus, a class of virus that includes the common cold and was already well known.) In contrast, the WHO's initial warning about an infodemic was as much about an "infoglut" (Andrejevic 2013) of potentially accurate information as it was about the spread of rumours, myths and conspiracy theories surrounding the new disease. The problem identified by the WHO was partly caused by the rapid production and widespread promotion by scientists, journalists and the public of preprints—academic articles that have not yet undergone peer review, but which are available in open access versions online. In their study of the role of the preprint in the early months of the pandemic, Gazendam et al. found that there had been an exponential increase in scientific publications relating to Covid-19, often with a quick turnaround time from submission to publication, with many of the articles taking the form of commentaries and opinion pieces rather than original research findings (Gazendam et al. 2020). The danger of this publishing process—not entirely new, albeit on a far greater scale than anything seen before—is that intriguing yet unconfirmed preliminary results can gain wide coverage, but any future clarifications, criticisms or retractions tend to receive less notice. For example, Gazendam et al. drew attention to a preprint article that claimed to have found similarities between SARS-CoV-2 and HIV, a finding which unsurprisingly fuelled conspiracy theories about bioengineering. Although the article was later withdrawn, it quickly became one of the most widely shared scientific papers in the last decade, rapidly moving far beyond medical circles.

As we have seen, however, most commentators use the term "infodemic" to mean not merely an overload of well-meaning information, but a potentially catastrophic explosion—to switch metaphors again—of either accidentally or intentionally misleading information. The suggestion is usually that the spread of mis- and disinformation has been at an unprecedented level. But is that true: has the epidemic of information reached pandemic proportions, and is this situation indeed unprecedented? Our starting assumption in this book is that the answer is not as obvious as it might at first seem. The feeling of being overwhelmed by information is not new, but, as Felix Simon and Chico Camargo point out (drawing on Hugo Mercier's recent book *Not Born*

Yesterday), many people have learned how to navigate their way through the contemporary mediascape by developing cognitive strategies such as selective attention (Simon and Camargo 2021; Mercier 2022). Indeed, some early studies in the pandemic indicated many people had a good idea of where to find reliable information around Covid-19, even if some of them chose to ignore scientific experts, national health institutions and the mainstream media in favour of folk remedies and conspiracy narratives (Nielsen et al. 2020). If, as some researchers have found, there has at the aggregate level been an increase in trust of science and trusted sources of information in a number of countries in the Global North (Nielsen, Schulz, and Fletcher 2021), the information ecosystem has also become increasingly polluted, politicised and consequently polarised. Determining whether we are currently living through an epidemic of online misinformation and conspiracism is also difficult because it relies not only on there being a clear distinction between high- and low-quality information, but also a transparent and complete account of what information and narratives individuals experience online, how they feel about it, and what they do with it. Neither is easily available. Although social media researchers can identify, for example, which posts have gone viral by tracking both volume and engagement metrics, the social media platforms do not provide transparent access to data that would show what actual users see on their feeds. Compounding this problem, it is becoming increasingly clear that engagement metrics are a poor proxy for actual engagement. People often share stories online that they have not even looked at, sometimes out of partisan cheerleading or polarisation, but at other times because conspiracy theories generate clicks and likes, or out of a desire to "burn it all down" rather than promote a particular position or simply from a motivation of interesting-if-true based on the headline alone (Gabielkov et al. 2016; Berinsky 2017; Petersen, Osmundsen, and Arceneaux 2018; Osmundsen et al. 2020; Altay, de Araujo, and Mercier 2021; Ren, Dimant, and Schweitzer 2021).

Setting aside these important caveats, it is nevertheless possible to produce some approximations of the size of the problem of online problematic information during the pandemic. A report from the Reuters Institute for the Study of Journalism (RISJ) in April 2020, for example, found that only a minority of respondents in its survey had come across a lot of misinformation concerning Covid-19 (Nielsen 2020). However, the RISJ study, and a similar one from January 2021 conducted by Daniel Allington and Siobhan McAndrew, found that young people and the less well educated are more likely to get their news and information from social media and, therefore, come across a significant amount of misinformation (Allington and McAndrew 2021). Some studies that focused on individual platforms understandably came to more pessimistic conclusions because they were not looking at the overall media diet of individuals. Yang et al., for example, found that low-credibility information on Twitter about Covid-19 circulates at roughly the same volume as information from the *New York Times* (Yang, Torres-Lugo, and Menczer 2020). That does not necessarily imply, however, that conspiracy theories and other forms of misinformation during the pandemic have outgunned reliable sources. A study by BBC Trending of the most popular, conspiracy-minded anti-vaccination accounts on Instagram, for instance, found that the number of followers of these accounts increased five-fold during 2020 ("The Anti-Vax Files: How Anti-Vax Went Viral" 2021). In contrast, using the Covaxxy Dashboard, we found that the *New York Times* was shared on Twitter ten times more than the conspiracy-leaning Zero Hedge website in the first week of April 2021. Yet this seemingly optimistic finding does not tell us the full story of the relative importance of good vs. bad information. On the one hand, conspiracy theorists will often link to an article from a reliable source such as the *New York Times* to back up their alternative interpretation of events or provide proof of what they perceive as the bias of the mainstream media. On the other, conspiracist articles from sites like Zero Hedge are shared by those debunking myths and rumours. The metrics of online media engagement do not necessarily provide a reliable measure of how widespread conspiracy beliefs have become during the pandemic.

The score card is therefore mixed, but many studies nevertheless concur in their assessment that, while the spread of low-quality information during the pandemic is a serious problem, it still has not drowned out high-quality sources of news and health information. Broniatowski et al., for example, argue that the idea of a "misinfodemic" (as they term it) has been exaggerated: there might be an excess of information about Covid-19 circulating online, but misinformation and disinformation are not winning out (Broniatowski et al. 2021, 2022). Nor is it clear that the problems of conspiracism and misinformation are significantly worse than prior to the pandemic. In fact, the studies by Broniatowski et al. found that links to high-quality information sources are *more* common in Covid-related online interactions than those relating to topics other than health or in comparison to previous episodes of disease outbreaks. The reason, the authors suggest, is that global health experts, in conjunction with the social media platforms, have done a comparatively good job in promoting authoritative sources of information during the pandemic, although their most recent research finds that interventions by the social media platforms do not appear to last in the long term (Broniatowski et al. 2022). It is important to note, however, that these kinds of study focus on the amount of supposedly problematic content rather than engagement with or belief in said content. The second part of this chapter will turn to the many opinion polls that were conducted during the pandemic which in broad terms confirm the conclusions of the content-based studies outlined here. As we will see, many opinion polls have shown that belief in particular conspiracy theories during the pandemic (e.g., that the virus was deliberately created in a lab) amounts to about 25% of respondents in the US and 20% in the UK. In a literal sense, then, the idea that the online spread of misinformation has reached overwhelming, pandemic proportions—an infodemic—is undoubtedly exaggerated. Nevertheless, it is still justified to be concerned at the prevalence of many harmless, bizarre or damaging untruths about Covid-19 among particular communities and sections of the population in individual countries.

What should we do about the term "infodemic"? Simon and Camargo argue that the metaphor is dangerous because it can push policy in ill-thought-out directions, for example by making illiberal disinformation counter-measures seem a matter of vital public health that are beyond discussion (Simon and Camargo 2021). Although we agree with many of their concerns, it is probably too late to put the genie back in the bottle. The term has gained too much traction, and, despite its flaws, it has the potential to suggest fruitful lines of inquiry. However, we can still insist that people should think about the implications of the metaphor, paying attention to when and why the analogy does not fit. More generally, there needs to be greater consideration of the range of metaphors that are being used to describe how ideas, images and narratives spread online, and the ideological baggage that each metaphor brings with it. The idea of escaping figuration altogether by using a scientifically objective language is naïve. Instead, we need to be alert to both the insights *and* the blind spots that different metaphors generate. In contrast to the medical, economic, meteorological and military figurative language sketched out here, there is increasing interest among digital media researchers in applying ecological metaphors to information dysfunction (Phillips and Milner 2021). Ecology provides a potentially productive way of thinking about the complex interactions between the content, the users, the technological infrastructure and the social dynamics of the different digital platforms, though it is not free of its own unspoken assumptions. Instead of simply replacing "infodemic" with a different coinage, then, researchers should make sure that they are more aware that all explanatory models have complex figurative entanglements.

Popularity vs. Visibility

So far, we have seen that the idea the Covid-19 pandemic has been accompanied by an infodemic of conspiracy theories and other varieties of misinformation cannot be taken as a given, not least because the analogy between the viral spread of information and the actual spread of the SARS-CoV-2 virus is problematic. We also have good reason to be suspicious of headlines warning of a dramatic increase in the volume or engagement of false and deceptive information about the causes, cures and consequences of the pandemic. In the second part of this chapter, we will examine the equally common claim that the level of belief in conspiracy narratives is disturbingly high. The lack of convergence in the results of the many opinion polls conducted during the pandemic reveals something significant about the nature of conspiracy belief, and the difficulty of measuring it. Our argument here is that survey data on conspiracy beliefs cannot be taken at face value, in large part because what it means to *believe* in a conspiracy theory (and what behaviour might result from that belief) is far from clear (Jerolmack and Khan 2014).

It seems intuitively plausible that there has been a dramatic rise in the level of popular belief in conspiracy theories since the spring of 2020. An analysis of the number of news articles in the UK mentioning the term "conspiracy theory," for example, shows that there has been a noticeable increase since the beginning of the pandemic, from roughly 3000 per year in 2015 to more than 8000 per year in 2019 and 2020 (there was a spike to 4000 per year in 2016, the year of Brexit in the UK and the presidential election in the US). An increase in news articles mentioning conspiracy theory might well be a good proxy for evidence of an increase in the popularity or significance of conspiracy theories in society more generally. But it might also be an effect of a self-conscious anxiety among the media that citizens are not merely turning to seemingly dangerous and deluded ways of interpreting events, but that they now increasingly view the mainstream media (often abbreviated to "MSM" in populist rhetoric online) as part of an established, Deep State conspiracy to hide the truth from the people. A detailed study of conspiracy beliefs in the US over time did not find evidence of any significant increase (Uscinski et al. 2022). If anything, the researchers found that belief in some coronavirus-related conspiracy theories has faded away as the pandemic has progressed. They found that in March 2020 31% of Americans believed that Covid-19 was "purposely created and released by powerful people as part of a conspiracy" (Drochon 2021), but by May 2021 the number declined slightly to 29%. Likewise for the 5G theory, support fell from 11% in June 2020 to 7% in May 2021, while the vaccine microchips theory declined in the same period from 18% to 12%. These results are intriguing, but are not necessarily evidence of a reassuring, gradual, popular rejection of conspiracy theories as the pandemic has unfolded; they ignore the possibility conspiracy theorists seem quite willing to latch onto and champion whatever new position becomes a matter of partisan faith in the culture wars. More importantly, however, these findings rightly lead the researchers to conclude that "conspiracy theories are more visible online, and journalists feel they need to report on them to help make sense of what is going on. But that doesn't mean there are more of them, or that belief in them has necessarily increased" (Drochon 2021). They suggest instead that there is a "conspiracy theory media bubble" (Drochon 2021). This suspicion is in keeping with Jack Bratich's observation that the increased focus on conspiracy theories in the public eye (since at least the 1990s) is evidence of a "conspiracy theory panic," a moral panic on the part of political, scientific and media authorities not about the threat of conspiracies from internal or external enemies but the dangers posed by the apparent mushrooming of conspiracy theories in the public sphere (Bratich 2008). Moreover, we need to always keep in mind that the first emergence in the 1950s and 1960s of academic interest in conspiracy theories as a distinctive sociological phenomenon arose out of an anxiety about mass political paranoia (Butter and Knight 2018; Thalmann 2019).

We cannot, however, simply dismiss the seeming proliferation of conspiracy theories during the pandemic (and on social media more generally in the last few years) as merely a "conspiracy theory media bubble." After all, there is some plausible evidence that there has indeed been an increase in the quantity and reach of conspiracist misinformation. For example, a study by Avaaz in 2020 found that health-related misinformation attracted four times as much traffic as official health sources on social media (Avaaz 2020a, b). Many reports by organisations investigating misinformation on social media have found similar patterns of greatly increased traffic and spread, although we need to remember that their studies are potentially influenced by starting from the assumption that there has been a worrying explosion of misinformation on social media. Like the conspiracy theorists they study, they are primed to find evidence for a narrative they already suspect to be true.

Polling and Trolling

There is now considerable evidence of the growth of problematic information, including conspiracy theories, related to the pandemic, even if we need to remain suspicious about the tendency to alarmism in these reports. However, these studies of the supply pipeline of misinformation and conspiracy theories do not necessarily confirm that people are any more likely to *believe* in the narratives that they come across on their social media feeds, on mainstream media or via personal interaction. Many news organisations, think tanks and academic researchers have attempted to determine the level of popular belief in the conspiracy narratives that have received such prominent attention in the media. They have drawn on a substantial body of political science and social psychology research into the demographics of conspiracy thinking (Douglas et al. 2019). This research has pursued two approaches to the problem of measuring how widespread belief in conspiracy theories is in society. Following the pioneering work of Ted Goertzel (1994), one strand has developed questionnaires based on lists of common conspiracy theories, ranging from a single-item scale (Lantian et al. 2016) to versions with multiple items (Douglas and Sutton 2008), and asked respondents which ones they endorse and to what extent on a five- or seven-point of agreement/disagreement, sometimes with a "don't know/no opinion" option and sometimes without. The more conspiracy theories that are added to the questionnaire, the more likely it is that a very high percentage of respondents will agree to at least one of the statements (Uscinski 2020). The other strand of research has focused on conspiracy thinking rather than conspiracy beliefs, in an effort to gauge a broader conspiracist mentality or disposition, rather than belief in particular theories, with scales such as the Belief in Conspiracy Theories Inventory, the Generic Conspiracist Beliefs Scale and the Conspiracy Mentality Scale (Brotherton, French, and Pickering 2013; Imhoff and Bruder 2014; Lantian et al. 2016; Uscinski, Klofstad, and Atkinson 2016). Surveys on Covid-19 conspiracy beliefs have drawn from both these approaches, as they seek to understand the popularity of individual conspiracy theories along with the underlying attitudes and dispositions.

The proliferation of methods of measuring conspiracy beliefs has not converged on a single standard. This is not surprising, because it would require agreement not only on what counts as a conspiracy theory but also what counts as conspiracy belief or conspiracy thinking. What does it mean to say in a survey that you "agree" with a one-line statement about a specific conspiracy allegation or a general conspiratorial proposition? There are also disagreements among scholars regarding whether the commonly used measures and methods in the surveys are underreporting or inflating conspiracy belief (Enders and Smallpage 2018). One study (Clifford, Kim, and Sullivan 2019), for example, examined the variation between giving respondents a sliding scale of agreement/disagreement and an explicit choice format, with a conspiratorial versus a conventional explanation for an event. The study demonstrated that changing to an explicit choice version not only removed the no-opinion group but also decreased the level of conspiracy belief, suggesting that the more usual sliding-scale method might be exaggerating the level of conspiracy belief in the population. In contrast, another recent study (Smallpage et al. 2021) investigated whether the perceived stigmatisation of conspiracy theories in the public sphere (Thalmann 2019) plays any role in how people respond to questionnaires, even if they are anonymous. By comparing results from a standard conspiracy belief survey with a control group who were asked merely the number of statements they endorsed (rather than which ones), they found a consistent underreporting of the level of conspiracy belief in the seven countries they examined. There is also the possibility that respondents to polls—especially in online polls that require no interaction with an interviewer—might be trolling the investigators and wilfully exaggerating their levels of belief, either out of ironic nihilism or partisan signalling (al-Gharbi 2022). One study found that survey trolling might account for up to half of all responses in some surveys, suggesting that the headline figures about conspiracy belief are considerably exaggerated (Lopez and Hillygus 2018). Given this lack of consistency in how conspiracy beliefs should be measured (and indeed, what counts as a conspiracy theory at all), it is no surprise that the findings from surveys conducted during the pandemic present a complicated picture rather than compelling evidence for an epidemic of conspiracism.

Pandemic Polls

One of the most widely circulated studies in the US was a poll conducted by the Pew Research Center in June 2020, which found that 71% of Americans had heard of the conspiracy theory that powerful people intentionally planned the coronavirus outbreak; 25% of all respondents found at least some truth in it (5% said it was definitely true and another 20% found it probably true (Schaeffer 2020)). The survey found that the level of belief varied by education and political affiliation, with 48% of Americans with a high school diploma or less finding the theory probably or definitely true, compared to 15% of those with a postgraduate degree, and 34% of those who support the Republican party agreeing with the theory, compared to 18% of those who lean towards the Democrats. The correlation in the Pew study between the level of belief and educational attainment is consistent with other studies into conspiracy belief which have found this to be one of the few significant demographic variables, with researchers in contrast finding little difference in the aggregate in the rate of conspiracy theory belief in terms of age, gender, race or class (Smallpage et al. 2020). However, there are often significant differences when it comes to individual conspiracy theories, some of which are far more likely to appeal to men or minorities, for example (Wang 2019). The role of gender and sexuality in conspiracy thinking and conspiracy communities in general has not yet received sufficient attention (Thiem 2020), but one small-scale study in April 2020 suggests that gender plays a more important role in Covid-19 conspiracy beliefs than most studies assume. It found that women were significantly less likely to endorse each of the 11 listed conspiracy theories than men, with an average gender gap of 10 percentage points (Cassese, Farhart, and Miller 2020). While women are more likely to identify as Democrats in the US, the study suggests the gender gap in Covid-19 conspiracy beliefs cannot be explained solely by political partisanship, not least because there are significant gender gaps both among Democrats and Republicans.

While other studies (Uscinski and Parent 2014) have shown that conspiracy beliefs are found across the political spectrum, the pandemic quickly became a partisan issue in the US and elsewhere. The September 2020 American Perspectives Survey, for example, found that close to half (48%) of Republicans, compared to 25% of Democrats, say Covid-19 is no more serious than flu (Cox and Halpin 2020). They also found that 42% of Republicans (compared to 5% of Democrats) believe that hydroxychloroquine is a safe and effective treatment. The findings of the Pew poll chime with a study published in the *Harvard Misinformation Review* in April 2020 by the political scientist Joseph Uscinski and his collaborators, who have been carrying out surveys on conspiracy beliefs more generally for the last decade. The main findings were that 29% of respondents agreed that the threat of Covid-19 has been exaggerated to damage President Trump, while 31% agreed that the virus was purposefully created and spread (Uscinski et al. 2020). The study also found—perhaps unsurprisingly in the context of the pandemic—that distrust of experts and a pre-existing disposition to believe in conspiracy were the strongest predictors of who believes in these theories. Although, as with the Pew report, the number of hard-core conspiracy believers in the Uscinski et al. study was quite low, it is still significant that less than half (44%) of those polled disagreed with the suggestion that the virus was deliberately spread. This corresponds with findings from later iterations of Uscinski's poll (Klofstad and Uscinski 2020), with less than half the respondents (49%), for example, disagreeing with the notion that the dangers of vaccines are being hidden by the medical establishment, while only 16% agree with the idea that the official government version of events (in general) can be trusted. To gauge the significance of beliefs about Covid-19 conspiracy theories, it is important to view them from a comparative perspective. While many studies during the pandemic have focused solely on conspiracist narratives relating to the causes and consequences of the virus, others have included coronavirus-related statements in surveys examining a range of conspiracy beliefs. In an investigation into the role of social media in spreading conspiracy theories, for example, the authors found that just under a third of respondents agreed with the idea that the coronavirus was purposely created and released by powerful people as part of a conspiracy (Enders et al. 2021). In comparison with the range of other conspiracy statements (both general and specific) included in the survey, the level of belief in the coronavirus statement was roughly mid-table, with agreement ranging from 15% for the notion that the number of deaths in the Holocaust has been deliberately exaggerated, to 54% for the idea that the richest people in the US control the government and the economy for their own benefit. In a large poll conducted by YouGov for *The Economist* in July 2021, respondents were asked about a wide range of political and social issues, of which conspiracy theories in general were only one section, and in turn pandemic conspiracy theories a small component of that ("The Economist/YouGov Poll" 2021). The story that the moon landing was a hoax polled at 12%, while the notion that the threat posed by Covid-19 has been exaggerated by the authorities reached 40%. Even the more far-fetched claim that the aim of the vaccination is to microchip the population scored 20%, with as many as 27% of white men with no college education (and 32% of Republicans in general) agreeing with that allegation, and another 11–12% unsure.

In addition to comparisons between different coronavirus conspiracy theory beliefs and comparisons with non-pandemic-related conspiracy theories, it is also important to place the US findings outlined above in an international perspective. Polling in the UK has also produced very mixed results. For example, a report by the campaigning charity Hope Not Hate in April 2020 found that "37% have heard about the 5G conspiracy theory and almost a third of people do not dismiss it: 8% believe it to be true, while 19% are unsure" (Hermansson 2020). They also noted that 45% of the UK population believes that the coronavirus is a manmade creation, while 18% agree that vaccines have hidden harmful effects. These figures are high compared to some other polls, particularly when framed in terms of the proportion of people who do not dismiss a conspiracy theory (i.e., aggregating those who agree and those who are unsure). This suggests that organisations whose remit is to warn of the dangers of extremism tend to highlight their results in more alarmist ways than polling firms without a specific agenda. Thus, a survey conducted by the market research company Opinium in April 2020 found that 7% of respondents agreed with the 5G conspiracy theory (3% believing it to be definitely true, and 4% probably true), which is in line with the 8% in the Hope Not Hate study. The latter emphasised the fact that nearly a third of people did not reject the theory out of hand, whereas the Omnium report placed the 5G figure in the context of other seemingly far-fetched conspiracy theories (for example, 7% for flat earth, and 8% that Elvis is still alive) (Opinium 2020).

Some studies start from the assumption and find evidence that conspiracism is bizarre and exceptional, while others view conspiracy beliefs as normal and widespread. Consequently, the kinds of questions asked by the surveys matter. In a poll conducted by King's College London and the University of Bristol in late 2020, for example, the researchers included a range of statements, from more overtly conspiracist ones such as "reporters, scientists, and government officials are involved in a conspiracy to cover up important information about the virus" (believed by 15% of respondents), to more socially acceptable statements such as "people need to wake up and start asking questions about the pandemic" (believed by 41%) (Allington and McAndrew 2021). Some of the statements blurred into potentially legitimate political critique of Boris Johnson's administration ("the authorities want us to think that coronavirus is much more dangerous than it really is" [20%]), while others are sufficiently ambiguous that both committed conspiracy theorists and those frustrated at the Conservative government's handling of the pandemic could endorse them ("the government is deliberately allowing vulnerable people to die" [19%] and "an impartial, independent investigation of coronavirus would show once and for all that we've been lied to on a massive scale" [26% of those aged 18 to 34]). The poll was mainly focused on investigating the potential connection between conspiracy thinking, social media use and vaccine hesitancy, but it also found some suggestive differences between demographic groups (as other polls have done, particularly around vaccine hesitancy). So, for example, the study found that "6% of those from white ethnic groups believe 'Bill Gates wants a mass vaccination programme against coronavirus so that he can implant microchips into people,' compared with 19% among those from other ethnic groups" (Allington and McAndrew 2021). However, this kind of poll finding lends itself to a framing of the issue in terms of the supposed pathology of non-white citizens, rather than a more historically contextualised understanding of why some social groups might have good reason to distrust the medical authorities (and in the case of the Gates conspiracy theory, as chapter 4 explains in more detail, it is connected to warranted suspicions of insensitive, neo-colonial practices on the part of governments in the Global North and charities in the Global South).

Numerous polls have been conducted on individual countries, both in Europe and elsewhere. For example, an Ipsos/Nieuwsuur poll in the Netherlands in May 2020 found marginally lower levels of conspiracy belief than the US and UK studies summarised above, with 4% believing the 5G conspiracy theory, and 5% the Bill Gates narrative (Ipsos 2020), while a poll in Switzerland found considerably higher levels, with a third of respondents entertaining various coronavirus conspiracy theories. A study in Germany conducted using the same methodology as Freeman et al. (2020a) also found comparatively high levels of belief in a range of both general and specific conspiracy statements, with on average 10% strongly agreeing and another 20% partially agreeing (Kuhn et al. 2021). In Eastern Europe, levels of belief are seemingly higher still. In Russia, for example, 64% of respondents said Covid-19 was artificially created as a new form of biological weapon (*Moscow Times* 2021), while in North Macedonia nearly two-thirds of citizens believe that coronavirus was created to control humans (Holroyd 2021). Outside Europe and North America, the picture is similarly mixed, with no consistent correlation in terms of GDP or level of democracy. In Australia, for example, the 5G theory polled at 12%, the Gates narrative at 13%, and the idea that the pandemic had all been orchestrated to force vaccination on the population also at 13% (Essential 2020). In Pakistan, a study found that 9% agreed with the idea that 5G theory with another 34% in the "maybe" category, while the figures for the theory that the Covid-19 vaccine was introduced to control the world's population polled at 18% and 28% respectively. Although these single-country polls allow for some rough-and-ready comparisons, often they are asking slightly different questions with different scales, and so accurate evaluations are not always possible. A few studies have, therefore, attempted to conduct multi-country surveys. A Cevipof poll conducted in a number of Western European countries, for example, found that 36% of respondents in France, 32% in Italy and Germany and 31% in the UK agreed that governments and pharmaceutical companies are covering up vaccine risks, with 42% in France, 41% in the UK, 40% in Italy and 39% in Germany believing that their government is using the pandemic to control and monitor citizens (Henley 2021). The large-scale, ongoing Cambridge/YouGov project on populism found a wide range of levels of belief in coronavirus-related conspiracy theories, with, for instance, 59% of respondents in Nigeria, 46% in Greece, 45% in South Africa, 38% in the US and 22% in the UK agreeing that Covid-19 death rate had been exaggerated by the authorities, and more than 20% in Turkey, Egypt, Saudi Arabia, Nigeria and South Africa believed it was definitely or probably true that Covid-19 symptoms were caused by 5G (Henley and McIntyre 2020). While in some countries a significant minority of respondents believed that Covid-19 had been deliberately created and spread by the Chinese government (over 50% in Nigeria, over 40% in South Africa, Poland and Turkey, over 35% in the US, Brazil and Spain, and 20–25% in France, the UK, Italy and Germany), at the same time many respondents also thought that the US was responsible (37% in Turkey, 20% in Greece and Spain, 17% in the US, 16% in Poland, 12% in France and 5% in the UK).

Penumbra of Uncertainty

In the US and the UK (our focus in this book), there are some broad areas of convergence in many of the studies, suggesting a sliding scale of belief from the far-fetched to the not-impossible: roughly 10% claim to believe in the 5G story, 20% in the microchips in the vaccine theory, 30% in the notion that the pandemic was planned, and 40% in the claim that the virus was manmade. However, two prominent studies came up with rather different findings, and mainly because they adopted a different methodology. The aim of a study led by Daniel Freeman (a psychiatrist at the University of Oxford) in the spring of 2020 was to examine the relationship between conspiracy beliefs and health behaviours, a vitally important matter of public concern during the pandemic (Freeman et al. 2020a). However, it was the headline findings about the level of conspiracy belief (rather than the correlation with a lack of compliance with health authority guidelines) that attracted considerable media and scholarly attention. The accompanying press release highlighted two findings in particular: "almost half of participants endorsed to some degree the idea that 'Coronavirus is a bioweapon developed by China to destroy the West' and around one-fifth endorsed to some degree that 'Jews have created the virus to collapse the economy for financial gain'" (Freeman et al. 2020a, 262). More broadly, the study concluded that "50% showed little evidence of conspiracy thinking, 25% showed a degree of endorsement, 15% showed a consistent pattern of endorsement, and 10% had very high levels of endorsement," and, significantly, "higher levels of coronavirus conspiracy thinking were associated with less adherence to all government guidelines" (Freeman et al. 2020a, 251). Other headline findings were that

> 60% of adults believe to some extent that the government is misleading the public about the cause of the virus; 40% believe to some extent the spread of the virus is a deliberate attempt by powerful people to gain control; 20% believe to some extent that the virus is a hoax.
>
> *(University of Oxford 2020)*

The survey asked participants about 48 conspiracy statements, using a five-point scale: do not agree, agree a little, agree moderately, agree a lot, and agree completely. The list of statements included suspicions about the government's response and rationale for the lockdown, conspiracist accounts of the cause and the spread of the virus, and some specific conspiracy beliefs. These views were then correlated to various cognitive and emotional conditions, demographic characteristics and self-reported compliance with health measures. The researchers found no difference by gender, but young people, ethnic minorities, those who get their news from social media or friends and those who think voting is a waste of time were more likely to believe in the conspiracy statements. In addition, the more people believe in conspiracy theories, the less likely they are to say that they will comply with health guidelines.

The finding that nearly half of the UK population believed to some degree a range of conspiracy theories about the pandemic made for disturbing headlines in the press, but other researchers suggested that the figures were too high because of the way Freeman's study was designed. They pointed out that the study was flawed because it offered only one disagree option but four categories of agreement, lacked a don't know/no opinion option and was compounded by the "acquiescence bias": if, as research has shown, people are more likely to agree with statements by default, then only choosing pro-conspiracy statements might produce unreliable results. According to one critique, Freeman's scale "makes agreement seem the norm and disagreement the exception" (Garry, Ford, and Johns 2020), while another insisted that "'findings' that indicate fringe beliefs are more widely held than they actually are can serve to normalise those beliefs. And can stoke fear among the groups being blamed. Misleading evidence can be more damaging than no evidence at all" (McManus, D'Ardenne, and Wessely 2020). Two teams replicated Freeman et al.'s study with more conventional scales, obtaining different results. Sutton and Douglas re-ran a mini version using three of Freeman's conspiracy statements (about Jews, Muslims and Chinese) that were highlighted in the press release, albeit on a smaller and less representative sample (Sutton and Douglas 2020). They used Freeman's scale in a control group, with a second group given a standard five-point scale (two agree and two disagree categories and a "don't know" option), and another group given a nine-point (matching Freeman's four gradations of agree with four disagree responses, along with a "don't know" option). They found considerably lower levels of agreement: 2–3% of participants agreed with the conspiracy theories about Jews and Muslims (compared to 20% in Freeman et al.), and 32% agreed with the Chinese lab theory (compared to 45% in Freeman). A more elaborate replication experiment was conducted by Garry et al. (Garry, Ford, and Johns 2020). They divided the cohort between a "best practice" scale (a five-point balanced scale with a "don't know" option), Freeman's positive-skew scale (with four agree and one disagree option) and a negative-skew version (with four disagree categories and a single agree choice). The study also used a balanced mix of pro- and anti-conspiracy theory statements, to obviate against any acquiescence bias. They found that Freeman's positive-skew version produced the highest scores and the negative skew the lowest, with the standard balanced version in the middle. They found that on average the scores in the "best practice" iteration were only 60% of those in the Freeman positive-skew version: where Freeman et al. found 23% agreed with the claim that Muslims are spreading the virus as an attack on Western values, Garry et al. found that with a more standard survey design that figure was reduced to 13%. In response to these criticisms, Freeman defended his team's original study, noting that "respondents were presented with stark beliefs and a clear decision to make about endorsement," and that, since the main focus was the link to behaviour, they were therefore interested in *any* level of agreement (Freeman et al. 2020b). They also observed that agreement and disagreement "are not genuine opposites of a single dimension and it creates difficulties in interpretation when they are treated as so." The critiques of Freeman et al.'s study make some valid points, suggesting that the level of belief might have been overreported. However, what these conflicting studies suggest is that what counts as conspiracy belief is an artefact of measurement. Although some of the replies to Freeman et al. claimed that they represent current "best practice" in survey design, they highlight the fact that not only is there no single correct way to measure belief but also that the very nature of popular conspiracy belief is not separate from the ways we choose to measure it. Opinion polls usually measure conspiracy belief as a sliding scale of agreement to a set of short propositions, but in the wild conspiracy theories are often embedded in complex narratives and can function as an expression of a tribal identity or a post-facto justification for behaviour (Berinsky 2018). Although the replication studies found lower scores when they used more usual scales, they do not necessarily provide a more accurate representation of popular belief in conspiracy theories during the pandemic.

What was particularly interesting about the Freeman et al. study was not its finding of a comparatively high level of positive belief in particular conspiracy theories, but the low proportion of the public who were confident enough to dismiss conspiracist explanations outright. Although in the replication studies the percentage of those responding "don't know" was quite small, by giving a single, clear option for disagreement Freeman et al.'s survey captured the notion that only half the population are willing to discount conspiracy theories completely (Freeman et al. 2020b). The other half of the population might not necessarily fully endorse the propositions, but they might find themselves identifying more with a set of options that in effect express a sense that "I don't know if this conspiracy theory is true, but nor do I know for certain that it's not true." This is not the same as a simple "don't know/no opinion." In a similar fashion, the report by Hope Not Hate suggested that the UK public can be divided into five broad categories: conspiracy theorists (21%), uncertain believers (21%), pop-conspiracy theorists (i.e., those who believe in one or two of the less far-fetched theories; 24%), strong sceptics (22%) and anti-conspiracy theorists (14%) (Hermansson 2020). What is significant about this typology of belief is that those who confidently reject conspiracy theories are in the minority.

A survey by Ipsos Mori in the UK in December 2020 set out to investigate in more detail the penumbra of uncertainty surrounding conspiracy belief in general and the pandemic more specifically. The starting assumption of the study was that there has been too much focus (in both the academic literature and media/political commentary) on the vocal minority of hard-core conspiracy believers, and not enough attention on the fact that to some degree conspiracy thinking is widespread and normal. "The danger of only focusing on the vocal minority," the report argued, "is that we have a skewed understanding of the issues and fail to act in an effective way to combat misinformation across the population" (Strong 2020). In line with other recent research, the study found that conspiracy beliefs are widespread, with the majority believing in at least one conspiracy proposition when asked about a range of popular theories. The poll found reasonably broad—but nowhere near universal—familiarity with (though not necessarily belief in) the range of conspiracy theories presented (the Princess-Diana-was-murdered theory at 81%, microchips in the vaccine at 59%, 5G masts spread coronavirus at 53%, information about UFOs being covered up by the authorities also at 53%, and 9/11 was an inside job at 40%). At the same time, however, it also discovered quite low levels of committed belief in many of the theories (for example, only 2% of those familiar with 5G theory considered it to be plausible, less than polls conducted in the spring of 2020). This suggests that the belief has waned over time—or, at the least, people are less willing to admit to believing it, even in an anonymous survey. The study highlighted that few people are committed conspiracy theorists (for instance, only 2% found two or more of the conspiracy statements they were presented with very plausible), but many more were in a grey zone of finding some of the explanations believable to some degree (49% agreed that at least one out of three conspiracy theories they were asked about was somewhat or very plausible). Or, to put it another way, they were not confident enough to rule them out entirely. As with the Freeman study, the significant finding in the Ipsos Mori report is not the number of committed believers, but the comparatively low proportion of people who were willing—whether for partisan signalling, trolling or genuine doubt—to agree that the conspiracy theory is implausible. For the Princess Diana story, only 27% found it implausible (compared to 40% who found it plausible); for 5G theories, 56% implausible (2% plausible); for 9/11, 29% implausible (14% plausible); climate change 48% implausible (14% plausible); and for the vaccine-microchip theory 60% implausible (4% plausible). These results are thus in keeping with the report's finding that the proportion of people who actively create and post content on social media relating to conspiracy theories is no more than 3%. In line with other research, the report found no significant difference in demographics except that "lower income households and those with fewer qualifications do seem to be slightly more likely to consider the conspiracy theory plausible" (Strong 2020).

One particularly fascinating section of the survey also asked respondents to consider not the strict truth of a conspiracy statement, nor even its plausibility, but the extent to which it conveys something meaningful about how the respondent views the world, even if it is not literally true: "It is not strictly accurate, but represents important issues" and "It is not strictly accurate, but is a reasonable challenge to official explanations." The results were Princess Diana conspiracy theories 34% and 39% (respectively); 5G 13% and 9%; climate change 31% and 25%, UFOs 22% and 29%; microchips in the vaccine 14% and 11%; and the 2008 financial crash 46% and 38%. Thus, even two of the more far-fetched conspiracy theories about Covid-19—5G and microchips—resonated with the public at levels far higher than a measurement of out-and-out agreement. While some might argue that the Ipsos Mori poll is in danger of stretching the definition of a conspiracy theory too far, the survey nevertheless manages to break away from the idea that conspiracy thinking adheres to a yes-no binary. The survey design helpfully highlights the possibility that, for some respondents, agreeing to a conspiracy theory proposition on a questionnaire might be a way of signalling frustration with the status quo or merely an increasing distrust of experts and authorities.

Often the issue is not that people believe things that are clearly untrue, but that people refuse to believe things that *are* true. Although there has been much discussion of the idea that we are living in a post-truth age, there is less a crisis of truth than a crisis of trust in authoritative sources of knowledge. Agreeing to a conspiracy proposition in an opinion poll might well be a way for some people to express their resentment about the authorities or their sense of being overwhelmed by conflicting sources of information with no easy way of knowing who or what to trust any more.

★

In this chapter we have laid out the varying claims, both conceptual and data-driven, that the Covid-19 pandemic has been accompanied by an epidemic of problematic information and belief in conspiracy theories. There is reasonably solid evidence to suggest that there has been an increase in the visibility and availability of conspiracy theories, mis- and disinformation, especially in the online sphere. There are also good grounds for thinking that a substantial minority of people report believing in particular conspiracy theories about the pandemic, but that does not necessarily tell us much about the nature of those beliefs, or indeed about the connection between belief and behaviour (Jerolmack and Khan 2014). Before the roll-out of the vaccines, many opinion polls warned that vaccine hesitancy (some—but by no means all of which—is based on conspiracy theories) was running at worryingly high levels, ranging from approximately 40% in the UK and the US to as high as 60% in France, for example (Chadwick et al. 2021; Guillon and Kergall 2021; Sallam 2021). However, the level of vaccine take-up has been much higher than those early surveys would have suggested (close to 90% in most nations in the Global North to date). But just as belief does not necessarily predict behaviour, so too does behaviour not preclude belief. It is entirely possible that people continue to believe in vaccine-related conspiracy theories even after they have been vaccinated—perhaps even precisely because they feel more distrustful of the authorities if they believe that they have in effect been coerced into getting the jab. In the same way that claims about an "infodemic" of mis- and disinformation should not be taken as given, so too should the opinion polls be taken with a pinch of salt. It is far from clear whether the coronavirus pandemic constitutes an unprecedented situation, with previously unseen levels of conspiracy theories in circulation and concomitant belief.

Note

1 We are grateful to Boris Noordenbos for this observation.

3

A YEAR OF COVID-19 CONSPIRACY THEORIES

Part 1

So far, we have examined both the deep background and the immediate context of the "infodemic" of conspiracy thinking, misinformation and disinformation surrounding the Covid-19 pandemic. This chapter and the next provide an account of the different conspiracy theories that developed during the pandemic, focusing primarily on the period from early 2020 to the summer of 2021. These findings are based on an immersive engagement by our research team in the emerging conspiracy culture across a range of media as the pandemic unfolded, coupled with digital methods analysis of the social media datasets that our team began to assemble from the outset of the pandemic. Our account is broadly chronological, yet the development is not a linear one with one theory leading to the next over time, but a complex, overlapping story in which conspiracy narratives emerge, get recombined and reused. The emergence of specific ideas, narratives, tropes, political positions and conspiracy communities does not lend itself to a straightforward timeline. Sometimes theories fade away but more often they return in a new guise and a new context. Although much of what emerged drew on a pre-existing repository of narrative building blocks, there have also been some surprising and significant new developments in conspiracy thinking during the pandemic. Contrary to claims that particular communities, political groups, influencers or social media pipelines are largely to blame for the seeming deluge of conspiracy theories, misinformation and disinformation during the pandemic, we found that conspiracy thinking emerged in complex ways across multiple sites.

There are, however, some broad trends that remain constant. The notions that "we are being lied to" and "THEY are trying to control us" were the governing ideas of many conspiracy theories about the pandemic, from the swirling community of QAnon to the prominent anti-lockdown and anti-vaxx movements. The pandemic provided "confirmation" to many conspiracy theorists of their existing

DOI: 10.4324/9781003315438-4

conviction that there is a vast conspiracy by globalist elites to remove individual sovereignty and freedom. It is also significant that many of the conspiracy narratives that have circulated during the course of the pandemic emerged early and were then retooled for new purposes. The reason (as we discuss in more detail in chapter 5) is that most of the underlying narratives and interpretive communities were already in place, and the pandemic was slotted into these existing frameworks. In addition, conspiracy theories about the pandemic (especially in the US) became incorporated into existing and emerging concerns such as QAnon and the fantasy that the US presidential election was rigged. The story of conspiracy theories about Covid-19 is thus part of a larger and longer story about the role of conspiracism, populism and new media in recent decades. To begin this account, we devote a fair amount of space to the lab leak theory before moving on to other key examples. As an origin story, this theory was kept alive because scientists, politicians in various countries, journalists and their sources in the world of intelligence were hotly debating it alongside disinformation agents and those we would more commonly label "conspiracy theorists."

Home-Grown Lab Leak and Bioweapon Theories

Although there were likely cases of Covid-19 circulating in the last two months of 2019 in China, the virus spread quickly in early 2020. On December 31, 2019, the Chinese National Health Commission alerted the regional WHO office to a cluster of pneumonia cases with unknown cause in a hospital in Wuhan. In an update on January 11, 2020, the Chinese authorities stated that the cases were linked to the Huanan wholesale market in Wuhan, and that genetic sequencing had identified the cause as SARS-CoV-2, a novel coronavirus. On January 21, the CDC confirmed the first US case: a resident of Washington state who had returned from Wuhan. With human transmission confirmed by January 21, the WHO declared a Public Health Emergency on January 31, with the US following suit on February 3. By March 11, the WHO had declared the situation a global pandemic. Conspiracy theories and other forms of misinformation and disinformation also emerged quickly, leading (as we saw in chapter 2) the WHO Director-General Tedros Adhanom Ghebreyesus to warn in a speech on February 15 that "we are not just fighting an epidemic" but "an infodemic" (Ghebreyesus 2020a). On platforms rife with conspiracy speculation such as 4Chan, Reddit and Alex Jones's Infowars, commentators had already in January 2020 latched onto the fact that the wet market (which Chinese officials believed to be the origin of the outbreak) was only a few miles from the Wuhan Institute of Virology (WIV), the only lab in China with biosafety level 4 (BSL-4) facilities, equipped to handle the deadliest of pathogens (Bandeira et al. 2021, 11). Moreover, one of the institute's labs specialised in research aimed at detecting new coronaviruses, especially from bats. Many conspiracy theories thus started from the assumption that it was no coincidence that the outbreak of the virus occurred close to China's only

BSL-4 lab, which was also working on novel coronaviruses. These appeared at first on fringe platforms but circulated in complex patterns in and out of more mainstream places. A thread titled "Chinese Chernobyl" on the /pol/ channel on the 4Chan message board from January 25, 2020, for example, began with the assertion that "Coronavirus is a BIOWEAPON." The poster went on to provide instant answers to questions many people had at the time:

- Why did the disease originate in Wuhan? Because China has a bioweapon lab there.
- Why does it have a 2 week incubation period? Because the disease was designed to spread as fast as possible prior to detection for maximum impact. [...]
- Why has China banned travel out of the country when the disease is within it? Because they are terrified that international governments will find out that the Coronavirus is man-made.

(see https://archive.4plebs.org/pol/thread/240889320/#240896751)

In a similar vein, but now straddling the divide between legacy and alternative media, in the online comment section of an article airing the lab leak theory in the conservative newspaper the *Washington Times*, one poster (BlueMustache) commented:

> I think [a lab leak] makes far more sense that it happening spontaneously. In this types of situations coincidences are never just coincidences! Its way too obvious that if they have this testing facility right there in Wuhan and they are dealing with such serious types of viruses etc then it had to have originated form this facility. It just makes sense. Although I do not think it was on purpose because that makes no sense at all to release it on their own population. They are reporting that China is not stating the real death toll and its far worse than what they are telling the world. Someone messed up in this facility and it got out and they couldn't contain it and they DEFINITELY do not want to admit to making a huge mistake like this so they blame it on the fish market or the USA.
>
> *(Gertz 2020)*

Another poster (RedQuill) went further in the conspiracy speculation:

> Concur 100% ... lets connect the dots shall we: 1. China was losing in Hong Kong and had to stop the rebels at all costs. 2. Trump beat them badly on the trade deals. They fear 'me too' from every other country they have ripped off. 3. Their economy is mostly stagnant. 4. China remains as one of the most polluted countries in the world. 5. The Chinese military remains on the move all over south Asia They want Taiwan back badly. These are just for starters. So for China the ends do justify the means even if they lose a few hundred thousand of their own. That is nothing

> more than collateral damage to a bunch of sick thug leaders hell bent on
> destroying the US.
>
> *(Gertz 2020)*

Confined at first to dedicated conspiracy forums and comment sections that leaned towards conspiracy talk, speculations about the origins of the virus quickly gained wider traction with two publications on January 26. First, a piece titled "Coronavirus Bioweapon: How China Stole Coronavirus from Canada and Weaponized It" was published by Great Game India, a comparatively obscure website that had prior form in publishing conspiracy rumours about geopolitics (GreatGameIndia 2020). The article claimed that two Chinese scientists had stolen the novel coronavirus from Canada's National Microbiology Lab in Winnipeg, where they had been working until they were dismissed under suspicious circumstances in July 2019. They then supposedly smuggled the virus to the WIV, where it was leaked. (Part of the story about the removal of the two Chinese scientists from the Canadian lab, possibly in connection with industrial espionage, turned out to be true, but the idea that they had smuggled samples of SARS-CoV-2 to the WIV has not been corroborated (Pauls and Ivany 2021)). The original item on the Great Game India website only gained 1600 interactions on social media (likes, shares and comments), but it was picked up the same day by Zero Hedge, a cult financial blog with more than half a million followers and a history of flirting with alt-right conspiracy theories (Hagan 2009).[1] The Zero Hedge piece was in turn reposted by Red State Watch, a popular partisan website that amplifies right-wing content (its Facebook page, @DonaldTrump4President, had more than four million followers at the time). From there the story went viral across social media, in particular Reddit, Facebook and Twitter, even after the Canadian authorities explained that the dismissal of the two Chinese scientists had nothing to do with coronavirus (Pauls and Yates 2020).

The second publication on January 26 that contributed to the lab leak/ bioweapon conspiracy theory going mainstream was a piece in the *Washington Times* (to which the posters cited above were responding). Based on an interview with Dany Shoham, a former Israeli military intelligence officer and (supposedly) an expert on Chinese biological warfare, the article repeated the story about the Canadian scientists, suggesting that the WIV had accidentally leaked the coronavirus as part of a "covert bio-weapons program" (Gertz 2020). The newspaper later added a correction to the article noting that scientists had since concluded that SARS-CoV-2 "does not show signs of having been manufactured or purposefully manipulated in a lab, though the exact origin remains murky" (Gertz 2020). Shoham himself also walked back his remarks, saying he had been misquoted, but by then the genie was out of the bottle. The spectrum of lab leak theories ranged from the comparatively plausible idea of an accidental leak from legitimate scientific research at the WIV to more far-fetched speculation that the virus was part of a covert biological warfare programme, and had either been accidentally leaked or deliberately released. Often the discussion online hedged its bets between all three positions, creating a heady brew of conspiracist conjecture. On January 31, into this mix was added the claim in a medical preprint article published by a group of Indian scientists that the SARS-CoV-2 genome contained a short sequence that was very similar to part of the HIV genome, leading them to conclude that the "uncanny similarity of novel inserts in [the Wuhan coronavirus] to [HIV] is unlikely to be fortuitous" (GreatGameIndia 2020; Deutch 2020). The preprint was widely criticised and was withdrawn on February 2, but not before the molecular biologist Anand Ranganathan sent out an alarmist tweet to his 200,000 followers, summarising that "they hint at the possibility that this Chinese virus was designed … Scary if true!" (Samorodnitsky 2020). The story of the supposed discovery by the Indian scientists was widely distributed, for example by David Knight, an online right-wing/libertarian radio host who was sacked from Infowars in December 2020. Knight shared the possibility of "Another connection to HIV & #Coronavirus" with his 232,000 followers on Twitter on February 2, 2020. But the story also travelled across partisan lines. The *New York Times* columnist Ross Douthat, for instance, retweeted Ranganathan's tweet to his 160,000 followers. In this way, a piece of shoddy and irresponsible science was amplified and legitimated both by online rumour-mongers and by more respectable scientists and journalists, which in turn became grist for the mill of conspiracy theorists.

The lab leak theory was repeated in many quarters including, for example, in an episode on March 11, 2020, of "Get Off My Lawn," by Gavin McInnes, the founder of the far-right group the Proud Boys (https://censored.tv/watch/shows /get-off-my-lawn/episode/s02e136). In the episode, McInnes interviewed Shiva Ayyadurai, who made the claim that Covid-19 is a Chinese bioweapon. In our study of coronavirus conspiracy theories month by month on the mainstream social media platforms, videos and posts by "Dr Shiva" were regularly in the top ten most engaged-with conspiracist items, promoting a range of conspiracy theories and other misinformation, along with miracle cures and a relentless anti-vaxx stance. A video by Dr Shiva posted on his Facebook page on February 19, 2020, for example, put forward the speculation that Covid-19 may have been released by China to stop the pro-democracy protests in Hong Kong at the time ("Did CHINA unleash #BioMediaWarfare on its OWN PEOPLE to CRUSH the Health & Freedom Movements in Hong Kong & Wuhan?"). In the comment thread accompanying the video, Dr Shiva's followers (all of whom in the following exchange seem to be women) threw out a range of conspiracy speculations: that the virus was a biochemical weapon to stop the Hong Kong protesters, that it was manmade, that it was a plan by Bill Gates and George Soros to depopulate the US (which is supposedly predicated by the Georgia Guidestones) and that 5G has killed people with the virus:

GG: WELL AS IT TURNS OUT, IM 100% CORRECT. THE CHINESE
      GOV ADMITTED THREE DAYS AGO THAT THIS DID NOT

ORIGINATE WITH BAT SOUP IN THE MARKET!! THEY NOW
SAY THEY'RE LOOKING FOR THE SOURCE.
GG: AND VIRUSES ARE TOO ALIVE. THEY REPRODUCE.
JS: where? Show me?
SA: man made virus
SS: that's Not what happened, gates & soros had the virus created & started it in
China, he even said last year at a conference they were going to do it, per
the Georgia guide stones, to depopulate US!!!!!!
SS: it was the 5G that killed them, the virus weakened the immune system, pls
the aluminium from the skies on us, the 5G fried them like being in a
microwave.
GG: JUST GOOGLE DR. CHARLES LIEBER AND ALSO HARVARD
UNIVERSITY AND IT SHOULD COME UP.
EY: I feel Trump released this virus, why I feel this way. I don't know! I just feel
he is behind it all
LB: I'm sorry, I have to disagree with you, because they have tried everything to
get our president empecshed right down to giving false statements to the
supreme Court!
LB: Big pharma did it. They sell fear, vaccine and pills […] they are the ones to
profit from all of this
(see https://www.facebook.com/va.shiva.ayyadurai/posts/2898381140218385)

In addition to the Dr Shiva posts, one particularly prominent video making the
claim that the Communist Party of China had created the coronavirus as a bioweapon was released in April 2020 by the *Epoch Times*, a site started by Chinese
Americans associated with Falun Gong. The video was viewed almost 70 million
times on Facebook according to a fact-checking report by the BBC, and, as of
July 2021, it was still available on various YouTube channels with around 10 million views (BBC News 2020a).

As with many conspiracy theories in the digital age, there is rarely a "patient
zero" post on social media that then spawns all subsequent "infections," as
the infodemic metaphor would suggest. Instead, the China bioweapon theory
emerged from several sources at the same time and was combined with other—
often contradictory—speculations from the outset. In addition to the posts
from Great Game India and *Washington Times*, the theory was given impetus by
Francis Boyle, a distinguished law professor at the University of Illinois, who
sent out a message to 300 contacts on January 24, asserting that the Chinese
had developed the coronavirus at the biosafety lab in Wuhan (Kinetz 2021;
Klepper, Amiri, and Depuy 2021). Boyle had previously championed human
rights causes such as Amnesty International and had been involved in the indict-
ment of war crimes in Bosnia, as well as drafting US legislation in connection
with the international Biological Weapons Convention in 1989. But he also has
a reputation for making unfounded conspiracy allegations, such as his claim
in 2014 on Alex Jones's Infowars show that the Ebola virus was a genetically

engineered bioweapon, followed by a similar assertion in 2016 about the Zika virus. An interview with Boyle on January 30, 2020, on the relatively obscure "Geopolitics and Empire" podcast was picked up by Jones on February 11, with Boyle's academic and political reputation, along with his citing of scientific studies, lending heft to the bioweapon theory that was already being discussed in the comments section on Infowars. The interview with Boyle on the "Geopolitics and Empire" podcast racked up nearly 300,000 views on YouTube before it was removed (Bandeira et al. 2021, 14, 26). Over the next few weeks, Boyle modified his theory, asserting instead that the Chinese had not engineered the virus themselves but had taken it from US Army's Fort Detrick biowarfare lab, which in reality was shut down after safety concerns in August 2019 (Klepper, Amiri, and Depuy 2021). In a pattern that was often repeated with Covid-19 conspiracist mis- and disinformation, the bioweapon theory spread within and between ultra-conservative, left-leaning and pro-Kremlin networks, via both social media and legacy media, creating odd allegiances and complex routes of transmission that are more circular than linear. One study found that the theory spread "via outlets like One America News Network, a pro-Trump channel, Iran's Press TV, Global Research and its erstwhile partner, the Strategic Culture Foundation, an online journal that masquerades as independent but is actually directed by Russia's foreign intelligence service, according to the U.S. State Department" (Kinetz 2021).

As early as January 2020, the bioweapon theory began to gain traction on conspiracy-leaning social media forums, in part by drawing on dubious scientific studies and tendentious journalism. Those more fringe discussions were picked up and amplified by partisan media outlets and political influencers, leading in turn to a further, much larger wave of online conspiracy talk, now "legitimated" by the appearance of previously marginal theories in more mainstream venues. It is not simply that politicians like Trump picked up on the rumour from social media (or even via Fox News), or that ordinary people responded to cues from the political elite. It is instead an effect of a revolving door of confirmation and amplification between all involved. Republican senator Tom Cotton was one of the most high-profile public figures to take seriously the possibility that the virus might have originated in the WIV, with the suggestion that it was not simply an accidental leak. In a tweet on January 30 that included a clip of him (Cotton 2020b) in a Senate committee, Cotton used the rhetorical pose favoured by conspiracy theorists of "just asking questions" and "innocently" raising a sceptical eyebrow at seemingly improbable coincidences: "We still don't know where coronavirus originated. Could have been a market, a farm, a food processing company. I would note that Wuhan has China's only biosafety level-four super laboratory that works with the world's most deadly pathogens to include, yes, coronavirus" (Bandeira et al. 2021, 22; Cotton 2020a). Coming under heavy criticism from Democrats and newspapers such as the *New York Times* and the *Washington Post*, Cotton subsequently dialled back his comments, instead listing the bioweapon hypothesis as one among a number of logical possibilities concerning the origins of the virus, which also included (as he noted) the prevailing scientific consensus of zoonotic transmission as still the most likely option.

Reporting on Cotton's speculations and providing considerable media amplification of them, on February 19 the conservative columnist Gordon Chang also floated the possibility of the lab leak/bioweapon theory on Fox News, without clearly dismissing it. If Cotton tried to seem measured, all the while hinting at conspiracies that had already been debunked by scientists, President Trump's estranged former adviser Steve Bannon had no such qualms. Bannon did an interview with his billionaire benefactor, the exiled Chinese businessman Guo Wengui, on G News, a website known for publishing fake news. In the interview, Bannon suggested that if the Chinese Communist Party did not actually manufacture the virus, its spread was nonetheless down to their incompetency. This rhetorical sleight-of-hand was repeatedly evoked in alt-right discussions of the lab leak and bioweapon theories: either the Chinese are conforming to the stereotype of a "backward" nation and are recklessly incompetent to have allowed a leak at the Wuhan lab, or the Chinese are living up to another, equally racist stereotype that they are fiendishly plotting the downfall of the white race through illegal experiments and scientific theft. Often these two contradictory positions are floated at the same time, held together by the master framing narrative that the Chinese are untrustworthy and constitute a "yellow peril" that endangers the West. In the spring of 2020, as the initial outbreak in Hubei province in China was brought under control while the pandemic spread rapidly across Europe and North America, the traditional conspiracist logic—working backwards from the question "who benefits?" in order to identify the conspirators and their plan—began to kick in. New versions of the bioweapon theory quickly gained ground, including the speculation that China had deliberately created a virus either to which Asian people were naturally immune, or for which the Chinese had already secretly created a vaccine. Most of the theories were also accompanied by the assumption that the Chinese government, possibly in collusion with the WHO, were involved in a conspiracy to cover things up.

What held these various conspiracy narratives together was an overriding suspicion of China. This was not a fringe position, but a key part of the Trump presidency. Trump had a track record of resorting to racism and conspiracy theory, often together. In 2016, he claimed that global warming is a hoax perpetrated by the Chinese to gain competitive advantage over the US, and his anti-China stance continued with his insistence on calling the coronavirus the "China virus," the "Wuhan flu" or the "Kung flu" (Wong 2016). At a press briefing on April 30, 2020, Trump claimed that he had seen classified information indicating that the virus had come from the WIV. But when asked what the evidence was, he said, "I can't tell you that. I'm not allowed to tell you that" (Singh, Davidson, and Borger 2020). Likewise, Secretary of State Mike Pompeo indulged in a mixture of bluster and obfuscation on the issue, at first maintaining that there was a "high degree of confidence" in the allegations. But he then walked back the claim, only to double down, insisting that there was "enormous evidence" for the lab leak theory (Finnegan and Margolin 2020; Bandeira et al. 2021, 29). Even if what Pompeo reported was correct, these were familiar rhetorical manoeuvres from Trump and his administration that have much in common with the posture of conspiracy theorising. When in 2011 Trump pushed the Birther conspiracy theory (that President Obama was not US-born), he told an interviewer, "I have people that have been studying it and they cannot believe what they're finding." Trump was the president who cried wolf, always hinting at vast conspiracies but never providing any concrete evidence (Muirhead and Rosenblum 2019). It is therefore understandable that in the spring of 2020 much of mainstream science and the media were initially sceptical about the lab leak theory, suspecting that it might just be part of an anti-Chinese propaganda campaign, aimed to deflect attention away from failings in the US response to the pandemic (Elliott 2021).

Scientists were quick to challenge conspiracy-minded speculations that the Chinese were to blame for the outbreak. First, on February 18, 2020, a group of prominent scientists signed a statement in *The Lancet* that warned against unfounded speculations about the origins of the virus: "We stand together to strongly condemn conspiracy theories suggesting that Covid-19 does not have a natural origin … Conspiracy theories do nothing but create fear, rumours, and prejudice that jeopardise our global collaboration in the fight against this virus" (Calisher et al. 2020). And second, in March, a high-profile article in *Nature* concluded that SARS-CoV-2 did not have any obvious tell-tale traits of genetic engineering (Andersen et al. 2020). Together these interventions by well-respected, mainstream scientists meant that much of the bioweapon talk was quickly framed by most of the liberal media as an unfounded conspiracy theory, motivated by anti-Chinese sentiment. The important thing to note here is that, even if the lab leak theory turns out to be true (and there are still good reasons to think it will not), the *way* in which the theory was promoted by both politicians and keyboard warriors in the spring of 2020 has all the hallmarks of conspiracy thinking: confirmation bias, claims to secret information, blaming all problems on a demonised enemy, sliding quickly from the idea of an accidental laboratory leak to a deliberate programme of bioweapon research, and so on.

Although the full-blown bioweapon theory continued to command respect on conspiracist forums, the potentially more plausible accidental lab leak theory became the fall-back position for right-wing politicians and their supporting media from April onwards. However, even the accidental leak narrative was rarely free of the insinuation of conspiracy because the assumption—sometimes spelled out but usually just implicit—was that the Chinese authorities had collaborated with the WHO to cover up the alleged leak. Under the guise of merely hearing out the other side of the story, the bioweapon theory was kept alive by prominent right-wing pundits. In September 2020, Bannon returned to the fray, now joining forces with Tucker Carlson on Fox News to publicise the whistle-blowing allegations from Li-meng Yan, a Hong Kong scientist who had worked at the WIV. In a series of pseudoscientific articles (designated as preprints, but unlikely to ever be published by a reputable journal), Yan laid out a dizzying account of how the virus had been engineered and the smoking gun evidence visible in its genome, which she then summarised in high-profile appearances on Fox News and similar right-wing and anti-Chinese partisan media outlets (Qin, Wang, and Hakim 2020).

Disinformation Campaigns

In addition to speculation that China had accidentally or deliberately released the coronavirus from the WIV, right from the outset there emerged a parallel set of conspiracy theories suggesting that it was the US that was to blame for the pandemic. Many of these conspiracy-minded accusations had their source in disinformation campaigns orchestrated either directly by Chinese or Russian state actors or by media outlets sympathetic (wittingly or not) to the CCP and the Kremlin. On January 20, for example, the Russian Army media outlet *Zvezda* published an item, including an interview by the supposed biologist and weapons inspector Igor Nikulin, speculating that the US might have created the virus as a biological weapon to attack China (Bandeira et al. 2021). In the coming months, Nikulin repeatedly appeared on Russian television to elaborate on these claims (Klepper, Amiri, and Depuy 2021). As with promotion of other conspiracist narratives in recent years, the aim of Kremlin-aligned disinformation is not necessarily to push a particular counter-narrative but to sow discord.

Conspiracy narratives about the coronavirus pandemic thus formed part of a larger revival of Cold War geopolitical struggles, this time staged through the proxy of online social media engagement. The covert sowing of disinformation rumours about the origins of an epidemic was nothing new, even if the technological means of transmission had changed considerably. For example, in the mid-1980s the KGB, in collaboration with the East German Stasi, quietly seeded the conspiracy rumour that HIV was manufactured as a biowarfare agent in Fort Detrick in Maryland (Selvage 2019). The story first appeared—with an uncanny presaging of the article about the origins of the coronavirus on the Great Game India website—in an anonymous letter by a supposedly "well known American scientist and anthropologist" to the editor of the *Patriot,* an obscure Indian newspaper set up to channel pro-Soviet, anti-Western stories to the subcontinent. The piece ("AIDS May Invade India") alleged that the US was spreading the new disease under the guise of a cholera vaccination programme in Pakistan and was thus warning Indian readers about the geopolitical threat posed in the region by the US collaborating with Pakistan. This letter was part of a much wider Soviet disinformation campaign (codenamed "Operation Denver," but also claimed to be called Operation Infektion by one Stasi officer), with letters and articles appearing in media outlets around the world that were covertly pro-Soviet (Selvage and Nehring 2019). The Soviets would then pick up on these publications—especially those from the West—and amplify the allegations with plausible deniability that they were in fact the original source of the conspiracy claims. Operation Denver was undoubtedly successful: according to a poll in 2005, a third of African Americans believe that HIV/AIDS was made in a government lab (The Lancet 2005). However, it would be a mistake to attribute the proliferation of conspiracy theories about the origins of HIV/AIDS solely to this single piece of covert propaganda. Belief in such rumours is rooted in a more complex history of medical neglect, along with attempts to provide folk explanations for institutional racism (Knight 2000, 143–67). Likewise, it is wrong to view the explosion of conspiracy accusations about the origins of the coronavirus pandemic in a US biowarfare lab as merely the product of anti-American disinformation. Although it is important to trace how these theories emerge, it is also necessary to understand both the networks of transmission and the cultural work that the theories perform for the various constituencies which circulate them.

Partly in response to the kind of story appearing in the *Washington Times*—alleging that the Chinese had created the coronavirus as a bioweapon—in February 2020, the Chinese began to push back with their own mirror-image conspiracy theory that the virus had been created as an American biowarfare agent in—of course—Fort Detrick. Although this tit-for-tat conspiracy-mongering played out in novel ways on social media, it was not in itself unprecedented. In the Korean War, for example, the Chinese accused the US of using germ warfare (an accusation which some historians suggest is accurate), while during the SARS outbreak of 2003 rumours that the US was behind the epidemic (based on a claim by two Russian scientists that the disease was man-made) circulated widely in China (Endicott and Hagerman 1998; Galloway and Bagshaw 2021), and the same accusation was made about China by the Taiwanese (Jennings 2008). The *People's Daily* ran a story on February 22, 2020, reporting on various speculations about coronavirus. It referenced an assertion (based on a mistranslation) that the CDC had acknowledged that 10,000 flu deaths were in fact caused by Covid-19 (and therefore the disease had been in the US earlier than the Wuhan outbreak), as well as an anonymous post on social media that the virus might have been brought to China by the US team as part of the Military World Games held in Wuhan in October 2019. In a commercial updating of the kind of "information laundering" that the Soviets used in Operation Denver, the *People's Daily* report was then carried as part of a reciprocal arrangement for free content in the *Helsinki Times* in Finland and the *New Zealand Herald* (Bandeira et al. 2021). In a similar fashion, the conspiracy-heavy Canadian think tank Centre for Research on Globalization (CRG) reworked a post from a Chinese WeChat account that had set out the hypothesis that the US had concocted the virus in its Fort Detrick Lab and released it via the Military World Games. In turn, Zhao Lijian—a spokesperson for the Chinese Ministry for Foreign Affairs—tweeted a link to the CRG website article along with a host of other accusations on March 12 and 13, urging his followers to read the articles: "When did patient zero begin in US? How many people are infected? What are the names of the hospitals? It might be US army who brought the epidemic to Wuhan. Be transparent! Make public your data! US owe (sic) us an explanation!" (Bandeira et al. 2021, 34–35). Zhao's accusations were widely decried as propaganda by Trump and others in the US, but they were picked up around the world by anti-American media outlets and state actors and, along with a host of related stories, were widely distributed within China in print, broadcast and digital media. Although the Military World Games scenario primarily played out in anti-American media in China, Russia and Iran (among others) as part of a geopolitical effort to deflect criticism and apportion blame, it was also flagged up by conspiracy theorists within the US—and, in turn, picked up by Chinese media as "evidence" that was being revealed within the US itself. The conspiracy YouTuber George Webb, for example, went so far as to doxx a US Army reservist who had been involved in the Games (and had fallen ill), claiming that she was the Patient Zero who had transmitted the virus in Wuhan in October. The story gained some attention in the US, but it was repeatedly amplified by Chinese media (Vallejo 2020). In this way, conspiracy theories about the origins of coronavirus circulated globally in a feedback loop of apparent confirmation, allowing state disinformation campaigns to engage in a form of "information laundering," with domestic conspiracy theorists in the West at times acting as unwitting collaborators (Kinetz 2021).

The Return of the Lab Leak Theory

By the summer of 2020, the idea that the coronavirus had escaped from a lab in Wuhan (whether accidentally or deliberately) had been dismissed by the vast majority of scientific experts and the mainstream media as not merely factually wrong but inevitably tied to racist and conspiracist assumptions about China. However, in May 2021, the lab-leak-and-cover-up theory came back on the agenda. On May 26, President Biden ordered the US intelligence agencies to deliver a report to him within 90 days, answering the question of whether the coronavirus pandemic emerged naturally from animal-to-human transmission or had leaked accidentally from the WIV. Various op eds (Allsop 2021) wondered if the mainstream media was guilty of "groupthink" in failing to take the possibility seriously:

> As we sift through the lab-leak debacle, the good news is that the healthy antibodies in the system are still strong enough to overcome the groupthink that produced the original error. News media are investigating a hypothesis they once dismissed, and the government has announced an investigation to find the truth.
>
> *(Chait 2021)*

In a similar fashion, editors behind the scenes at Wikipedia debated whether they needed to now include an entry on the lab leak theory as a viable scientific hypothesis or continue to ignore it as misinformation (Ryan 2021). In late May, Facebook reversed its policy of removing posts which claimed that the origin of the virus was manmade (Hern 2021). More worrying, Trump and his supporters were quick to claim that they had been right all along and should not have been dismissed as crazy conspiracy theorists. Trump acolytes also made the speculative leap that if they were right about the lab leak theory, then they would be proved correct in their other assertions—not only about the "Big Lie" that the 2020 election was stolen but also the whole QAnon narrative about a massive conspiracy of Satan-worshipping paedophiles. The return of the lab leak theory therefore raises an important question: if a conspiracy theory turns out to be true, are we still justified in calling it a conspiracy theory?

Although some researchers take an agnostic approach to whether a conspiracy theory is, by definition, false, often the default assumption is that the theory is unwarranted (Pigden 1995; Keeley 1999). In effect, the usual definition is that a conspiracy theory is merely an unfounded (or not yet proven) hypothesis that a particular event is the result of a secret conspiracy. The implication is that if experts come to the conclusion that the theory is in fact correct, then it is no longer called a conspiracy theory. Watergate is the most commonly cited example of a conspiracy theory that turned out to be true. A more recent and more fraught example is the case of Weapons of Mass Destruction (WMD) in the lead-up to the Iraq war: those who were sceptical about the claim by the Bush and Blair governments that the Iraqis had the capability of launching a nuclear attack were dismissed at the time as conspiracy theorists. In contrast, few at the time accused Woodward and Bernstein of dabbling in conspiracy theory in their reporting on Watergate (the *Washington Post* came under fire from the Nixon administration for spreading false stories, but its reporters were not labelled "conspiracy theorists"). One reason for this is that the very term "conspiracy theory" was only beginning to gain popular usage in the early 1970s, having emerged as a term in social science in the 1950s and 1960s, along with other discussions of the dangers of the "paranoid style" in American politics. Conspiracy theory as a recognisable way of making sense of the world began to be stigmatised as a pathology at the tail end of the 1950s, with the discrediting of McCarthyism as a mass delusion (Thalmann 2019). The term "conspiracy theory" has thus tended to function as both a seemingly neutral description of a style of historical explanation and an accusation that the proponent not only fundamentally misunderstands how history works but is aligned with harmful politics. On the one hand, the minimalist definition of a conspiracy theory as merely a theory of conspiracy fails to understand why they are a distinctive, problematic and seductive form of narrative explanation. On the other hand, the pathologising of conspiracy theories tends to dismiss them as deluded, but it fails to see that they are not mere fantasies. As Mark Fenster puts it,

> overarching conspiracy theories may be wrong or overly simplistic, but they may sometimes be on to something. Specifically, they may well address real structural inequities, albeit ideologically, and they may well constitute a response, albeit in a simplistic and decidedly unpragmatic

form, to an unjust political order, a barren or dysfunctional civil society, and/or an exploitative economic system.

(Fenster 2008, 90)

We therefore need to be aware that labelling a particular view as a conspiracy theory is not simply a neutral and objective act of classification. However, as we outlined in the introduction, there is a cluster of identifiable characteristics that we can point to in terms of rhetorical style, logical assumptions, psychic investment and political functions that makes conspiracy theories distinctive— even if they are also closely related to other ways of making sense of the world, legitimate and otherwise (Birchall 2006). We also need to think about the affective force of conspiracy belief. Conspiracy theories are not simply propositions that can be cast aside if new evidence comes to light but are more usually part of a broader, deeply held worldview. We need to consider the psychic investment that believers have in their theories: why do people hold onto beliefs, even when the evidence is speculative, at best, and often contradictory, at worst? To explain this, we can turn to Slavoj Žižek's discussion of a story told by Jacques Lacan about a pathologically jealous husband who, Žižek argues, should still be considered paranoid even if all his accusations turn out to be true (Žižek 2019). The husband's jealousy at the time was based not on falsifiable reason and evidence but an obsessive, emotional commitment to a particular interpretive framework—whatever the facts might have been. On this line of thinking, the reason conspiracy theorists believe and cling to their beliefs is not warranted by the evidence (which would lead people to change their mind if new evidence comes to light) but by a deep-seated, affective commitment to the belief, which is fuelled by an intense need to blame and scapegoat (Andrejevic 2013).

It therefore still makes sense to characterise a particular view as a conspiracy theory, even if it turns out to be true. The crucial point is that we need to examine closely how and why people adopted a conspiracist stance *at the time*, rather than retrospectively reclassifying it as not a conspiracy theory in the light of new evidence. When we look back at the way the lab leak theory emerged in the spring of 2020, then, what stands out is that the hypothesis was rarely propounded on its own. As we have seen, talk about a possible leak from the WIV was often bound up in speculations about the virus as a bioweapon and other implausible narratives. This is a signature feature of the online conspiracy theory ecosystem during the pandemic (and is becoming the default mode of conspiracy theorising in general): conspiracy theories rarely come as a single, separate claim, but are instead integrated into endlessly shifting mega-conspiracy theories that tie together all kinds of details and episodes into one overarching theory. In addition, conspiracy talk is often gestural, hinting knowingly about a grand plan while providing little in the way of detail. For example, in the discussion thread following Dr Shiva's video ("We Are at War. #FireFauci. End the Shutdown") posted on April 4, 2020, there was the following exchange: "China made the virus and spread it on purpose with the help from WHO AND THE GATES

FOUNDATION," one poster asserted, while another replied that "The reason why is because of Rothschild's Rockefellers and Bill Gates and Tesla all of them combined is the reason why the world is going the way it is" (see https://www.facebook.com/watch/live/?ref=watch_permalink&v=807183449773495).

The turn to a gestural but all-encompassing conspiracism can, in part, be explained by the fact that the more complicated versions of the story (as told in lengthy, multi-part videos on YouTube or in long blog posts, websites and books) are often distilled down into a single meme. One widely circulated meme, for example, distilled the supposed conspiracy plan into a story-board with six panels: "create virus, lockdown, go cashless, install 5G, create RFID, inject as vax" (see Votta 2021). Another meme offered a similar eight-point plan of "How to Ransom the World," which supposedly explains everything that is happening (see Figure 3.1). In this version, the grand plan involves crashing the stock market rather than using the vaccine to implant 5G-controllable chips: "1. Engineer a virus 2. Release virus 3. Use media to create a panic 4. Control the narrative 5. Drive the stock market down 6. Buy up all the cheap stock 7. Release vaccine 8. Enforce mandatory worldwide vaccine … for a man-made retro virus that shouldn't exist."

In many cases, the specific lab leak theory was quickly glossed over as it became inserted into a far larger story that the pandemic was planned in advance by an all-powerful conspiracy whose ultimate aim is to control the world through implanting chips in the vaccine or to engage in mass depopulation. In effect, the idea of an accidental leak is replaced by the conviction that the release of the virus—perhaps made to look accidental—was part of an expertly orchestrated master plan for world domination (a notion which often has antisemitic undertones). As a detailed digital methods analysis has shown, in conspiracy forums

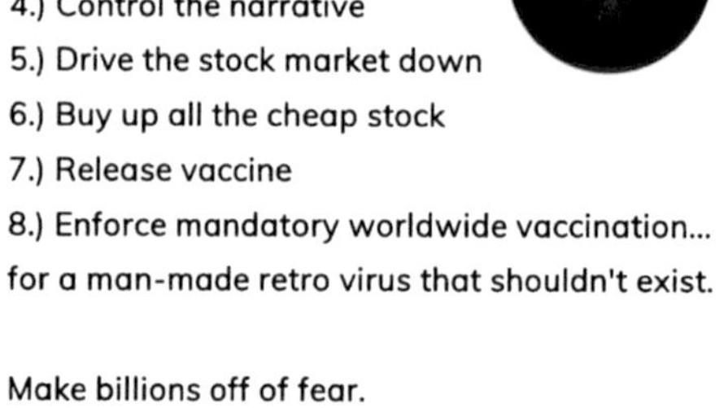

HOW TO RANSOM THE WORLD

1.) Engineer a virus
2.) Release virus
3.) Use media to create panic
4.) Control the narrative
5.) Drive the stock market down
6.) Buy up all the cheap stock
7.) Release vaccine
8.) Enforce mandatory worldwide vaccination...
for a man-made retro virus that shouldn't exist.

Make billions off of fear.

FIGURE 3.1   Meme from the Infodemic Project's dataset. *Source: Available online, see Votta 2021.*

the discussion of the origins of the novel coronavirus was dominated by talk of deliberate engineering rather than accidental leak (Marcellino et al. 2021). Online debate about the origins of the coronavirus—especially in the first few months of the pandemic—involved a scattergun blast of different speculations in endless combinations: both accidental and deliberate, both hoax and manufactured, enemies both within and without. An analysis of our Twitter dataset, for example, indicates how both lab leak and bioweapon talk can branch off in many different directions (see Figure 3.2).

On its own terms, the lab leak theory is not necessarily implausible, even if most experts continue to agree that the scientific evidence indicates it is unlikely.[2] But the way the notion was discussed on social media in the spring of 2020 was often very much part of a recognisable conspiracy culture. When the lab leak theory returned in May 2021, the accusation from some critics of the liberal media in the US was that there was not much in the way of new revelations, so it was merely a result of the shift from a bias against Trump to a bias in favour of Biden. However, there were three potentially significant new leads in the case. First, the Nobel prize-winning biologist David Baltimore was quoted in an article in May 2021 in the *Bulletin of the Atomic Scientists* (written by the controversial science writer Nicholas Wade) that the furin cleavage site of SARS-CoV-2 was a "smoking gun" that indicated that the virus was not solely a result of natural mutation (Wade 2021). However, Baltimore quickly issued a clarification, explaining that the genome's sequence is compatible with both the natural origin and lab leak theories (Beaumont 2021). Other scientists with more direct expertise in coronaviruses, though, have pointed out that the lab leak theory is still very unlikely given the furin cleavage site and other features of the SARS-CoV-2 virus, and new research (February 2022) provides stronger evidence that the Wuhan market was indeed the source of a zoonotic outbreak (Lewandowsky, Jacobs, and Neil 2022; Zimmer and Mueller 2022).

Second, there are uncorroborated intelligence reports of several lab workers at the WIV getting sick with coronavirus-like symptoms in November 2019. If true, this would be compelling evidence for the lab leak theory, given that it also strongly suggests that the institute itself, as well as the local and national Chinese authorities, were involved in covering up the story. However, we need to exercise some caution in accepting these intelligence reports blindly on trust, even if they turn out to be true. The claim was included, for example, in an article in the *Wall Street Journal*, with the journalist briefed off the record by intelligence officials. The author of the piece, Michael R. Gordon, was the co-author of a notorious article in the *New York Times* in 2002 in the build-up to the Iraq war (Gordon and Miller 2002; Calame 2005). That article had also relied on an off-the-record briefing from intelligence officials about the supposedly confirmed existence of WMD, including the influential claim that the discovery of aluminium tubes in Iraq strongly suggested that Saddam's regime had the capability of carrying out a nuclear attack. The much-quoted punchline of the article was that the first sign of a smoking gun would be a mushroom cloud. As was later

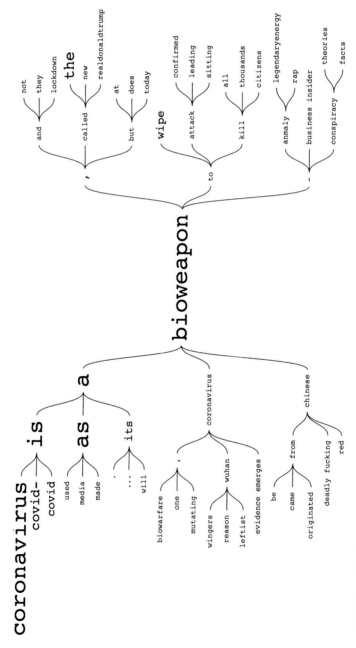

FIGURE 3.2 Word tree from the Infodemic Project's Twitter dataset. *Source: Image created by Marc Tuters. Published with permission.*

revealed, the claim about WMD had been exaggerated, and the scaremongering line about the mushroom cloud had been fed to reporters by Vice President Dick Cheney. This is not to say that the new intelligence report about the lab staff in the WIV is wrong, but we need to make sure that we are not being played.

The third set of new revelations is about the way that the statement in *The Lancet* was put together in the context of the wider international scientific collaborations with the WIV, especially those involving controversial "gain-of-function" research, which had been the subject of a moratorium from 2014 to 2017. (Many of the details about the cooperation between the US, France and the WIV were in fact reported on in the spring of 2020, but they only gained significant attention in conspiracy forums, especially concerning the role of CDC director Anthony Fauci in channelling funds for research to the WIV.) In particular, as detailed in a lengthy article in *Vanity Fair*, we now know more about the role of Peter Daszak, head of EcoHealth Alliance—a scientific organisation which had secured US National Institutes of Health grants for collaborations with the WIV involving gain-of-function research on coronaviruses (Eban 2021). It turned out that Daszak had not merely signed the statement in *The Lancet* but had been pivotal in getting prominent scientists to add their names, all the while downplaying his own role. As the *Vanity Fair* article also documents, there were many competing interests at work as various US intelligence agencies have investigated the lab leak claims, with some preferring "not to pursue an investigation into the origin of Covid-19" because it would "open a can of worms" if it continued (Eban 2021). Gain-of-function research in itself is nothing new or secret, but it raises complicated ethical issues that have previously received little wider public discussion or scrutiny. As the *Vanity Fair* article explains:

> investigators inside the U.S. government asking similar questions [about a potential lab leak] were operating in an environment that was as politicized and hostile to open inquiry as any Twitter echo chamber. When Trump himself floated the lab-leak hypothesis last April, his divisiveness and lack of credibility made things more, not less, challenging for those seeking the truth.
>
> *(Eban 2021)*

In terms of international politics, it will of course be very significant if the lab leak theory—involving either the WIV or Fort Detrick—turns out to be true. But, even if it does not, focusing all our attention on conspiracy speculations means that we are in danger of failing to raise other, more important questions—not least about the safety and ethics of virus research around the world. The return of seemingly more warranted versions of the lab leak theory has also been accompanied by the kind of exaggerated speculation and dubious self-promotion that are often found in conspiracy culture. For example, an article in the *Daily Mail* in May 2021 featured the work of two scientists, Angus Dalgleish and Birger Sørensen (Boswell 2021). They asserted not only that had they found smoking-gun evidence that the coronavirus genome had been deliberately engineered, but that their as-yet-unapproved vaccine candidate—a poor cousin to the other vaccines already approved by health agencies around the world—was the only one that could be truly effective and safe because it had been designed to take into account the supposedly peculiar and unnatural features of the genome.

What the investigation into the lab leak hypothesis uncovered is not really a tale of conspiracy and cover-up, even if that turns out to be true. Instead, it revealed a complicated story of competition, complicity and conflict of interest. The Trump administration presented China as a threat and a rival to US hegemony, but, in the case of the WIV, there was considerable cooperation in scientific research, even if the Chinese were less than transparent about all the activities taking place at the institute. One of the problems with conspiracy theory in general is that it drowns out the more nuanced analysis of forms of collective action that sit somewhere between the usual two poles of a conspiracy or a cock-up (Knight 2021). If we insist on framing events simply in terms of conspiracy or no-conspiracy, we will fail to make sense of the messier ways in which history—including global pandemics—unfold. Legitimate concerns get tarred with the brush of paranoid delusion. Some conspiracy theorists seem to get close to asking the right questions, yet their insistence on trying to find a hidden masterplan behind everything that is happening distracts us not only from the more painstaking work of genuine investigative journalism but also from the more complicated analysis of our interconnected world. It also precludes the development of modes of political engagement that do not succumb to either naïve complacency or obsessive paranoia.

Hoax and False Flag Theories

The lab leak and bioweapon theories placed the blame for the pandemic on a foreign enemy. At the same time, however, another strand of conspiracy talk took aim at enemies within. These narratives drew on and resonated with the populist political rhetoric that (as chapter 1 sketched out) was a conspicuous feature of both the Trump administration in the US and the climate of political polarisation surrounding Brexit in the UK. In addition to the many misleading and outright false claims made by Trump about the pandemic (Milman 2020; Stolberg and Weiland 2020), at the outset the president framed it in terms of one of his existing pet themes: the notion that Democrats and the mainstream media were using "fake news" to criticise his administration and damage his chance of re-election in November. As fact checkers later pointed out (when the claim cropped up in the presidential debates in the autumn), Trump did not directly claim that the virus or the pandemic was a hoax:

> Now the Democrats are politicizing the coronavirus, you know that right? … We did one of the great jobs. You say, "How's President Trump doing?" They go, "Oh, not good, not good." They have no clue … . They tried the

impeachment hoax … . They tried anything. They tried it over and over
… . Think of it. And this is their new hoax.

(Yen 2021)

However, throughout the last year of his presidency, Trump downplayed the
seriousness of Covid-19, declaring confidently in February 2020, for example,
that it was "going to disappear. One day it's like a miracle—it will disappear"
(Qiu, Marsh, and Huang 2020). In private, however, Trump expressed far more
concern about the seriousness of Covid-19 (BBC News 2020b).

While it is true that Trump did not actually call the virus a hoax, he continued to insist that any media accounts critical of his administration's response to
the pandemic were part of a conspiracy against him. On October 26, in the run
up to the election, Trump tweeted about the "Fake News Media Conspiracy,"
insisting that the US had the most cases in the world only because it carried
out the most tests and that, instead, it was the "Corrupt Media conspiracy" that
was "at an all-time high" (Lovelace 2020b). Subsequent accounts have also suggested that the view that the pandemic was an exaggerated threat—perhaps even
a hoax—was prevalent in the Trump White House, along with the abiding suspicion that he was the victim of internal enemies ("Dr. Deborah Birx on 'Face
the Nation'" 2021).

#FilmYourHospital

Even if Trump himself was circumspect about directly calling the pandemic a
hoax, some of his loyalist followers—especially those into QAnon—took this
view literally, incorporating it into a range of conspiracy narratives. Some
of the talk about coronavirus being a hoax was little more than a claim that
the authorities (in the person of Fauci or state governors mandating lockdowns and mask wearing) were inflating the seriousness of the pandemic.
In effect, it was a politicised and deliberately provocative way of expressing
disagreement with public health measures, and in some versions it formed
part of a legitimate debate about the balance between individual freedom
and collective security. However, much of the hoax talk was quite literal. For
example, in response to an article shared by Zero Hedge about US hospital
beds rapidly filling up with Covid-19 patients, a tweet from the account @
MAGA2ARIGHTS on March 7 remarked, "Call me crazy but this feels like
a false flag!" In a similar vein, the @MRROYALBADNEWS account, on
March 10, drew attention to the "Coronavirus Impeachment Scam," noting
that "POTUS has already called corona a hoax," and "We have been calling corona false flag and a distraction from the start" (Argentino 2020a).
Accusations that the pandemic was a hoax drew on the right-wing conspiracist narratives of "false flag" events and "crisis actors," which have become
an increasingly common stock reactions to events such as mass shootings,
especially since the Sandy Hook Elementary School shooting in 2012 (Mason

2019). False flag and crisis actor claims are, in part, driven by a knee-jerk cynical distrust of official versions of events, but they are also fuelled by a familiar conspiracist cult of the amateur expert. Why trust evidence from supposedly reputable media and scientific sources, the argument goes, if it contradicts your own personal experience or the first-hand experience of like-minded "citizen journalists" you follow online?

One of the oddest strands of conspiracy-themed discussion during the spring of 2020 was the #FilmYourHospital craze. The theory was that the pandemic was wildly exaggerated, if not entirely invented. The "proof" was that hospitals were not overwhelmed with Covid-19 patients but were quieter than usual. Social media users began posting their own drive-by videos with voiceovers, showing how the hospital car parks were empty; some even filmed themselves walking into the hospital and showing empty corridors and waiting areas. The reason for the disconcerting quietness was that many hospitals cancelled non-emergency appointments and banned visitors in order to make space (and consolidate staff resources) for Covid-19 patients, many of whom were being treated on intensive care units far from the public gaze. The trend began on March 28 with a tweet of a clip filmed outside a New York hospital. It was made by Todd Starnes, a former Fox News commentator, and was viewed 1.3 million times that weekend (Zadrozny and Collins 2020). Although researchers did not find evidence of automated bots or other coordinated inauthentic behaviour in the spread of the hashtag, it was, nevertheless, amplified by conservative politicians such as Deanna Lorraine (who encouraged her 150,000 followers to "get #FilmYourHospital trending"), partisan media figures, including Fox News contributor Sara Carter (who retweeted it to her 1 million followers), and prominent right-wing social media influencers such as Candace Owens (who shared the hashtag with her 2 million audience).[3] The #FilmYourHospital trend spread quickly among Trump supporters in the US, with a typical comment on Twitter agreeing that "We are being lied to … The deep state wants maximum panic" (Orr 2020). The hashtag spread quickly on English-language social media (Ahmed et al. 2020) as well as in other online language spaces—most notably through pro-Bolsonaro accounts in Brazil (Gruzd and Mai 2020).

QAnon and Deep State Theories

Although the QAnon community engaged in a variety of conspiracy speculations right from January 2020, the person (or people) posting as Q were actually late to the game. In January and February, Q continued to post the usual fare of ominous-yet-vague prophecies, attacks on the so-called Deep State and pro-Trump statements, but ignored the emerging global health crisis—which, like pretty much everything else of significance, Q had failed to predict. The first post, or Q drop as they came to be called (Q drop #3896) about the coronavirus from Q appeared on March 23, endorsing, in suggestive fragments at least, the conspiracy theory that Covid-19 is a bioweapon produced by China, which was also covering up the scale of the outbreak (Q 2020):

"the CHINA virus"
Worth remembering:
 [link to YouTube video]
Wuhan Institute of Virology [geo location]?
[1st biosafety lvl 4 lab – 2015]
City/Province origin – hot zone [geo location]?
*[link to Justice Department item about a Harvard professor charged with espionage relating
    to Wuhan]*
[…]
[link to Epoch Times *article claiming that the Chinese were underreporting the Covid
    death toll]*
> End POTUS rally(s)?
> End POTUS econ gains?
> End POTUS unemployment gains?
> End POTUS [A, B, C, D, …]?

With its highlighting of a story about Chinese scientific intellectual property theft, the post was consistent with the anti-China stance of the Trump administration (Q also calls SARS-CoV-2 the "China virus"). There were only four Q drops in April that mentioned the pandemic, eventually rising to 20 in May. However, in keeping with the predominant notion that the pandemic was engineered by the Deep State to disadvantage Trump, Q speculated, for example, that the pandemic would conveniently allow campaign rival Joe Biden to avoid public events. With Q comparatively silent, QAnon "bakers" (as these Q-decoders were called) were active in interpreting the pandemic. At first, many QAnoners pushed the line that the virus was a hoax designed to crash the economy and ruin Trump's chance of re-election. For example, the major QAnon promoter Joe M (@StormIsUponUs) tweeted on February 20 that "The #CaronaVirus was a deliberate biological terror attack by the globalist cabal which they are using as the pretext to make massive simultaneous stock sell-offs to crash the economy in the run-up to the 2020 election to hurt Trump. Simple as that" (Argentino 2020a). Others in the movement interpreted the pandemic as the "Storm" that Q had prophesised and which would lead to mass arrests of all the traitors in the Deep State. The prolific conspiracy theorist Liz Crokin stated that:

> if you've been following Q since 2017, Q has been talking about these mass arrests, and Q has also been talking about how, when these arrests happen, then there will probably be many days of darkness, social media might go down, the National Guard's going to come in, the military will be used to arrest these people, and that is what I believe is happening right now.
>
> *(QAnon Anonymous 2020)*

After the WHO declared a pandemic on March 11 and the Trump administration began taking it more seriously, some in the QAnon community suggested that the pandemic and the ensuing lockdown was not a hoax by Trump's political enemies to damage his chance of re-election but a clever cover story created by Trump and his fellow "white hats" in their counter-conspiracy struggle against the Deep State and global elites. The idea was that stay-at-home orders would ensure that the supposed conspiracy of paedophile Satanists would not be able to flee the country as the mass arrests were to begin imminently. For example, self-styled "Prophet" Mark Taylor speculated in an interview on the online McFiles radio show in March 2020 that "they are using this corona-virus as a cover to go in, shut places down, and start making arrests" (Right Wing Watch 2020). The increasing presence of police and military personnel in enforcing lockdown orders and assisting in relief efforts was taken by some QAnon watchers as a sign that Trump had personally taken charge of the mili-tary, in a prelude to the fantasised "Coming Storm" of a "second civil war" that would see the final, apocalyptic defeat of the Democrats, Hollywood elites and Satanists, in keeping with the recurrent strand of evangelical belief in the QAnon community.

Some in the QAnon movement suggested that the pandemic was unfolding according to "the Plan" that would see the white hats triumph. Others, however, were concerned that the mobilisation of the state in response to the pandemic— which many liberal commentators decried as far too slow and too small—was a forerunner of the removal of individual liberty and mass incarceration of "patri-ots" in FEMA camps—a long-running fear in conspiracy communities since the 1980s. This alarmist interpretation is possibly what led Eduardo Moreno, a train driver with the Pacific Harbor Line in Los Angeles, to attempt to crash his loco-motive at speed into the USNS Mercy, a Naval hospital ship sent to the city to free up space for Covid-19 patients in regular hospitals. When arrested, Moreno hinted ominously (with several echoes of posts that Q had recently made) that he wanted to "wake people up" and "bring attention to the government's activi-ties," including a "government takeover," but without specifying exactly what he meant (Zaveri 2020; Amarasingam and Argentino 2020).

The idea of the pandemic as a hoax remained a default suspicion for many of the Make America Great Again (MAGA) faithful throughout 2020, even when it came up against the most confounding counter-evidence. For example, when it was announced on October 2 that Trump had been taken to hospital because of Covid-19, a Trump-supporting truck driver in Missouri insisted that "it's a hoax. There's no pandemic. As Trump said, how many millions die of flu?" Struggling to square this view with the information about Trump's hospitalisa-tion, the Trump supporter speculated instead that "if he's sick, then they planted it when they tested him" (McGreal 2020). In a similar fashion, others sympa-thetic to QAnon insisted that the president was not in hospital but aboard a US naval warship, orchestrating the much-anticipated round-up and execution of the Deep State. At first, the QAnon community struggled to interpret the pandemic through the lens of their existing narrative, not least because Q provided little of substance on the issue. But, by the summer of 2020 (as we will see in chapter 4), some in the movement began to frame events in terms of the master narrative of Satanic-worshipping paedophiles and child trafficking.

Far-Right Accelerationism

At first, QAnon supporters continued to engage mainly in the collective online interpretation of Q's enigmatic statements. Although their forums often contained rallying cries to action, usually this involved nothing more than the injunction to "do your own research" or "#FilmYourHospital." In contrast, ideologically motivated extremists issued more direct calls for action in response to what they viewed as an overweening curtailment of individual liberty with government mandated lockdowns and mask wearing. As we'll see in more detail in chapter 4, these far-right and libertarian groups reworked traditional scare-mongering conspiracy theories, in effect using the pandemic to opportunistically recruit new members to their cause. On platforms such as 4Chan, 8kun and Telegram, where the alt-right congregated, participants coined the hashtag "corona-chan" for coronavirus. "Corona-chan" was used 13,000 times on 4Chan in February and March 2020, for example, while on Facebook there was a twentyfold increase of the term in March alone (ISD 2020, 3). The discussion often returned to an idea—half-ironic, but increasingly taken at face value—that had become prominent during the Trump presidency and the ascendency of QAnon, namely an impending second civil war or American revolution, dubbed the "boogaloo." The boogaloo movement encompassed a loose cluster of libertarians, gun rights activists, militias, anti-government nationalists, white supremacists and neo-Nazis. What they had in common was a conviction that the US government was dangerously restricting the rights of the sovereign individual, contributing to an "accelerationist" stance that openly fantasised about a coming race war. It therefore came as little surprise that the "boogaloo boys" viewed the pandemic as a plot by the government to further erode individual liberty, and heavily armed groups associated with the boogaloo movement became an increasingly visible and active presence during the summer of 2020 at anti-lockdown gatherings and agitating against Black Lives Matters protests, culminating in the storming of the Capitol on January 6, 2020. Although the boogaloo boys' rhetoric was often couched in gamified terms of "players" and "points," their call for violent action against those they viewed as enemies (the police, liberals, Muslims, Jews and Black Americans) was taken seriously by some of their fellow travellers. On March 24, for example, law enforcement officers in Belton, Missouri shot and killed a man, Timothy Wilson, suspected of plotting to attack a hospital in the Kansas City area treating Covid-19 patients (Goldman 2020). Affiliated with the neo-Nazi group the Atomwaffen, Wilson had posted on Telegram shortly before the shoot-out with police that the coronavirus pandemic was being controlled by Jews (Makuch 2020). In October

2020, 14 men (half with ties to a paramilitary militia group) were arrested on suspicion of plotting to kidnap Gretchen Whitmer, the Democrat governor of Michigan, and overthrow the state government. The inept yet disturbing plot was seemingly in reaction to the strict coronavirus pandemic lockdown measures in Michigan ordered by Whitmer. Indeed, encouraged by an incendiary tweet by Trump on April 17 ("LIBERATE MICHIGAN!"), heavily armed anti-lockdown protesters had stormed the Michigan state capitol building on April 30. In the UK, similar narratives about Covid-19 were pushed by various far-right extremist groups, which promoted conspiracist misinformation far more than any other political persuasion (Miller 2020). Many on the far right interpreted the pandemic in terms of their existing ideology: some claimed it was the fault of immigrants, part of a supposed plot of a "Great Replacement" of white Christians in Western societies by Muslims; others specifically blamed Jews; some saw it as the outcome of liberal policies towards LGBT communities; and others identified globalist elites as the culprits (often with the inclusion of antisemitic bogeymen such as the Rothschilds and George Soros). Research by the BBC in collaboration with the counter-extremism think tank ISD Global found that of these five themes, narratives about elites increased the most in the spring of 2020. As Chloe Colliver of ISD explained, "anti-elite conversations have escalated dramatically, especially driving home the idea the lockdown is a tool of social control" (Miller 2020).

★

In this chapter we have examined the emergence of both home-grown conspiracy talk and global disinformation narratives about the pandemic resulting from a bioweapon or a lab leak in Wuhan. We then tracked the return of the lab leak theory in the spring of 2021, arguing that the initial development of these stories should continue to be regarded as forms of conspiracy theorising, even if there are now more reasonable grounds for believing in the claim. We also traced the proliferation of conspiracy theories based on the idea that events were being manipulated as part of a political plot to undermine Trump. Along with conspiracist calls to "Do Your Own Research," the rallying cry of #FilmYourHospital was fuelled by a populist distrust of mainstream media and experts. We also documented how the pandemic was incorporated and utilised by QAnon and other right-leaning political movements. In the next chapter, we continue the story with conspiracy theories that focused on mistrust of medicine and science.

Notes

1 Although it had published many other pieces of disinformation, Zero Hedge was banned from Twitter on January 20, 2020 for violating their platform manipulation policy: in addition to reprinting the Great Game India article, it had doxxed a Chinese scientist at the WIV in an article provocatively titled "Is This the Man Behind the Global Coronavirus Pandemic?" However, Twitter rescinded the ban in

June 2020 after an appeal from Zero Hedge, saying that it had made an error (Reuters 2020a; Reuters 2020b).

2 And by the time this book is published, the lab leak hypothesis might even have been proven correct, although at the time of writing—February 2022—we doubt it. Zoonotic origin continues to seem more likely (Lewandowsky, Jacobs, and Neil 2022). It is also important to note that we are unlikely to ever get final, definitive proof that would satisfy everyone. After all, conspiracy theorists are distrustful of all experts and authorities, so a definitive finding one way or the other by the US or Chinese government, or even by seemingly objective and neutral scientists, is unlikely to persuade them.

3 The role of bots in promoting Covid-19 conspiracy theories and other misinformation in the online environment is not clear. One study by researchers at Carnegie Mellon University, for example, reported that 45% of Twitter accounts spreading messages about the pandemic are likely to be bots; it also found the level of bot activity twice that of other recent disasters (Huang and Carley 2020). In contrast, Ferrara (2020) found that although bots play a significant role in partisan, political conspiracism in the US (e.g. QAnon and "Reopen America"), health misinformation (e.g. anti-vaxx) during the pandemic is spread primarily by humans.

4

A YEAR OF COVID-19 CONSPIRACY THEORIES

Part 2

The Covid-19 conspiracy narratives we examined in the previous chapter mainly revolved around existing concerns of domestic and international politics. This chapter examines theories that focus primarily on imagined medical and scientific plots. Many of the theories explored in chapter 3 begin from the assumption that Covid-19 is *not* dangerous and, therefore, it is a hoax or a result of some other nefarious, political machination. In contrast, the first section of this chapter will examine conspiracy theories which concede that Covid-19 *is* in fact dangerous but also characterise it as part of a sinister medical or scientific plot to harm the unwary. The second section explores a different cluster of conspiracy speculations which begin with the premise that it is not Covid-19 that is dangerous, but the *vaccine* and other public health measures (Center for Countering Digital Hate 2020b). The final section will turn to the increasing prominence of "superconspiracy theories" (Barkun 2013) that combine aspects of the political and medical plots analysed in both chapters.

Miracle Cures

Although there are many varieties of medical and scientific misinformation, the notion that "you are being lied to" is at the heart of many, whether explicitly or implicitly. During the pandemic, as we will see in more detail in chapter 6, many prominent conspiracy theorists built on an existing explanatory framework and marketing infrastructure to exploit the crisis for self-promotion and profit. There has been a long tradition of snake oil, miracle cures and alternative therapies (more so in the US than the UK), but, in recent decades, these have turned increasingly conspiratorial (Oliver and Wood 2014; Whorton 2002). In the 1970s, for example, the chemical compound laetrile (found in apricot pits) was widely championed in alternative health circles as a miracle cure for

DOI: 10.4324/9781003315438-5

cancer, but, if taken in high doses, it could also induce cyanide poisoning. The suspicion was that it was being deliberately kept secret by the authorities (Merlan 2021). Often the governing idea behind miracle cures is that doctors, medical researchers, "Big Pharma" and now "Big Tech" are plotting to keep from the public knowledge of these cheap, alternative (and usually "natural") treatments, supposedly because "They" want to keep a monopoly on profit and prestige. Instead, as with so much conspiracy culture, those promoting alternative remedies challenge the knowledge of mainstream experts, favouring instead their autodidactic wisdom. Although there are valid criticisms to be made of the pharmaceutical industry, the public health policy choices made by governments and global institutions and the failure of science to communicate with the public effectively, much of this alternative health conspiracism is animated as much by grift as it is by a genuine resentment against powerful and insufficiently democratic organisations.

Right from the outset, conspiracy theorists touted alternative cures for the novel coronavirus. Even before the pandemic, many prominent conspiracy theorists such as Alex Jones had already heavily promoted "Miracle Mineral Solution" (MMS) on the e-commerce section of his Infowars website. With the news about the new virus others jumped on the bandwagon. Sodium chlorite, the active ingredient of MMS, when coupled with citrus extract produces chlorine dioxide, an industrial bleach. Proponents claim that spraying yourself with, gargling or even taking small doses of MMS solves many medical complaints. In reality, however, MMS is not merely ineffective in curing the various diseases it is claimed to combat (including HIV, malaria and cancer), but it is actively dangerous if ingested. Despite warnings from the FDA, advocates for MMS are still convinced of its healing powers. Conspiracy talk usually takes the FDA's efforts to regulate or ban it as proof that the authorities are concerned that ordinary people have seen through their supposed lies. For example, prominent YouTuber and QAnon advocate Jordan Sather repeatedly tweeted his followers and uploaded videos touting the benefits of MMS, in particular the brand marketed by the Genesis II Church of Health and Healing, a church led by a man named Jim Humble, who styles himself "Archbishop" of the Genesis II Church and currently resides in Mexico (Dickson 2020a). Sather's populist narrative of a cheap cure hidden from ordinary people by Big Pharma is the flipside of his conspiracist claim that the elites have secret access to exclusive medicines against Covid-19. Sather's claim was based on the widely shared but mistaken "discovery" that the Pirbright Institute in the UK, which conducts research on animal disease, had filed a patent in 2015 in conjunction with the Bill and Melinda Gates Foundation for a vaccine against coronavirus. As fact-checkers soon pointed out, it was not a vaccine for SARS-CoV-2, but for a type of coronavirus that affects poultry livestock (ISD 2020, 13).

Claims about the healing powers of MMS made their way through the right-wing media ecosystem, possibly as far as Trump. In a White House press briefing on April 23, 2020, Trump wondered aloud in a very garbled manner whether ultraviolet light and chemicals such as disinfectant might be part of a cure for Covid-19:

> And then I see the disinfectant, where it knocks it out in one minute. And is there a way we can do something like that, by injection inside or almost a cleaning, because you see it gets in the lungs and it does a tremendous number on the lungs, so it'd be interesting to check that, so that you're going to have to use medical doctors with, but it sounds interesting to me.
>
> *(PolitiFact 2020)*

(Trump later unconvincingly rowed back on the remarks, to suggest that it had been a sarcastic question at the expense of the press.)

Hydroxychloroquine and Ivermectin

Others on the conspiracy circuit—including most notably Alex Jones on his Infowars platform, and the QAnon YouTuber Dustin Nemos—plugged colloidal silver and vitamin supplements as the "suppressed" miracle cures of choice (Smith, McAweeny, and Ronzaud 2020; Merlan 2022). Yet it was two existing, licensed therapeutics that gained most attention around the world in 2020 as potential Covid-19 cures, nearly always with the populist insinuation that there was a conspiracy of silence on the part of medical authorities and politicians regarding the miraculous efficacy and low cost of the medicines. The first drug to be hyped was hydroxychloroquine (often abbreviated to HCQ in conspiracist talk) and its related compound chloroquine, a medicine used to prevent malaria and treat other conditions such as lupus. Because of its known effectiveness against some autoimmune diseases, it was not unreasonable for doctors to experiment with the drug as a preventative or treatment for Covid-19, the most serious cases of which seem to involve disturbances of the autoimmune system. Some early, small-scale experiments suggested positive results but later, more rigorous trials indicated that it not only failed to provide any benefit in combatting Covid-19 but it was potentially dangerous for some patients, and it was therefore withdrawn as an emergency-use treatment in most countries in June 2020 (Lovelace 2020a; Rogers 2020b). The waters were muddied when a study published in *The Lancet* in May 2020, which reported higher death rates caused by use of hydroxychloroquine, was retracted in September because of faulty data (Davey 2020). However, the scientific debate was almost beside the point: much of the popular discussion about HCQ was framed in terms of a vast conspiracy by Big Pharma to suppress a cheap and effective cure. Q posted multiple times about hydroxychloroquine in April and May, and the narrative spread widely in QAnon communities online which were monetised (as usual) with ads from well-known brands (GDI 2020). Unsurprisingly, one social psychology study found that "conspiracy beliefs predicted support for chloroquine as a treatment for Covid-19" (Bertin, Kenzo, and Delouvée 2020, 1).

As with so much else in the pandemic, HCQ quickly became politicised and polarised, boosted by Trump in the US and Bolsanaro in Brazil. Trump began to promote the use of HCQ in March 2020, presumably on the back of considerable traffic on right-wing conspiracist social media and reports on Fox News. According to several accounts, he tried to pressurise the FDA into granting approval without going through the usual process (Rogers 2020b). The online promotion of the miracle powers of HCQ had their origins in a "research document" written by a self-styled philosopher (with a habit of antisemitic tweeting) and two cryptocurrency enthusiasts, which was then amplified by Elon Musk and others in Silicon Valley (Robins-Early 2020). Fox News ran a story with one of the authors, and, at a press briefing the very next day, Trump suggested that hydroxychloroquine was a "very powerful" cure (Ball and Maxmen 2020). On May 17, Trump announced that he was actually taking it himself as a preventive measure against Covid-19 (Beauchamp 2020). In response to a warning issued a few days later by the FDA about hydroxychloroquine, Trump dismissed the federal agency's notification as a "Trump enemy statement" (Rupar 2020). Inevitably, some Trump supporters preferred to follow his advice rather than that of health experts, and in one tragic case in March 2020, an Arizona man died (and his wife was hospitalised) after ingesting chloroquine phosphate, a compound related to chloroquine, but which was in fact a treatment for parasites in fish tanks (Associated Press 2020).

The second drug to be championed by right-wing populists and alt-health gurus—not just in the US but in South Africa and many South American countries—was ivermectin, a treatment used (in both human and veterinary medicine) against parasites. Many of the websites and organisations presenting misleading pseudoscientific information about its benefits were related to the ones that had also promoted HCQ (Merlan 2021). As with other cases of conspiracy theories in the pandemic, the rumours spread from the margins to the mainstream (and back again) through a complex mixture of social media, broadcast media and unwise comments from politicians and other influencers. A study by the *Guardian* in conjunction with digital methods researchers from the Queensland University of Technology, for example, tracked the way that a single Facebook post touting ivermectin by former Australian Liberal party MP Craig Kelly in December 2020 rippled out across social media in the ensuing months (Evershed, McGowan, and Ball 2021). Although (as of February 2022) the potential benefits of ivermectin for preventing or treating Covid-19 are unconvincing and are still undergoing scientific trials, some of the earlier studies have already been discredited, most notably a report by Egyptian doctors which had then fed into several meta-analyses (Davey 2021). The narrative being pushed by ivermectin's champions is the familiar one about a potentially "game-changing" cure for the pandemic being suppressed by powerful financial and political figures. On an episode of Joe Rogan's very popular podcast, for example, the host included a conversation with Dr Pierre Kory and Bret Weinstein, two of the people most heavily involved in promoting ivermectin. "You have a drug that's good enough to end the pandemic at any point you wanted," Weinstein claimed. "Who decides to prioritize business interests ahead of that? I find it hard to imagine." He went on to claim that because "there's no profit to be made" for the pharmaceutical industry from a generic drug like ivermectin, its benefits are being deliberately ignored (Merlan 2021). Populist conspiracy theories about the suppressed truth of ivermectin have spread widely on social media, with Facebook groups such as "Fauci, Gates & Soros to prison worldwide Resistance" sharing posts that mix pro-ivermectin claims with other Covid-19 related hoaxes and anti-vaccine misinformation (Sharma 2021).

Some of the promotion of HCQ and ivermectin has been well-intentioned and willing to follow the science, but much of it has been driven by a populist fantasy that the medical experts, government authorities and Big Pharma are conspiring to keep affordable solutions from the people. While these conspiracy theories are often delusional, they nevertheless resonate with frustrations and anxieties about the healthcare system, especially in the US. They also speak to justifiable concerns about the role of the profit motive in the creation and distribution of medicines. As mainstream a publication as *Rolling Stone*, for example, ran a story titled "Big Pharma's Covid-19 Profiteers" (Taibbi 2020). Although conspiracy theorists make vague accusations of plotting, legally defined conspiracies—in the form of price fixing—do occur in the pharmaceutical sector. For example, in August 2020 the US Department of Justice announced price fixing charges against Teva Pharmaceuticals as part of a wide-reaching antitrust investigation (Kuchler 2020). Making health and medicine subject to competitive open markets invites conspiracist reactions. Rather than focusing on the all-too-obvious ways in which the worst excesses of capitalism exploit people, conspiracy theorists instead insist not merely that pharmaceutical companies will profit from the pandemic, but that they caused it in the first place for that very reason.

5G

Like miracle cure conspiracy theories, conspiracist suspicions about 5G mobile phone technology were already circulating before the pandemic. But their proponents opportunistically used fears about coronavirus to promote them to new audiences. There were different variations of the 5G–coronavirus conspiracy theories, sometimes overlapping but also sometimes making contradictory claims. As we have seen, one of the first versions of the theory falsely claimed that it was no coincidence that 5G technology was trialled in Wuhan, where the pandemic began (in reality, 5G was already being rolled out in a number of locations around the world). Some claimed that the coronavirus crisis was deliberately created in order to keep people at home while 5G engineers installed the technology everywhere. Others insisted that 5G radiation weakens people's immune systems, making them more vulnerable to infection by Covid-19. Another variation asserted that 5G directly transmits the virus—a claim usually coupled with a conspiracist narrative about a plan by global elites to bring about mass depopulation. These different 5G stories were often combined together with other Covid-19 conspiracy theories into a toxic cocktail of disinformation. The usual conspiracy theory bogeymen George Soros and Bill Gates were also woven into the narratives, along with transnational institutions like the United Nations and the World Health Organisation. The Illuminati, as a convenient signifier of a secret elite, also frequently appeared in these allegations.

Conspiracy theories about a link between Covid-19 and 5G began to appear online in late January 2020. Starting the cascade was a post on January 20 on "Les moutons enragés" (a French conspiracy website), speculating about a link between the coronavirus outbreak in Wuhan and the rollout of new 5G masts in that city. The idea was then repeated in an interview with a Belgian doctor in a regional version of the Flemish newspaper *Het Laatste Nieuws* on January 22, although the paper soon retracted the article (Temperton 2020). From there, the conspiracy-minded story spread, first among Dutch-speaking social media, and then rapidly in other languages, especially on YouTube and Facebook. In January, it was mainly confined to existing anti-5G groups, with 1,000 posts leading to 45,000 interactions on Facebook, according to one study (Temperton 2020). Then, on January 30, the far-right conspiracy theory website Infowars announced that "5G launches in Wuhan weeks before coronavirus outbreak," with the article claiming that this fact "connects the dots" between the coronavirus, the Gates Foundation and 5G. This claim then moved beyond those conspiracist echo chambers, as it became amplified by conspiracy celebrities, social media influencers and anti-vaxx activists (Heilweil 2020). In addition to veterans of the conspiracy world such as David Icke, the 5G–coronavirus conspiracy theory was promoted by self-proclaimed telecommunications expert Mark Steele and Kate Shemirani (a British nurse who has since been struck off), both of whom went on to become central figures in the conspiracist anti-lockdown movement in the UK (BBC News 2021). All of them have been making money from peddling misinformation (Broderick 2020b).

The 5G story was also promoted by others less associated with conspiracy theories, such as the actor Woody Harrelson and the boxer Amir Khan. The singer Keri Hilson, for example, tweeted in March 2020 to her 4.2 million followers:

> People have been trying to warn us about 5G for YEARS. Petitions, organizations, studies … what we're going thru is the affects of radiation. 5G launched in CHINA. Nov 1, 2019. People dropped dead. See attached & go to my IG stories for more. TURN OFF 5G by disabling LTE!!!
>
> *(Tiffany 2020a; Heilweil 2020)*

Hilson also included a link to a widely circulated online video made by Thomas Cowan, a holistic medical practitioner from California (Wynne 2020), who claimed that each pandemic in the modern age had preceded by the introduction of new electromagnetic technology, including the widely repeated canard about the invention of radio and the 1918 flu pandemic (Frith 2020). Whipping up instant controversy, the British television presenter Eamonn Holmes supported if not the 5G conspiracy theory itself, then at least the right to question what he called "the state narrative" concerning Covid-19 on live television (Robinson 2020). Although much of the spread of 5G conspiracy theories was organic, involving the usual circuit of social media, broadcast media and celebrities, there is also evidence of coordinated inauthentic behaviour. RT (the media agency for Russian soft power and propaganda) had already been spreading numerous conspiracy stories about the dangers of 5G since 2019, and in the spring of 2020 researchers found plausible evidence of a concerted campaign of amplification of the coronavirus–5G conspiracy theory (Temperton 2020; EUvsDisinfo 2020b; Gallagher 2020).

The 5G conspiracy theory is notable for the way in which it spilled over into offline activism and malicious vandalism, at times fuelled by familiar antisemitic conspiracism (Davis 2020). In the Netherlands, the UK and elsewhere, there were a number of arson attacks on 5G masts (often masts erroneously thought to be 5G, including those serving an emergency Covid-19 hospital in Birmingham in the UK) and communication infrastructure engineers. Videos of some of these attacks went viral, most notably a film by an anti-5G protester confronting two bemused telecommunications engineers (who were installing fibre optic cables and not even working on 5G) (Waterson 2020a). Understandably, social psychologists have found that "belief in 5G Covid-19 conspiracy theories was positively correlated with state anger, which in turn, was associated with a greater justification of real-life and hypothetical violence" (Jolley and Paterson 2020; van Prooijen 2020).

Although the seeming sudden emergence of the 5G–coronavirus conspiracy theory baffled many commentators, conspiracist suspicions about mobile phone technology have been circulating since the 1990s and have long historical roots (Rahman 2020). Doctors first talked of "radiophobia" as early as 1903, although their concern was more about X-rays (*Los Angeles Times* 1903). Following on from fears about power lines and microwaves in the 1970s, opponents of 2G technology in the 1990s suggested that radiation from mobile phones could cause cancer and that this information was being covered up (Burgess 2003). Other conspiracy theories about 5G include the idea that it was responsible for supposedly unexplained deaths of birds and trees (Full Fact 2019a, b). The theory about 5G radio waves transmitting or activating the virus, for example, is a reworking of long-running conspiracy fears about mind control experiments, subliminal messaging and supposed secret US military weapons projects (all ripe topics for Hollywood's movie industry) (Melley 2012). The 5G story shares similarities with rumours that date back to the 1990s about HAARP (the US military's High Frequency Active Auroral Research Program) (NBC News 2014). HAARP was a large radio transmitter array located in Alaska and funded by the US Department of Defence, in conjunction with a number of research universities. The programme conducted experiments into the ionosphere (the upper layer of the atmosphere) using radio waves. It was closed down in 2014. Conspiracy theorists, however, claimed that it was actually still operating in secret and developing a weapon for weather control, as well as mind control.

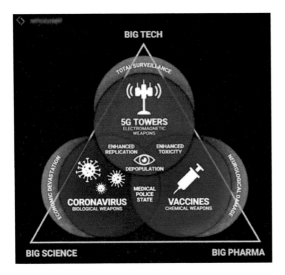

FIGURE 4.1   Image shared on Instagram, May 3, 2020, and included in the Infodemic project's dataset. *Source: Available online, see Votta 2021.*

During the pandemic, 5G conspiracy theories gained much visibility, as they circulated between the margins and mainstream, crossing the increasingly porous boundary between online and offline activism. They created cognitive maps that weave together the collusion of Big Pharma, Big Tech and Big Science. They mix medical fears about the invasion of one's body, with grand geopolitical conspiracy theories about global depopulation (see Figure 4.1).

They combine understandable concerns about unknown health risks and conditions, such as electromagnetic hypersensitivity (EHS), with the cynical commercial exploitation of those fears in the flourishing alternative health online marketplace (Tiffany 2020a). While often ludicrous in their assertions, 5G conspiracy theories nevertheless emerge out of and speak to justifiable unease about the privatisation and lax regulation of telecommunications, the overweening power of mobile phone companies, and anxieties among policy makers in the US and UK about the threat of espionage from Huawei, the Chinese telecommunications giant. These legitimate concerns are, however, inevitably eclipsed and ignored, as much discussion during the pandemic about communication technology was sucked into the vortex of conspiracist claims about vast plots and sci-fi powers.

Pastel Q

In the same way that 5G conspiracy theories combined fears about personal health and global politics, so too did an important strand of QAnon discussion as the pandemic progressed during 2020. Although (as we saw in chapter 3) Q and QAnon devotees at first interpreted the coronavirus crisis in terms of familiar domestic and geopolitical conspiracy theories about a Deep State plot to undermine Trump, in the summer of 2020, some within the QAnon movement (but, conspicuously, not Q) began to pivot towards a different narrative framework. Online talk increasingly viewed the pandemic through the lens of speculation about a global cabal of elites engaged in the mass trafficking and Satanic sexual exploitation of children. In effect this shift was a return to some of the themes of the #Pizzagate trend that began during the US election campaign of 2016 (and which, in turn, was a reprise of earlier Satanic panics). Based on a fanciful interpretation of innocuous phrases from the leaked emails of Hillary Clinton's campaign manager John Podesta, the conspiracy theory claimed that Clinton and other Democratic Party leaders were engaged in the trafficking and ritual abuse of children, all run out of the basement of a Washington DC pizza parlour called Comet Ping Pong. The bizarre theory was heavily promoted—at first in a spirit of ironic outrage—on alt-right platforms such as 4chan, but then it began to move from the margins to the mainstream (Tuters, Jokubauskaitė, and Bach 2018). The popularity of the theory waned after a man from North Carolina—convinced of the truth of the story—staged an armed raid on the Comet Ping Pong restaurant in December 2016, only to find it did not even have a basement. However, the story returned in the summer of 2020 during the pandemic, fusing with a wider set of claims about a vast, secret ring of child sex traffickers that saw QAnon themes appeal to a new, broader audience (Kang and Frenkel 2020), even if Q hardly posted about paedophiles and Satanists. As Mike Rothschild puts it in his study of QAnon,

> a new coalition of Instagram influencers, wellness devotees, and far-left anti-vaxxers flocked to QAnon's simple explanations for complex and fast-moving events. Many did not even know anything about the mythology underlying the group, but liked the anti-authority and anti-expertise messages they saw in it. Thus QAnon, a movement that had been founded on the promise of a great and bloody reckoning for liberals, somehow absorbed progressive wellness moms and Bernie Sanders voters.
>
> *(Rothschild 2021, 104)*

There was thus an uneasy convergence between alt-right anti-lockdown protesters and "pastel Q" who rallied under the banner of "#SaveTheChildren" (Argentino 2021b; Gillespie 2018; Tiffany 2020b; Bloom and Moskalenko 2021).

Early on in the pandemic, some QAnon supporters suggested that celebrities such as Tom Hanks getting sick with coronavirus was part of "the Plan," a harbinger of the "Coming Storm." They explained that the elites were unwittingly injecting themselves with adrenochrome that was tainted with Covid-19 (Mantyla 2020). The theory was that a cabal led by George Soros had funded a secret adrenochrome manufacturing plant in Wuhan with the aim of supplying the drug to the cabal of the global elites, but it had somehow (possibly as part of a "white hat" operation against them) become contaminated with coronavirus. In reality, adrenochrome—the oxidised form of adrenaline—is produced naturally by the adrenal gland, and the synthetic version is sometimes used as a blood-clotting agent. Drawing on some outdated and inconclusive scientific research into schizophrenia from the 1950s into adrenochrome's hallucinogenic properties, along with a mention of it in Hunter S. Thompson's novel *Fear and Loathing in Las Vegas*, QAnoners developed the speculation that the elite go to great lengths to acquire a pure organic version. Such purity, they claim, is achieved by harvesting adrenochrome from children, whom the elite traffic, sexually abuse and murder. Theories about adrenochrome appeared in QAnon chatter before the Covid-19 pandemic, but they have adapted to the new crisis. The mention of Soros in this context draws on established antisemitic tropes, not least a history of "blood libel," which accused Jews of using the blood of Christian children in religious rituals (Simonsen 2020). The focus on the sacrifice of children, and vague talk about child trafficking and paedophilia, enabled the influence of QAnon to spread to new demographics during the pandemic, particularly women (see chapter 5). Various new Q-related speculations emerged as the pandemic unfolded in the US, such as the idea that the lockdown was a cover story to allow the "white hats" in the US military to organise a secret rescue mission of the thousands of children who had supposedly been kidnapped.

This newer, Q-adjacent community are not the usual demographic of conspiracy theorists. However, in lifestyle, wellness and alternative health spaces—especially on Instagram—they have combined an existing distrust of medical experts with an emotive, moral outrage about an imagined vast conspiracy of global child trafficking.[1] In effect, they form a bridge between the alt-right (and often hypermasculinised) universe of the original QAnon following and the more liberal, yoga, alt-health and anti-vaccination world of "QAmom" (Guerin 2021; Dickson 2020b; Greenspan and Landsverk 2020; Wendling and Spring 2020). The activism began to move from the online world to IRL ("in real life") meet-ups, not just in the US but around the world. The movement combined with other anti-lockdown, anti-5G, anti-vaxx and anti-globalist protests in the spring and summer of 2020. In the most extreme cases, this led to violence. For example, on April 29 Jessica Prim, a woman from Illinois with seemingly unstable mental health, was arrested in New York near a ship that she mistakenly thought was the USNS *Comfort* (a hospital ship sent to help with the pandemic), which Prim believed was being used to hold children who had supposedly been liberated from underground bunkers in the city. In the days leading up to her arrest, Prim had been live-streaming her journey, seemingly inspired by QAnon #savethechildren theories, to rescue the children and assassinate Joe Biden (Amarasingam and Argentino 2020).

As we describe in more detail below, often Bill Gates became the epitome of evil for these various groups. They imagined Gates to be at the heart of a global paedophile ring that was also supposedly plotting to introduce mandatory vaccinations as part of a grand plan to control all people and/or bring about mass depopulation. Ultimately, what united these disparate communities and issues was a deep-seated sense that the authorities are lying and that people's individual freedoms are being assaulted. Conspiracy theories provided both an explanation for the pandemic, and a sense of community for the like-minded who felt they had managed to see through the lies they were being fed by the mainstream media and scientific authorities.

Anti-vaxx

Pastel Q was often closely connected to anti-vaccination activism. Anti-vaxx conspiracy theories emerged early in the pandemic, but they spread far more widely later in the year as the rollout of the vaccines came closer to reality. Of all the varieties of disinformation that circulated during the pandemic, conspiracy theories about vaccines attracted the most public concern and were at the centre of political debates about the responsibilities of social media platforms for stopping their spread. While some conspiracy theories about vaccines are on the distinctly implausible end of the spectrum, the world of anti-vaxx is a complicated one that cannot simply be dismissed as the work of a few unhinged conspiracy fantasists. As indicated by the pausing and restarting of the vaccination campaigns in many countries in the spring of 2021, amid fears about rare adverse reactions to each of the approved vaccines, for example, the line between justifiable caution and unwarranted fear is not always easy to establish—especially with the fast-moving and endlessly changing nature of the coronavirus pandemic. There are genuine, important debates to be had about balancing individual risk against collective benefit, but the anti-vaxx movement often muddies the waters by mixing those issues with more fanciful conspiracy theories.

Suspicions about vaccines have a long history, from ridicule of Edward Jenner's work on smallpox in the eighteenth century, to organised resistance against the introduction of mandatory vaccinations in the middle decades of the nineteenth century in Britain, and the formation of the American Anti-Vaccination League in 1908 (Durbach 2004; Kitta 2012). After the successful vaccination campaign against polio in the early 1950s, vaccination resistance dwindled, but it emerged again in the 2000s with the claims in a 1998 article by a British doctor, Andrew Wakefield, about a link about the MMR combined childhood vaccine and autism. Although Wakefield was eventually discredited and struck off, vaccine hesitancy did not disappear. Instead, it has continued to grow, with an active community both online and offline. The anti-vaxx movement is diverse and complex. Vaccine hesitancy and refusal are not simply a result of a lack of education or limited access to accurate information. Researchers have found that, in general, people in the anti-vaxx movement tend to have a higher level of education and are more likely to be liberal in their political outlook than other conspiracy-minded interest groups, and women outnumber men three to one. They therefore do not fit the usual stereotypical image of a conspiracy theorist (Smith and Graham 2017). In addition to an emphasis (like many conspiracy-inclined communities) on "doing your own research," there is also a strong faith in the authority of personal experience, often in opposition to established medical wisdom. Unlike some conspiracy forums online which are animated by an alt-right trolling sensibility, the anti-vaxx movement is marked out by its earnestness and grass-roots activism.

At the same time, however, the world of anti-vaxx—like other conspiracy communities—has its fair share of influencers and grifters. A study by the Center for Countering Digital Hate (CCDH), for example, found that a dozen anti-vaccination campaigners are responsible for 65% of all the vaccine-related disinformation appearing on Facebook, Instagram and Twitter (CCDH 2021b). Prominent figures include Joseph Mercola, an osteopath from Florida, who runs a multi-million dollar venture that involves selling all kinds of dubious wellness products. He also employs dozens of staff who quickly generate anti-vaxx content, which is then shared and engaged with at considerable volume around the world. A study in July 2021 by the *New York Times*, for example, found that Mercola had posted to his 1.7 million Facebook followers more than 600 pieces of misinformation about coronavirus vaccines since the pandemic began (Frenkel 2021). Many of Mercola's posts insinuate that there is a vast conspiracy involving the CDC and pharmaceutical companies to conceal the shocking truth about the dangers of the vaccines. Anti-vaxx is big business, both for the conspiracy entrepreneurs and the platforms: one report estimated that "the Anti-Vaxx industry boasts annual revenues of at least $36 million and is worth up to $1.1 billion to Big Tech with 62 million followers across their platforms" (Center for Countering Digital Hate 2021a).

However, it is not just individual "superspreaders" who have pushed anti-vaccination disinformation during the pandemic. As we will see in more detail in chapter 7, the platform design—in particular, the recommendation algorithms—of the social media companies have contributed to the growth of anti-vaxx narratives, especially the more extreme and "sticky" conspiracist versions. A study conducted by CCDH using simulated user accounts found that Instagram's recommendation algorithm (introduced in August 2020) is designed to increase engagement in order to boost ad revenue. It does this by promoting high engagement content such as conspiracy theories, misinformation and extremism: "if a user follows anti-vaxxers, they are fed QAnon conspiracism and antisemitic hate; if they engage with conspiracies, they are fed electoral and anti-vaxx misinformation" (CCDH 2020a, 4). Other researchers found a similar pattern with Facebook: if you search for wellness and alternative health information, you quickly get recommended ever more extreme (and inevitably conspiracist) anti-vaccination groups. There is also evidence of coordinated inauthentic behaviour campaigns by right-wing groups who have promoted anti-vaccination disinformation along partisan lines, for example, by cynically exploiting the fears of conservative anti-abortion groups or whipping up opposition to Bill Gates when he remarked in March 2020 that it was unwise for Trump to remove the US from the WHO (Wakabayashi, Alba, and Tracy 2020). As an investigation by the *New York Times* found, after the defeat of Trump in the election and the dismaying spectacle of the storming of the Capitol of January 6, some far-right extremists have pivoted from "Stop the Steal" to "Stop the Vaccine" (MacFarquhar 2021).

The social media platforms have come in the firing line for their perceived lack of action to remove harmful misinformation. The US surgeon general, Vivek Murthy, issued a report in July 2021 that declared that "misinformation poses an imminent and insidious threat to our nation's health," with President Biden distilling the message to the claim that Facebook "is killing people" (Guardian 2021). For their part, the social media firms have pointed out the volume of potentially dangerous material they have removed, although their claims cannot be independently verified. For example, in response to the CCDH report about the "disinformation dozen" (upon which Biden and Murphy were drawing), Facebook stated that "in total, we've removed more than 16 million pieces of content which violate our policies and we continue to work with health experts to regularly update these policies as new facts and trends emerge" (Bond 2021). Yet researchers have repeatedly found that a considerable amount of misinformation remains online, in part because so much of it has moved to private groups and channels: one estimate suggests 90% of anti-vaxx content on Facebook is now in non-public spaces (Ball and Maxmen 2020). It is also because anti-vaxx activists have become more skilled in disguising their discussions to avoid moderation and deplatforming, especially of the automated kind—some anti-vaxx groups, for example, have taken to using code names such as "dance party" to evade bans by Facebook (Collins and Zadrozny 2021).

Therefore, when the coronavirus pandemic began, there was already a well-developed anti-vaxx community which was quick to interpret it through their existing narrative frameworks. But those groups have swelled during the pandemic. A report by the CCDH, for example, found that 147 of the leading anti-vaxx accounts gained more than 10 million followers since 2019—an increase of 25%, primarily on Instagram and YouTube (CCDH 2020c).[2] Contrary to Facebook's claim in the spring of 2020 that they had quickly and effectively taken measures to contain the spread of misinformation, research by the online activist network Avaaz identified 104 pieces of misinformation in six different languages that had been labelled false and misleading by fact-checkers. They found that "millions of the platform's users are still being put at risk of consuming harmful misinformation on coronavirus at a large scale," and that "the pieces of content we sampled and analysed were shared over 1.7 million times on Facebook, and viewed an estimated 117 million times" (Avaaz 2020b, 2), indicating that Facebook's efforts were insufficient. Of particular concern is the fact that "of the 41% of this misinformation content that remains on the platform without warning labels, 65% has been debunked by partners of Facebook's very own fact-checking program" (2). Over the course of their research (from January to April 2020), much of this content remained on the platform despite Facebook's reassurances to the contrary, and there were significant delays (or up to three weeks) in Facebook's response times when it came to implementing measures to contain misinformation on the platform. Moreover, misinformation in certain languages—Spanish, Portuguese and Italian content in particular—appeared to evade warning label mechanisms. While Facebook did remove some content flagged as harmful, cloned versions remained on the platform and continued to spread. A further report by Avaaz concluded that Facebook failed to protect people from misinformation during the pandemic (Avaaz 2020a). Already by August 2020, Avaaz researchers identified posts of health misinformation garnering 3.8 billion views globally, and health misinformation sites at the centre of this network peaked at 460 million views on April 20, 2020, at the very moment the pandemic was escalating worldwide. Content from the top ten health misinformation sites on Facebook had four times as many views than content from the top ten global health authority websites such as the WHO and the CDC, while only 16% of those posts identified as health misinformation had a warning label from Facebook.

Early in the pandemic, several alarming surveys suggested that high numbers of people would refuse a vaccine, should one become available. However, vaccine resistance takes many forms, ranging from hesitancy to outright refusal, and (as we argued in chapter 2) these kinds of surveys should therefore be interpreted cautiously. The headlines of media reports of polling on vaccination intention often lump all forms of vaccine hesitancy together. For example, in Germany one poll in the spring of 2020 indicated that 84% of people would not accept a vaccine, even if it were guaranteed to have no side effects (Callison and Slobodian 2021); by February 2022, however, 89% of adult Germans had actually been vaccinated. Some surveys attempted to distinguish between different varieties of vaccine resistance. A poll conducted by Surgo in May 2021 in the US, for example, divided people into five groups in terms of their attitudes to vaccination: enthusiasts, watchful, cost-anxious, system distrusters (people suspicious of government/health authorities), and Covid-19 sceptics (those more aligned with a conspiracist view) (Surgo Ventures 2021). The survey found that vaccine hesitancy and conspiracy belief varied state by state, with no clear indication—in contrast to the assumption made by many commentators—that people of colour were uniquely prone to conspiracy-minded vaccine resistance. (Rates of vaccine take-up among Black Americans remained lower than for whites or Latinx for various reasons, but not necessarily because of conspiracism.) Instead, as other surveys have noted, the one significant outlier group is Trump supporters (Ivory, Leatherby, and Gebeloff 2021). With the approval of various vaccines by medical authorities, and the (comparatively) successful rollout of the vaccination campaign, the reported level of vaccine hesitancy fell dramatically in most countries, to roughly (as of July 2021) 5% in the UK (Office for National Statistics 2021a), but closer to 25% in the US (and three quarters of the hesitant say they are unlikely to change their minds) (Durkee 2021).[3] While some of the responses to the more alarming surveys earlier in the pandemic were undoubtedly prompted by a desire to "perform" a political position when stating intended action, people's attitudes understandably began to change as more information and first-hand experience regarding the vaccines was shared.

Anti-vaxx sentiment ranges from principled and well-informed resistance to ideologically motivated conspiracism. Some anti-vaxx concerns are framed in terms of a desire to lead a more "natural" lifestyle that favours alternative health therapies. Other anti-vaxxers emphasise the idea of individual freedom and bodily sovereignty and lean towards the conspiratorial. As we explore in chapter 5, in one of the many ironic turns that the pandemic has produced some libertarian and conservative opponents of vaccinations, masks and lockdowns appropriated the slogan of the feminist pro-choice movement, "my body, my choice" (Blom 2020). Some anti-vaxxers have moral and religious concerns based on the fact that some vaccines are derived from cells of aborted foetuses or contain ingredients contrary to religions proscriptions, although neither is the case with the Covid-19 vaccines. Others take issue with the racial ethics of how vaccine testing programmes are conducted. Many anti-vaxx groups dispute the safety, efficacy and necessity of particular vaccines.

However, unlike vaccine resistance in earlier decades, the contemporary anti-vaxx movement often also includes the assumption that the scientists and pharmaceutical companies are engaged in a massive cover-up, and even that they are actively conspiring against the people. For example, a documentary made in 2016 by the disgraced anti-vaccine activist, Andrew Wakefield, was titled "Vaxxed: From Cover-up to Catastrophe." During the pandemic, the ideas dominating much anti-vaccination discussion have been that the danger of Covid-19 has been deliberately exaggerated, and therefore vaccines are not necessary; that the vaccines are not safe (especially those involving the comparatively new mRNA approach); and, finally, that medical, pharmaceutical and political authorities have questionable motives at best, and might be involved in a sinister cover-up at worst (Smith, Cubbon, and Wardle 2020; Center for Countering Digital Hate 2020b). In an analysis by EU DisinfoLab of disinformation claims on Facebook in December 2020, for example, researchers found that 69% of the posts suggested that Covid-19 vaccine is dangerous, 28% that the vaccine is part of an evil plan, and 3% that the vaccine is not effective (Sessa 2021). However, many posts about the dangers of the vaccine also imply a conspiracy in some shape or form—and are certainly taken as saying that, by the online audience. Despite claims to the contrary, the anti-vaxx movement regularly relies on a conspiracy narrative, whether explicit or implicit.

Medical Mistrust

During the pandemic, anti-vaccination talk has drawn on a cluster of overlapping conspiracy narratives. Some have suggested that the pandemic has been deliberately engineered by Big Pharma, either to generate untold profit from selling vaccines and endless booster jabs or (in a grander scheme) to make *all* vaccines mandatory. Narratives about the medical sector seeking to profit from the pandemic resonate more strongly in the US than other countries because of its for-profit healthcare system (one persistent conspiracy-minded rumour, for example, has been that hospitals are mis-recording deaths as caused by Covid-19 in order to illegitimately access government compensation). Likewise, it is not unreasonable to ask questions about the chequered history of pharmaceutical companies and the regulatory agencies in prematurely licensing some drugs that went on to cause harm, or to examine the role of private profit in the distribution of vaccines that were developed in large part through considerable state funding.

However, many of the anti-vaccination conspiracy theories go well beyond asking these necessary questions. Other stories have focused instead on the suspicion that the vaccine was tested unethically on people of colour (especially in Africa) or that minorities in the US will be used as guinea pigs by rolling out the vaccine to them first. Other variations are that the vaccine will interfere with women's fertility or make men who take it sterile, and even that the vaccination programme is part of a sinister plot to bring about a genocide of people of colour. These vaccination rumours conjoined fears in urban African American communities about the accidental or even genocidal sterilisation of black men with fears from primarily affluent white women about the effect of the vaccine on their fertility. Conspiracy-minded fears about sterilisation have long featured in African American popular culture (Turner 1993). Taken at face value, these allegations are not factually accurate, but they nevertheless resonate with those communities, especially African Americans, who have suffered a long history of medical neglect and mistreatment—from James Marion Sims's pioneering work in the nineteenth century on gynaecology, which was based on unethical experiments on enslaved black women without anaesthesia, to the Tuskegee syphilis study in the twentieth century, which continued to carry out an experiment on black men to determine the effects of untreated syphilis, long after an antibiotic treatment was available (Washington 2007; Knight 2000). During the pandemic, conspiracist mistrust of medical authorities on the part of communities of colour has at times been pathologised. Although many of the specific allegations are unwarranted, focusing on an imagined paranoid lack of trust on the part of particular communities detracts from the historical and ongoing untrustworthiness of actual medical institutions and practices.

Microchips and Bill Gates

Some anti-vaccination conspiracy theories have latched onto the unfounded (but understandable) fear that the mRNA technology involved in some of the Covid-19 vaccines will change the recipient's DNA. Other theories have posited that the vaccine contains a microchip that will be used to track and control the world's population. Sometimes this theory is framed in terms of a familiar right-wing conspiracist narrative about the incipient introduction of a globalist, godless New World Order that will bring about totalitarian enslavement of the masses. The Illuminati are often imagined to be the ultimate puppet masters. In our team's analysis of the emergence and convergence of conspiracy tropes on Instagram during 2020, the Illuminati are a central node in the cluster of interconnecting themes, indicating their recurring importance (Tuters and Willaert 2022). The idea of an apocalyptic New World Order often draws on evangelical Christianity and its notion of the End Times. These religious myths are found, for example, in claims that Bill Gates and Microsoft have a patent numbered 060606 for an injectable microchip, which recalls the (possibly mistranslated) prophecy from the Book of Revelation that the antichrist will be marked with the "number of the beast" 666. (While Microsoft did indeed file a patent in 2018 whose number included the figures 060606, it was never granted, and it was for an admittedly troubling idea of an implant that would reward physical activity with cryptocurrency payments.) Other theories see the vaccine as a Trojan horse that will enable the evil, globalist elites to carry out their secret plan for depopulation, with the kill switch (in some versions of the theory) being activated by 5G waves.

Many of the vaccine-related conspiracy theories revolve around Bill Gates as the arch-conspirator pulling the strings—although the details about the ultimate purpose of Gates's plan are often surprisingly hazy (Wakabayashi, Alba, and Tracy 2020). These theories are not confined to the fringes: according to a Yahoo News/YouGov poll carried out in June 2020, 44% of Republicans in the US believe that Gates plans to use a Covid-19 vaccination to implant microchips in people and monitor their movements (Romano 2020). One popular rumour that circulated early in the pandemic was that Gates had planned the pandemic in advance. Conspiracy theorists have latched onto accounts of pandemic preparedness exercises that took place before the outbreak of Covid-19, most notably Event 201, organised in October 2019 by Johns Hopkins Center for Health Security in conjunction with the Gates Foundation and others. Likewise, a 2015 TED talk by Gates—in which he warns of a new pandemic—fanned the flames and bolstered fictitious claims that Gates had foreknowledge of the Covid pandemic or even purposely caused it. For those who had not taken much notice of conspiracy theories before the pandemic, these far-fetched narratives about Gates plotting the pandemic in advance and planning to use the vaccine to microchip millions seemed to come out of nowhere. But many of the narrative tropes were already circulating before the pandemic, and, in any case, draw on a deep wellspring of fears about surveillance, bodily control and the megalomaniac power of plutocrats. For example, already before the pandemic there was a conspiracist take on ID2020 (an NGO formed in 2016 to improving access to digital IDs for the many undocumented people around the world), but it went viral during the pandemic, and became amalgamated with other conspiracy theories about Gates and vaccines. The theory suggests that Gates is using the pandemic to institute mandatory vaccinations, and to thereby implant a digital tracking device. In some versions of the conspiracy narrative, this is the fulfilment of the prophecy about the "mark of the beast." As one post put it:

> The ID2020 Alliance, as it's being called, is a digital identity program that aims to "leverage immunization" as a means of inserting tiny microchips

into people's bodies. In collaboration with the Global Alliance for Vaccines and Immunizations, also known as GAVI, the government of Bangladesh and various other "partners in government, academia, and humanitarian relief," the ID2020 Alliance hopes to usher in this mark of the beast as a way to keep tabs on every human being living on Earth. Similar to how cattle are marked with ear tags, this globalist alliance wants all humans to be "vaccinated" with digital tracking chips that will create a seamless monitoring system for the New World Order to manage the populations of the world with ease. Vaccines now being used to harvest biometric identities of everyone; Big Brother merges with Big Pharma.

(Thomas and Zhang 2020, 3)

Some of the Gates microchip conspiracy theories are based on the ID2020 story. Others—often unknowingly—are based on a different kernel of truth. In 2019, the Gates Foundation funded some blue-skies research at MIT to explore ways of recording vaccinations by including readable imprints under the skin using a novel method of vaccine delivery by means of a patch with microscopic needles delivering quantum dots of invisible ink (Weintraub 2019). The research aimed to provide a solution to the very real problem of keeping accurate vaccination records in developing nations around the world. In a similar vein, conspiracy theories about Gates planning to conduct a campaign of depopulation were not invented out of thin air but are elaborations on a false claim in a Ghanaian tabloid in 2010 about a programme of testing—funded by the Gates Foundation—of the Depo-Provera contraceptive on unwitting villagers in a region of Ghana (Joyce 2020). The story was taken up by both anti-abortion and social justice organisations in the US, with two reports from the Rebecca Project, for example, alleging that international charities such as the Gates Foundation were "outsourcing Tuskegee" and in effect carrying out a black genocide. While some parts of the story about unethical and ill-considered practices by Western charities in Africa were justified, the specific claims about the Gates Foundation and the Depo-Provera trials were most likely fabricated by a disgruntled former employee of the foundation. It turned out the man who had written the Rebecca Project reports had failed to declare a conflict of interest, as he was romantically involved with the dismissed employee-turned-whistleblower. The spread of anti-Gates conspiracy theories, therefore, made some kind of sense—even if they were not literally true—because they chimed with specific elements of the way the pandemic and the vaccine development happened. Although there are thus real-world origins to some of the Gates/vaccine conspiracy theories, the actual form they take on social media is often far removed from the backstory, as they become part of baroque conspiracy speculations.

As we have seen, versions of the Gates stories had been circulating before 2020, but they received a turbo boost with the pandemic. The Harvard disinformation researcher Joan Donovan identified as the starting point of the Gates conspiracy theories taking off an AMA (Ask Me Anything) with Gates on Reddit in March 2020, in which he predicted that in the future we will all carry digital health records (Ball and Maxmen 2020). A Swedish biohacker website, with an existing fascination with implantable technology, speculated on the Gates comment and connected it to the quantum dot research project. They then reached the unwarranted conclusion that there was already a plan for an injectable microchip that might be used as part of the Covid vaccination plan (Sriskandarajah 2021). In turn, the biohacker post was picked up by a Baptist pastor from Jacksonville, Florida, whose YouTube video translating the microchip theory into the Biblical language of the "mark of the beast" soon racked up 1.6 million views. From there, the rumour spread to a wide variety of different constituencies, from earnest evangelical Christian posts on Facebook to ironic TikTok videos (Gerts et al. 2021). As we have seen in the other cases, the story was then given a further boost when it was picked up by those in Trump's circle. In April 2020, Roger Stone (Trump's former campaign adviser) latched onto the story: "Whether Bill Gates played some role in the creation and spread of this virus is open for vigorous debate. He and other globalists are definitely using it in a drive for mandatory vaccinations and microchipping people" (Sriskandarajah 2021). Stone's disingenuous remarks were in turn reported by the *New York Post*, and from there the story went mainstream—with the newspaper publication then providing renewed "confirmation" for the circulation of the rumour on social media. Some on the right wing were using the conspiracy theory as a way of getting back at Gates after he criticised Trump's withdrawal from the WHO (Wakabayashi, Alba, and Tracy 2020), while others were using the rumour to stoke conservative, Christian opposition to the vaccines.

As we will see in more detail in chapter 5, the Gates–vaccine conspiracy theories served to bring together seemingly unlikely bedfellows, including 5G, QAnon, New Age, and anti-vaxx constituencies. As the pandemic progressed, Gates became the shared antagonist who served as a focal point for disparate conspiracy communities. At the same time, the Gates-is-planning-to-microchip-us-all claim became the example of choice for those "normies" who found themselves completely baffled by the bizarre conspiracy theories circulating during the pandemic. However, as we have seen, in even the most fanciful narratives there is usually an original kernel of truth, which then often results in what Richard Hofstadter called "the curious leap in imagination" from provable facts to paranoid conjecture (Hofstadter 1964). Moreover, like many conspiracy theories, the Covid microchip stories resonate with longer histories of medical mistrust and racial inequalities and cannot, therefore, be dismissed as merely crazy. At the same time, however, they distract us from asking other important questions, such as whether we should be relying on individual billionaire philanthropists to fund global vaccine distribution and to plug the shortfall when the US withdrew from the WHO.

Plandemic

Many of the pandemic conspiracy narratives and many of the patterns of circulation we have explored in this chapter came together in the online documentary *Plandemic: The Hidden Agenda Behind Covid-19*, which we outlined in the introduction. The video was billed as a trailer for a feature-length documentary

(*Plandemic: Indoctornation*), which was eventually released in August 2020. The original *Plandemic* video consists of an interview with Judy Mikovitz, a discredited medical researcher who claims (falsely) that her PhD research had revolutionised the treatment of HIV/AIDS. She had been dismissed from her research post after her publication claiming a link between a particular virus and Chronic Fatigue Syndrome was retracted amid allegations of falsified data. Instead, Mikovitz alleges in the film that Anthony Fauci (at the time the director of National Institute for Infectious Diseases) had conspired to destroy her reputation. *Plandemic* throws all the conspiracy theories circulating at the time into the mix: Bill Gates planned it all, Big Pharma is pushing unsafe vaccines for profit, the establishment are suppressing hydroxychloroquine as a miracle cure, the virus is a bioweapon made in Wuhan and Fort Detrick, masks are not merely unnecessary but positively lethal, and so on. Although made on a small budget, the video is in the style of a professional television documentary interview. Like many conspiracy theory videos online, the allegations in *Plandemic* come thick and fast in a "Gish gallop," overwhelming viewers who have no time to contemplate or fact-check a particular claim before the film rushes onto the next. It relies on a love-hate relationship with credentialed scientists, with some being dismissed as part of an imagined vast conspiracy, while others are cited to back up the scientific claims being made. *Plandemic* invites viewers to identify with Mikovitz's story of having uncovered hidden knowledge that means she is ignored and ridiculed by the mainstream, in the same way that those conspiracy theorists who buy into the film's argument will both feel themselves unique but also find themselves marginalised.

The rapid spread of the film caught social media companies off-guard. (They were better prepared for the follow-up film, which received far less engagement online.) However, an analysis by DFRLab showed that the video migrated to alt-tech platforms, not in reaction to attempts by major social media platforms to remove the video once in circulation, but beforehand, "in anticipation of future removals" (DFRLab 2020). This suggests that the removal of the video created a Streisand Effect, when attempts to suppress online content backfire leading more people to seek out the content. It also highlights the problem of confining content moderation to a single platform approach, because "harmful content … moves to find niche refuges on the internet in order to meet demand" (DFRLab, Kharazian, and Knight 2020). The research also showed that, despite the relative isolation of these communities from one another, the most active accounts from each cluster promoting the film tended to have QAnon-related information in their profile bios as well as frequently use QAnon-themed hashtags. An article in the *New York Times* traced how *Plandemic* went viral, starting on May 5 with QAnon groups. It then spread via a celebrity women's health doctor, whose half a million followers then seeded it into numerous anti-vaccination groups. Next, it was picked up by right-wing and libertarian anti-lockdown activists; then it was endorsed by celebrities such as a mixed martial arts fighter. It was also highlighted by a Republican political candidate, and by May 7 it was on the radar of media outlets such as Buzzfeed. It then came to the attention of fact-checking organisations and the content moderation teams of the social media platforms, who then started to try and remove it. Despite this organic, rhizomatic spread, there is also some evidence that the campaign to make *Plandemic* go viral was carefully orchestrated. One study of how the film was spread on Twitter, for instance, concluded that there was "a sophisticated disinformation campaign" which was accomplished by "coaching citizens toward activism to maximize the speed at which the documentary propagated and decrease positive sentiments toward public health interventions" (Nazar and Pieters 2021). The scattergun claims in films like *Plandemic* allowed it to speak to and bring together seemingly incompatible audiences. At the same time, however, it also served as a prime exhibit for those disturbed by the power and reach of conspiracist misinformation on social media.

Great Reset and Beyond

As we discuss in more detail in chapter 5, in the autumn of 2020 the "Great Reset" conspiracy theory became a central star in the Covid conspiracy cosmos, with its gravitational pull drawing other conspiracy narratives into its orbit. Covid scepticism joined climate denialism to create a swirling mass of fears about a global elite plotting to control our lives. The Great Reset refers to the theme of the World Economic Forum's fiftieth annual meeting, which presented the idea that unfettered capitalism needed "resetting" in order to now include stakeholders and environmental concerns. The WEF's rhetoric about a Great Reset is little more than vague idealism at best and corporate greenwashing at worst, but in the eyes of conspiracy theorists of many different political persuasions it is a frightening master plan for total domination by the globalist elite. The conspiracy interpretation of the Great Reset includes tropes familiar to Covid-19 such as 5G, microchips and population control, but now inserts them in a dystopian master narrative of mass surveillance, forced vaccination and erosion of individual liberty that extends far beyond the pandemic. As our team's data analysis showed, a key hashtag in this conspiracy narrative is #agenda21, which becomes increasingly central in the Covid conspiracy universe (see Tuters and Willaert 2022). Agenda 21 is an existing intergovernmental initiative for sustainable growth, but conspiracist critics view it as the sinister extension of global corporate power into all aspects of our lives. Many commentators have assumed and hoped that Covid-19 conspiracy theories would begin to fade, with the successful roll-out of vaccines, the reduction of restrictive measures and increased medical knowledge about the causes and treatments of the disease. However, the convergence of conspiracy theories about the pandemic with ones about the climate crisis suggests that there is unlikely to be a reduction in online conspiracism any time soon.

★

In the previous chapter and this one, we have provided an overview of the interconnecting conspiracy narratives that have emerged during the pandemic. After a year of tracking Covid-19 conspiracy theories in the online environment, we identified a number of key themes, patterns and modes.[4] Many of the conspiracy theories were not in themselves especially new, but they did combine their building blocks (images, metaphors, narratives, fears and antagonists) in sometimes surprising ways. Conspiracy thinking in the online sphere during the pandemic has involved modularity, incorporation, integration, convergence, cross-pollination, distribution, mobilisation, influence, pollution and monetisation. The next chapter provides a taxonomy of these and other elements.

Notes

1 Child trafficking and the sexual exploitation of minors (including by elite figures such as Jeffrey Epstein) are indeed real, but happen at nowhere near the scale that is imagined. The hijacking of the #SaveTheChildren hashtag by QAnoners only served to hinder the vital work of charity campaigners.
2 The CCDH report is hard-hitting and well researched, but it must be noted, however, that it is itself framed in somewhat sensationalist and conspiratorial terms: "Drawing on access to a private conference attended by the world's leading anti-vaxxers, CCDH has been able to reveal their plan to use social media to spread distrust about the Covid vaccine and recruit new supporters to their cause" (Center for Countering Digital Hate 2020b).
3 These figures need to be taken with caution. According to a longitudinal study of attitudes to Covid-19 vaccination, in the UK and the US 19% and 25% (respectively) of respondents still—as of February 2022—say that they are unvaccinated and unwilling to be vaccinated, with a further 3% and 5% (respectively) uncertain ("Willingness to Get Vaccinated against COVID-19" 2022).
4 Now, at the time of final revisions before publication, it is two years since we first started tracking Covid-19 conspiracy theories in January 2020.

5

COALITIONS OF DISTRUST

Features of Coronavirus Conspiracy Theories

In the previous two chapters, we catalogued the conspiracy theories that emerged and converged during the first year and a half of the pandemic. To do this adequately, we included the longer histories of those conspiracy theories. This might give the impression that there is nothing new under the sun when it comes to conspiracism—and documenting that longer history helps correct the widespread but inaccurate claim that conspiracy theories exploded on social media during the pandemic in a way that had never been seen before. In this chapter, however, we counter the equally misleading claim that the circulation of conspiracy theories in the online environment during the pandemic was merely business as usual. This chapter is concerned with identifying what is distinctive about Covid-19 conspiracy theorising, over and above some of the general mechanisms and features of conspiracy theories we outlined in the introduction. If the content is not necessarily new—as we have seen, many of them reuse tropes, fears and rhetoric—what tendencies can we see emerging in the creation and circulation of pandemic conspiracy theories, and the uses to which they have been put? In what follows, we consider some key characteristics.[1] Not all these characteristics are unique to the pandemic; what we see, rather, is that existing trends intensify, accelerate and/or mutate during the pandemic. Yet, when considered together, a definite shift in conspiracism seems clear. Consequently, our focus is less on the narratives that we tracked in the previous chapters and more on form, function and flow. In recognising how conspiracy theories related to Covid-19 operate, we can better appreciate what such narratives do for those who engage in them, how they shape the cultural understanding of events and power relations, the conditions of knowledge production today, and the role of technology in the contemporary information ecology. It will also tell us something about why most attempts to curb online conspiracism are flawed, which we will turn to in the conclusion.

DOI: 10.4324/9781003315438-6

We have divided the key characteristics of Covid-19 conspiracy theories into two categories. The first cluster includes mechanisms that are identifiable in the form and content of conspiracy theories: convergence, modularity, incorporation and integration. The second includes characteristics that relate more to the function or social contexts of conspiracy theories: expressive, enmeshed, distributed, mobilising, diverse, celebrities and superspreaders, opportunism, adjacency, moderated and monetised. Studied together, they offer a rounded picture of how conspiracism has developed under Covid-19.

Convergence

As a highly contagious virus, Covid-19 necessitated the curtailment of personal liberties in the form of lockdowns that restricted movement and contact. The popular reaction to the situation realigned traditional political identifications, drawing together those from both the left and right who prioritise personal sovereignty. In their analysis of the German context, William Callison and Quinn Slobodian call this process of political realignment "diagonalism." For Callison and Slobodian, diagonalism comes about through transformations in technology and communications, a contestation of the left/right axis, an ambivalence towards parliamentary politics and an affinity with holism and spirituality. Stoked by conspiracy entrepreneurs and narratives, concerns about freedoms become fused with a stance that considers all power as conspiratorial, according to Callison and Slobodian. What we are calling "convergence" is directly related to these new alliances and adjacencies based on shared fears and frustrations, because those alliances allow for the combination of previously distinct conspiracy theories and the communities they engender.

For example, a text-based post on Instagram from March 17, 2020 with 15,207 likes and 2,354 comments (as of February 2021) begins "Let's see what you all make of this …" and goes on to claim the arrests of a number of high-profile figures supposedly involved with different conspiracy theories including the elite paedophile rings of Pizzagate, theories surrounding the death of Jeffrey Epstein, propositions that Covid-19 was man-made in a lab to mandate vaccines (and therefore connecting to pre-existing anti-vaxx conspiracy theories), and QAnon (see Votta 2021). The post mixes classic conspiracist revisionist history with the prophesising characteristic of QAnon to weave together the "real story" behind events many are familiar with. It also includes predictions about the breakdown of society as we know it. Anti-elitist sentiment draws in the real names of actors, CEOs and politicians who are being opposed by a "white hat" Deep State plot, a clandestine operation led presumably by Trump as per the QAnon narrative.

While Bill Gates is just one name among many in this example, he is a key antagonist for Covid-19 conspiracy theories. One representative tweet from May 1, 2020, reads: "Bill obviously has magical powers of foresight or … he planned it all and more plandemics to come. We know Bill, we are watching. #WWG1WGA #ArrestBillGates." A meme from our Instagram dataset depicts a devil-horned Gates holding a syringe dripping with blood with the words

"CHIP YOU, VACCINATE YOU, TRACK YOU," a reference to eugenics and the phrase "I'M GOING TO SAVE THE WORLD! BUT I'M NOT RESPONSIBLE FOR ANYTHING I DO" (see Votta 2021). A BuzzFeed investigation found that "the pushback against [Gates] is a focal point for several previously unlinked misinformation communities, such as anti-vaxxers, 5G truthers, New Agers, and QAnon supporters" (Broderick 2020a). Given that Gates has funded research into the viability of invisible ink vaccines, had offered prescient warnings about a pandemic, and was accused of enforcing population control when his foundation rolled out contraception in Ghana, not to mention his immense wealth as well as his reach in the fields of technology and health, it was perhaps inevitable that Gates would be positioned as a super-villain in different conspiracy strands during Covid-19, the very personification of conspiracy.[2] The figure of Gates in conspiracy theories serves to draw those strands closer together, prompting new narrative alignments and converged conspiracy strands.

This observation is corroborated by our team's research into the role of shared antagonists in the process of convergence, as part of the University of Amsterdam Digital Methods Summer School in 2021 (Tuters and Willaert 2022). The researchers found that Bill Gates became a key figure within Instagram conspiracy theories with different foci during the second quarter of 2020 as the pandemic took hold.

In our dataset, the name of Gates co-occurs with hashtags related to anti-5G, anti-vaxx, "Plandemic," Event 201, QAnon, the New World Order and other conspiracist takes on the pandemic. Figure 5.1 shows the hashtag co-occurrences in our Instagram dataset for the first three quarters of 2020, coded into seven overarching narratives: Trump/QAnon, Pizzagate, Conspirituality, New World Order, Covid, Bill Gates and 5G. The data visualisation shows how the narrative clusters increasingly converge, with shared hashtags pulling them together. By the autumn of 2020 (the third image), hashtags involving Gates move to centre stage, creating the most overlap.

QAnon is what we term an integrationist theory (see below), a convoluted story that incorporates other conspiracy theories, with much of its narrative focusing on the accusations of paedophilia and sex rings familiar from a connected band of conspiracy theories (Pizzagate and QAnon, but also the Satanic panic of the 1980s and 1990s). However, during the Covid-19 pandemic we also see a more general aversion to elites that has long characterised conspiracy theories and anti-vaxx sentiments. A global pandemic offered a perfect occasion for a Deep State plot narrative such as QAnon and health-focused anti-vaxx narratives to align. The pandemic brought together different narrative worlds to produce new fantasies about the operation of power.

There have been other crises that have brought together different elements from the universe of distrust. The attacks of 9/11 are perhaps the most striking as they coalesced left-wing suspicion of the Bush government with right-wing fantasies of the Deep State (see Merlan 2020). Previous episodes such as 9/11 have certainly produced some convergence of disparate conspiracy theories. But the Covid-19 pandemic has intensified this process, drawing together in sometimes

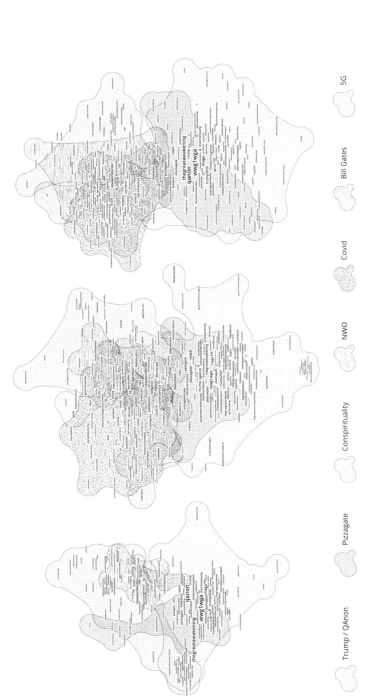

FIGURE 5.1   Side-by-side graphs of hashtag co-occurrences in posts from the Instagram dataset in the first three quarters of 2020. The size of the node labels represents the number of posts that contain the hashtag in the description. *Source: See Tuters and Willaert 2020. Republished with permission.*

surprising ways diverse conspiracy theories that at heart share a deep concern with autonomy and a fear of control. Many conspiracy theories express forms of what Timothy Melley calls "agency panic" (2000)—which causes people to project the agency they feel they have lost onto organisations and institutions—but shared experiences of agency panic have not always brought disparate theories together. The pandemic was an event that necessitated pronounced forms of state intervention, where life-changing decisions really were out of the hands of ordinary people. Under such extreme circumstances—which laid bare the far-reaching powers of even liberal states—conspiracy narratives that tried to make sense of the situation from different angles found common ground and produced new convergences.

Modularity

As we saw in chapters 3 and 4, few of the Covid-19 conspiracy theories are entirely new. We use the term "modularity" to describe how many conspiracy theories under Covid-19 are assembled out of ready-made narratives or tropes that are cobbled together. While "modularity" might connote an efficient, Ikea-designed system that can be arranged to accommodate different requirements, often the result in terms of conspiracy theory is more of a Frankenstein's monster. The parts, that is to say, fail to operate holistically. We can see this in the far-reaching Instagram example we opened this chapter with in which threads are not entirely integrated and some accusations, such as those related to "mandatory vaccines," are invoked without being fully explained.

   The re-use of tropes has long been a feature of conspiracy theorising and is part of what makes it a recognisable genre. This feature has been utilised and gamified by several automated projects. For example, there are a number of conspiracy theory generators online that allow users to input key names and words that are subsequently processed by proprietary AI and word-matching algorithms to produce a series of tropes connected by a narrative, the logic of which follow the rules of conspiracism as laid out by Matthew Barkun (2013): everything is connected, nothing is as it seems and nothing happens by accident. The frenzied production of conspiracy theories under Covid-19 sometimes produced results akin to these automated generators. What we see happening in some examples of Covid-19 conspiracy theories is a willingness to use many different conspiracy building blocks in order to account for the pandemic, even where this leads to narrative incoherence—a conspiracy overload. This suggests high levels of conspiracy literacy among some posters of online conspiracy theories. While some conspiracy theories during the pandemic might have been proposed in a haphazard way by those unfamiliar with the genre, for the most part the conspiracy theorising showed a working knowledge of both the tropes and the conventions of this interpretive mode. In this way, conspiracy theories that are modular serve as repositories of conspiracy histories. This repurposing, iteration, borrowing and adaptation also tell us something about the way that conspiracy theories develop online. One big data study of 120 million tweets from the first five months of the pandemic confirms that "as conspiracy theories evolve, they pick up details from unrelated conspiracies" (Gerts et al. 2021). Given what we know about the virality and speed of conspiracy theories circulating online (see Vosoughi, Roy and Aral 2018), we can assume that they can mutate rapidly, adding ever more modular elements (tropes and narrative snippets) into the mix.

Modularity comes sharply into focus when we consider hashtag usage. It is important to acknowledge that not all uses of hashtags directly correspond to the content of a post (especially with the tendency of "hashtag stuffing" on Instagram and other platforms to game the recommendation algorithm), nor should they be read as earnest representations of what the poster believes. Nevertheless, they do offer an insight into how conspiracist elements become articulated together to create if not a complete narrative, then at least an impression of one. For example, one Instagram post from January 27, 2020, titled "This is just my take on the Corona Virus" (which received 7,804 likes and attracted 481 comments as of February 2021), consists of a five-minute video in which the presenter warns about the mainstream narrative concerning the origins of Covid-19 and suggests that it is more likely that Covid-19 was created as a bioweapon. The presenter points towards shadowy plots by Bill Gates and Big Pharma to profit from the virus, as well as a larger plot by an unnamed entity to depopulate the planet. In a "conspiritual" swerve, the poster encourages us to develop immunity to mainstream news and to Covid-19 (the former through doing our own research and the latter through taking turmeric). Alongside more New Age hashtags (#thirdeye, #pinealgland, #conscious, #awareness), the post includes #populationcontrol #newworldorder #wakeupsheeple #secretsocieties #elite #mindcontrol #illuminati #depopulation #coronavirus #bigpharma. Read together, they fill in the gaps left by the video—for example, that the shadowy, all-powerful group orchestrating depopulation is the Illuminati. More importantly, these hashtags operate synecdochically, gesturing towards different (though in some instances overlapping) conspiracy corpora.

Jo Fox, a historian in the UK, led a research team that built a database of historical rumours and conspiracy theories about health that have re-surfaced during the pandemic. Such projects are essential if we are to understand both the continuities and ruptures, the repetitions and innovations—the genealogies, no less—of Covid-19 conspiracy theories. The concept of modularity reminds us to think about conspiracy theories historically, even when we can also recognise novel developments.

Incorporation

Many conspiracy theories that predate the pandemic have adapted to absorb the turn in events. This is what we call "incorporation." Previous crises have mainly only prompted related conspiracy theories to adapt. For example, it is obvious why any Deep State or transnational secret society conspiracy theory of the 1990s might want to respond to the events of 9/11 given the latter's geopolitical significance. But the far-reaching ramifications of the pandemic—political, economic, societal, medical—have meant that few existing conspiracy threads have not had to incorporate elements of it. Even some "flat-earthers," for example, insist that consensus reality regarding both Covid-19 and the shape of the earth is produced by mental trickery (see Breathnach 2020).

Incorporation requires a conspiracy theory to bend around current events and make sense of them according to the laws of the existing conspiracist cosmology. QAnon, for example, with its theory that an elite cabal of paedophiles have been orchestrating events to their advantage, pre-dates the pandemic by several years, but during 2020 the already highly flexible and reactive narrative adapted to incorporate Covid-19. Consider the many twists and turns of the narratives produced by the Q community during the pandemic covered in chapters 3 and 4. While QAnon gurus played down the threat of the virus and claimed it was a hoax to derail Trump's presidency early in the pandemic (Argentino 2020a), the narrative changed course when the WHO declared Covid-19 a pandemic to suggest lockdowns were being implemented not because of a virus but as a smokescreen for the military to rescue children from the sex-trafficking trade (Rothschild 2021, 124). It was even a Q account that started the #FilmYourHospital hashtag that we discuss in chapter 3 (Argentino 2020b). It was Q influencer Jordan Sather who claimed that a patent filed in 2015 by the Pirbright Institute covered a potential vaccine for Covid-19 (ISD 2020). As Mike Rothschild points out, it was easy for QAnon followers to incorporate conspiracy theories about Big Pharma in relation to Covid-19 even without the guidance of Q at the beginning of the pandemic because previous drops had offered a template: QDrop #252 from 2017, for example, hinted that AIDS had been manufactured by elite and powerful families (Rothschild 2021, 124).

When a QDrop finally arrived, it pushed the oft-repeated bioweapon theory, suggesting that a conspiracy between the Chinese and the American Democrats was seeking to spoil Trump's chances of re-election and that Covid-19 would allow Biden to avoid public debates and enable votes by mail, which Q claims is "unsecure" [sic] (QDrop 3869). Drawing Covid-19 further into the mythology of QAnon, others claimed that Wuhan was also home to a lab owned by George Soros that produced adrenochrome for the pleasure of the elite (ISD 2020). As John Bodner et al. write,

> QAnon slowly transformed parts of its sprawling narrative to respond to Covid-19 by politicizing the pandemic in favor of President Trump … QAnon either had to integrate and explain the crisis, or risk irrelevance of internal dissonance within their interlocking narratives.
>
> *(2020, 187)*

As it spread to different national contexts, QAnon became an umbrella theory under which perceived government overreach concerning the pandemic—lockdowns, mask-wearing, vaccinations—were read as proof of Deep State plotting.

Taken up by various wellness and lifestyle influencers on social media, at least in diluted form, QAnon hashtags and gesturing became shorthand for all kinds of frustrations under Covid-19 and an anti-lockdown stance.

QAnon is just one of the pre-existing conspiracy theories that integrated Covid-19 into their narratives. Theories about 5G (or former incarnations of communication infrastructure) being associated with mind control, surveillance or health concerns were also easily adapted early in the pandemic to stand as the "real" cause of Covid-19 symptoms, with claims of a connection between the roll-out of 5G and Covid-19 (see Bruns et al. 2020). A study of existing anti-5G groups, for example, found that during the pandemic their discussion shifted from focusing strictly on 5G to more scientific-populist and conspiracist claims that incorporated "5G technology, vaccines and the pandemic crisis as parts of a global transhumanist plan" (Tosoni in Bory et al. 2021). The prominent conspiracy theorist David Icke likewise quickly incorporated the pandemic into his existing conspiracy framework. His anti-elite cosmology, which weaves a yarn about lizard people plotting to control all humankind, swerved seamlessly towards the pandemic to capitalise on people's sense that someone other than themselves stood to gain from it and to exploit experiences of restriction. In a similar fashion, pre-existing anti-vaxx theories that allege Big Pharma orchestrates illnesses in order to profit from vaccinations found a golden opportunity in Covid-19 given that vaccinations had to be developed at record speed and were the only viable way to curb the pandemic in an era of global travel and trade.

As we have seen with the modular Instagram example above, theories about the Illuminati have also incorporated Covid-19 (the Illuminati hashtag becomes increasingly central and overlapping in the cluster graph in Figure 5.1). In the video, the Instagrammer repeats a phrase made popular in conspiracist circles by David Icke: "problem, reaction, solution." Icke uses this debased version of Hegelian dialectics in his books and lectures to explain how the ruling elite garner support for social control (e.g., Icke 2003). The phrase has been echoed by many different Illuminati conspiracy theorists during the pandemic, including a Nigerian ex-minister on Twitter (see Nwachukwu 2020). As per Icke's blueprint, they are suggesting that the pandemic has been engineered by the Illuminati to implement social controls; this has prompted the public to call for a solution in the form of a vaccine; and the Illuminati deploys the vaccine in order to achieve mass depopulation. The pandemic is merely one more event in the life story of the Illuminati's bid for world domination under this logic. In all these examples, the pandemic is positioned as further proof or vindication of the former theories.

Integration

During the pandemic, we have also seen high levels of integration where individual conspiracy theories are combined into Grand Unified Theories of

Everything. There have long been a number of these "superconspiracies" (Barkun 2013), such as the Illuminati conspiracy theories outlined above that hold the secret society responsible for many different events, and include stories of alien technologies from Roswell, rumours of faked celebrity deaths, and theories about the New World Order, black helicopters and "men in black." Such superconspiracies pluck low-hanging fruit to make what Naomi Klein has called a "conspiracy smoothie" (2020). QAnon, too, should be considered an example of such integration—a feature that has been especially evident since Covid-19.

There is, however, a "born-Covid" superconspiracy that we want to consider as exemplary of the genre as it has evolved during the pandemic. (Of course, "born-Covid" should not obfuscate the ways in which this conspiracy theory, like so many others, draws on and echoes prior theories.) The "Great Reset" is a conspiracy theory that, through a process of *détournement* (creative hijacking), has resignified a phrase promoted by Klaus Schwab of the World Economic Forum in the summer of 2020. Originally intended to encourage governments around the world to consider the pandemic an opportunity to refocus economic priorities towards more sustainable options, conspiracy theorists argue that it is actually a globalist plot to "turn the world into a high-tech dictatorship that will take away your freedom forever" (Klein 2020).

This narrative about how elites are using the pandemic as a pretext to secure more power and transform life is one echoed in two of the most popular Covid-19 conspiracy theory videos on YouTube—*Plandemic* and *Hold-Up*. Therefore, even when the Great Reset is not named, those on the lookout for corroboration can find it in almost every anti-elitist, Deep State conspiracy theory produced during the pandemic. But it is not just these kinds of conspiracy theories that get woven into the narrative. In his mixed quantitative and qualitative analysis of 9,574 comments below the World Economic Forum's promotional video for the Great Reset on YouTube, Michael Marshall found mentions of a number of different conspiracy theories, some of which fit the bill of Deep State (QAnon, Pizzagate, NWO, and Icke's lizard people), but also flat earth and climate denialism (Marshall 2021). Given the Great Reset's ability to integrate other integrationist theories, like the Deep State conspiracy theories Marshall observed appearing in the comments section, we can see a seemingly never-ending extension of its narrative reach.

The Great Reset conspiracy theory has become popular. Research by the BBC found that "great reset" received more than eight million interactions on Facebook and was shared almost 2 million times on Twitter between June 2020 and May 2021 (BBC Monitoring 2021). This might be because it operates as a repository of frustration with the rigged system, or game of speculation, of financialised capitalism (see Haiven, Kingsmith and Komprozos-Athanasiou 2021b). The curtailments of what were already compromised forms of freedom that came with the pandemic, and the rise in fortunes of Big Tech bosses as well as cronyism and corruption, amount to what might be termed "late disaster capitalism," to conjoin Klein (2007) and Fredric Jameson (1991). In right-wing versions, such crony capitalism is in the service of a socialist, technophilic left determined to requisition property, rescind rights and impose a Green New Deal and cashless state on a reluctant populace. Indeed, in a video post about the Great Reset from October 11, 2020, which garnered 695 retweets, 153 quote tweets, 883 likes and 40,300 views as of February 2021, one Twitter user claims that "Covid-19 has been a green socialist's dream." As Klein puts it, "the Great Reset has managed to mash up every freakout happening on the internet—left and right, true-ish, and off-the-wall—into one inchoate meta-scream about the unbearable nature of pandemic life under voracious capitalism" (2020).

The "Great Reset" offers a narrative hook for new, distorted forms of anti-globalisation, showing how populist narratives migrate between political communities. The fact that the conspiracy theory builds upon and integrates other existing theories produces an apparent contradiction. Talk and text about the Great Reset often contains many layers, gesturing towards a vast prehistory, and yet the narrative is, by necessity, simplified. It sheds or subsumes that prehistory to secure maximum reach. Posted in response to a suspicious tirade by London Real's Brian Rose against lockdown on October 1, 2020, one typical Facebook comment only has to gesture towards forms of social control to get traction. It reads: "The Great reset. All part of the plan, don't think its going to get any better either, expect permanent restrictions on your liberty and greater control from the government and watch as the facial recognition cameras start to appear every where" (https://www.facebook.com/LondonReal/posts/3313085625405345). It received 60 reactions—thumbs up and crying face—and 22 replies.

A second example comment, posted on the same page, is more developed. It uses the tropes of New World Order and Illuminati conspiracy theories without mentioning them by name. The "plan," in this post, is to

> destroy the economy, destroy livelihoods, force people to use up their cash reserves … force people into debt … force them into being dependent on state benefits and then push the vaccine and vaccine passport to receive these benefits, it is all part of the WHO, UN, IMF plan to bring about a global financial reset.

This whittled down dystopian, anti-globalist account garners the most engagement on the page, in terms of emoji responses (153) and replies (38).

Brian Rose's original post under which these comments appear only airs frustration at the second British lockdown. His text-based post includes statements such as: "We are killing the economy and the livelihoods of millions of people based on policies with NO SCIENCE-BASED DECISIONS. We are witnessing yet again a COMPLETELY DISPROPORTIONATE RESPONSE TO THE VIRUS. We see a TOTAL LACK OF LEADERSHIP FROM OUR ELECTED OFFICIALS." In response, his conspiracy-literate following—primed by London Real's guests (such as David Icke) rather than Rose himself, careful as he is to avoid social media moderators—funnel this frustration into conspiracy templates. The latter absorb the different historical or contemporary grievance users invoke.

Writing about the US context during the summer of Black Lives Matter protests and the impending election, Anna Merlan coined the phrase "the Conspiracy Singularity" (2020). She observed how "the trend towards a kind of disturbing unity is distilled in the hashtag #Covid911." The hashtag was endorsed, she writes, by anti-vaxx and QAnon influencers alike. "It holds that what we're living through—the pandemic and the protests against police brutality alike—is all a massive hoax, designed to sway not just the 2020 elections but usher in the New World Order." This idea of the conspiracy singularity helps to explain how challenges to or curtailments of "freedoms" secured via uneven distributions of privilege and power are seen as threats so existential in nature to some that they can occasion coalitions of previously distinct conspiracy communities and narrative threads (see "convergence" above and "adjacency" below). The different challenges Merlan describes (the pandemic, as the name suggests, is global, affecting every area of life; and the demands of BLM protests would involve deep, structural change) are met by conspiracy theories of equal scale. The trend towards large, integrated superconspiracy theories that can explain not just one or two events but the entire trajectory of human civilisation seems necessary, at least in the eyes of those who propagate them, to explain the world historical events unfolding in the time of Covid-19.

Expressive

It has become increasingly clear during the pandemic that conspiracy theories have to be understood not necessarily as statements of belief but as symptomatic expressions of resentment, frustration, disgust, fear, anxiety or partisan belonging. We are wary of approaches that always seek to tell people what they are *really* saying, what they *really* mean. This kind of "false consciousness" argument is particularly problematic in relation to conspiracy theory given that it is a popular and populist discourse centred on concerns about authority, expertise and the production of knowledge. We instead draw on approaches in anthropology, folklore studies, and audience and fan studies that engage seriously with what their research subjects say without interpreting it straight away as merely a symptom of something else. Nevertheless, the need to contextualise Covid-19 conspiracy theories within the larger forces at work, to see these theories as speaking to events and pressures that linger on the edges of what conspiracy theorists write and say, feels more necessary than usual. This is partly because the stakes seem that much higher than some other conspiracist-rich moments; but it is also because the responses to Covid-19 conspiracy theories, which we turn to in the conclusion, are based on the assumption that all Covid-19 conspiracy theories are simply statements of belief. Such an assumption can make us fail to tune in to what else such theories might be expressing and also fail to understand when the theories are proposed with less than full seriousness.

Thinking about conspiracy theories only as statements of belief underpins the way many data-led initiatives approach the "problem" of conspiracy theory. For example, deplatforming initiatives that use automated detection of certain words, word combinations and/or hashtags in order to eradicate or suppress conspiracist sentiments might miss the way that a conspiracy claim functions as an affirmation of partisan belonging (or even a desire to entrench polarisation and operate in ideologically insulated spaces) over and above what it declares on the surface. (We acknowledge that this is a difficult balance to get right; the storming of the Capitol arguably caught security services off guard because they weren't reading conspiracist sentiments literally *enough*!) Deplatforming and fact-checking strategies might misunderstand that conspiracy theories are not simply factual errors that can be corrected. Rather, they articulate deep-seated forms of agency panic specific to the era in which they arise (Melley 2000). In chapter 1, we explored many of the social, political and economic factors contributing to the grievances and frustrations that may have shaped Covid-19 conspiracy theories. Here, we want to simply remark on the fact that so many Covid-19 conspiracy theories (both those about the pandemic and those that incorporate the pandemic into their existing narratives) express concerns about a loss of sovereignty. In some of these theories, the focus is on the sovereignty of the state, which is seen to have been compromised by a powerful, supra-national, Deep State elite. In others, the focus is on the sovereignty of the body, whether this manifests as concerns about vaccinations, about masking up, with being told where one's body can and cannot safely go or about the bodies of children being violated. Any approach to Covid-19 conspiracy theories needs to address why a concern over sovereignty of the body politic and the body is so prominent in conspiracy theories today.

The concern with personal sovereignty should not be surprising at a time when states have had to curtail freedoms under pandemic conditions. In such circumstances, personal sovereignty must be sacrificed to preserve the health of the nation. In the US, this should also be understood within longer histories of individualism, libertarianism, gun laws and the sovereign citizen movement. (The anti-vaxx movement in the UK spawned an increasingly militant version of the latter in the autumn of 2021, with a series of misguided attempts to invoke ancient common law in an effort to shut down vaccination centres and "arrest" police officers (Coleman and Sardarizadeh 2022).) We also need to see how a sense of personal sovereignty and agency is threatened by the financial conditions outlined in chapter 1. Within a system characterised by highly limited social mobility and a widening gap between rich and poor, personal agency might not offer the rewards promised by myths of meritocracy. If the only choice one can make is between two paths that have equally bad outcomes, the capacity for decision-making feels like a poor form of freedom. This might lead some to identify threats to personal sovereignty other than those presented by inequitable economic conditions. There is certainly a great deal of nostalgia in agency panic, harking back to an imagined time when power over one's own destiny delivered returns.

In terms of bodily autonomy, we need to situate these concerns within histories of medical experimentation and exploitation. We also need to take into account Cold War narratives of brainwashing; the battle over which bodies—those of women or unborn foetuses—have legal priority; and even an obesity epidemic that renders bodies as the object of a number of discourses and as subject to multiple interventions. In addition, a concern with bodily autonomy that arises in many conspiracy theories today can also be usefully understood within the ascent of post-feminism, an ideology that perpetuates the idea that equality has been achieved and feminism is no longer needed.

When second wave feminist arguments about women's rights concerning bodies and consent are side-lined, such concerns re-emerge in untethered, conspiracist form and appeal to certain women who might traditionally avoid feminism and feminist agendas (see "Diverse" below). For example, the second wave feminist mantra, "My body, my choice," has been appropriated by many anti-vaxx and anti-mask protestors (see Figure 5.2).

The desire for political sovereignty has galvanised a variety of campaigns and movements. Most recently in the UK and US, it has become commandeered by nationalist and isolationist agendas. In the UK, the pro-Brexit arguments that preceded the pandemic mostly hinged on ideas of "protecting" borders to limit immigration, and of not taking orders from seemingly remote bureaucrats in Brussels. In the US, Trump promised to "build a wall" to keep illegal immigration to a minimum as well as retreating from international treaties and organisations. On the one hand, the pandemic, during which borders effectively

FIGURE 5.2   Protestors take to the streets of London for an anti-lockdown protest on Saturday, April 24, 2021. *Source: Photograph by Tejas Sandhu, MI News & Sport/Alamy Live News. Credit: MI News & Sport/Alamy Stock Photo.*

closed in unprecedented ways and nation states made decisions that were in their own best interests, has strengthened these sovereign imaginaries. On the other hand, the global scale of the pandemic has necessitated co-ordinated responses guided by the World Health Organisation, members of the scientific community and COVAX. This geopolitical reality—which rests on a fine balance between autonomy and interdependence—is ignored by conspiracy-oriented folk who present power as residing with supra-national covert networks. Any display of sovereignty by the state under this logic is at risk of being undermined by the Deep State (if one supports the display of sovereignty) or is the work of the Deep State (if not).

Enmeshed

It has become difficult to isolate conspiracy theories from other modes of information and forms of knowing even though boundary maintenance tactics like "fact-checking" and "deplatforming" are based on the ability to do just that. Covid-19 conspiracy theories live alongside, borrow from, appear with, and are often inseparable from more legitimated genres of information.

During the pandemic, conspiracy theories have been found among more legitimated information for two main reasons. First, because the pandemic was caused by a novel coronavirus, scientific research was conducted and published rapidly, often in pre-print form before being subject to peer review. This meant that some of the findings were provisional and later superseded by further research. Conspiracy theorists latched onto some of these findings, ignoring caveats and qualifications. Contradictory evidence and opinions in the scientific community also affected state responses. For example, the decision to require mask-wearing came late in the day in the UK due to differences of scientific opinion (which fed into conspiracist stories about masks making people ill). Similarly, many states in the Global North were caught off guard in terms of pandemic preparedness, meaning their responses were characterised by U-turns which, again, undermined confidence and allowed conspiracist explanations to take seed. Second, there were plenty of legitimate questions to ask about how governments were handling the pandemic. How were contracts for PPE, ventilators, vaccine research etc. being awarded? What were the criteria determining which industries would receive support? How were deaths being recorded? And what was the rationale behind certain restrictions? A lack of transparency regarding official decisions bolstered the conspiracist cause.

It has never been easy to separate out conspiracy theory from knowledge proper. Despite some defining features that we have outlined throughout this book, conspiracy theories imitate and even exaggerate more legitimate discourses (see Birchall 2006). For example, long conspiracy tracts that circulate on the internet often use that most academic of conventions—footnotes—to the hilt. But the way in which the pandemic highlighted the provisional rather than permanent nature of scientific enquiry and proof fuelled the conspiracist fire. It also encouraged the miscegenation of scientifically rooted hypotheses and conspiracist hermeneutics in online discourse. If ontological flatness in Actor Network Theory indicates a radical equivalence between human and non-human agents in the assessment of any network, we can fashion the situation under discussion as epistemological flatness, whereby knowledges and knowing practices with very different provenances and protocols become intertwined in ways that make it hard to make decisions about their veracity or helpfulness.

Such epistemological flatness is not only shaped by the particular circumstances of the pandemic but also by the experience of digital media today. The media studies concept of "flow" is helpful here. Raymond Williams (1975) originally used the term to capture the experience of watching television across time (as opposed to focusing on individual programmes). Subsequent refinements have differentiated between channel flow and viewer flow (Jensen 1994: 291). If we extend viewer flow to the admittedly more complex information-entertainment ecology of the internet, what we could refashion as "user flow" is important to consider when thinking about the enmeshed nature of online conspiracism. This flow captures the personalised experiences of users as they travel across different digital platforms and experience a variety of digital content (video, text, audio, memes, etc.).

For conspiracy-curious users, the flow can include both legitimate/credible and illegitimate/untrustworthy sources seamlessly. Indeed, "online conspiracies often share real information, such as legitimate media reporting or official documents, presented in a misleading or conspiratorial frame. This has two effects: it helps to create an illusion of legitimacy, and it complicates the efforts of social media platforms to moderate conspiratorial content" (Thomas and Zhang 2020). Moreover, the high production values of some conspiracist platforms and products make the distinction between outfits that *are* subject to certain regulations and *do* adhere to journalistic ethics and those that *are not* and *do not* much more difficult to discern. Alex Jones's site Infowars, for example, is a slick, expensive operation. Both its landing platform and the live talk show streams are impossible to fault in terms of production values. Equally, the conspiracy video that we opened this book with, *Plandemic*, is indiscernible aesthetically from high-specification documentaries. In addition, as we will see in chapter 6 when we turn to monetisation, conspiracist marketplaces associated with key conspiracy entrepreneurs mirror more hegemonic digital marketplaces. This is not to suggest that all users are unaware of what kind of site they are on. Often, conspiracy theorists deliberately seek out spaces that are *not* the "mainstream news" which they have learnt to distrust. The point, rather, is that we must take into consideration a media ecology that is shot through with conspiracist stories. This is different from the 1970s–1990s when conspiracist content needed to be sought out in obscure and esoteric zines (see Ivan Stang's 1988 collection of listings for alternative magazines, newsletters, cassettes and catalogues in *High Weirdness by Mail*).

Even if it were possible to separate out conspiracist platforms from those of legacy media in terms of aesthetics, some highly partisan branches of traditional media are sources of conspiracy theories. As Yochai Benkler notes,

> If you're trying to understand what causes tens of millions of people to believe that Democrats stole the election, or that Hillary Clinton runs a pedophilia ring out of a basement of a pizza parlor, that's not coming from social media. That's coming from Fox News and Sirius XM Radio, Bannon and Breitbart, Rush Limbaugh and Sean Hannity on radio.
>
> *(quoted in Sweet 2021)*

Joan Donovan in the same piece argues that there is no point in debating whether social media or traditional media are more to blame for disinformation. Instead, we must recognise that people both watch Fox News and scroll through Twitter, for example, or they post a link in a Facebook group to a YouTube video and flood the review section of a conspiracy book on Amazon to boost it up the charts. Conspiracist messaging is repeated and reinforced across the user flow which switches between traditional and social media often via the same digital screen and sometimes via the same platform (as traditional media can be embedded and shared on social media).

Distributed

Since the advent of social media, it has become harder to find examples of coherent and contained linear conspiracy narratives that are confined to one text or "space." This, along with the conspiracy gesturing characteristic of Trump, has led Russell Muirhead and Nancy L. Rosenblum to declare that conspiracism today is more accurately captured by the phrase "conspiracy without the theory" (Muirhead and Rosenblum 2019), which, they argue, is marked by a lack of evidence and argument in comparison with more traditional conspiracist texts. However, what we have found studying Covid-19 conspiracy theories is that users with digital literacy and conspiracy literacy can assemble parts of the narrative from different sources. There are, as Muirhead and Rosenblum claim, plenty of conspiracy fragments to be found on social media. But the theory is there for the conspiracists who know not just where to look but how to read. That such theories might not be offered in one linear story becomes part of the genre. Indeed, conspiracy literacy comes through "doing your own research" and being "red-pilled," as Q followers put it. Part of the allure is putting together an overarching narrative from different sources. The user flow, in this scenario, becomes a hyperlinked, algorithmically guided, search optimised narrative.

Consider, for example, a comment on Facebook under a post about the Swiss roll back of 5G due to health concerns made on the "Stop5G Legal Resistance – Research Stop5G(dot)net Group" page in February 2020 (https://www.facebook.com/groups/374394582995703/permalink/861049347663555).

The comment is really a series of statements and introductions to video evidence (e.g., "Bill Gates predicts his pandemic") punctuated by links to YouTube videos. It ends by stating: "This is absolutely vital information please review immediately." Following the threads, a complex, and at times contradictory, modular conspiracy theory emerges that posits Bill Gates as the orchestrator of the "plandemic," 5G as the source of illness and as a control technology, and Agenda 21 as the larger context or superconspiracy. Instead of writing a linear narrative, the poster offers hyperlinks to visual texts that weave their own conspiracy web. Such "writing" cannot be explained away as "lazy" or evidence of a post-truth disregard for the possibility of truth, evidence and argument—after all, finding and ordering links is an investment in time and energy, and the assemblage of links suggests a continuing desire to reveal supposedly hidden ("vital") information, or a larger truth hidden in plain sight. Rather, we should think of this practice of citation as the hyperlinked version of that classic trope of conspiracy and detective fiction: the "crazy board" filled with pictures of suspects and places, snippets of evidence, and lines of string to connect them. For the keyboard warrior, the conspiracy is to be found in the complex array of linkages, rather than in a simple set of propositions or linear narrative. The conspiracy theory in this Facebook comment example can only be identified as such if one looks across distributed nodes. Other users who follow the links may make new connections between the different threads or find new sources online, perhaps recommended alongside the suggested videos. Rather than conspiracy without the theory, the "new conspiracism" (as Muirhead and Rosenblum name it) is characterised by its distributed, decentralised nature—a form that invites and enables re-workings and endless interpretation.[3]

As well as these hyperlinked narrative structures, the distributed character of online Covid-19 conspiracy theories can be identified in the ways that the latter emerge in the margins of otherwise moderated spaces. For example, while YouTube itself has deplatformed many videos that explicitly promote Covid-19 conspiracy theories, our research team have found the comments sections under both conspiracy clickbait videos (YouTube videos that signal conspiracy theories in the title only) and conspiracy evidence videos (legitimate videos that conspiracy theorists analyse) rife with conspiracy theories (see Sheppard-Dawson 2021; de Keulenaar, Burton and Kisjes 2021). We also considered conspiracist content in Amazon reviews under certain books and videos (Scott 2020; Scott 2021; Silverman and Lytvynenko 2021; Gray et al. 2021).[4] In these examples, elaborate and sustained theories appear in places not often considered central to the exchange of conspiracist ideas. Effectively, to study conspiracy theories today, it is necessary to see how different kinds of digital spaces are made to function like social media, something that is certainly true of Amazon reviews, which include embedded links to recommended conspiracist content such as videos in much the same way as Twitter or Facebook posts do.

There is one last angle to the distributed nature of Covid-19 conspiracy theories worth considering. This one is less about the narratives being distributed across platforms and media forms and more about how old and new media forms cross pollinate—a tendency that echoes those discussed in relation to the category of "enmeshed" above. The distribution (and redistribution) of conspiracy theories between media has been harnessed by savvy conspiracy theorists intent on spreading the word while evading moderation on social media platforms. Physical copies of *The Light* newspaper, a conspiracist publication produced in the UK, had a print run of 100,000 and was distributed to letterboxes by volunteers recruited via *The Light's* private Facebook page (see Waterson 2020b; Dacombe, Souter and Westerlund 2021). This traditional mode of distribution soon extended to digital spaces as people receiving the "truthpaper" uploaded pictures of particular headlines to social media. A picture of one article from *The Light* claiming that masks can damage the brain was shared on Facebook 64,000 times (Goodman 2021). As *Guardian* journalist Jim Waterson reports, "flyers and fringe conspiracy newspapers are nothing new but the ability to build a real-world, low-cost newspaper distribution network is, perhaps ironically, made easier by tech companies, which are trying to clamp down on disinformation hosted directly on their platforms" (2020b).

Mobilising

The way *The Light* recruited volunteers on Facebook points to the mobilising force of Covid-19 conspiracy theories. During the pandemic, those harbouring conspiracist sentiments have taken to the streets in collective displays that have historically been rare in conspiracy circles. As conspiracy theories were delegitimised in the public sphere in the post–Second World War period, conspiracy theorists were often isolated (Thalmann 2019; Butter 2020). (Members of cults or extremist organisations based on conspiracist tenets are important exceptions to this.) As well as the distribution of hard copy conspiracist material, street protests and rallies, mobilisation has also taken other forms of real-world interventions, such as the destruction of communication infrastructure by 5G conspiracy theorists (see Figure 5.3), the filming of hospitals by those who believe the pandemic is a hoax (see chapter 2), and later, the deliberate sabotaging of vaccine supplies as well as disruption of vaccination distribution sites. One action against a vaccination distribution site was organised on Facebook and advertised as "Scamdemic Protest/March" (see Network Contagion Research Institute 2021).

While extremist violence from different ideological positions is often accompanied by conspiracy theories, the latter have only infrequently appeared within the sphere of legitimate peaceful political protest or inspired otherwise law-abiding citizens to destroy property, trespass or break the law. The heightened tensions created by pandemic restrictions and deprivations and, in the US, a highly partisan election and a democratic system under strain, provide the context for the shift towards increased in-real-life mobilisation. It was private messaging apps and private groups on social media, however, that provided organisational and communication infrastructure to put otherwise unconnected folk in touch

FIGURE 5.3   5G conspiracy image shared on Twitter, March 26, 2020.

(see O'Connor 2021). What such groups offer is not only a constant stream of disinformation, but also a social community that reaches beyond conspiracist concerns. As new social fields liable to displace those more traditional ones based on class or geography, these groups become difficult to leave because they engender meaningful relationships and social networks, as well as habits, skills and dispositions (see Chloe Colliver interviewed by Mariana Spring, Colliver 2020).

Investigative journalists point to the power of Telegram to organise anti-lockdown, anti-vaxx protests (Coleman and Sardarizadeh 2022). We should not misread the rallies as an absolute move from online to offline, resisting what Nathan Jurgenson refers to as "digital dualism"—the "habit of viewing the online and offline as largely distinct" (2012). The events are filled with people filming and live-streaming images of themselves and other protestors. Private messaging channels and social media are not left behind once street action begins; rather, such modes of communication remain central to tactical organisation, arranging social meet-ups on the day, and spreading the conspiracist word beyond the real-life event. There is, we could argue, no offline space. (Moreover, we might also want to register the fact that conspiracy theories, like other fantasies and fictions, are always already "mobilising" in a near incantatory or performative function, generating affects and creating new knowledge pathways.[5]) Nevertheless, the fact that real-life interventions arise from online conspiracist activity is noteworthy as a characteristic more prominent under Covid-19 than in previous historical moments.

On the surface, the anti-lockdown protests in the UK resemble any other political mobilisation. Organisers choose, for example, key locations of democratic protest such as Westminster, Whitehall and Trafalgar Square and iconic backdrops, like the National Gallery, for their staged rallies. There is much talk about fighting for "freedom." One rally in July 2021, for example, was even called the Worldwide Rally for Freedom. They have appropriated the language of the "99 percent" from the Occupy movement and the V for Vendetta mask from the Anonymous movement (subsequently taken up by Occupy and other protest movements); concern about future generations from the ecological movement; and the language of consent and rights from various identity-based movements. Interspersed with this more familiar political protest language, however, are the signs of conspiracist rather than structural sources of the perceived exploitation: signs referencing QAnon or the Illuminati, a sign that warns us "Covid is a hoax to usher in the new world order and mark of the beast," and a banner that reads "The Covid Lie: Jail Bill Gates; Jail Matt Hancock for crimes against humanity… Governments start working for the people and stop working for the elite agenda" (Nsubuga 2020). Positioning themselves as victims of totalitarian governments, participants carry signs that read "Covid-1984," "No Gestapo Policing," and, more controversially, protestors have appropriated the star of David (see Figure 5.2).

The real-world assemblies introduce those who might disagree with one aspect of lockdown to more all-encompassing interpretations. Having been exposed to conflicting scientific information, some attending these rallies understandably feel that they are being lied to by the government and other authorities. They might not be able to articulate exactly what they believe is happening, but their sense of unease can be stoked by prominent and persuasive speakers using incendiary language and populism to appeal to a range of grievances. The anti-lockdown rally in London in July 2021, for example, featured former nurse, Kate Shemirani calling Covid vaccines "Satanic" and claiming that masks are "subjugation tools used by the Freemasons;" German lawyer, Reiner Fuellmich claiming that "there is no evidence for the pandemic;" and prominent conspiracy theorist, Mark Steele asserting that the "virus is a hoax" and calling the Scientific Advisory Group for Emergencies (SAGE) "a terrorist organisation" (reported by Sardarizadeh 2021). The gatherings serve to shape or affirm sceptical views about the pandemic and give those with oppositional views strength in numbers. One protestor at a London anti-lockdown rally in April 2021 said, for example, "we all know the tin-foil hat conspiracy theory nut [stereotype], but there are thousands of us here" (interviewed by Annie Kelly for the QAnon Anonymous podcast). What is important about these events is that they put on display a conspiracy convergence (see above) and/or adjacency (see below). They have solidified coalitions of distrust.

Diverse

In the Anglo-American conspiracist imaginary, the dominant stereotype of a conspiracy theorist is an "unwashed, middle-aged white male" (Uscinski and Parent 2014: 73). Even though several quantitative studies argue that this is inaccurate (finding, rather, that gender has little effect on conspiracy beliefs, or that women are more susceptible, and that ethnic minorities sometimes demonstrate higher levels of conspiracy belief), there are good reasons behind the stereotype. First, far-right American militia movements in the 1980s and 90s, which weaved conspiracism into their mythologies, were obviously hostile to people of colour. Second, conspiracism is a key part of many racist narratives that at once denigrate and fear the power of a racialised other. Third, some conspiracy theories, like the Great Replacement theory, are racist and misogynist, implicitly blaming both multiculturalists (for celebrating immigration) and feminists (for untethering women from reproductive, domestic roles). Fourth, cultural production and representation has reinforced the stereotype: a majority of postmodern "paranoid" literature, so central to cultural configurations of conspiracy, was produced by white male writers (with Ishmael Reed and Joan Didion offering important exceptions); and conspiracy films of the 1970s and key television shows from the 1990s, such as *The X-Files* (1993-2016), were almost exclusively interested in white worlds. Fifth, key conspiracy influencers such as Alex Jones in the US and David Icke in the UK reinforce the message that conspiracy theories are produced by and for white men. Lastly, as Timothy Melley convincingly argues, post-War conspiracy theories often dramatise a perceived threat to masculine notions of individuality and autonomy by "*feminising*" social forces (2000, 32).

Conspiracy imaginaries, as repositories of culturally produced assumptions and tropes, do not necessarily reflect the cohorts of people who actually harbour conspiracist beliefs and narratives. But they do indicate who is addressed and invited in—who has easy access to, and affinity with, dominant conspiracist messages—and which conspiracy theories and theorists assume culturally hegemonic positions. We argue that, despite the growing influence of the Islamophobic "Great Replacement Theory" and the continued antisemitism in much conspiracism during this period, Covid-19 has shifted the axis of this conspiracy imaginary to address, invite in and represent more ethnic minorities and women. Unlike other instances of widening representation, there is little to celebrate here. It is, nevertheless, important to recognise what difference Covid-19 has made to the conspiracy imaginary.

Before exploring this claim, it is necessary to again acknowledge that conspiracy beliefs beyond the white, male conspiracy imaginary have long been held and utilised by ethnic minorities and women. When particular conspiracy theories are considered, a more diverse picture emerges. Opinion polls that measure general conspiracy beliefs according to gender and ethnicity are thus not especially insightful (even while this approach might tell us something about other markers of difference like education levels or political orientation). It is more helpful to consider individual narratives: for example, women have always been active in anti-vaxx conspiracy circles, in those that configure children as victims, and in conspiracy theories regarding the deaths of female icons such as Marilyn Monroe and Princess Diana; and African Americans have long resonated with any conspiracy theory that suggests the US government is conspiring against black people (Crocker et al. 1999).

Moreover, it is crucial to think about what conspiracy theories *do*—about the different roles particular conspiracy theories might play in communities, and the cultural work they perform. Those circulating among African Americans have offered a way to articulate and explain deeply entrenched racism (see Knight 2000). As we describe in chapter 4, these theories have roots in experiences of discrimination (Simmons and Parsons 2005) and real plots of violence, exploitation, discrimination and neglect (such as the Tuskegee syphilis experiment, the practice of "redlining," enforced sterilisation, segregation and, of course, the brutal conditions of surveillance and control suffered by the enslaved). In this context, Patricia Turner calls such theories "tools of resistance" (1993) because of the way in which they warn others to distrust systems, knowledges and organisations that have subjugated black people. The circulation and use of conspiracy theories by ethnic minorities in this vein has continued to be true under Covid-19, not least because of the way that the virus has disproportionately affected ethnic minorities in the UK and US due to underlying health, economic and housing inequities. Historical examples of anti-blackness in medical and scientific contexts offer proof enough for many black Britons and black Americans sceptical about Covid-19 and vaccinations. A survey by Pew Research from July 2020 found that roughly a third of black (33%) and Hispanic adults (34%) in the US say that the theory that powerful people planned the outbreak of Covid-19 is probably or definitely true, compared with 22% of white adults (Pew 2020).

Examples of historical malpractice are cited by cynical anti-vaxx influencers trying to nudge vaccine hesitancy and what has been identified as (entirely understandable) "system distrust" (Surgo Ventures 2021) in ethnic minority communities towards a more militant and conspiracist anti-vaxx stance (see CCDH 2020c). This is true not only for those anti-vaxx influencers of colour, such as Rizza Islam and Kevin Jenkins, but also for figures like Robert F. Kennedy Jr. One Instagram post with 22,000 likes reproduced in a report by the Centre for Countering Digital Hate (2020) advertises an anti-vaxx event with Kennedy and the black minister Aboul Malik Sayyid Muhammad with the words: "Smallpox Infested Blankets, Tuskegee Experiment, Forced Vaccinations and Hidden Agendas."

As we emphasise in chapter 4, it is important not to elide vaccine hesitancy with anti-vaxx conspiracy theories. Equally, it would be wrong to ignore differences *between* ethnic minorities in terms of vaccine hesitancy (a subsection of which would count as conspiracist Covid scepticism). For example, UK government data shows that 30% of black British respondents were vaccine hesitant, a much higher figure than other ethnic minorities (Office for National Statistics 2021b). Keeping these caveats in mind, the higher levels of vaccine hesitancy among some ethnic minorities, even when this was eventually reduced in practice, needs to be factored in when thinking about the changing parameters of conspiracist constituencies during Covid-19.

Many fears about the virus and the vaccine held by black Britons and Americans offer continuity with previous conspiracy theories about "black genocide," such as those about AIDS being engineered to target the black community and those that claim the US organisation, Planned Parenthood, is a white supremacist plot.[6] What is new, however, under Covid-19, is the way in which such black genocide narratives align with aspects of those anti-elite and/or Deep State populist theories more associated with white conspiracist cultures including some far-right, nationalist conspiracist groups that would historically exclude people of colour by placing an emphasis on racial "purity."

There are several possible reasons for this. First, Deep State conspiracy theories and anti-lockdown/anti-vaxx protests have appropriated the language of rights and freedom that animates legitimate civil rights movements and vernacular theories of black genocide alike. Such appropriations create false equivalences and make narrative alliances where none, on ideological grounds, should exist. Second, rumours of black genocide and conspiracy theories about depopulation share a common adversary. Above, we examined the role of Bill Gates as a lightning-rod antagonist in anti-elite conspiracy theories concerning the pandemic. Gates also serves as the evil conspirator in many African American and black British conspiracist imaginaries.

One meme reproduced in a report on "Covid-19 Misinformation and Black Communities" by Harvard's Shorenstein Center uses a photograph of the artist Cardi B as a child with some words of warning imposed: "my mama said nobody elected Bill Gates to do anything and we ain't takin no vaccine from some shady ass nerd that wants to depopulate the planet" (Collins Dexter 2020). One UK based survey conducted in late 2020 found that 19% of ethnic minorities, compared with 6% of white ethnic groups, agreed with the statement "Bill Gates wants a mass vaccination programme against coronavirus so that he can implant microchips into people" (Allington and McAndrew 2021). While ethnic minorities have not constituted a large proportion of anti-lockdown protestors in the UK and US, it is clear that conspiracist narratives have been present at the level of personal narratives, in-person community interactions and online activity. By contrast, women, including some women of colour, have been overrepresented at anti-lockdown, anti-vaxx, Q-adjacent events according to some journalists (e.g., Kelly 2021). Moreover, Pew Research in the US found that "women are slightly more likely than men (29% vs. 21%) to see at least some truth in the conspiracy theory that powerful people planned the outbreak" (2020).[7]

Again, women harbouring conspiracy theories is nothing new, but they are not often included in meaningful ways within the conspiracy imaginary. Indeed, in popular cultural texts such as *Conspiracy Theory* (1997) and *The X-Files*, as well as literature such as Umberto Eco's *Foucault's Pendulum* (1988) or Hari Kunzru's *Red Pill* (2020), women repeatedly figure as the rational counterpart to the male conspiracy theorist. What is it about the Covid-19 conspiracy imaginary, therefore, that has addressed women and invited them to participate?

At least three converging factors are pertinent here. First, childcare responsibilities during school closures and lockdowns disproportionately fell upon women (McMunn and Xue 2021). As Lorna Bracewell argues, the multiplication of caring duties and the general alarm caused by the health crisis left many mothers feeling helpless. Conspiracy theories offered them a chance to "regain a sense of maternal efficacy in a moment when both of these things have been severely destabilized by the global pandemic" (2021, 2). This goes some way to explain why, as investigative journalists have shown, the pandemic turned mothers' groups on Facebook and Instagram towards ever more conspiracist content (Butler 2020). Second, as a conspiracy theory that has integrated the pandemic into its narrative, QAnon has appealed to many women because of the emphasis it has placed on the safety of children. Annie Kelly points out that QAnon has been less insular than other far-right communities which "make an attempt to draw their digital borders along race- or gender-based lines by emphasizing purity," making for "a hostile environment for non-white, non-male newcomers" (2020). Moreover, Bracewell argues convincingly that, because populism imbues "the people" with traditionally feminine character-istics (purity, innocence, vulnerability), "populists are able to target women with the kind of explicitly gendered appeals we see at work in the QAnon movement with relative ease" (2021, 2). Third, since it became clear that vac-cines were the only way to manage the threat, the female dominated anti-vaxx movement has become central to Covid-19 conspiracism. The predominance of women in the anti-vaxx movement is well documented (e.g., Smith and Graham 2017; Robertson 2020) and the reasons for this help us to understand some women's involvement in Covid-19 conspiracism as a whole. Women, who make the majority of health decisions concerning their children, reportedly have less faith in the medical establishment because, as Jessica Valenti (2019) points out, they are "more likely than men to be disbelieved or not taken seriously when they report chronic pain or fatigue, among other symptoms, and to have their concerns written off as 'all in their head.'" As the second wave feminist classic, *Our Bodies, Ourselves* puts it: women have experienced male doctors as "con-descending, paternalistic, judgmental and non-informative" (Boston Women's Collective 1973). Moreover, when women's experience is side-lined and their intelligence underestimated, the anti-vaxx movement offers them an opportu-nity to feel like an expert (Valenti 2019).

As we saw in the "Expressive" section above, some conspiracist discourses might be thought of as weak postfeminist invocations or emaciated versions of second wave feminist tenets. *Our Bodies, Ourselves* called on women to educate themselves about their bodies, medical institutions and the law. Covid-19 anti-vaxx conspiracy theories answer that call without any of the ideological com-mitments of the Boston Women's Collective. Such appropriations are explicit in some online posts. For example, one tweet from April 3, 2020, states, "I call for @BillGates to NOT call for what HE wants for #Americans. Remember the #WholeMyBodyMyChoice … well, this is where it comes back to bite #Democrats in the ass. You can take that 'call' and shove it up your #OWO ass. #NotThisWhiteGirl #QAnon2020 #Trump2020NowMoreThanEver."

As well as shaping right-wing discourse, (post)feminist remnants concerning bodily autonomy and scepticism about health institutions have become a key feature of "conspirituality," a term coined by Charlotte Ward and David Voas (2011) to refer to a convergence of spirituality, wellness, alternative health and conspiracism. For example, Dr. Christiane Northrup, OB/Gyn author of the holistic women's health book *Women's Bodies, Women's Wisdom* (1994) describes herself as "a visionary pioneer and a leading authority in the field of women's health and wellness, which includes the unity of mind, body, emotions, and spirit." Northrup's posts on different social media platforms, once a blend of natural childbirth advocacy, anti-childhood vaccinations and conventional medical advice, featured coronavirus conspiracy theories, including QAnon videos, since the beginning of the pandemic (Butler 2020). She has posted a series of videos entitled the "Great Awakening" and praises *Plandemic* in another.

Some posters on Instagram have developed a particular aesthetic to house this conspiritual mash-up. The disinformation researcher Marc-André Argentino has named this aesthetic, and those "lifestyle bloggers, fitness instructors, diet influencers, esoteric spiritualists, promoters of alternative healing" that use it, "Pastel QAnon" because of the soft tones and uplifting images that it borrows from more inspirational and aspirational female Instagrammers (2021b) (see Figure 5.4).

Argentino shows that between March and September 2020, 76 accounts of women posters he identified as pastel-QAnon collectively increased their

FIGURE 5.4   Instagram post by "Pastel QAnon" influencer. *Source: Marc-André Argentino, 2021b.*

followers by 160%. One of his conclusions is that "QAnon is gender inclusive and women play an important role in disseminating and creating QAnon propaganda" (2021b). Such aesthetic developments have allowed conspiracism during the pandemic to reach new cohorts. The emergence of Pastel Q has also significantly altered and expanded the kinds of people included in the conspiracy imaginary; or, rather, it has significantly multiplied the number of different conspiracy imaginaries out there.

Celebrities and Superspreaders

Prior to the pandemic, celebrities from the world of mainstream entertainment rarely and only playfully referenced conspiracy theories, unless their chosen medium was versed in aesthetic incarnations of the paranoid style, such as rap (see Quinn 2002). Plenty of pop stars intrigued fans with Illuminati symbology in music videos, but few stars of stage and screen openly endorsed a conspiracy theory. Doing so would have been to risk being stigmatised. Those that did express earnest affinity with conspiracy theories, such as Rosanne Barr who tweeted in support of QAnon in 2018, were side-lined (though in Barr's case, the final straw for producers of her television show was a racist comment).

During the pandemic, conspiracy theories about the role of 5G drew in A-List actors Woody Harrelson and John Cusack and the boxer Amir Khan. In response to a story about 5G, the UK television presenter Eamonn Holmes defended the right to question "the state narrative." Even Madonna posted a conspiracy theory about elites holding back a vaccine to her 15 million Instagram followers; and racing driver Lewis Hamilton shared an anti-vaxx post alleging Bill Gates was lying about vaccine trials, before quickly removing it (Carroll 2020). This type of celebrity intervention had a disproportionate influence in the (dis)information ecology during Covid. One study conducted in April 2020, for example, found that while "top-down misinformation from politicians, celebrities, and other prominent public figures made up just 20%" of misinformation, it "accounted for 69% of total social media engagement" (Brennan et al. 2020).

Alongside the role played by celebrities and public figures, we also need to consider so-called disinformation superspreaders (acknowledging that these can sometimes be one and the same). In chapter 2, we cautioned against uncritically importing viral metaphors to understand how information circulates, but the term "superspreader"—if used with caution—does capture the amplification role played by certain figures. (The key difference between viral superspreaders and disinfo superspreaders is that the former do not necessarily know they are infectious and presumably do not intend to infect others, whereas the latter hope that their posts gain traction.)

The Centre for Countering Digital Hate identified 12 online anti-vaxx figures, many of whom propagate conspiracy theories, and who are responsible for 65% of anti-vaxx content on the four largest social media platforms (CCDH 2021b). However, Donald Trump surpassed the conspiracist influence and reach of any self-appointed gurus. One study by researchers at Cornell University (of traditional media this time) found that mentions of Trump featured in 38% of the overall misinformation conversation. The researchers concluded that "the President of the US was likely the largest driver of the COVID-19 misinforma-tion 'infodemic'" (Evanega et al. 2020). Moreover, as Astrid Taylor puts it, while Trump "condemn[ed] millions to disease and destitution," he "told his followers they were victims … of public health protocols and marginalized groups seeking equal rights; he comforted those afflicted with delusions that a reassertion of white supremacy and a revolt against a spectral 'deep state' could cure the crisis" (2021).

While conspiracy influencers precede the pandemic, then, Covid-19 coincided with the presidency of a man whose whole rhetorical and political strategy relied not merely on a refusal to correct misinformation but on endorsing it. He nailed his colours to the mast of conspiracism by launching his presidential bid on the racist "birther" conspiracy theory about Obama's citizenship, and his term in office ended with accusations of voter fraud and an appeal to "stop the steal." The top-down nature of much Covid-19 conspiracism is certainly significant for what it tells us about the changing locus of power in this discourse, which, during the post-War period (and even more so in the post-Cold War period), was largely the preserve of those marginalised, epistemically and culturally, in the public sphere (see Thalmann 2019; Butter 2020).

Opportunism

One of the first studies of extremism and conspiracy theories in 2010 found that, although "conspiracy theories are not a necessary condition for extreme beliefs or action," they certainly "play an important social and functional role within extremism" (Bartlett and Miller 2010, 4). The report, produced by the UK thinktank Demos, describes conspiracy theories as a "radicalising multi-plier" (4) because of how they help extremist groups to demonise others, del-egitimise oppositional opinions by casting them as part of the conspiracy and position violent action as the only way to get the masses to see what is really going on (5). The authors warn that because conspiracy theories held by groups of different ideological stripes all break down trust in government, "extreme groups may be able to draw on a larger counter-culture of conspiracies as a pool of possible recruits" (5). The opportunism shown by existing extremist groups to attract newcomers during Covid-19 sees this warning come to fruition. As well as extremist organisations, political interest groups have also used a shared conspiracist vocabulary and common grievances to increase their reach during the crisis. Opportunism, therefore, plays a part at different stages in what could be thought of as a radicalisation pipeline.[8]

For example, US far-right organisations such as the Boogaloo movement and the Proud Boys exchanged their "Stop the Steal" campaign for an attack on the vaccine after Biden's inauguration (MacFarquhar 2021), bringing them into contact with anti-vaxx conspiracy theorists. In a similar fashion, conspiracist anti-vaxx groups sought to influence people who are vaccine hesitant or distrustful of the state. In their quantitative study of how "online hate communities are weaponizing COVID-19," Nicolas Velásquez et al. (2020) find that "the rise of fear and misinformation around COVID-19 has allowed promoters of malicious matter and hate to engage with mainstream audiences around a common topic of interest, and potentially push them toward hateful views."

Because lockdown orders during the pandemic threatened to disrupt the usual, real-world recruitment paths of violent extremist organisations— outreach, grooming, vetting (Argentino 2021b), social media, prior to a crackdown, and Telegram and Gab afterwards, proved crucial to continuing recruitment work.[9] As well as the result of active recruitment, engagement with extremist groups also occurred because of the way in which some of their anti-elite, anti-state con-spiracist ideas have resonated beyond extremist groups during the pandemic. The increased prominence of such ideas meant that interest in extremist groups grew in the first half of 2020. A briefing by ISD Global, for example, reported that public Facebook groups associated with the Boogaloo movement received sig-nificant increases in engagement during March 2020, with Covid-19 a key topic. During the same period, far-right groups set up Telegram channels specifically for discussion of Covid-19, such as one called "Corona-chan news" (ISD 2020; O'Connor 2021). One white supremacist channel that made its focus Covid-19 increased its users by 800% in March 2020 (Perrigo 2020). It is important to note that the interconnections between different strata of the internet mean that the leap from conspiracy theory to conspiracist-fuelled calls for violence is not so far. Because moderated social media spaces dedicated to borderline—but largely non-extremist—content can easily link to unmoderated deep vernacular web spaces focused on explicitly extremist content, opportunistic fishing expe-ditions to find those curious or sympathetic to extremist causes can yield results (Velásquez et al. 2020).

As Argentino's study of Pastel QAnon found, new recruitment pools have been created in which violent organisations and non-violent actors share the same infor-mation-communication channels (2021b). While it is too early to say how lasting and deep any "recruitment" from these new adjacencies might be, this presents a slight but nevertheless significant shift in the role of conspiracy theories in extrem-ist organisations. It is tempting to read the situation as simply an intensification of the role the Demos report recognised in 2010. Yet, conspiracy theories are not only a potential "radicaliser" for any new recruit once in; rather, they serve as the very reason for encountering the extremist organisation in the first place.

The attraction of anti-vaccine, lockdown-resistant narratives for groups like the Boogaloo Bois, advocating for civil war, is clear: the longer herd immunity is delayed, and disruption continues, the greater their chances of undermining faith in the state (MacFarquhar 2021). White supremacist groups, like the Patriot Front in the US, have used the social upheaval prompted by the pandemic more generally to promote an impending race war. The ideologies of such groups are shot through with conspiracy theories of "white genocide" and "the great replacement" (Moonshot 2021). Of course, it is not only extremist groups and interest groups that have exploited the pandemic via conspiracist narratives. In his role as president, Trump also attempted to leverage the pandemic in this manner. While he ultimately failed in his endeavour to utilise fear, distrust and conspiracy theory to secure a second term in office, it was a strategy that mobilised enough people, some of whom belonged to the organisations discussed above, to storm the Capitol building on January 6, 2021.

Disruptive

At one time, conspiracy theories would encourage us to believe untruths; they now seem more intent on making us disbelieve truths. Some commentators argue that this erosion of trust in facts, truth and institutions—often referred to as "post-truth" during the rise of Trump—endangers liberal democracy. With caution, given the way that this word has become a celebratory business buzzword, we call this tendency in contemporary conspiracism "disruptive." It is another shift that predates but becomes fully realised during Covid-19. The grave conditions of the pandemic have certainly raised the stakes of a disruptive approach which were already high: think of what Steve Bannon's strategy to "flood the zone with shit" (quoted in Remnick 2018) did to the idea and standing of the fourth estate in the US or how a disruptive conspiracism regarding climate change has delayed crucial action.

While any conspiracy theory can disrupt in the way we define this term, in this section we focus on the conspiracism that is generated by two kinds of actors: domestic agents of chaos, and disinformation operatives sponsored by foreign states. Disruptive conspiracy theories draw together several other characteristics we have outlined in this chapter, because they are sometimes peddled by opportunists and superspreaders, some of whom encourage offline mobilisation.

Trump, his entourage and the conspiracist groups that supported him proved to be exemplary domestic agents of chaos in the US. While it was often others who generated the conspiracy theories, the Trump administration amplified them as a way of deflecting attention from its own actions, undermining trust in media outlets that were exposing those actions, stoking grievances and creating confusion and fear to promote acquiescence to illiberal policies towards, for example, immigrants. Writing about the post-truth, disruptive strategies of figures associated with the alt-right, Naomi Klein writes,

> [the Great Reset conspiracy theory] makes no sense, and that's just fine by the likes of [Steve] Bannon … Because if you want to keep waging war on the Earth's life-supporting ecology, a great way to do it is to deliberately pollute its democracy-supporting information ecology. In fact, the pollution is the point.
>
> *(Klein 2020)*

Indeed, doubt sowed by conspiracism can be a political tool. Whitney Phillips and Ryan M. Milner (2021) also use this metaphor of information or media pollution in relation to conspiracy theories. Their book on polarised speech and conspiracy theories describes the media environment as caught in its own media-ecological crisis, polluted by toxic information. They write, "polluted information is a public health issue" (2021, 5). However, they do not only blame the biggest polluters, "the white nationalists and supremacists, clickbait sensationalists, state-sponsored propagandists, and unrepentant chaos agents" (6), but also smaller actors. This is because big and small polluters are fundamentally intertwined. In fact, their focus for change rises above actors altogether towards macro-structural solutions. We, too, will address some of these issues in chapter 6, but here we want to stay with those actors and features that can tell us about the climate of conspiracism under Covid-19.

The work of domestic chaos agents is aided by that undertaken by foreign state-sponsored disinformation campaigns. In chapter 3, we outlined the conspiracy theories concerning the origins of Covid-19 coming out of China and Russia. Such outputs serve as a particularly cynical extension of propaganda operations—cynical because they are often intended to sow discord rather than persuade audiences of an alternative ideology. These well-funded campaigns produced multiple, sometimes contradictory stories to undermine trust during the pandemic. As the European Union's specialist unit tasked with combatting Russian disinformation put it: "pro-Kremlin disinformation outlets expose the target audience with dozens of different statements, versions, explanations, 'leaks,' 'sensational revelations,' conspiracy theories. All this aims to diminish the trust in the efforts of the health care system, the authorities, national and international institutions" (EUvsDisinfo 2020b). As well as the push towards general discord, some Covid-19 related conspiracist disinformation was more about gaining recognisable global advantages through vaccine diplomacy. For example, a swathe of disinformation denigrating different western vaccines and/or vaccination strategies was produced by pro-Kremlin and pro-Chinese Communist Party units (EUvsDisinfo 2020a). At the same time, however, the pandemic has also made clear that conspiracist disinformation cannot solely be blamed on foreign agents, as much of it has been home-grown—sometimes as part of populist, grassroots resistance, but at other times prompted by an array of conservative think tanks and funders. For example, support for the Great Barrington Declaration—which recommended a herd immunity strategy and, in turn, underpinned protests against lockdowns—drew together a disparate range of political groups and interests. Yet these media talking points and public demonstrations have also been subtly promoted and funded by an intersecting network of right-wing organisations opposed to government control, whether in the realm of personal freedom or business activities (especially in the US, but also in the UK). For example, the "Koch-backed group Americans for Prosperity (AFP) filed an amicus brief with the state supreme court challenging the authority of the governor and the health department to continue to require people to stay home without sign-off from the Republican-controlled legislature" (Holden 2020). An array of organisations—many of which have ties to the Koch and Mercer family foundations—were already agitating against climate crisis mitigations, and swiftly pivoted to resisting public health measures that involved, in their view, unwarranted restriction of individual or corporate liberty (Bragman and Kotch 2021).[10] There are, thus, close connections between Covid denial, climate denial and "Stop the Steal" in terms of both content and personnel, with some of the same conspiracists, both domestic and foreign, now also peddling the disinformation that the Russian invasion of Ukraine is a hoax. In each case, the motivation behind such claims seems as much about disruption as promoting a specific set of "alternative facts."

Adjacency

While the term "convergence" captures the merging of different narrative strains of conspiracism, "adjacency" describes the encounters created by such convergence. Some Covid-19 conspiracy theories have allowed seemingly incompatible social and political groups to become adjacent. As well as breaking down the binaries of traditional political divides, such adjacency can bring together under a common cause people with vastly different concerns and values. For example, anti-lockdown protests and the conspiracist messages that fuel them have seen anti-vaxx mothers march alongside antisemitic neo-Nazis, or QAnon patriots alongside homeopaths in some instances. We call this "adjacency" because the different foci of the groups remain distinct even while they share the same physical or digital space.

The case of what happened on yoga Instagram during the pandemic is revealing. Cecile Guerin, for example, writes about her experience of watching her feed, which followed yoga accounts, turn from miracle cures in the early stages of the pandemic to anti-vaxx content, Covid denialism and "calls to 'question established truths' and wilder conspiracy theories" such as QAnon (2021). Some yoga accounts, like that belonging to Krystal Tini, gained thousands of followers once she began posting support for QAnon. Figure 5.5, created by Eleni Maragkou, shows the shift towards more conspiracist, QAnon-related themes in @KrystalTini's posts from 2019 to 2020 (before deplatforming processes made explicit promotion of QAnon difficult).

In a discussion of conspirituality under Covid-19, Maragkou points out that "influencers' reactionary epistemologies do not stem from the traditional underpinnings of the far right, but from the relatively innocuous promises of spirituality-inflected self-fulfilment" (2021). While conspiracists take different journeys, however, they can sometimes end at the same physical place. For example, the January 6 pro-Trump rallies that turned into riots at the Capitol coincided with an anti-vaxx event nearby. One prominent anti-vaxxer, Dr Simone Gold, was charged with breaching the Capitol. She bridged the anti-vaxx and pro-Trump worlds easily, appearing in a video that spread misleading claims about Covid-19 that was shared by Trump on Twitter. Later, in April 2021, a conference with the

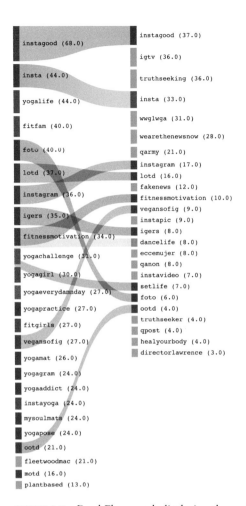

FIGURE 5.5   RankFlow graph displaying the evolution of conspiracist themes on @kri-staltini's account between 2019 and 2020. *Source: Copyright Eleni Maragkou, 2021. Reprinted with permission.*

tagline "Learn How to Fight Back for Your Health and Freedom" placed anti-vaxx figures and Trump allies on the same platform (see MacFarquhar 2021).

While Covid-19 conspiracism has created some odd bedfellows, what becomes clear in online and offline spaces, where people of different ideological leanings might gather under a conspiracist banner, is that the sense that there *is* a conspiracy is more powerful than any differences of opinion about the details of that conspiracy (or the different reasons that brought them to that conclusion). The challenge of this is clear. As the Network Contagion Research Institute at Rutgers University points out, new adjacencies have the potential "to meld disparate factions into a large anti-government movement united around public health issues" (Ross et al. 2021). However, as Jack Bratich points out, we should be wary of any legal framework or government discourse that attempts to demonise or legislate against "anti-government" movements because of the way, historically, such moves have disproportionately been used against the left rather than right (2021).

Moderated

Moderation policies of social media platforms have put new pressures on online conspiracism during Covid-19. The risks presented by conspiracy theorising to public health and—during the heated election in the US—democratic institutions have forced social media platforms to act. While we consider the efficacy of various interventions in the conclusion, it is worth noting in this chapter on the characteristics of conspiracism under Covid-19 that moderation policies shaped online conspiracism. For example, Instagram users took to embedding QAnon messages in images rather than texts and then in stories rather than posts (see Argentino 2021b); QAnon Twitter and Instagram users both morphed hashtags and appropriated neutral hashtags (#savethechildren) to stay ahead of moderators; anti-lockdown conspiracy theorists posted pictures of printed material; producers and consumers of conspiracy content turned to more niche, moderation-free apps and channels; some conspiracy theorists turned to more generic theories, spreading memes that refer to the New World Order rather than QAnon or vaccinations, for example (Network Contagion Research Institute 2021); and conspiracists made non-conspiracist online spaces (Amazon reviews and the comments sections of non-conspiracist YouTube videos) function like social media. Moreover, such moderation practices have become absorbed into conspiracy narratives, as the platforms are configured as part of a conspiracy to silence the truthtellers (see de Keulenaar, Burton and Kisjes 2021).

Monetised

Our final distinctive characteristic of Covid-19 conspiracism is that it has become increasingly monetised. It is undeniable that conspiracy entrepreneurs and social media platforms have profited from stoking conspiracist controversy. Like other characteristics outlined in this chapter, this tendency pre-exists but has intensified during the pandemic. Because we consider this to be vital to understanding Covid-19 conspiracy theories, we devote the following two chapters to examining the different ways in which the latter have been rendered lucrative.

Notes

1 Other researchers have identified key features of Covid-19 conspiracy theories. Shadi Shahsavari et al. (2020), for example, recognise 5 features: 1) the attempt by some conspiracy theorists to incorporate the pandemic into well-known conspiracy theories; 2) the emergence of new conspiracy theories; 3) the alignment of various

conspiracy theories to form larger ones; 4) the nucleation of potential conspiracy theories that may grow into a larger theory or be subsumed in one of the existing or emerging theories; and 5) the interaction of these conspiracy theories with the news, where certain factual events are linked to conspiracy theories.

2 In singling out Gates as the arch-conspirator, Covid-19 conspiracism follows a recurrent trend in conspiracy thinking. As Michael Butter (2016) points out in his analysis of Dan Brown's novels, what is often initially presented as a vast, interconnected conspiracy turns out in the end to be the work of a single, criminal mastermind. However, as the focus on Gates and Soros during the pandemic makes clear, these figures stand as both specific individuals and the personification of nefarious plotting by global elites in general.

3 On conspiracy as distributed system, see Knight 2008 and 2021.

4 Our research team and students attending the Amsterdam Digital Methods Winter School 2021 who looked at Amazon reviews were Veronika Batzdorfer, Liliana Bounegru, Yingying Chen, Tomasso Elli, Zeqing Feng, Alex Gekker, Jonathan Gray, Ekaterina Khryakova, Mingzhao Lin, Matthew Marshall, Thais Lobo, Dylan O'Sullivan, Erinne Paisley, Lara Rittmeier, Nahal Sheikh, Adinda Temminck, Marc Tuters, Fabio Votta, Arwyn Workman-Youmans, Jingyi Wu.

5 We thank Marc Tuters, one of the researchers on the project, for prompting this observation.

6 Like so many conspiracy theories, narratives about Planned Parenthood and black genocide contain a kernel of truth. The founder of the organisation that later became Planned Parenthood, Margaret Sanger, was involved in the eugenics movement, gave a speech at the women's auxiliary of the Ku Klux Klan and had a relationship with a Klansman (see Collins-Dexter 2020).

7 However, we should point out that the quantitative data on gender differences in relation to conspiracy thinking is notoriously inconclusive (see Thiem 2020). Contradicting this Pew research, an earlier study finds that women are "significantly less likely to endorse each of the 11 conspiracy theories [about the pandemic] than men" (Cassese et al. 2020, 3). Of note is the fact that the latter study was conducted early in the pandemic before conspiracy theories concerning vaccination, in which women play a key role, were dominant.

8 This is not to suggest that all conspiracy theories "radicalise"—a view that woefully misunderstands not only the range of relationships people have to conspiracy theories, but also the ludic or ironic nature of some conspiracy fantasies.

9 In fact, one off-line tactic—flyering—increased, although extremist groups targeted public spaces rather than campuses given the move to online teaching (see Bates and Gale 2021).

10 Research into these influence networks itself comes dangerously close to conspiracism, with its talk of shadow forces, guilt by association and diagrams of hidden connections; while these speculative investigations may indeed be accurate, they also overstate the ability of think tanks and similar organisations to manipulate the masses.

6
CONSPIRACY ENTREPRENEURS AND MARKETPLACE BOTS

While much activity in conspiracist milieus is conducted by people who are motivated by nothing more than a desire to be heard, this chapter is concerned with the financial incentives of conspiracism. Certain public figures who promulgate conspiracy theories, so-called conspiracy entrepreneurs (Campion-Vincent 2015), have long made a profit from such activities. But they have become of particular concern during the pandemic, as their ability to reach wide audiences positions them as potential "superspreaders" of conspiracist misinformation and disinformation that could be harmful physically (rather than only epistemically). As this chapter is concerned with the monetisation of conspiracy theories, it will consider both the activities of conspiracy entrepreneurs and the role that digital marketplaces play. What we will see in this chapter and the next is that the business models of digital platforms and the design choices that support them shape the availability and flow of conspiracist ideas.

It would be impossible to find the first instance of someone profiting financially from a conspiracy theory. Conspiracy narratives being used for political rather than financial gain are more familiar, but they often go hand in hand. Rather than looking at cases where financial gain is secondary, this chapter focuses on the purposeful commodification of conspiracy theories. We can, therefore, identify when and how conspiracy theories move from the marketplace of ideas (which may or may not bring some form of financial reward) to the marketplace proper. Instead of falling into the trap of identifying origins, we trace a line through the contemporary period that shows the development of conspiracist cultural commodities. While our focus is on English-language Covid-19 conspiracy theories rather than the US specifically, the global influence of American culture during the twentieth and twenty-first centuries is undeniable. Although we are therefore mindful of local variations in content and homegrown conspiracist commodities, understanding the longer trajectory of American conspiracist

DOI: 10.4324/9781003315438-7

cultural production can help to contextualise the commodification of conspiracy theories under Covid-19 in the US and beyond.

Conspiracy Inc.

Speculation concerning the assassination of President Kennedy in 1963 soon turned conspiracist in nature, with many claiming that the CIA had been involved. Mark Lane's conspiracist take on the assassination, *Rush to Judgment* (1966), spent 29 weeks on the *New York Times* best-seller list. A veritable industry of books questioning the lone gunman theory grew in the years that followed (see Knight 2007). The event even spawned early (though far less cynical) examples of conspiracy entrepreneurs such as the housewife-turned-radio-host, Mae Brussell, whose syndicated show, "Dialogue: Conspiracy" (later renamed "World Watchers International") centred on conspiracy theories about JFK (see Olmsted 2008).

In terms of fictional cultural production, a genre of conspiracy film influenced by events like the assassination of JFK and the later Watergate scandal evolved in the 1970s. Literary fiction by authors like Joan Didion, Don DeLillo, Thomas Pynchon and Ishmael Reed became infused with new reflexive forms of paranoid thinking. While the mid-century Cold War fear of communism also produced its cultural commodities, the cultural paranoia that developed after the JFK assassination diverged from the "official" government narrative, commodifying distrust of those very institutions previously meant to provide ontological security from the threat identified. Paranoia became more "a default attitude for the post-1960s generation, more an expression of inexhaustible suspicion and uncertainty than a dogmatic form of scaremongering" (Knight 2000, 75). The ubiquity of a postmodern paranoia meant that all kinds of highbrow cultural forms were infused with its sensibility, its style, but it was not yet part of a fully-fledged mass market. It was yet to become a staple of popular culture.

At the end of the twentieth century, "a postmodern form of paranoid scepticism [had] become routine in which the conspiratorial netherworld has become hyper-visible, its secrets just one more commodity" (Knight 2000, 75). In the ensuing decades, a formerly marginal paranoid style of politics became suffused into the culture at large. Indeed, the 1990s drew on the still somewhat counter- or subcultural and, in the case of literature, high cultural status of conspiracy theory and postmodern paranoia and turned them into popular forms of mass culture. *The X-Files* (Fox 1993–2002 and 2016–18) offers the best-known example. This long-running television show packaged its conspiracy theory about a Deep State faction within the US government and its coverup of an extra-terrestrial invasion in a unique blend of conspiracy thriller and the speculative genres of horror and science fiction. The show's mixed tones of sincerity and irony garnered widespread appeal. Galvanised by this show, copycat series and countless television documentaries, conspiracy theories became part of the cultural conversation so that theories about JFK, Roswell, alien abductions, black helicopters, AIDS, flat earth and the Illuminati had common popular currency even while conspiracy theories became politically less influential and were delegitimised overall (see Butter 2020).

By 1997, the box office flop, *Conspiracy Theory* (dir. Donner), could use the signifier without any explanation. The film failed not because it assumed a readymade audience but because it did not incorporate any of the postmodern paranoia, playfulness, self-referentiality and irony that rewarded consumers of other conspiracy texts. It is an overly literal interpretation of a phenomenon that had come to primarily resonate, in such fictions, at the allegorical level. The film is nevertheless notable because it registers conspiracy theory as a marketable category rather than either as purely political rhetoric or as a counter- or subcultural marker. The committed Cold-Warrior who espoused the "paranoid style" (Hofstadter 1964) had "become an armchair consumer of *The X-Files* in the 1990s" (Knight 2000, 45) as conspiracy theory became mass entertainment.

The popularity of conspiracy fictions, earnest or playful, continues to the present day. Following and extending *The X-Files'* successful formula, sophisticated conspiracy narratives such as *Watchmen* (HBO 2019), *Westworld* (HBO 2016–), *Lost* (ABC 2004–2010), and *The OA* (Netflix 2016–19) reward avid fans and attentive audiences with so-called easter eggs (self-referential gifts that encourage intense hermeneutic activity), online fan semiotic production and opportunities to buy associated merchandise. But a new development in the commodification of conspiracy theory has emerged in the last two decades because of the democratisation of digital production and broadcasting, the opportunities for self-promotion offered by social media platforms, new avenues for monetisation online and an emboldened populist politics that encourages conspiracist subjectivities that can be affirmed through forms of consumption. We will examine these developments in the context of a continuously evolving conspiracy market that has, most recently, extended to conspiracy theories concerning Covid-19. As we argued in chapter 1, this conspiracism is stoked by a strand of populism that capitalises on ethnonationalism and associated feelings of relative depravation, a perception that "the wider group … is being left behind relative to others in society, while culturally liberal politicians, media and celebrities devote far more attention and status to immigrants, ethnic minorities and newcomers" (Eatwell and Goodwin 2018, 31). Part of the appeal of conspiracist populism in the age of digital media is the promise that passive "armchair consumers" of entertaining conspiracy fictions can become at the same time active producers of alternative knowledge, or "prosumers" as this hybrid mode has been termed (Ritzer and Jergenson 2010). While conspiracists can indeed become active in the co-production of alternative cosmologies through social media and other communal platforms, only certain online conspiracists will make money from this activity. Because of this, an asymmetry between producer and consumer is affirmed at a time when other configurations are technologically more possible than ever.

Conspiracy Entrepreneurs

As part of the logic of neoliberalism, the figure of the entrepreneur has increasingly focused on the self as the prime enterprise-unit. As Michel Foucault notes, "the stake in all neo-liberal analysis is the replacement every time of homo œconomicus as a partner of exchange with homo œconomicus as entrepreneur of himself, being for himself his own capital, being for himself his own producer, being for himself the source of [his] earnings" (Foucault 2008, 226). The rational management of one's own human capital involves not renting oneself out for wage labour but, rather, investing in oneself in order to constantly be at an advantage within the market. This "rational actor"—a new and improved homo economicus—is able to thrive amongst the ruins of liberal democracy through modes of self-reinvention and self-exploitation.

Given this hyperrational attention to self-exploitation and modulation, we might consider the entrepreneur of the self as the opposite of the apparently hyper-irrational conspiracy theorist.[1] While the entrepreneur is identified with jujitsu moves up the ladder of opportunity, constantly optimising themself as a commodity, the conspiracy theorist is associated with downward class mobility and stuck in forms of negative, enervating grievance. Both subjects seem to emerge out of precarity—job insecurity and increased exposure to risk—but one is a resilient go-getter, willing to align their sensibility with the market and, therefore, beating the system at its own game while the other becomes paralysed within loops of paranoid logic and feels defeated or controlled by invisible forces. Both subjects also exude a kind of anti-state sensibility: the entrepreneur because s/he thrives in unregulated spaces of capital where each person is responsible for themself; the conspiracy theorist because s/he fears being thwarted by its machinations. In fact, these figures are not so far apart. The commodification of conspiracy theory today is led by conspiracy entrepreneurs whose personalities and experiences are central to their market success. They combine a conspiracy theorist sensibility, a traditional entrepreneurial spirit and the neoliberal entrepreneurialism of the self which fashions personhood as an enterprise. William Callison and Quinn Slobodian call such figures "agents of disinfotainment" who deal in "gig conspiracies for the gig economy" (2021). The force of the entrepreneurial imperative of neoliberalism extends to monetise even an apparent counterforce to it.

The flow of neoliberal entrepreneurialism into the conspiracist landscape is both fitting and surprising in terms of ideology. On the one hand, many Anglo-American conspiracy entrepreneurs are aligned with a neoliberal self-responsibilised subjectivity that finds itself in market relations with others rather than within the social field of the state. But because this often manifests as far-right or libertarian ideas of sovereign citizenship and extreme forms of individualism, in which the government and/or elites are blamed for one's woes, such a position diverges from globalised neoliberal marketisation. The most ambitious right-wing conspiracy entrepreneurs today therefore find themselves having to reflect a revanchist or xenophobic politics while trying to appeal and trade across national boundaries.

Conspiracy entrepreneurs and influencers profit from conspiracist merchandise and broadcasting in ways that "hucksters" and "quack doctors" have been doing for years. But there is a difference. As "alternative influencers" (Lewis 2018) having to operate in a digital attention economy, their identities are extensions of the commodities being sold.[2] They themselves are brands that have to quickly adapt to emerging conspiracy narratives and developments—this is why the already-established conspiracy entrepreneurs were well placed to take advantage of Covid-19 uncertainties (Jackson and Heal 2021). Particularly adept conspiracy entrepreneurs, who can create value for their currency of the self, attain the status of conspiracy guru. As such, they create complex conspiracy cosmologies and, on the back of this, sell books, merchandise and services. Such status is reserved for those conspiracy entrepreneurs most able to adjust their provision to the desires of the market or who can stay in the game for the longest time.

In the same way that fake news sites are often aesthetically indistinguishable from legitimate news outlets because of lowered costs and ease of use of publishing packages, the marketplaces produced by the most successful conspiracy entrepreneurs and gurus closely resemble any other online market space. While a do-it-yourself, anti-establishment aesthetic might work for certain forms of populist provision, these web interfaces employ high production values and aim for frictionless consumer experiences. On David Icke's website (davidicke .com), for example, users can follow breaking news with a conspiracist twist, navigate to the chat forum, subscribe to Ickonic—Icke's conspiracist streaming service—for £9.99 a month and purchase Icke's books, tickets for events or pro-biotics. Advertisements for various conspiracy-adjacent media, services and products adorn the page. The pandemic, and Icke's conspiracy theories about it, have been good for business. One report shows that traffic to davidicke.com increased to 4.3 million in April 2020 from 600,000 in February of the same year. We will turn to the role of platforms themselves in the commodification of the paranoid style later in this chapter and the next, but here it is worth noting that 31% of the increased traffic to Icke's portal came from social media websites (see Turvill 2020). Icke's book sales and public speaking have also been a lucrative source of revenue over the years. One report noted that sales for a single show during an international speaking tour totalled £83,000 (Alexander 2011). Equally, from a case Icke brought against the US distributor of his books in 2008, it is clear that sales figures in the US alone were in the millions of dollars (Icke v. Adams 2008).[3]

Conspiracy theory veteran Alex Jones attracts more than 8 million visitors a month to his Infowars platform through conspiracist content (news items and a live stream of the show), but two-thirds of his revenue is from online sales (see Medik 2018).[4] Jones hawks an extensive range of survival gear (including prepper food), t-shirts, conspiracist videos, wellness supplements and unverified cures including—until the FDA demanded they be removed in April 2020—many products containing colloidal silver, which Jones claimed in a live stream on March 20, 2020 could kill "the whole SARS-corona family at point-blank range" (quoted in Marantz 2020). Such products are "intended to assuage the same fears he stokes" (Williamson and Steel 2018). The interlinked companies that make up Infowars do not publicly report their finances, but the *New York Times* has reported on its finances for 2013–2014: "One entity—created to house the supplements business—generated sales of $15.6 million and net income of $5 million." During the same period, the piece notes, another entity of Infowars recorded net income of "$2.9 million and sales of $14.3 million, with merchandise sales accounting for $10 million, advertising for nearly $2 million and $53,350.66 in donations, according to an unaudited company statement" (Williamson and Steel 2018). These figures regarding site traffic and profits were gathered before Jones was deplatformed by various social media sites in 2018 and 2019 (decisions that will have certainly curtailed revenue Jones would have earned from those sites and reduced traffic to the Infowars website and online store).

While Icke and Jones are two of the most prominent conspiracy entrepreneurs, their digital offering is replicated at more modest scales across the internet. For example, a study by student researchers at King's College London considered the profiles and homepages of 102 YouTube conspiracy influencers.[5] Many of these influencers have homepages that use various monetisation strategies: 56% offer goods or services for sale, while 41% offered memberships and subscriptions using direct payments through PayPal, crowdfunding sites like Patreon or cryptocurrencies like Bitcoin.

Selling Freedom: The Case of Dustin Nemos

Dustin Nemos (whose real name is Dustin Krieger) is one such influencer seeking to maximise profits. In his thirties, Nemos is younger than veterans like Icke and Jones and a relative newcomer to the conspiracy marketplace. Mixing the populist and pretentious, the folksy and fanciful, Nemos describes himself as "a freedom-maximalist, Voluntaryist, Autodidact Polymath, Husband, Father, Entrepreneur, Farmer, Trend Watcher, Avid Researcher and hobbyist Economist, holistic researcher, Philosopher, and Political Talking Head" [capitalisation in original] (https://fos.news/channels/dustinnemos/). Despite these eclectic interests, his offering—at the level of content at least—does not veer too greatly from the "conspiritual" cocktail of anti-government, anti-elitist conspiracy theory and alternative remedies (which often verge on "New Age") mastered by Jones and Icke.[6]

Unlike Jones and Icke, however, Nemos's favoured conspiracy theory is QAnon. His co-authored book, *QAnon: Invitation to the Great Awakening*, rose high in Amazon's categories for "Politics" and "Censorship" and appeared on its "Hot New Releases" section on the landing page in March 2019 before being banned in January 2021 (see Collins 2019). Alongside a crowded "news" oriented site (nemosnewsnetwork), a sister marketplace, Red Pill Living, sells ingeniously branded products such as "Sleepy Joe Supplements" and "Great Awakening Coffee." QAnon merchandise thus acts as an extension of online research, "[binding] adherents to the conspiracy theory just as powerfully as do memes and online catchphrases," according to Lisa Kaplan of the counter-disinformation consultancy, Alethea Group (quoted in Timberg and Stanley-Becker 2020). Even the name of Nemos's marketplace, Red Pill Living, is a conspiracist trope derived originally from the deep vernacular web "manosphere" (Nagle 2017, 88), which then subsequently filtered into "surface" conspiracist web spaces.[7] Crucially, this is Red Pill *living*—Nemos is trying to sell a lifestyle, not simply individual commodities. In this way, Nemos tries to foster loyal communities that can offer ongoing financial support, rather than one-time purchases. Amusing though the labels are, the products need to be more than a gimmick if Nemos is to secure repeated sales. After all, one bag of Great Awakening coffee might make a witty gift, but the brand needs to resonate on a more sincere level to turn a profit.

Nemos positions himself and his brand as on the side of all kinds of freedoms: freedom of information, freedom of speech, and what it calls medical freedom: "the right to be informed about health, and make the right decisions for their own health—without being told what they can or cannot do by overzealous or corrupted bureaucrats" (RedPillLiving n.d.). As we have seen in the case of other conspiracy entrepreneurs, Nemos creates alarm over such infringements, capitalising on the deep frustrations QAnon and Covid-19 scepticism tap into, while offering apparent solutions on the same website. As well as selling colloidal silver as a supposed treatment for Covid-19 early in the pandemic (Hanoki 2020), Nemos promises to reveal the "truth" about election fraud, Covid-19 vaccinations and social media censorship. In terms of health freedoms, he tells customers that "it starts with the highest quality, vetted holistic and health products on the planet," sold on his platform. Through this marketplace, Nemos invites customers to assert freedom through consumption.

Nemos was once able to use various social media platforms to direct traffic to his online store. However, he has been deplatformed during purges of QAnon-related accounts on the major social media platforms on various occasions and barred from the crowdfunding platform Patreon. Since the storming of the Capitol in January 2021, Nemos's merchandise has also been de-listed by Shopify and his QAnon book removed from Amazon (Dastin, Dang, and Irrera 2020). Consequently, he has been forced to move to less mainstream and less lucrative social media options, like Bitchute and Parler, and use a less familiar crowdfunding site, Donor Box (https://donorbox.org/dustinnemos). While Nemos has attained Bitchute badges for having over 10,000 subscribers and over a million views, suggesting he must receive some income from viewers through its "tip/pledge" button and direct traffic to his marketplace, research into the revenue opportunities of alternative social media sites points out how difficult it is to replicate the rewards of mainstream social media. The organisation Hope Not Hate, for example, collated remarks by alt-right figures such as Milo Yiannopoulos on their reduced influence (Mulhall 2019). Yiannopoulos claims to have lost four million followers during a round of purges on mainstream social media and says that he cannot match that success on platforms such as Telegram and Gab: "I can't make a career out of a handful of people like that. I can't put food on the table this way." He complains that "none of [these platforms] drive traffic. None of them have audiences who buy or commit to anything" (Quoted in Mulhall 2019). Richard Rogers reports that "when Alex Jones was banned from Facebook and YouTube, his Infowars posts, now only available on his websites (and a sprinkling of alternative social media platforms), saw a decline in traffic by one-half" (2020, 215; drawing on Nicas 2018). Assuming attention and traffic translate into financial gain, such measures are significant. Indeed, Nemos told reporters from Reuters that he had lost between one and two million dollars in revenue because of the crackdowns (Dastin, Dang, and Irrera 2020).

However, in promotional material, Nemos contradicts this admission and boasts of having tripled his income since being deplatformed by YouTube by creating the WhiteHat Movement—a network of businesses and services that identify with "patriot values" and want to support and advertise on the sites of deplatformed figures (whom he refers to as "independent media voices" (Nemos 2020)). Before the end of Trump's presidency, there were nine businesses listed, but once Biden took office, Magazon (an online marketplace dedicated to all things Trump) and an associated company were no longer listed, and their sites no longer functioning. While Nemos's own marketplace uses a similar recipe to those belonging to more established conspiracy entrepreneurs, his turn to this ambitious venture is notable, whether it is as successful as he claims or not. (It is hard to see how such a limited network of businesses could achieve his vision for an alternative consumer experience or the profits he claims).

Clearly, Nemos's vision has not been realised. Nevertheless, his venture indicates a shift in conspiracy entrepreneurialism as it attempts to exploit the populist wave to ask businesses to identify under a political banner and steer would-be supporters towards a branded consumer experience, creating what Nemos grandiosely calls the "patriot economy" (Nemos 2021a). Just as we might find some consumers looking for signs of ethical or green merchants to ensure that their shopping experiences align with their values, Nemos is trying to establish a network of online services and marketplaces that subscribe to "freedom of speech, individual liberty, and marketplace freedom" (Nemos 2021b) as he frames it in the promotional literature. The WhiteHat Movement's tagline is "Support free speech—shop patriot." In addition, Nemos has made several attempts to branch out beyond the marketplace and the WhiteHat venture. *The Washington Post* reports that he "has also sought to create a health insurance company trading on the 'Make America Great Again' slogan, as well as an independent cellphone service" (Timberg and Stanley-Becker 2020).

Here it is worth considering a rudimentary but telling illustration that Nemos uses to accompany an account of Red Pill Living's profits in promotional literature for the WhiteHat movement. In the Western movie genre, white Stetsons delineate the admirable and honourable hero; consequently, "white hat" crops up in deep vernacular web spaces to mark out "good guys" or patriots. The trope has also been used to refer to ethical hackers, which is not dissimilar to the way in which Nemos presents himself to prospective collaborators: as an insider who understands the various online factions of the patriot and conspiracy communities, and who can use this knowledge to good effect. The illustration, showing a number of white-capped figures helping each other to climb a mountain with a WWG1WGA flag being waved triumphantly at the summit, implies that noble WhiteHat-affiliated companies can help each other succeed by working together (though it might unintentionally connote an arrangement more akin to a pyramid scheme). By citing the QAnon rallying cry "Where we go one, we go all" in this context, Nemos explicitly seeks to connect a statement of solidarity among believers of a conspiracy theory with a bold business opportunity. He is using the vernacular and logic of QAnon to create alternative economies and shape consumer experiences. Nemos presents his "patriot economy" as playing its part in the great awakening—after all, patterns of production and consumption, and the economy in general, are a part of the consensus reality that has been challenged by QAnon and other conspiracy theories during the pandemic. It follows that a challenge to reality involves changes to commerce.

Echoing ethnonationalist cries heard in conspiracist populism that great swathes of Americans have been left behind economically, Nemos describes his venture as a "Patriot-First marketplace." Nemos's rhetoric speaks to the 90% of core Trump supporters who believe that "discrimination against whites is a major problem in America" (Eatwell and Goodwin 2018, 31). The "patriot" will be prioritised in Nemos's vision—he or she will be first in line. Just as the alt-right has appropriated so many progressive arguments, memes and tropes, Nemos's idea of "patriot-first" inverts the redistributive goals of racial justice and even programmes like affirmative action. Nemos wants to construct a trading network that privileges the desires of, and rewards for, right-wing, white Americans (who have commandeered all talk of patriotism).

These marketplace examples and business ventures tell us that the commodification of conspiracy theories now reaches beyond products (whether goods or media content). Conspiracy entrepreneurs attempt to use identifications with conspiracism to develop producer and consumer pathways and loyalties that can be translated into profit in various ways. We know that conspiracist media can change the way people perceive reality, but it can also guide modes and patterns of production and consumption (as well as "prosumption"). These tendencies were evident before the pandemic, but they have intensified with the convergence of more traditionally political forms of activism with lifestyle conspiracism. Despite the vaunted idealism of anti-vaxx and anti-lockdown campaigns during the pandemic, they are often tied up with attempts to monetise their efforts. At the end of the day, it is nearly always about the grift.

Crowdfunding: Affective Patronage and Digital Tithing

Deplatforming was already becoming an issue before the pandemic in the wake of a series of high-profile mass shootings in which it became apparent not only that the gunmen had histories of online conspiracist radicalisation, but that the platform recommendation algorithms contributed to the amplification of misinformation surrounding the events. YouTube, for example, changed its algorithm in 2017 in response to the public outcry following the killing of 58 people at a music festival in Las Vegas (Levin 2017), and again in 2019, partly in response to the Parkland High School shooting in Florida the previous year (Lapowsky 2019). Deplatforming rapidly gathered pace during the pandemic as the major social media firms bowed to public and political pressure to take action against health misinformation (Krishnan et al. 2021). Deplatforming makes it more difficult for conspiracy entrepreneurs to ensure a steady stream of traffic to their marketplaces. It also eliminates the opportunity to receive payments from the platforms themselves (such as revenue from AdSense on YouTube) or from supporters on hegemonic platforms (using, for example, Facebook's "creator" or "fundraiser" tools or selling goods to supporters using Facebook's shopping facilities). Therefore, during the pandemic, conspiracy entrepreneurs have come to rely on direct donations from supporters using bespoke fundraising services. Though it is more usually associated with charity initiatives or with entrepreneurs seeking to raise funds from communities rather than venture capitalists, "crowdfunding" is the contemporary term for raising money in this way, including in conspiracist communities.

Many creatives and content producers use sites like Patreon to process voluntary contributions, given the difficulties of monetising online content without installing paywalls. While most crowdfunding sites process single payments, Patreon asks donors to commit to a monthly contribution, meaning that it is an ideal solution for those wanting to generate a regular income. It was, therefore, popular among conspiracy entrepreneurs before the platform cracked down on QAnon-related ventures and other varieties of problematic information at the height of the pandemic (in the US) in October 2020. The appeal of this mode of financing for supporters is that they feel directly involved in the success of their chosen conspiracy content producer. Donors are flattered by the allusion to a venerable history of arts patronage, whereby figures of influence and wealth provided security for creatives. However, while crowdsourcing sites like Patreon might appear to cut out any third party, creating an affective bond between patron and content creator, the site itself is a third party keeping a percentage of the income—Patreon keeps between 5% and 12% of donations, depending on the package (Patreon n.d.).

Crowdfunding can be lucrative. One conspiracy entrepreneur going under the name of Neon Revolt raised $150,000 to publish a QAnon book (Dastin, Dang, and Irrera 2020) and raised £115,000 on IndieGoGo for pre-orders in the UK alone. In terms of the conspiracy entrepreneurs we have considered in this chapter, they use a variety of methods to solicit regular and direct donations. Icke, for example, points users towards the *Ickonic* monthly or yearly subscription to access premium content. Jones asks supporters to sponsor the Infowars project as a recurring commitment or one-off payment ranging from $25 to $1000 by using the site's own credit card payment system. Such schemes eliminate the necessity of a crowdfunding site and allow conspiracy entrepreneurs themselves to retain more of the profits. Because of various bans by payment platforms and Patreon, Nemos News Network has resorted to asking for donations by mail, but, as mentioned above, Nemos also has a donation page on Donor Box. Moreover, those wishing to purchase Great Awakening Coffee on Red Pill Living can do so on a monthly subscription basis and pay for this through Visa-owned Authorize .net using major credit card networks.

While we have outlined the problems faced by conspiracy entrepreneurs when they are banned from crowdfunding platforms, they also benefit from the platforms' ad-hoc and inconsistent approach to content moderation and deplatforming. According to a report by Disinfo.eu, crowdfunding platforms rely heavily on user reporting to moderate content. On Patreon, for example, conspiracy entrepreneurs can publish private posts to their financial supporters who are less likely to report content that violates community guidelines. In effect, this "creates a loophole whereby users can spread and finance disinformation without moderation" (Disinfo.eu 2020).

Rather than patronage, which suggests a bestowing of a gift upon someone less affluent or powerful, it might be more accurate to think of the crowdfunding of conspiracy entrepreneurs as a form of faith-based tithing. Tithing—a regular offering, traditionally 10% of earnings, to the Church—features in most Abrahamic religions. It demonstrates commitment to God and adherence to guidance in the Bible. Some conspiracy theories like QAnon borrow from evangelical language and have been likened to a religion or cult. While it is beyond the scope of this book to consider that analogy in any depth, it gives us a way to understand the support some people offer conspiracy content makers through donations.[8] When a conspiracy theory like QAnon or Icke's convoluted conspiracy cosmology offers meaning and purpose to adherents, making financial contributions becomes a self-interested investment rather than an act of charity. Donors are ensuring the continuance of the world view in which they are so heavily invested. They are feeding their faith.

The Myth of the Non-conspiracist Marketplace

Above, we remarked on how the marketplaces belonging to conspiracy entrepreneurs use high production values to rival those of more mainstream marketplaces. However, that might wrongly suggest that mainstream e-commerce sites are free of conspiracy content. In fact, plenty of products relating to conspiracy theories are available on Amazon and, before belated (and incomplete) action was taken by Amazon and other marketplaces, it also sold a great deal of QAnon and anti-vaxx merchandise. Third-party sellers on Amazon, for example, offered more than 8,000 individual QAnon-branded products in Autumn 2020, according to an analysis conducted by Alethea Group and the Global Disinformation Index (see Timberg and Stanley-Becker 2020).

Michael Barkun suggests that conspiracy theories display three main assumptions: first, nothing happens by accident; second, nothing is as it seems; and third, everything is connected (2013, 3–4). If we take this as a guide to demarcating conspiracist from non-conspiracist material, we can see that they appear side-by-side on mainstream online marketplaces. Indeed, the recommendation algorithm for Amazon ensures that conspiracy books show up alongside non-conspiracist material in ways that create false equivalences between positions, arguments and texts. After searching for "children's vaccination and immunisation" and being delivered a lot of dystopian fiction, Benedict Evans points out that Amazon's recommendations result from a system that "turns products into packets in a network, and the whole point of a packet-switched network is that you don't have to know what the payload is" (2021). This system of agnotology (the wilful spread of ignorance for political or financial gain) is exacerbated by Amazon's inclusion of third-party sellers, which account for 60% of Amazon's trade.

A team of researchers on the Digital Methods Initiative Winter School at the University of Amsterdam in January 2021 usefully distinguish between books that are conspiracist because of how they are written (which they call, after Roland Barthes (1975), "writerly"), books that are connected to conspiracy through the way they are read ("readerly"), and books that are algorithmically associated with conspiracism "through an interplay between recommendation features and user practices."[9] The researchers also found that the space for consumer reviews can introduce conspiracist content to the platform even when the product is not ostensibly about conspiracy theory. Reviews for *Covid-19: The Great Reset*, a book by Executive Chairman of the World Economic Forum, Klaus Schwab, for example, are shot-through with a conspiracy theory that finds a sinister plan in "the Great Reset." For example, one reviewer on Amazon.co.uk from September 6, 2020, who gave the book one star, writes,

> the WEF is an exclusive club and, by its very nature, excludes the majority of the citizens of the world. It's [sic] real aim is global control of the billions of ordinary people and the destruction of nation states. In other words, the imposition of a totalitarian government. The Great Reset is a sham of epic proportions. Read this book with extreme caution. It is a Trojan horse.

The review appears near the top because it has been voted as "helpful" by 590 people (as of February 2021). Another from October 8, 2020, claims that "this has all been in the planning for a long time and Covid was deliberately used to force the Reset." Other reviews mention Agenda 21 or talk about the New World Order (NWO), not as they were originally intended (Agenda 21 is the name of a 23-year-old non-binding UN resolution, and "the new world order" is a phrase used by politicians throughout the twentieth century at moments when global co-operation was called for) but as they have come to signify within conspiracist circles (Agenda 21 is reimagined by conspiracy theorists as a plot by eco-totalitarians to subjugate humanity and the NWO as a totalitarian one-world government). One review from October 26, 2020 points people towards the discredited disinformation film about Covid-19, *Plandemic*, offering a link in a manner that ensures the reviews operate in a similar way to social media platforms. However, these reviews are less ephemeral than social media and leave a conspiracist trace on the marketplace. Crucially, the conspiracist reviews attached to readerly conspiracist books remain, even while writerly conspiracist books and products are removed.

Such marketplaces offer third-party sellers, who do not have to be fully-fledged conspiracy entrepreneurs and who do not have to cultivate a following in order to profit from conspiracy theory. Apart from books, most of the conspiracist QAnon merchandise for sale on hegemonic marketplaces, for example, were in the form of baseball caps, phone cases or t-shirts emblazoned with QAnon emblems like the letter Q or a rabbit. Initially, it seems as though these products are symptomatic of the shedding of explanation and political theory that Russell Muirhead and Nancy L. Rosenblum diagnose as the new conspiracism (2019, 19). Their thesis, that we now have conspiracy without the theory, in which allegations never backed up by evidence have taken the place of argumentation, seem to be given form here. And yet, many of the products operate synecdochically. The symbols they display must be understood as nodes in a distributed network of conspiracy theories (recall how the distributed nature of Covid-19 conspiracism is one of the key features that we identify in chapter 5). While this merchandise may not itself display the qualities of what Muirhead and Rosenblum name "classic conspiracism" (29)—which for them aligns with Richard Hofstadter's paranoid style—it gestures towards the larger QAnon movement and related forms of conspiracy theorising in the pandemic and their reams of "research," which very much illustrates a belief that conspiracy is "the motive force in history" (Hofstadter 1964, 29). The theory might be "elsewhere," that is, but this merchandise appeals and speaks to conspiracy literate consumers who know where to find it.

One way in which this merchandise significantly diverts from Hofstadter's paranoid style, however, is that the proponents—here the merchants themselves—are far from the passionate and invested spokesperson he focused on. Indeed, it makes no sense to use such terminology in the context of hegemonic online marketplaces, for conspiracy commerce relies on mechanical or algorithmic reproduction. This suggests a radical distance between merchant and merchandise, between producer and consumer. Rather than a conspiracy entrepreneur or guru, what we are faced with on these marketplaces is a conspiracy bot. In certain cases, the bot, the merchant, and therefore the platform, are deeply disinterested in what the product communicates as long as the product sells. (This is the case until platforms are made to care via pressure from interest groups.) James Bridle writes about algorithmically generated content and products. Automation has led to disturbing examples of t-shirts and other apparel with offensive slogans. Bridle describes a t-shirt on Amazon that reads "Keep Calm and Rape a Lot." He writes, "nobody set out to create these shirts: they just paired an unchecked list of verbs and pronouns with an online image generator. It's quite possible that none of these shirts ever physically existed, were ever purchased or worn, and thus that no harm was done." However, the point is that "the scale and logic of the system is complicit in these outputs" (Bridle 2017). These slogans are not glitches, but necessary possibilities of automation. Looking at YouTube and its hosting of unsettling algorithmically generated content for children, Bridle calls this form of content agnosticism "infrastructural violence."

The content agnosticism and the logic of infrastructural violence evident in this algorithmic generation of Q content and similar conspiracist fare are key elements of the commodification of conspiracy theory today. The pandemic did not create this economic logic but it has intensified the trend. Conspiracy entrepreneurs profit from paying lip service to online cultures of conspiracist pro-sumerism while maintaining an asymmetry between producer and consumer in practice. Automated conspiracy commerce on mainstream marketplaces presents us with an even more pronounced gap between conspiracy theorist consumers (many of whom are deeply invested in the alternative cosmologies offered by the theories they engage with) and the merchants that seek to capitalise on that engagement. Such asymmetries are only further exacerbated when we turn in the next chapter to the differences between conspiracy consumers and the social media platforms whose business models depend on attention and engagement regardless of content (beyond what that content can contribute to profitable audience profiling).

Notes

1 Some of these observations were made by Sean O'Brien, a research assistant on our AHRC-funded "Infodemic" project, who has kindly allowed us to explore them here.
2 The term "alternative influencer" is from Rebecca Lewis. She uses it to describe how "a particular network of political influencers perpetuates far-right ideology on YouTube and other social media platforms. Specifically, individuals from academic and media institutions and reactionary or extremist movements have used participatory digital media to broadcast to new audiences and rebrand old, often bigoted and discriminatory ideas. Content creators have employed the tactics used by brand influencers, along with social networking, to establish an alternative to mainstream news, convey their ideas to audiences, and monetize their content. As a result, audiences and influencers alike are accessing, producing, and supporting extremist and often harmful content" (2018, 43).
3 However, less impressively, the most recent filing to Companies House in the UK tells us that equity in Ickonic Enterprises Inc. amounted to £194,589 in the tax year 2018–2019.
4 Visitor figures are from Quantquast.

5 Jingyi Chen, Wei-Lun Huang, Haoxiang Ma, Hongyi Ren, Haiqi Zhang, "Monetization and Social Merchandise." MA Digital Methods, King's College London, Autumn Term 2020, taught by Liliana Bounegru and Jonathan Gray.

6 The term "conspiritual" is from Charlotte Ward and David Voas (2011) and is useful for thinking about how the conspiracy entrepreneurs under consideration here move between and help to merge different and sometimes apparently incompatible markets.

7 "Redpilling" references the well-known scene in *The Matrix* where the protagonist Neo is asked whether he wants to take the blue pill or the red pill. Only the red pill will puncture the simulacrum and allow him to see the world as it really is. "Redpilling" has subsequently been used as shorthand for enlightenment and is a key component of conversion narratives within conspiracist circles.

8 For a critique of the argument that conspiracy theory is "bad religion" see Aupers 2014.

9 Veronika Batzdorfer, Clare Birchall, Liliana Bounegru, Yingying Chen, Tommaso Elli, Zeqing Feng, Alex Gekker, Jonathan Gray, Ekaterina Khryakova, Peter Knight, Mingzhao Lin, Matthew Marshall, Thais Lobo, Dylan O'Sullivan, Erinne Paisley, Lara Rittmeier, Nahal Sheikh, Adinda Temminck, Marc Tuters, Fabio Votta, Arwyn Workman-Youmans, Jingyi Wu. "Investigating COVID-19 Conspiracies on Amazon", Digital Methods Winter School.

7

INFRASTRUCTURAL DESIGN AND DISINFO CAPITALISM

In chapter 6, we examined the way that individual conspiracy entrepreneurs have found ways to monetise their content in recent years (and increasingly so during the pandemic) amid the shifting terrain of deplatforming and the emergence of alternative platforms. In this chapter, we shift the focus from the money-making strategies of the conspiracy promoters to the financial incentives that are built into the way that particular platforms and other online spaces operate. In doing so, however, we want to avoid a technological determinist approach that positions conspiracy theorising merely as a direct result of platform affordances. After all, conspiracy theories have existed and thrived long before the internet. Indeed, historians convincingly argue that conspiracy theories were probably more widespread before the twentieth century when they were considered orthodox knowledge (Butter 2020; Thalmann 2019). However, it is also clear that digital communication technologies have helped those sympathetic to conspiracist explanations or who enjoy conspiracy narratives to find each other, share ideas and, in some cases, form counterpublics based on idiosyncratic forms of research and ludic engagement. Social media (as we argued in the introduction) have been a significant—but by no means the only—factor in the unwitting creation of a "perfect storm" for conspiracy theories to thrive under pandemic conditions. If there is still some doubt whether conspiracy theories are more popular now, it is indisputable that they are more visible and amplified. However, we need to develop a more nuanced notion of visibility, given the moves that social media platforms have made to deplatform or demote conspiracist content, particularly when related to Covid-19 or QAnon. As a consequence of deplatforming, conspiracy talk has increasingly migrated to what Jing Zeng and Mike Schäfer (2021) call "dark platforms": those online spaces that are less regulated than mainstream social media, but which also have less engagement. Nevertheless, it remains the case that the visibility of conspiracy theories has been assisted by

DOI: 10.4324/9781003315438-8

digital infrastructure design and by a data-driven business model geared towards customer profiling and targeted advertising known as "surveillance capitalism" (Zuboff 2019). In chapters 3 and 4, we considered the main conspiracy theories circulating online during the pandemic; and in chapter 5, we examined the key characteristics of online Covid-19 conspiracy theorising. Together these chapters build a picture of the content, form and function of online conspiracy theories during the pandemic. Existing research also makes clear that conspiracy theories constitute a small, but surprisingly "sticky" and adaptive, component of the total information circulating online (Islam et al. 2020). Drawing on some of our observations in other chapters about how conspiracy theories have circulated during the pandemic, this chapter focuses on the technological conditions that assisted those conspiracy theories to have the reach that they did.[1]

Designed for Disinformation?

Sometimes it can seem as though certain social media platforms are uniquely suited to the creation and circulation of all kinds of dis- and misinformation. However, it is important to remember that social media affordances are the result of activity by both engineers *and* users, and they have evolved relationally. That is, while it is tempting to think of social media platforms as producing rigid experiences and pathways, users are far from passive and have played a key role in developing how communication works on such platforms. For example, protocols for using the @, # and retweet functions on Twitter evolved through user deliberation and were fashioned according to user needs (see Burgess and Baym 2020). On one hand, the mutual construction of platform affordances undermines accounts that posit an all-controlling design or designer—not only because such a narrative ignores how social media change in practice, but also because it risks emulating the logic of conspiracy thinking. On the other hand, it would be a mistake to overstate the agency of users in the face of powerful Big Tech platforms. Thus, affordances that might have been driven initially by users are "ultimately appropriated by the platform to generate metrics that favor commercial logics and open doors to antisocial uses and manipulative practices" (Burgess and Baym 2020, 18). Relationality rarely means that agency is evenly distributed.

People have long suspected a general confluence between the internet and conspiracy theories. Well before social media, Kathleen Stewart observed that "the internet was made for conspiracy theory" (1999, 18). Going further, she claimed that the internet "*is* a conspiracy theory" in as much as "one thing leads to another, always another link leading you deeper into nothing and no place, floating through self-dividing and transmogrifying sites until you are awash in the sheer evidence that the internet exists" (Stewart 1999, 18). From one perspective, the convergence between the experience of surfing the hyperlinked web 2.0 and the construction of conspiracy theories is heightened today because the ubiquity of smart technologies means that there is little sense in talking about a difference between online and offline realms when we are always connected and when algorithms can make it seem as if platforms link us up with what we want before we have fully articulated it. And yet, from another perspective, it is arguable that the internet today is less rather than more connected. The increasing use of encrypted messaging apps, paywalls, firewalls and censorship in certain countries, and the existence of the deep web, dark platforms and spaces not searchable by mainstream engines, introduces friction into the mantra "everything is connected"—used to sum up the logic of both conspiracy theories *and* the internet.

The reality of connectedness falls somewhere between these two poles—a state we could reflect by proposing that everything *seems* connected for users of digital media technologies and for conspiracy theorists even though, in fact, not everything is (or rather, not in the way people often assume). Rather than posit an essential character of the internet or social media (and, hence, an essential relation to conspiracy theories), what we are interested in are those platform affordances, protocols and design choices that assisted the spread of Covid-19 conspiracy theories in the early days of the pandemic.

Platform Affordances

Because education, socialising and some forms of work moved online in the early stages of the Covid-19 pandemic, the default mode of living for many with the means of access became digital. In a heightened state of anxiety, looking for news, seeking advice and reaching for connection, entertainment and community in atomising times of mandated social retreat, many spent more time online than ever. While the increase in digital usage was largely due to video conferencing platforms like Zoom and Teams, people also turned to social media.[2] For example, 51% of the American adults polled by Harris between March 14 and May 3, 2020 reported an increased use of social media (Harris 2020); Twitter reported a record number of users by April 30, 2020 (Washington Post 2020); and the number of people checking one of the apps owned by Facebook every day rose by 15% in 2020 to more than 2.6 billion worldwide (Statt 2021). Given the increased exposure to, engagement with and reliance upon various forms of social media during the pandemic, it is necessary to consider not only the amount of time spent online, but how platforms shaped encounters with and experiences of content as well as the nature of that content itself. The increasing reach of social media is important because research has shown that people who consume their news about the pandemic on social media platforms are more exposed to conspiracy theories and other forms of problematic information (e.g. Baum et al. 2020), with the proviso that increased exposure to online misinformation in itself does not necessarily entail changes in belief or behaviour—though many studies have found evidence of such a correlation (see e.g. Allington and McAndrew 2021 Chadwick et al. 2021; but also the recent revisionist takes by Valensise et al. 2021; Broniatowski et al. 2021, 2022).

As the name suggests, *social* media enable forms of sociality and community, even though the forms these take might be a world away from offline modes, those specific to other historical periods or even those enabled by other media. Twitter allows users to coordinate according to different interests using the # function; the @ sign allows users to directly address other users; and the retweet function cites other posts, continuing a conversation, or allows a user to post a longer thread of connected thoughts that exceed the confines of the 280 characters allowed in the standard tweet. Facebook allows for varied forms of engagement at different levels of intimacy and publicness. Private and public groups create spaces of sustained interactivity based on explicit criteria and interests. Personal feeds offer the opportunity to post content (videos, links, images, memes, opinions, news items etc.), which invites engagement from friends in ways that create flurries of connection and concentrations of communion. Users navigate Instagram through following certain users and/or via hashtags. Conversations take place below an initial image prompt, text-based graphic or meme, although an increasing concentration on the more ephemeral "Stories" feature invites shorter forms of communication from followers who are only visible to the poster. YouTube's comments section allows for opinions to be expressed and exchanges to occur around specific content. This is particularly important for those interested in discussing conspiracy theories because, even when conspiracist videos are deplatformed or hard to find, comments around key texts (such as the World Economic Forum's promotional video concerning "the Great Reset") introduce spaces of conspiracy tolerance. (As we saw in chapter 5, a similar strategy has turned Amazon from a purely marketplace platform into a de facto social media platform where "Reviews" become spaces of congregation for those with beliefs that might otherwise not be featured there.) "Subscribing" to particular channels on YouTube can ensure a continuity of provision and the ability to engage in an ongoing conversation. YouTube's recommended viewing panels can convey the impression that there is a canon to be mastered by a community, even though listed videos will be different for every user depending on their viewing history and user profile.

The semi-curated nature of a user's feed or interface might produce a perception of agency over what one encounters on the platform (seeing content of those we choose to follow or that we have "liked" before). Such feelings might also be enhanced by the ability to leave comments. However, recommendation algorithms and targeted advertising mean that the feed (and therefore any sociality and community) is also curated by automated processes that users have little to no control over. Users interested in conspiracy theories are much like any other interest group, seeking out like-minded users/groups and media content that speaks to their concerns. In this sense, the technological affordances described here support communities interested in "good faith" causes/arguments and "bad faith" causes/arguments alike (although waves of deplatforming and content moderation attempt to intervene). As people spent more time engaging with social media during lockdowns, it was easy to find groups of people questioning the veracity of the pandemic and proposing alternative explanations for the trajectory of world events. Sharing, extending, debating, crowdsourcing, "liking" and engaging with such ideas offer a markedly different experience to lone speculation or vague scepticism. Social media are "infrastructures of our everyday lives" (Sujon 2021, 99) and so the conspiracist communities and content encountered there can confer identity, foster belonging, elevate suspicion to intractable belief and construct archives of alternative evidence to fall back on in moments of doubt. Such processes of affirmation are important to the formation of communities of contested and stigmatised knowledges.

Constructed to facilitate experiences of sociality (even when this might involve negative affects and bonds) in order to secure attention and engagement, social media also allows for rapid circulation. This speed facilitates the spread of content, like conspiracy theories, before there is any chance of fact-checking or deplatforming. Retweeting or reposting takes seconds; cloning content is easy online; and the use of moderation-avoidant tactics, such as morphing hashtags, is standard procedure for developers of borderline and problematic content. In this way, Covid-19 conspiracy theories can be spread despite deplatforming. For example, in a study of one conspiracist article about Bill Gates profiting from Covid-19, Avaaz (2020a) found that the article appeared in its entirety or partially multiple times on different Facebook accounts. The original article reached 3.7 million viewers and a further 4.7 million through republished versions.

An affordance that is important for sustaining conversations and debates, for sharing content of interest, makes the dissemination of problematic information especially easy. Social media platforms value this rapid multiplication as it signals engagement; and, as a consequence, rapidly shared content is, in turn, more likely to be recommended. Noortje Marres notes: "online platforms, then, reward messages that spread instantly and widely with even more visibility," and notes that "sensational rather than factual content turns out to satisfy this criterion of maximal 'share-ability' best" (2018, 430–31). Moreover, Marres argues that in privileging a conception of the user in behavioural terms (focusing on what they do—link, like, share), social media have privileged preference and opinion over knowledge (437). Social media, therefore, constitute a "truth-less public sphere by design" and this "behavioral vision that has informed the design of social media architectures … encourages a conception of users as influenceable subjects, not knowledge agents" (435). While we might argue that Marres is side-lining the role users have played in the development of key affordances, even that limited form of agency fits in with this vision of users being important for how they behave online. When platforms focus on behavioural and engagement metrics in the promotion of their services and benefits to both advertisers and businesses, the subjectivity of users is very much positioned as people whose behaviour can be nudged, shaped and harnessed.

Algorithmic Amplification

There are plenty of users intent on "self-radicalisation," searching for conspiracist content and communities with increasing intensity, following the call to "do your own research." But others appear to be led to conspiracist content via the recommendation algorithms of certain social media spaces. In fact, there is much scholarly debate about how platform algorithms work, not least because they are black box technologies that platforms do not share with researchers. The problem is compounded by the fact that, to date, there are also only a few digital ethnography (netnographic) studies (e.g. Munn 2020), journalistic accounts (e.g. Roose 2019) and first-hand testimonies (e.g. Faraday Speaks 2019) of the negative effects of such exposure to ever-more-extreme content. Becca Lewis (2018), for example, places far more importance on the role of influencers than on the algorithm. What we do know, however, is that, even if other criteria contribute to algorithmic recommendation and networks of influencers also lead users to different conspiracist content, all social media algorithms are employed to maximise the time a user spends on the platform in order that the platform can collate user data and deliver advertising. Ultimately, this is what shapes online experiences with conspiracist content.

To take the example of YouTube, some researchers have found its recommendation algorithm to "systematically [amplify] videos that are divisive, sensational and conspiratorial" (Lewis 2018). If YouTube offers a user similar or ever-more-extreme content, this might not matter if the original content searched for and viewed is a cute kitten video, because the algorithm will simply deliver even cuter kittens. But such processes matter more when the original content viewed is conspiracy adjacent or conspiracy curious because of the way this might lead to conspiracism that has consequences for public health or democratic institutions.[3] It is quite possible that within a few recommendation steps, a video that asks legitimate questions over how death tolls should best be counted during a pandemic, for example, could lead a user to a video like *Plandemic* (before it was deplatformed). In 2017, Zeynep Tufekci found that YouTube delivered ever more extreme content, remarking, "you're never hardcore enough for YouTube" (2017). In fact, YouTube responded to such criticisms in 2018 by introducing links to Wikipedia pages on contested conspiracy theories and again in 2019 by promising to limit "recommendations of borderline content and content that could misinform users in harmful ways" (YouTube 2019a). As a result, YouTube estimated that its measures led to a 70% reduction in view times of these recommendations (YouTube 2019b).

Research by Marc Faddoul et al. (2020) provides partial confirmation of these claims, but they also found that the reduction slipped back to 40% over time. While general recommendations of ever-more-extreme content might have been dampened, meaning that radicalisation is less of a feature, Faddoul et al. point out that "for those with a history of watching conspiratorial content, the filter-bubble effect is strongly reinforced by personalized recommendations" (6).

They point out that conspiracy content is perhaps unlike other political content: "the repercussions of selective exposure may be stronger with conspiracy theories than they are with more typical political content, because conspiratorial narratives are rarely challenged or even addressed on other media" (7). When it comes to conspiracist content, therefore, the algorithm ensures a limited informational diet for those who have already expressed interest.

On Instagram, once a user's feed reaches the end of accounts followed, it is extended with content based on interests that have been identified by AI. As one report notes, "users are being encouraged to view radical material, and then, once hooked, cross-fertilized with content from other limbs of the radical worldview. If a user follows anti-vaxxers, they are fed QAnon conspiracism and antisemitic hate; if they engage with conspiracies, they are fed electoral and anti-vaxx misinformation" (Centre for Countering Digital Hate 2020). It found that even following a "wellness" influencer who posted innocent material about growing vegetables led to recommendations of anti-vaxx material and conspiracy theories about Covid-19.

In 2019, users noticed that Twitter's algorithms were inserting tweets from accounts followed by those they follow. A CNN report noted that this meant that some users experienced "more extreme content" including extreme political rhetoric and conspiracy theories. It added that such content is "posted by media or internet personalities who hold fringe views (many are also verified, giving them an added sense of credibility to people who may not be familiar with them), exposing users on the platform to radical content they may otherwise have not encountered" (Darcy 2019). Such levels of algorithmic curation of the feed can catch unaware users who imagine they have high levels of control over what they experience on Twitter (in contrast to YouTube, which has long recommended content). New "Trending" and "For You" curated feeds on Twitter also offer different pathways to material users might not have explicitly sought out.

An internal report by Facebook in 2018 admitted that "Our algorithms exploit the human brain's attraction to divisiveness. If left unchecked, Facebook would feed users more and more divisive content in an effort to gain user attention and increase time on the platform." An earlier internal report from 2016 had found that "64 percent of people who had joined an extremist group on the platform did so because the group was promoted by Facebook's automated recommendation tools" (quoted in Engineering and Technology Staff 2020). Facebook's algorithm can find lookalike audiences for advertisers or groups, filtering out certain demographics and even linking users to content via prejudices and fears as much as positive affiliations and interests. Equally, its algorithms arrange the order of posts in a feed to entice users to engage for longer (Tufekci 2017). In fact, contentious content, including conspiracy theories, might not only be amplified by algorithms guided by user interest and the influencers or friends they follow; Facebook might also, as Kevin Roose (2019) argues, be "designed to amplify emotionally resonant posts" because "controversy wins." This is because "all attention looks good to an algorithm." In relation to Covid-19 conspiracy theories, the top performing conspiracist content on Facebook Pages in terms of engagement metrics according to our data methods research consisted of provocative talking head videos or interviews by figures like London Real's Brian Reed. One of his highly engaged-with videos from March 20, 2020, for example, is an interview with conspiracy guru David Icke which asks the question, "Is this the truth about 5G technology?" with a prod to comment below: "What do you think?" This gives rise to 217,013 likes and almost 2000 comments, many of which prompt further comments, shares or reactions. To fully understand the reasons behind this "attention economy," and why algorithms are designed around securing attention, we need to consider the business models of social media platforms.

Data Disinfo Capitalism

In general, user attention, engagement and traffic are valuable to online platforms regardless of what is holding that attention or generating engagement because those platforms are reliant on monetising data extraction, using "tracking infrastructures and practices that underpin audience commodification" (Bounegru, forthcoming). Crucially, data about users have, according to scholars like Shoshana Zuboff (2019), been fed back into the system to not only serve targeted adverts, but also predict and modify human behaviour. This means that platforms can encourage the continued engagement and attention of users to generate ever more user data in an optimising feedback loop. Social media platforms certainly collect plenty of data on their users. Facebook, for example, collects "user posts, reactions to posts, profile information, social connections, data extracted from photographs and video (including facial recognition data), information on user logins, and, at least at one point in time, posts that users 'self-censored' (i.e., composed but did not actually publish)" (Crain and Nadler 2019). Third-party data can then be added to Facebook's first-hand data to produce granular profiles to assist advertising systems.

Under "surveillance capitalism" (Zuboff 2019), conspiracy theories are commodified by infrastructure that is largely concerned with content only for the data points it yields. To illustrate the depths of the content-agnostic approach that we touched upon in chapter 6, we only need to consider the case of Facebook including the category "antisemite" for potential advertisers to target until it was brought to their attention (Angwin, Varner, and Tobin 2017). Facebook's defence rested on the fact that the category had been generated by an algorithm—as though the role of AI absolves the platform that utilises it of responsibility. Employing an algorithm that recognises any marketing category no matter how problematic is a design choice. Luciano Floridi and J.W. Sanders (2004) usefully distinguish between accountability and responsibility in systems of distributed agency. While the algorithm may be accountable in this example, the engineers (and the platform) are responsible.

Social media platforms, search engines, data brokers and any other entities whose business models rely on the efficacy of data extraction infrastructure stand to gain the most in financial terms from the proliferation of Covid-19 conspiracy theories in the datafied era. In part, this is because the novelty of false rumours (of which conspiracy theories are a subcategory) ensures that they travel faster, farther and deeper than the truth on, for example, Twitter (Vosoughi, Roy and Aral 2018).[4] Speed and reach mean that conspiracist mis- and disinformation are generating a great deal of monetisable attention and engagement for platforms. To give an indication of the value of a conspiracy influencer like David Icke to social media platforms, the Center for Countering Digital Hate (CCDH 2020a) estimates that Icke's following could be worth up to $23.8 million in annual revenue for tech platforms that rely on advertising and marketing revenue.

This content-agnostic business model extends to the adverts themselves on these platforms. A *BuzzFeed* report shows how Facebook profits from disinformation adverts. For example, it banked "almost $10 million in advertising revenue from the Epoch Times, a pro-Trump media organization that spreads conspiracies, before banning the outlet's ads for using fake accounts and other deceptive tactics" (Silverman and Mac 2020). The report collates previous *BuzzFeed* investigations to remind its readers that in 2020, Facebook "took money for ads promoting extremist-led civil war in the US, fake coronavirus medication, anti-vaccine messages, and a page that preached the racist idea of a genocide against white people, to name a few examples" (Silverman and Mac 2020). Even when checks are put in place, they are often conducted by "low-paid, unempowered contractors" rather than workers who are valued and are central to operations (Doctorow 2020). This, too, is a choice integral to Facebook's approach to problematic content. Far from anomalies, adverts for disinformation and scams are endemic on Facebook, arising from "a deliberately constructed system designed to maximize profits from [such] ads" (Doctorow 2020).

To give another example of platforms profiteering from disinformation, we can look to the case of fake news (while acknowledging that conspiracy theories are a particular sub-set of both). Many platforms, as well as digital advertising and marketing companies do not discriminate between mainstream and junk news. Their trackers operate indiscriminately across the (dis)information ecosystem, scraping data wherever users go. Liliana Bounegru, Jonathan Gray and Tomasso Venturini point out that while scandals regarding fake news and other forms of disinformation have "prompted numerous remedial projects, policy consultations, startups, platform features and algorithmic innovations … there is also a case for—to paraphrase [Donna Haraway]—slowing down and dwelling with the infrastructural trouble" (2020, 334). Only by taking this time will we be able to begin to imagine how to "re-align infrastructures with different societal interests, visions and values" (334). In the case of conspiracist content, this might mean reconfiguring the relationships between users, data, infrastructure and content as well as determining what place paranoid reading, scepticism and popular knowledges should have in digital sociality.

There are policy recommendations and infrastructural fixes that could interrupt the commodification of online conspiracism. We have seen that deplatforming conspiracy entrepreneurs from the main social media platforms has certainly made it more difficult to make money. The campaigning organisation Avaaz, for example, recommends demonetising disinformation by demoting and decelerating disinformation actors. It argues that this method does not impact on free speech, but instead disincentivises users to promote misleading content. Alternatively, the Global Disinformation Index encourages brands to put pressure on the ad-tech industry, particularly ad exchanges, to not allow their adverts to appear on domains that contain disinformation (Fagan and Melford 2019). Facebook, Google and Twitter, for example, agreed a joint statement with the government in the UK that "no user or company should directly profit from Covid-19 vaccine mis/disinformation" (UK Government 2020), although a report by the Bureau of Investigative Journalism found violations of this agreement on a mass scale. This demonstrates the limitations of leaving the platforms to create their own voluntary agreements, rather than requiring action through regulation (Jackson and Heal 2021).

We will turn to a range of targeted interventions to contend with Covid-19 conspiracy theories more specifically in the conclusion, but here we want to reiterate the need for a "whole-of-society" approach that involves "stakeholders in the private sector, public sector and civil society" (Donovan et al. 2021) and understands online conspiracism as a complex ecosystem. Such an approach involves a reassessment of the political economy that lies behind and shapes the infrastructural choices made by the platforms. Deplatforming conspiracy entrepreneurs from, and tweaking the algorithms of, hegemonic social media and online marketplaces might be good publicity for those platforms, but it will take a bolder approach to address the role of Big Tech as an industry and the technological infrastructure through which conspiracy theories spread. As well as data capitalist imperatives and the "infrastructural violence" we considered in chapter 6, it is the "passive ecosystem" that requires most attention. This includes "the mechanisms that allow this content to be hosted and spread, and sometimes to hide ownership, such as DNS infrastructure, adtech, and algorithmic recommendation" (Alaphilippe 2021).

For society as a whole, we also need to consider our own attachments to social media and responses to their affordances; our apathy about data extraction models; and our own tendencies towards conspiracist framings, including the very notion of surveillance capitalism, at least in the apocalyptic, Manichean terms that Zuboff uses. Indeed, the story of surveillance capitalism put forth by Zuboff holds certain similarities to Richard Hofstadter's paranoid style. The subtitle of her book is "The Fight for a Human Future at the New Frontier of Power," and she locates the exact nature of the exploitation as "the rendering of our lives as behavioral data for the sake of others' improved control of us" (2019, 94). Zuboff names and shames the enemy: "The world is vanquished now, on its knees, and brought to you by Google" (2019, 142). Ultimately, Zuboff warns readers of the unprecedented asymmetric power yielded by data capitalists with the ominous repeated refrain: *"Who knows? Who decides? Who decides who decides?* [italics in original]" (521), a phrase which echoes the graffiti derived from Juvenal—"Who watches the watchmen?"—in Alan Moore and Dave Gibbons's graphic novel of conspiracy and paranoia, *Watchmen* (1987). What is at stake, Zuboff writes, "is the human expectation of sovereignty over one's own life and authorship of one's own experience" (522). She warns "those who would try to conquer human nature" that they should expect to "find their intended victims full of voice, ready to name danger and defeat it" (525). Some might consider such rhetoric "overheated, oversuspicious, overaggressive, grandiose, apocalyptic" (Hofstadter 1964, 4). It is shaped by righteousness and moral indignation—all characteristics that, according to Richard Hofstadter, constitute "the paranoid style" used by conspiracy theorists. Zuboff's central image is certainly "that of a vast and sinister conspiracy, a gigantic and yet subtle machinery of influence set in motion to undermine and destroy a way of life" (29), as Hofstadter put it in the 1960s.

Part of the issue is that Zuboff's concerns are shared by conspiracy theorists like the anti-vaxxer Robert F. Kennedy Jr. In an interview from May 2020 with Daniel Liszt on YouTube titled "Medical Tyranny Big Pharma Bill Gates AI Immunity Passport Surveillance State!" RFK Jr warns that the hidden purpose of 5G is to develop an infrastructure for AI, which will assist surveillance and data harvesting. He discusses the internet of things and its role in tracking people until Bill Gates "will have all this data about you that will make you into a permanent consumer." He discusses data as the new oil, facial recognition technologies, and the power of large data centres, much of which also appears in Zuboff's analysis (as well as other work by scholars of digital culture).

Zuboff does not succumb to the tell-tale "curious leap of imagination" (Hofstadter 1964, 37) that often appears in conspiracy theories, nor does she start from the assumption that conspiracy is "*the motive force* in historical events" (29) in the way someone like RFK Jr does—for Zuboff, a more likely candidate would be technology in general or Google in particular. Nevertheless, the convergence in rhetoric between Zuboff's surveillance capitalism and Hofstadter's paranoid style highlights the difficulty of separating out a critique from a conspiracy theory of Big Tech's use of data. Moreover, the risk of mirroring some of the features of the paranoid style and presenting the social media moment as a narrative of "Us versus Them" is that it obscures the ways in which users actually experience social media and, indeed, data. Concerns about the way that platforms are driven by data extraction might miss the precise ways in which we live inside and alongside, and are subjectivised within, "data worlds" (Gray 2018). They might obscure "how data infrastructures may be involved in not just the representation but also the articulation of collective life" (Gray 2018). And because we are not completely rendered passive and dispossessed, because "we get to keep our own feelings even as Google gets them too," the concept of "incitement capitalism" might better describe the situation (Slobodian 2019). The idea of "surveillance," as Philip E. Agre (1993) points out, is tied to technologies like photography rather than the computer, which might be better described as an apparatus of "capture." If there is some kind of generalised conspiracy (built into operating systems and infrastructure) against users to commodify attention and capture their data, engagement can also forge meaningful connections and groupings. This would have to include those conspiracist communities, or counterpublics, that coalesce around the most cynical (or even the most algorithmically governed) conspiracist marketplaces and social media spaces.[5]

While we should accept that users can have meaningful experiences even under conditions of exploitation and surveillance, it is still important to consider alternative infrastructure. This means thinking not only about ownership, design and regulation, but about the forms of meaning-making we want to prioritise. As Richard Seymour writes, "the problem is not the lies. It is the information reduced to brute fact, to technologies with powers of physical manipulations by means of information bombardment" (Seymour 2019, 162). He turns to the French state-owned Mintel as an example of information infrastructure not reliant on attention and engagement to remind us that there have been alternatives, and that the current model is tied to a particular political and economic ideological formation (209). The call for a public service internet is loud in academia, best represented by the "Public Service Media and Public Service Internet Manifesto," which has over 500 international signatories (Fuchs and Unterberger 2021). The advantages of this model are clear: infrastructural choices would align with and support democratically agreed-upon values, delivering content that helps to build consensus rather than division, that prioritises the public good over sensationalism, that "bakes in" ethical concerns from the beginning or that is not driven by pressures to increase engagement and reduce people to data. Such shifts in infrastructural design and regulation would play a part in a wider reconfiguration of the role that experts, knowledge and trust should play in the information ecology. They would also contribute to debates about whether there are other ways to meet the concerns, fears and needs that are currently met through consuming conspiracy. Deplatforming the most immediately harmful content might be a necessary measure in the middle of a pandemic, but it is only a temporary and blunt-edged fix if we do not also address the underlying reasons why Covid-19 conspiracy theories have spoken to many different individuals and social groups.

Notes

1 It is also important to keep in mind the role of mainstream media in the (perhaps unintentional) amplification of conspiracy theories. Whitney Phillips (2018) has warned journalists against the "oxygen of amplification." Covid-19 conspiracy theories as well as QAnon (some elements of which incorporated the pandemic) became a major topic for journalists to report on, framing them as a socio-political problem, an "infodemic." The framing allowed news outlets to perform boundary maintenance, to enact a "politics of demarcation" (Marres 2018), while at the same time gaining interested readers and increasing literacy in Covid-19 conspiracy theories.

2 According to MarketWatch, Zoom's daily users quadrupled in March 2020, for example (Bary 2020).

3 This point was originally made by our research assistant, Fabio Votta.

4 Other recent research specifically on Covid-19 misinformation in the online environment challenges some of the conclusions of Vosoughi, Roy and Aral (2018). Broniatowski et al. (2022), for example, found that "during the earliest stages of the pandemic, when claims of an infodemic emerged, social media contained proportionally less misinformation than expected based on the prior year. Our results suggest that widespread health misinformation is not unique to COVID-19. Rather, it is a systemic feature of online health communication that can adversely impact public health behaviors and must therefore be addressed." Likewise, Pulido et al. (2020) found that, during a health emergency like the Covid-19 pandemic, "false information is tweeted more but retweeted less than science-based evidence or fact-checking tweets, while science-based evidence and fact-checking tweets capture more engagement than mere facts."

5 Our focus on social media in this chapter is not intended to misrepresent the varied nature of the conspiracist digital ecosystem. The latter spreads across the open web (website, blogs), hegemonic social media (Twitter, Instagram, Facebook etc.), private Facebook groups and "dark platforms" (Zeng and Schäfer 2021) such as encrypted messaging apps (Telegram, Signal etc.), the deep vernacular web (4Chan, 8kun), and alternative web apps (Parler, Gab etc.). An adequate representation of the conspiracist landscape during the pandemic would therefore need to think about the ways in which users encounter conspiracy theories and conduct research within and between these different online spaces. Not all of these spaces operate under a logic of data extraction and surveillance (or capture or incitement) capitalism, and we would need to think about what difference this makes to the circulation and exchange of conspiracy theories. When algorithms are not employed to promote content, how do community practices (like upvoting on Reddit) resist or replicate their logic?

CONCLUSION

Confronting Conspiracism

Not all conspiracy theories pose a risk, and sometimes paranoia is a reasonable response to concentrations of power and experiences of powerlessness. Much of this book has been arguing for the necessity of contextualising conspiracy theories, whether within political and social histories, the discursive terrain of contested knowledges or the design of digital infrastructure. However, during the year we spent studying Covid-19 conspiracy theories, it often seemed that such theories at best distracted people from the real challenges of the pandemic and at worst created obstacles to containment and recovery. Conspiracy theories in the online environment did not inevitably lead to a crisis of trust in governments and health authorities, but nor did they remain merely harmless or ironic fun. While it is important to consider the way conspiracy theorising can serve as a creative form of worldmaking that responds to the cultural and political anxieties and economic pressures of the day, there are times when it is more appropriate to interrupt or challenge them. Intervention is prudent when lives and livelihoods are threatened by conspiracist denialism. The challenge, however, is how to limit the negative consequences of conspiracy theories without reinforcing a normative position or endorsing a political status quo that might further the structural conditions that help to produce populist, conspiracist thinking in the first place.

Before outlining some general conclusions of this book and the research that guides it, therefore, we want to assess some of the ways that have been mooted for curbing conspiracy theories during the pandemic.

Fact-Checking and Debunking

In the wake of the 2016 election in the US and the Brexit referendum in the UK, a great many fact-checking organisations were established to contend with the distorted facts and lies being told by politicians and other prominent public

DOI: 10.4324/9781003315438-9

figures. Fact-checking was also a response to the broader emergence of so-called post-truth phenomena (including fake news websites and conspiracy theories). Interventions vary. Some focus on directly correcting factual inaccuracies; some on pointing out the logical inconsistencies and errors in reasoning; and others on discrediting the sources of dubious information and conspiracy theories. Likewise, in some cases users have to seek out a service such as the BBC's Reality Check (established in 2017); but social media platforms have also teamed up with other fact-checking services to experiment with pop-ups or tags to flag up dubious claims in social media posts. Facebook, for example, collaborated with fact-checking organisations in 2016 to offer users more information about the claims made in posts before being shared. The attractions of such interventions are clear: they offer some form of corrective to factually flawed viral information and potentially introduce alternative views into otherwise epistemically homogenous spaces (so-called echo chambers). Fact-checking, at the very least, asks users to pause before spreading fake news, disinformation or conspiracy theories.

The limitations are perhaps equally as clear as the attractions. Offering correctives to false information of the kind to be found in the BBC's Reality Check is based on a model from print journalism. Legally, printed corrections are important to those whose reputations are at risk from uncorroborated claims, lies and mistakes in newspapers. But such an approach has a limited effect in the face of the scale and speed of social media. Besides, journalistic corrections are produced by the very media outlet that printed the error in the first place; they are a form of apology, a signal that the publication is taking responsibility. However, the kind of fact-checking under discussion here is carried out by an external organisation in a watchdog capacity. This can feed the feeling conspiracy theorists might have that they are being censored by "the establishment," which is, to their mind, part of a conspiracy. In the current culture wars in the US and the UK, organisations like Facebook and the BBC are viewed by many conspiracy theorists as organs of censorship, and so fact-checking corrections issued by them are automatically discounted. A "disputed content" banner might make one user question the information and yet serve as a badge of honour or even signify legitimacy to a more conspiracy-minded user. Unorthodox knowledge is prized precisely because it is eschewed by the "mainstream."

More than this, fact-checking assumes that everybody cares about facts or cares about them in the same way. More accurately, it assumes that everyone has the same criteria for facticity. Though the term "truthiness" was used in jest by Stephen Colbert back in 2005, it anticipated the sentiment, widely espoused today, that it is acceptable to pay more attention to the way a fact might *feel* right or wrong rather than whether it adheres to criteria for truth established by logical reasoning, empirical research or scientific rationalism. Trump's one-time press secretary, Kellyanne Conway, coined the term "alternative facts" in 2017 to capture the mood. In light of this, fact-checking corrections are unlikely to change a conspiracy theorist's mind not only because of confirmation bias but also because they tend to distrust the very institutions that produce credentialled, fact-based knowledge. In opposition to scientific systems for deriving knowledge, dana boyd therefore calls conspiracy theories and other post-truth ways of seeing "experience based epistemologies" (2018). This suggests that conspiracy theories are less about erroneous facts in need of correction and more about knowledge construction: not about *what* is known but *how* it is known.

Fact-checking can also be difficult in cases where the science is quickly changing and highly contested. David Spiegelhalter argues, "behind closed doors, scientists spend the whole time arguing and deeply disagreeing on some fairly fundamental things … The binary idea that scientific assertions are either correct or incorrect has fed into the divisiveness that has characterised the pandemic" (quoted in Clarke 2021). In chapter 3, for example, we considered what happened when the speculation that Covid-19 was developed in a lab, rather than naturally occurring in an animal habitat, changed from conspiracy theory to scientific possibility. In cases like this, fact-checking risks misrepresenting the provisional nature of scientific research and undermining its own legitimacy when people wonder how "facts" can change. Fact-checking, therefore, is difficult when scientific hypotheses are still in dispute and evidence from intelligence gathering is not verifiable.

During the Covid-19 pandemic, the visibility and volume of fact-checking in many countries around the world has increased considerably (Oledan et al. 2020). In this regard, the pandemic has produced a step-change in the capacity of an array of government agencies and civil society organisations to engage in fact-checking (Siwakoti et al. 2021). Because of the speed and scale of factually incorrect information being circulated, fact-checking organisations and social media platforms are increasingly turning to automation to keep up (Volpicelli 2018). The holy grail of research in this area is the use of machine learning to enable automated detection and removal of misinformation, disinformation and conspiracy theories (Tangherlini et al. 2020; Shahsavari et al. 2020; Moffitt, King and Carley 2021; Centre for Data Ethics and Innovation 2021). There are, however, potential problems with the turn to algorithmic content moderation. In practical terms, most of the research currently focuses on English-language content, and thus fails to engage with content circulating in other languages. As we saw in chapter 4, making the situation harder is the deployment of obfuscation techniques by those posting conspiracist content, as they are now alert to the keywords and hashtags that trigger automated detection and removal (see Collins and Zadrozny 2021). In some cases the AI fails to distinguish between the promotion and debunking of problematic information, and ends up removing content, groups or sites which are explicitly aimed at criticising misinformation and conspiracy theories. Likewise, machine learning can fail to spot the difference between ironic mimicry from actual conspiracism. As we have been arguing in this book, the distinction between those categories is ever more fluid. Given that what counts as a conspiracy theory is historically shifting and politically contested, it is difficult to teach a computer to reliably sift examples into clear categories. Some impressive work is being carried out in this area, using innovative approaches derived from, for example, narratology (e.g., Tangherlini et al. 2020) and corpus linguistics coupled with sentiment analysis (Miani, Hills and Bangerter 2021). The problem, however, is that the nature of conspiracy theories is always evolving; the turn to more fragmentary and distributed forms of conspiracism, for example, means that automated detection may fail to "see" the conspiracy talk in these subtle traces.

At a more fundamental level, as Noortje Marres argues, there are problems with AI approaches that rely on the "correspondence model of truth," a logical positivist approach to demarcating valid and invalid statements that "draws a normative boundary" (Marres 2018, 428). For Marres, this "politics of demarcation" (429) effectively distinguishes between those capable of knowledge and those susceptible to manipulation in terms of an "opposition between educated progressives and … less educated supporters of populist and nationalist causes" (430). First, such an approach fails to address how social media algorithms are designed to share sensational messages. Second, demarcation side-lines the relationship between technology and the status of knowledge as such. In other words, the correspondence model of truth, which relies upon stable referents for validating empirical statements, is "ill-adjusted to the dynamic model of information, communication and feed-back that is today implemented across society by computational means" (434). A more dynamic approach to public truth is therefore needed. Lastly, as we point out in chapter 7, Marres shows how social media designers themselves view users as influenceable subjects rather than knowledgeable agents (435–36). This means that coercion is baked into the system from the very beginning and is not something that can be weeded out by fact-checking manipulative false claims that might circulate on the platform. As an alternative, Marres advocates the recovery of "experimental facts." Facts, she argues, "are too important to be reduced to vehicles of the restoration of authority: their validity is always experimentally acquired, and the experimental validation of public facts must today happen in the public domain" (441).

Marres's work is careful and nuanced, but the overall argument and approach comes with risks. Anyone wanting to exploit constructivist logic could use her call for experimental facts to justify the idea of "alternative facts." Moreover, in the current culture wars, it can unwittingly provide ammunition for free-speech absolutists. Nevertheless, it remains helpful for thinking reflexively about the problematic assumptions upon which fact-checking practices might unwittingly rely. This is especially useful when considering the desire for, and experiments with, automated, real-time detection, categorisation and removal of problematic content. Such aims are often based on unexamined assumptions not only about the nature of facticity itself and a politics of demarcation in Marres's terms but also about the political neutrality of the machine learning algorithms that are deployed, whether by researchers, fact-checking organisations or the platforms themselves. Work by scholars such as Safiya Umoja Noble (2018) has shown that algorithms reproduce and amplify rather than escape social inequalities. Automation might create or consolidate certain problems even as it tries to solve others.[1]

Prebunking and Inoculation

Whereas fact-checking and debunking focus on challenging particular pieces of conspiracist information after they have already begun to circulate, the aim of inoculation ("prebunking") is to bolster the cognitive immune system of recipients in advance so that they are more able to resist infection by these messages. Researchers have experimented with different forms of prebunking interventions (see, e.g., Cook et al. 2017; van der Linden et al. 2017, 2020; Vivion et al. 2022). One involves giving people pre-emptive factual corrections of likely conspiracy theories and other forms of misinformation, with the aim that they will be more sceptical of those narratives when they subsequently encounter them. The other approach provides a broader form of advanced warning, equipping people with knowledge about the kinds of logical fallacies and rhetorical strategies that conspiracy theories employ in general, in the hope that people will then be able to identify conspiracist misinformation whenever they come across it.

Both these forms of "immunological" intervention have produced some promising results, individually and in combination. Likewise, studies have found that in some cases debunking is more effective, and at other times prebunking works best (for a literature review of this research, see Ecker et al. 2022). However, the effects of information inoculation seem to wear off quickly. This makes sense if we think that conspiracy beliefs are the result not simply of false information, nor faulty reasoning that can be corrected. If conspiracy theories are narratives that emerge from and help shape the worldview of an individual or a group, then it is understandable that people revert to their position despite— and, in some cases, precisely as a result of—attempts from experts (academics, fact-checking organisations and the media) to convince them otherwise (on this kind of "backfire effect," see Hart and Nisbet 2012; Nyhan, Reifler and Ubel 2013). Moreover, as we argued in chapter 1, the turn to medical metaphors in media research risks introducing misleading analogies. In particular, it suggests that the recipients of conspiracy theories, misinformation and disinformation are passive victims, whereas, in much of the Covid-19 conspiracy culture we have analysed in this project, those who circulate these forms of problematic knowledge are often co-creators of it (even when they merely like and share items that they do not necessarily believe in).

Deplatforming

Another approach to reducing the circulation or visibility of conspiracy theories is deplatforming. If fact-checking and debunking seek to correct or warn about information after it has entered the online ecosystem, deplatforming seeks to prevent that information from being posted in the first place by suspending or removing accounts that break the platform's terms of service (or "community standards"). At their inception, social media companies ducked responsibility by positioning themselves as the neutral providers of micro-publishing platforms rather than curators or editors of content. However, the presence of Islamic

State accounts nudged social media platforms towards greater intervention. In addition, as "fake news" and "bots" became a concern during the Brexit campaign in the UK and the lead-up to the 2016 election in the US, many social media platforms started to remove accounts associated with co-ordinated inauthentic behaviour. Increased pressure from governments and campaigners forced more concerted sanctions against users who violated the platforms' community standards. Figures deplatformed in this way include alt-right agitators such as Milo Yiannopoulis (banned from Twitter in 2016 and Facebook in 2018); conspiracy gurus such as Alex Jones (removed from YouTube, Twitter and Facebook in 2018) and David Icke (removed from Facebook and YouTube in 2020); and political figures like the QAnon-supporting congresswoman Marjorie Taylor Greene (permanently banned from Twitter and suspended from Facebook in January 2022 for spreading Covid-19 misinformation) and, notoriously, Donald Trump (barred from Twitter and Facebook following the storming of the Capitol in January 2021). In 2021, in the midst of the Covid-19 crisis, many social media platforms updated their community standards to reflect concerns about problematic information and public safety. For example, Facebook made a commitment to remove "misinformation [that] has the potential to cause imminent physical harm" (Facebook 2021). The pandemic caused social media platforms to change their approaches to content moderation far more quickly and far more extensively than had seemed imaginable prior to 2020 (Scott and Wheaton 2021). Faced with a public outcry and with governments in the US, the UK and the EU threatening tighter regulation, the platforms took action—although, as we have seen, it was often more a case of "performative transparency" than a genuine culture shift.

Some research suggests that deplatforming can be successful in reducing the circulation and visibility of disinformation. As a strategy, deplatforming has influential advocates such as Joan Donavon from Harvard's Shorenstein Center on Media, Politics and Public Policy and crisis informatics expert Kate Starbird. Deplatforming works, they argue, because it takes away the financial incentives to produce disinformation and reduces engagement with it. One data-analytics project by Adrian Rauchfleisch and Jonas Kaiser (2021) shows how deplatforming leads to a significant reduction in traffic to the content creators' new channels on alternative platforms (like Gab, Bitchute etc.) and, therefore, their financial revenue. Alex Jones, for example, had 2.4 million subscribers on YouTube, but only 125,000 subscribers on Bitchute as of June 2021 (Rauchfleisch and Kaiser 2021, 22). As further proof of the financial impact of deplatforming, we can look to Milo Yiannopoulos, who complained that being deplatformed left him bankrupt (quoted in Beauchamp 2018). One study by Zignal Labs, for example, suggested that the circulation of disinformation concerning election fraud across social media sites decreased by 73% when Twitter deplatformed Trump (as well as 70,000 QAnon related accounts) in January 2021 (see Garrett 2021). While it is relatively easy to prove the positive short-term effects on the circulation of disinformation that deplatforming can have, what remains uncertain in all the research are the long-term effects. One study (Broniatowksi et al. 2022) found that although Facebook managed to reduce the engagement with anti-vaxx pages by 29%, within six months those gains had been wiped out; more worryingly, Facebook's new policy on harmful vaccination information also managed to reduce engagement with pro-vaccine information by half. Much depends on whether platforms can prevent old networks from rebuilding and, therefore, effectively "re-platforming" certain key figures, groups, or messages (see Starbird 2021).

While effective in the short term at reducing the visibility of disinformation, including conspiracy theories, deplatforming has some undesirable unintended consequences. Most notably, it forces key content creators to migrate to alternative apps like Bitchute, Voat, Parler or Gab, increasing the visibility and profits of platforms that have little to no moderation and as such are, potentially, more radicalising spaces (Rogers 2020a). Such cross-platform presence and diversification "may ultimately increase the resilience of the target group" (Innes and Innes 2021, 15), even if it renders them less visible to the "normies." Equally, the move to alternative platforms for many content creators of the far right, a category known to engage in forms of conspiracism, has led to an increase in activity and a darkening of tone (Ali et al. 2021). And if it is not alternative social media to which deplatformed content creators and their followers turn, it is encrypted messaging apps like Discord and Telegram. Because groups on these messaging apps are often private, they may be more at risk of operating as epistemically, informationally and ideologically homogenous "echo chambers." It also means that they exist beyond the purview of moderators, regulators, researchers and monitors of extremism.

Deplatforming is a blunt instrument. It is a whack-a-mole approach that requires constant vigilance on the part of moderators, or updates to detection algorithms (to identify new influencers, pages or accounts and to keep up with an ever-evolving disinformation landscape, including hashtags that are constantly morphing in order to evade detection). Deplatforming key figures can produce a multiplication of pages dedicated to them. Helen Innes and Martin Innes (2021) highlight the role of "minion accounts" in the event of deplatforming: these "are clearly associated with the de-platformed 'leader' and continue to perform their ideological mission, albeit not under their personal direction and control" (10). Conspiracist content can therefore be replatformed even when key conspiracists are banned.[2] Moreover, as with fact-checking, deplatforming risks confirming the sense a conspiracist might harbour that they are being censored. Alex Jones, for example, warned that "America has been sold out" and the Infowars Twitter account railed against "communist style censorship" after Jones was deplatformed by YouTube (quoted in Tsioulcas 2018). This is often a tactical move on the part of conspiracy gurus, a way of gaining credibility by reinforcing their defiance of the mainstream. For their followers and other conspiracy sympathetic users, it is further proof of a conspiracy of silence. In their study of the reactions of YouTube users to deplatformed Covid-19 conspiracist content, Emillie de Keulennar, Anthony Glyn Burton and Ivan Kisjes note that some conspiracy-minded internet users "claim that video testimony of doctors and nurses disappear as part of a general cover-up for the spread of crowdsourced information" (2021, 129), viewing YouTube as part of a wider conspiracy against the truth. These form what they call "folk theories of Big Tech persecution" (118). Even when overtly conspiracist content is removed from such platforms, conspiracism can remain on the platforms in the comments sections under authoritative primary sources that conspiracists contest. (As explored in chapter 5, we found the same phenomenon within customer review spaces on Amazon.)

Deplatforming works, and, in some situations, it may be the best solution. But in the long term other options need to be explored. Demoting (i.e., not removing problematic content, but altering the recommendation algorithms to make it harder to find) can provide a better solution than deplatforming because it does not raise the spectre of censorship to the same degree (on the perils of deplatforming as censorship, see Royal Society 2022). After all, the right to free speech is not the right to algorithmic amplification. However, perhaps one of the most troubling aspects of deplatforming and demoting is that it leaves key decisions about the parameters of acceptable speech in the hands of private companies. This might be fine while such companies adhere to a broadly liberal consensus on such issues, but this is not always in evidence, nor is it guaranteed for the future.

Digital Literacy and Critical Thinking

Another solution often suggested for tackling mis- and disinformation including conspiracy theories is to teach greater digital literacy and critical thinking skills (for overviews in research in these areas, see, e.g., Machete and Turpin 2020; Jones-Jang, Mortensen and Liu 2021). In an article for Learning for Justice, an initiative of the Southern Poverty Law Center, for example, Cory Collins (2021) positions digital literacy as central to the fight against disinformation of the kind that led to events at the US Capitol building in 2021 or the most extreme forms of Covid-19 conspiracism. The thinking behind this is clear: better skills to navigate the information encountered online increases the ability of individuals to discern mis- and disinformation from the truth.

While empowering people to evaluate information is obviously useful, too much reliance upon a digital literacy approach tends to responsibilise individuals for the quality of the information environment when in fact, such responsibility lies with platforms as well as state regulatory bodies. Moreover, as dana boyd (2018) points out, the tenets of digital literacy also risk mimicking the questioning, critical logic of conspiracist scepticism and the QAnon rallying cry to "do your own research!" boyd thinks that it is highly risky to challenge students' "sacred cows" without offering "a new framework through which to make sense of the world" because they will look for that framework in untrustworthy spaces (2018). Digital literacy advocates often underestimate the affective connection people have to the emotive issues on which mis- and disinformation often focus—especially when they involve, as conspiracy theories so often do, weaponising the act of asking questions: "this is about making sense of an information landscape where the very tools that people use to make sense of the world around them have been strategically perverted by other people who believe themselves to be resisting the same powerful actors that we normally seek to critique" (boyd 2018).

boyd's concern with digital literacy echoes a connected set of issues we have with all of the approaches mentioned so far when we focus specifically on conspiracy theories rather than mis- or disinformation more generally. None adequately address the motivations of conspiracists, the link between conspiracy theorising, identity and belonging which has been intensified by rampant culture wars, nor the deep-rooted causes and histories of conspiracy theories. In effect, they fail to see what is distinct about conspiracy theories that mean they cannot be treated in the same way as "fake news" or other forms of mis- and disinformation. They fail to understand why these narratives and social practices are meaningful here and now (as well as in other locations and historical periods). Because they promote scepticism about the very authority of institutions tasked with separating fact and fiction, conspiracy theories are not simply a false belief in need of correction; because they are evolving, creative endeavours, they cannot easily be identified by algorithms or human moderators; and, because they share or even "weaponise" the same tactics as rational, critical thinking, they cannot easily be separated from it.

Approaching Conspiracism

There are no quick fixes to conspiracism, especially in the middle of pandemic when the terrain can shift so quickly. Yet we suggest that any proposed solution must pay adequate attention to the following:

1. **The structural conditions that contribute to the attraction of conspiracy theorising in the first place.** Developing empathy for conspiracists—as many "How to Talk to a Conspiracy Theorist" guides suggest—is all well and good, but this tends to set up individuals as figures in need of rescuing when it might be better to consider the technological and social inequalities that feed into feelings of scepticism and grievance in the first place.[3] We might then consider what structural changes are necessary for people to see the state and democratic institutions as at least benign and at best trustworthy, as well as to create positive and supportive forms of sociality that are not based on grievance or denialism. The point is to understand the demand side of the conspiracy theory pipeline rather than only trying to curb the supply or coax the wayward back to the fold of mainstream rationality through behavioural nudges or emotional connection (necessary though those might be). Conspiracy theories themselves often come close to naming structural causes and confronting real problems, but through deflection and distortion they end up pointing the finger at imagined evil

villains. Any approach to conspiracy theories must tune in to the pressing issues upon which conspiracist fantasies build.

2. **The different investments people place in conspiracy theories.** Some of those who engage regularly with conspiracy theories value them less as information and more for how they confer identity (defined in contrast to the establishment or mainstream) and belonging (to an alternative community). Those less invested—the conspiracy curious or simply confused, such as the "don't know" category we discussed in chapter 2—might share theories online not because they think they are completely true but because they cannot be certain that they are completely false. Moreover, as various studies of "deep vernacular web" conspiracist culture confirm (de Zeeuw and Tuters 2020), some users' relationship to conspiracy theories is diffracted through layers of irony, dissimulation and play. This renders problematic any "solution" to conspiracy theories based on a simplistic notion of "gullible believers," or on the idea that people turn to conspiracy theories because of a deficit of information or having accidentally consumed the wrong information. It also suggests that there are many different kinds of sociality facilitated by conspiracy theories, some of which are based on shared aesthetic tactics rather than clearly articulated beliefs.

3. **The particular kinds of discourse, forms of knowledge and modes of interpretation provided by conspiracy theories.** Conspiracy theories are not the same as other forms of mis- and disinformation because they are not simply false stories, knowingly or unknowingly shared. In contrast, they often stem from a kernel of truth or collect distorted facts along the way. Moreover, it is important to recognise that conspiracy theories are not easily distinguishable from more legitimated forms of knowing and interpreting (see Birchall 2006). The line between a conspiracy theory and a theory of conspiracy is slippery; the relationship between a hermeneutics of suspicion employed by literary and cultural theorists like us and the paranoid style of a conspiracy theorist is closer than academia would like to admit. Moreover, research shows that conspiracy theorists are not victims of a bizarre psychology but have cognitive traits that most people share to a greater or lesser extent. These cognitive habits include the tendency to both find patterns amid randomness and also assume that all effects must be the result of intentional agency. Likewise, the underlying psychological motives for believing in conspiracy theories are shared by most people to some degree: anxiety about a loss of control (both individually and socially), a desire to make sense of how everything fits together, the temptation to think that you are special (for being able to see through the lies) and the need to belong to a community of like-minded people. Until we recognise the ways in which conspiracy theories and theorists are not wholly other, discrete categories nor pathological, but are, rather, always already a part of more "rational" ways of thinking, being and knowing, we are on shaky ground when it comes to decision making about what narratives and logic we do and do not want to circulate in the public sphere.

4. **The ways conspiracy theories offer collective experiences of enchantment and spiritual affirmation.** This is clear in the case of QAnon, which has been likened to a Live Action Role Play game (LARP) because of the levels of world-building it requires and to a religion because of how it promises deliverance by Trump the saviour; these elements have continued with the shift to Pastel Q and the wider convergence provided by conspirituality. It is important to recognise the rewards and attractions of conspiracism alongside the risks. As well as bringing immediate pleasures, "the worlds conspiracists build often express a longing for pleasure, collective fun and connection" (Haiven et al. 2021a, 23). The challenge, therefore, is to think about how society might better address such desires and needs.

5. **The emotional dimension of conspiracism.** Conspiracy theories often work less by the power of argument than the intensity of the emotions that they evoke. They can involve feelings of resentment and righteous injustice, express and provoke excited optimism and crushing pessimism as well as cynicism about the corrupt nature of the world. They often reject an image of dispassionate rational logic and trust gut feelings and instincts. This means that any solution that fashions conspiracy theories as an information problem will miss the affective bonds people have with conspiracy theories and the emotional registers in which they operate.

6. **The shifting characteristics of conspiracy theories in each historical conjuncture.** We have tried to do this for the Covid-19 context in this book by identifying key features of contemporary conspiracism such as modularity, incorporation, integration and convergence and by thinking about the political, social and digital environment in which conspiracy theories circulate.

7. **The current culture wars.** This involves situating the role of conspiracy theorising within highly charged debates that cut to the core of identity and belonging. Doing so might cause us to reconfigure what is "dangerous" about conspiracy theories. That is to say, conspiracy theories might not be inherently dangerous; rather, it is the way they become enlisted within polarised issues (about, for example, immigration or race) and used to demonstrate an existential threat to a way of life. What makes this situation more complicated is that the term "conspiracy theory" itself is not a neutral moniker but is usually applied as a term of denigration to undermine the credibility of one's opponent. It is always someone else who is a conspiracy theorist. Such rhetorical sparring can often take place within the polarised space of the very culture wars that also deploy conspiracism.

8. **Regional differences and contexts.** Much conspiracy theory research, including our own, tends to focus on the US, the UK and, to a lesser extent, Europe. Universal claims are then made, and solutions drawn up, based on these context-specific examples. The internet allows conspiracy narratives (especially in English) to spread globally, but they are often adopted

and adapted in local contexts in sometimes quite surprising ways. Moving forward, it is important to take into account regional political histories of propaganda, press freedoms, democratic and epistemic norms, levels of state control, conflict and authoritarianism to understand how such histories shape conspiracy theories.

9. **The limitations of technological fixes.** Some researchers and platforms have had success employing machine learning to identify conspiracy theories (Tangherlini et al. 2020; Coan et al. 2021), and algorithms built by the social media platforms themselves are no doubt even more sophisticated. However, in general, technological approaches to conspiracy theory miss nuances of tone (particularly irony), intent, context and creativity. Some of these approaches reduce conspiracy theories merely to a set of keywords, hashtags and phrases, whereas conspiracy theories can be narratively complex, distributed across a number of nodes, informing intricate cosmologies and entrenched world views. Such approaches also tend to assume the harm of *all* conspiracy theories (or that "harmful" conspiracy theories are harmful to all, in every circumstance, in the same way).

10. **The design, political economy and infrastructure of platforms.** To understand contemporary conspiracism, we need to focus more on how platform affordances and financial incentives shape online communication and sociality and how they intersect with legacy media and the offline world. This involves looking not at isolated pieces of conspiracist misinformation but adopting a "whole-of-society" approach (Donovan et al. 2021) to the "media ecosystem" (Phillips and Milner 2021). Instead of a short-term fix centred on the removal of problematic content or tweaking particular features of individual platforms, the necessary next step is to think about how social media (and the internet in general) might be organised with different priorities. As Jenny Rice puts it, we need to address "the material structures that allow certain figurations to become thick evidence in the first place: websites, social media platforms, funding sources" (2020, 176). The reorganisation of platforms around the monetisation of user data in the twenty-first century has meant that whatever procures attention and engagement is valued by them even while it might cause reputation damage. It is not a coincidence that conspiracy theories travel well over social media. Such platforms are designed to support emotive and inflammatory speech styles.

All these considerations will help us to understand conspiracy theories as a sui generis sub-set of problematic information and help create bespoke responses to them.

Lessons from the Pandemic

What has the pandemic taught us about conspiracy theories? Although the WHO's use of the term "infodemic" is helpful for highlighting the danger of the proliferation of narratives that undermines robust and trustworthy information in the face of global threats and health challenges, it places too much focus on the production of, rather than desire for, conspiracy theories. It does not capture why a conspiracy theory about tracking microchips planted in vaccines or one which suggests the whole pandemic was orchestrated for evil or profit might resonate more than the truth. Throughout this book we have tried to contextualise Covid-19 conspiracy theories so that they can be understood as socially and politically embedded narratives rather than dismissed as purely false information or as paranoid delusions. We have tried to understand how they resonate with genuine and even legitimate concerns, confusions and resentments, even if the specific claims they make are wide of the mark.

During the first two years of the pandemic, the time we spent researching and writing this book, it became clear that a convergence of previously distinct narratives, and the identification of key antagonists (like Bill Gates) as the personification of the conspiracy, brought together groups that might otherwise not have shared common ground. Evidence of narrative convergence in the online world was, then, mirrored by adjacency of seemingly opposed groups (such as wellness communities and neo-Nazis) in real-world, anti-lockdown protests. This means that it is difficult to locate the original source of Covid-19 conspiracy theories or to pin the blame on any one group. We have long known that conspiracy theories are tied to and consolidate the political identity of individuals, but the ideological miscegenation, appropriation and confusion evident in Covid-19 conspiracy theories means that the political identities conferred by conspiracy theories need to be understood beyond left and right and more in terms of the populist vectors of "the elite" and "the people." Indeed, we need to think of conspiracist movements during Covid-19 as engaging in what Gideon Lasco and Nicole Curato (2019) call "medical populism." "While some health emergencies lead to technocratic responses that soothe anxieties of a panicked public," they note, "medical populism thrives by politicising, simplifying, and spectacularising complex public health issues" (1).[4]

A mundane point about conspiracy theories brought into sharp relief by the pandemic is that they become particularly vivid and visible at moments of crisis and social upheaval (van Prooijen and Douglas 2017). Covid-19 was the first global pandemic of the twenty-first century and the only pandemic within living memory. It is hardly surprising that people seeking to make sense of the crisis looked to all kinds of explanations—some more outlandish than others. But conspiracy theories do not only occur during crises; they last through times of stability and turmoil. They offer ready-made frameworks and tropes that can be activated and animated by new and pressing concerns.

It has been hard not to become frustrated with conspiracy theories during the pandemic. There are, indeed, urgent questions that people must ask of governments implementing unprecedented measures that curb freedom of movement, adjust working conditions and keep children from face-to-face teaching. Governments must be held accountable when they ask people to make great sacrifices (such as missing out on key life events like the funeral of a loved one or a graduation, or not being able to celebrate a wedding, a birthday or religious festival with family and friends). People have a right to know that the spending of public funds during crises is allotted fairly and transparently. As the opioid crisis in the US clearly demonstrates, there are also good reasons to be suspicious of pharmaceutical companies and the regulatory bodies established to keep them in check. It is also perfectly logical to question the concentrations of power that characterise the political economy of media. Conspiracy theorists concerned about vaccines, masks, the "mainstream media" and lockdowns are right to exercise vigilance and raise questions. But in doing so, they pass over everyday collusion, corruption, spin, hypocrisy, cronyism and abuse of monopoly power in favour of more spectacular or dramatic stories.

One modest way forward would be to encourage paranoia about paranoia, scepticism about scepticism, while acknowledging the value of vigilance and questioning. How would conspiracy theorists respond if they were encouraged to refocus their critical approach towards, say, "mainstream media" back on to conspiracist explanations and the entrepreneurs who peddle them? Erik Davis, a key figure in and commentator on the counterculture, says that when he gets challenged about his take on conspiracy theories, he responds, "I'm so paranoid that I'm even paranoid about your paranoia" (Davis 2020). This is not the same as encouraging information or digital literacy, but rather, seeking to redirect rather than dismiss scepticism, vigilance and concern.

Max Haiven, Aris Komporozos-Athanasiou and Alex Kingsmith have come up with a novel approach that could enact such redirection. They found that existing online educational games concerned with conspiracy theories and mis- or disinformation (like Harmony Square, created by the US Departments of State and Homeland Security (https://harmonysquare.game; or the Go Viral Game, created by Sander van der Linden at Cambridge University https://goviralgame.com/en) reinforced the erroneous sense that conspiracy theories are simply anomalies to eradicate from an informational, economic and political system that is otherwise functional and fair. They argue that the enchantment and play offered by conspiracy theories needs to be matched by "countergames." With this aim, they have created a board game, Deep State (https://conspiracy.games#game), to help people understand the lure of conspiracy theories, and to game them, where others have only tried to debunk them. Their proposition is to show how today's forms of conspiracism "are connected to broader systems of financial capitalism" and offer "dangerous play" in a gamified era "where life feels like a game only the rich can win" (Haiven et al. n.d.). In a utopian vein, they argue that countergames "need to offer players the resources for better, more hopeful fantasies of a different socioeconomic system, and give them the tools to create it" (Haiven et al. 2021b).

Developing paranoia about paranoia and offering experiences of countergaming to challenge the neoliberal status quo are long-term projects. In the short term, even taking into consideration all of the points we outline above, in some cases, it will still be worth limiting the circulation of certain conspiracy theories, given the role they can play in spreading dangerous health behaviours, undermining democracy, fuelling political polarisation and socially debilitating discontent. An astute article in *Project Syndicate* proposes we create an independent monitoring body, funded by the platforms, to focus on detecting and removing content if it ticks any of these boxes: "Does the theory fuel hatred, divide society, or incite violence? Does it seek to delegitimize political opponents with baseless allegations of treason or other crimes? Does it encourage general distrust of expertise and fact-based policymaking and administration without evidence of its own, thereby eroding the basis of public debate?" (Anheier and Roemmele 2020). But, as we have shown throughout this book, there are no quick technological fixes, and removing content online only treats the symptoms, not the cause. Moreover, even sensible suggestions like those made in *Project Syndicate* could be used to enforce bland political centrism intent on maintaining the status quo of a system that gives rise to conspiracy theories. In the long term, the only solution to the spread of conspiracist cynicism is to address deep structural inequalities in order to enact institutions that are built on concepts of fairness. Rather than creating schemes to promote trust in government (which can ironically end up provoking anti-government conspiracy theories), we should concentrate more on how we can create institutions worthy of trust.

Will conspiracy theories about Covid-19 fade away, perhaps as the virus itself (hopefully) becomes less of a problem? This seems unlikely any time soon. As we complete this book (March 2022), it is clear that Covid-19 conspiracy theories are already being integrated into the overarching framework of the Great Reset as the master narrative that supposedly explains both the pandemic and climate change. And with the Russian invasion of Ukraine, there is the unsavoury but unsurprising spectacle of a convergence between right-wing conspiracists and pro-Putin propagandists, with both groups pushing the story, for example, that the invasion is really a campaign to destroy US-funded biolabs in Ukraine where (so the claim goes) Covid-19 was manufactured as a bioweapon (Ling 2022). This convergence is based partly on a shared fantasy of the Russian leader as the embodiment of anti-woke traditional values; partly on the logic that the pandemic is a hoax and so too is the war in Ukraine; and partly on the idea that the war is a harbinger of the Great Reset. Conspiracy theories never really disappear entirely. Instead, they are revamped and reframed for new battles within wars both cultural and all too material.

Notes

1 On the flipside, human content moderation is also problematic. A plethora of research exists on the poor labour conditions and negative psychological effects endured by content moderators (e.g. Roberts 2019). The work of content moderation for social media platforms is often outsourced to companies based in developing countries that offer low wages and poor worker protections.

2 Some platforms have had success in removing persistent, problematic conspiracy groups through a combination of vigilance on the part of the platform and crowd-sourced moderation by the users. Reddit, for example, managed to remove QAnon content before the other platforms, and long before the storming of the Capitol (see Tiffany 2020b).

3 As part of the "Infodemic" and previous projects, we have contributed to some of these guides. See, for example, "Talking about Covid Conspiracy" (https://senseaboutscience.org/activities/talking-about-conspiracies/) and "Guide to Conspiracy Theories" (https://conspiracytheories.eu/_wpx/wp-content/uploads/2020/03/COMPACT_Guide-2.pdf).

4 Although medical populism might have thrived in some contexts during the pandemic, there is evidence that (a) trust in scientists in some countries has increased (Mede and Schäfer 2021); and (b) the wave of political populism that has hit the US, Europe and elsewhere in the 2010s is beginning to recede (Centre for the Future of Democracy 2022).

APPENDIX

The research for this book was based on a number of intersecting research projects carried out by the "Infodemic: Combatting Covid-19 Conspiracy Theories" team; researchers at the various Digital Methods Initiative (DMI) data sprints at the University of Amsterdam; and projects conducted by the Department of Digital Humanities at King's College London (KCL). We also drew on datasets and projects conducted by other teams working on related queries. In this appendix, we describe the datasets assembled by the "Infodemic," DMI and KCL researchers.

We began gathering data from social media platforms related to conspiracy theories about the emerging Covid-19 pandemic in January 2020. As we explain in the introduction, our main aim was to assemble a manageable and broadly representative dataset of the most engaged-with content on each of the major platforms, divided up by quarter during the course of 2020 (with the scraping continuing, in some cases, into 2021). Much of the content was subsequently deplatformed, so the datasets became a useful repository of primary source evidence that enabled us to build up a picture of how conspiracy talk developed during the pandemic. The scraping was carried out using seed lists of hashtags, keywords and channels based on our existing subject knowledge of the field, along with inductive, snowballing techniques of identifying additional terms and channels to include. Our research assistants then cleaned the data, primarily identifying false positives, leaving us with a manageable set of individual posts, pages and videos from each platform. The research assistants then did a preliminary trawl through the resulting datasets for each platform, labelling each item according to the categories of Covid-19 conspiracism we developed in chapter 5. This was an iterative, inductive process, involving fine-tuning of the categories in discussion with the rest of the team. In most cases, we scraped considerably more data but we narrowed this down to the top 20 items for each platform for each quarter. Although, for this book, the research principally involved contextualised close reading of the resulting sample, other teams affiliated to the project used the datasets to conduct quantitative digital methods queries (see e.g. Tuters and Willaert 2022).

When we include primary source examples from websites and social media in the text, we have removed, anonymised or abbreviated the usernames (unless they are public figures). We give links to the original URL or an archived version (where available). In the case of Instagram, we give the link to our dataset (https://favstats.github.io/corona_conspiracyland). The Twitter examples are from our dataset, which researchers can request permission to access (https://4cat .oilab.nl). For quotations from social media sources, we give them verbatim, with no "[sic]."

University of Amsterdam Digital Methods Initiative Projects

As part of the "Infodemic" project, we collaborated on a number of projects conducted as part of the DMI data sprints in 2020 and 2021: "COVID-19 Conspiracy Tribes Across Instagram, TikTok, Telegram and YouTube" (https://wiki.digitalmethods.net/Dmi/SummerSchool2020Conspiracytribes); "An Exploration of Named Entities and Epistemic Keywords in Conspiratorial Instagram Posts" (https://wiki.digitalmethods.net/Dmi/WinterSchool2021Inf odemicInstagram); "How Interpretative Frames are Co-articulated on Social Media? An Instagram versus Parler Case Study" (https://wiki.digitalmethods .net/Dmi/WinterSchool2021Infodemic5G); "Authority and Misinformation in the Process of COVID-19 Sensemaking" (https://wiki.digitalmethods.net/Dmi /AuthorityandModeration); and "Demoting, Deplatforming and Replatforming COVID-19 misinformation" (https://wiki.digitalmethods.net/Dmi/SummerS chool2020ModeratingCovidMisinfo);

Facebook

Using the Crowdtangle tool, we assembled a dataset based on 176 groups and 281 pages. The list of conspiracy-related Facebook groups and pages was "snowball" generated by entering a set of basic Covid conspiracy search phrases into Crowdtangle and then collecting every page that was returned with more than 100 followers ("coronavirus 5g," "covid 5g," "new world order," "reopen," "against excessive quarantine," "liberty militia," "bill gates," "agenda 21," "qanon," and "wwg1wga"). Beginning in April 2020, we captured all the text and metadata for all the resulting groups and pages, then filtered them quarter by quarter for 2020.

Instagram

Instagram data was collected at four points during 2020 (May, June, August and October) by our research associate, Fabio Votta of the University of Amsterdam, using the Instaloader tool from the Python library. The queries were based on a seed list of 82 hashtags related to Covid-19 conspiracy theories identified by the team early in the pandemic and from the accounts of 66 known conspiracy influencers that frequently post using similar hashtags. We used this set of keywords and hashtags as the basis for querying other platforms (for a list of the search terms, see Tuters and Willaert 2022). The resulting dataset of 478,154 posts and accompanying comments was designed not to be comprehensive but to capture a broadly representative sample. (It appears that Instagram changed its API in October 2020, making it more difficult to collect data.)

Using the same seed terms and accounts, Votta assembled a set of 14,259 Covid-19 conspiracy images posted on Instagram between January and September 2020 into a custom-built visualiser (available at https://favstats.github.io/corona _conspiracyland/#). This set of images received a total of 4.2 million likes and 260,000 comments on Instagram in that period.

TikTok

Using the same criteria, we assembled a dataset of 38,000 TikToks using the "tiktokr" R library tool. The data was collected at the end of June 2020.

Twitter

Using the same set of Covid-19 conspiracy hashtags and keywords, we used the programming language R to query the Academic Twitter API and retrieved all unique tweets (no retweets) with the hashtags and keywords. The resulting dataset contains 15,175,179 Tweets.

YouTube

The team used the YouTube video downloader youtube-dl. The script returned the first 60 results for 98 keywords and phrases every day between April and October 2020 (the repeated querying allowed the team to identify which videos had been deplatformed). This resulted in a dataset of 108,537 videos and 39,531,963 comments. The list of Covid-19 conspiracy search terms (such as "wwg1wga," "id2020" and "covid depopulation") was based in part on the team's existing knowledge of conspiracy buzzwords from previous research on conspiracist sites such as the /pol/ board on 4chan and 8kun (e.g. de Zeeuw et al. 2020) and on keywords that emerged from the team's monitoring of known conspiracist channels and media reports on Covid-19 conspiracy theories during the first quarter of 2020. The choice of search terms was designed to capture the different emerging narratives. (For the complete list of keywords and categories, see de Keulenaar, Burton, and Kisjes 2021.)

The team then filtered the results to produce subsets of: (1) the top 20 most viewed results for the whole time span (the 20 videos that had the most aggregate views; these included all videos, except music and other entertainment contents); (2) the top 20 most viewed conspiracy (i.e., "borderline") and deleted results; (3) the top 20 most viewed results per month; (4) top 20 most viewed conspiracy and deleted results per month; (5) the comments accompanying each of the videos from these four categories; (6) the deleted videos that made it to the top 20 lists (as the most likely to be "borderline" content). Our research assistants then manually combed through the results to remove false positives (i.e. videos that were not obviously about Covid-19 conspiracy theories) to leave us with a comparatively manageable dataset for close reading.

Websites

The team at KCL also compiled several sets of websites. One was a list of conspiracy websites from a dataset assembled from 4chan/pol/ Corona Virus General discussion. A second list consisted of URLs from 4chan/pol/ discussions of 5G, Bill Gates, Illuminati, New World Order and related conspiracy theories. A third list focused on anti-vaxx websites.

BIBLIOGRAPHY

Ahmed, Wasim, Francesc López Seguí, Josep Vidal-Alaball, and Matthew S. Katz. 2020. "COVID-19 and the 'Film Your Hospital' Conspiracy Theory: Social Network Analysis of Twitter Data." *Journal of Medical Internet Research* 22 (10, October): e22374. https://doi.org/10.2196/22374.

Agre, Philip E. 1993. "Surveillance and Capture: Two Models of Privacy." *The Information Society* 10 (2, April): 101–127. https://doi.org/10.1080/01972243.1994.9960162.

Alaphilippe, Alexandre. 2021. "Disinformation Is Evolving to Move under the Radar." Brookings Institute, February 4, 2021. www.brookings.edu/techstream/ disinformation-is-evolving-to-move-under-the-radar/.

Alexander, Harriet. 2011. "David Icke: Would You Believe It?" *Telegraph*, December 4, 2011. www.telegraph.co.uk/news/religion/8933565/David-Icke-would-you-believe -it.html.

al-Gharbi, Musa. 2022. "No, America Is Not on the Brink of a Civil War." *Guardian*, January 27, 2022, sec. Opinion. https://www.theguardian.com/commentisfree/2022 /jan/27/no-america-is-not-on-the-cusp-of-a-civil-war.

Ali, Shiza, Mohammad Hammas Saeed, Esraa Aldreabi, Jeremy Blackburn, Emiliano De Cristofaro, Savvas Zannettou, and Gianluca Stringhini. 2021. "Understanding the Effect of Deplatforming on Social Networks." In 13th ACM Web Science Conference (WebSci '21), Association for Computing Machinery, New York, 187–195. https:// doi.org/10.1145/3447535.3462637.

Allington, Daniel, and Siobhan McAndrew. 2021. "Coronavirus Conspiracies and Views of Vaccination." University of Bristol/King's College London. https:// www.kcl.ac.uk/policy-institute/assets/coronavirus-conspiracies-and-views-of -vaccination.pdf.

Allsop, Jon. 2021. "The Lab-Leak Mess." *Columbia Journalism Review.* June 2, 2021. https://www.cjr.org/the_media_today/lab_leak_theory_credibility.php.

Altay, Sacha, Emma de Araujo, and Hugo Mercier. 2021. ""If This Account Is True, It Is Most Enormously Wonderful": Interestingness-If-True and the Sharing of True and False News." *Digital Journalism* 0 (0): 1–22. https://doi.org/10.1080/21670811.2021 .1941163.

Amarasingam, Amarnath, and Marc-André Argentino. 2020. "*The QAnon Conspiracy Theory: A Security Threat in the Making?*" *CTC Sentinel* 13 (7, July): 37–44. https://ctc .usma.edu/the-qanon-conspiracy-theory-a-security-threat-in-the-making/.

Andersen, Kristian G., Andrew Rambaut, W. Ian Lipkin, Edward C. Holmes, and Robert F. Garry. 2020. "The Proximal Origin of SARS-CoV-2." *Nature Medicine* 26 (4, March): 450–452. https://doi.org/10.1038/s41591-020-0820-9.

Andrejevic, Mark. 2013. *Infoglut: How Too Much Information Is Changing the Way We Think and Know.* Abingdon: Routledge. https://doi.org/10.4324/9780203075319.

Andrews, Travis. 2020. "'Plandemic' Conspiracy Video Removed by Facebook, YouTube and Vimeo." May 7, 2020. https://www.washingtonpost.com/technology/2020/05 /07/plandemic-youtube-facebook-vimeo-remove/.

Angwin, Julia, Madelleine Varner, and Ariana Tobin. 2017. "Facebook Enabled Advertisers to Reach 'Jew Haters'." *Propublica*, September 14, 2017. https://www .propublica.org/article/facebook-enabled-advertisers-to-reach-jew-haters.

Anheier, Helmut, and Andrea Roemmele. 2020. "The Q-ing of the West." *Project Syndicate*, September 11, 2020. https://www.project-syndicate.org/onpoint/ conspiracy-theories-qanon-from-america-to-germany-by-helmut-k-anheier-and -andrea-roemmele-2020-09.

Applebaum, Anne. 2020. "Trump is Putting on a Show in Portland." *Atlantic*, July 23, 2020. https://www.theatlantic.com/ideas/archive/2020/07/trump-putting-show -portland/614521/.

Argentino, Marc-André. 2020a. "1/ Stories Have Been Circulating Today That 'Beijing is Pushing a Conspiracy Theory That the US Army Brought the Coronavirus to China'.... ." *Twitter thread (@_MAArgentino)*, March 13, 2020. https://twitter.com/ _MAArgentino/status/1238537205225795591.

———. 2020b. "QAnon Conspiracy Theories about the Coronavirus Pandemic Are a Public Health Threat." *The Conversation*, 8 April, 2020. https://theconversation.com /qanon-conspiracy-theories-about-the-coronavirus-pandemic-are-a-public-health -threat-135515.

———. 2020c. "Quick Recap of Qanons Relationship with the Coronavirus. Two Weeks Ago the Narrative Was That the Virus Was a Deep State/Globalist Cabal Plot to Take Down POTUS." *Twitter Thread (_MAArgentino)*, March 13, 2020. https:// twitter.com/_MAArgentino/status/1238345556038168576.

———. 2021a. "1/ For Those Who Missed My @GNET_research Panel I'm Going to Share My Slides Here with Some of My Comments on How Violent Extremist Organizations Have Leveraged the COVID-19...." *Twitter Thread (@_MAArgentino)*, 26 May 2021. https://twitter.com/_MAArgentino/status/1397578321182044166.

———. 2021b. "Pastel QAnon." *GNET* (blog), March 17, 2021. https://gnet-research .org/2021/03/17/pastel-qanon/.

Associated Press. 2020. "Arizona Man Dies after Attempting to Take Trump Coronavirus 'Cure.'" *Guardian*, March 24, 2020. http://www.theguardian.com/world/2020/mar /24/coronavirus-cure-kills-man-after-trump-touts-chloroquine-phosphate.

Aupers, Stef. 2014. "Conspiracy Theories: Between Secular Scepticism and Religious Salvation." *Conspiracy and Democracy (YouTube channel).* Filmed January 21, 2014 at Cambridge University, Cambridge, UK. Published September 1, 2014. www.youtube .com/watch?v=VtrjL_SzkfU.

Avaaz. 2020a. "Facebook's Algorithm: A Major Threat to Public Health." https://secure .avaaz.org/campaign/en/facebook_threat_health/.

———. 2020b. "How Facebook Can Flatten the Curve of the Coronavirus Infodemic." https://secure.avaaz.org/campaign/en/facebook_coronavirus_misinformation/.

Ball, Philip, and Amy Maxmen. 2020. "The Epic Battle against Coronavirus Misinformation and Conspiracy Theories." *Nature* (news feature), May 27, 2020. https://www.nature.com/articles/d41586-020-01452-z.

Bandeira, Luiza, Nika Aleksejeva, Tessa Knight, and Jean Le Roux. 2021. "Weaponized: How Rumors about COVID-19's Origins Led to a Narrative Arms Race." *The Atlantic Council's Digital Forensic Research Lab*, February 14, 2021. https://www.atlanticcouncil.org/in-depth-research-reports/report/weaponized-covid-19/.

Barkun, Michael. 2013. *A Culture of Conspiracy: Apocalyptic Visions in Contemporary America*, 2nd ed. Comparative Studies in Religion and Society. Berkeley: University of California Press. https://www.ucpress.edu/book/9780520276826/a-culture-of-conspiracy.

Barnes, Julian. 2021. "Origin of Virus May Remain Murky, U.S. Intelligence Agencies Say." *The New York Times*, October 29, 2021, sec. U.S. https://www.nytimes.com/2021/10/29/us/politics/coronavirus-origin-intelligence-report.html.

Barthes, Roland. 1975. *S/Z*. Translated by Richard Miller. London: Macmillan.

Bartlett, Jamie, and Carl Miller. 2010. "The Power of Unreason: Conspiracy Theories, Extremism and Counter-terrorism." Demos, August 2010. https://www.demos.co.uk/files/Conspiracy_theories_paper.pdf?1282913891.

Bary, Emily. 2020. "Zoom, Microsoft Teams Usage Are Rocketing during Coronavirus Pandemic, New Data Shows." *MarketWatch*, April 1, 2020. https://www.marketwatch.com/story/zoom-microsoft-cloud-usage-are-rocketing-during-coronavirus-pandemic-new-data-show-2020-03-30.

Bates, Lydia, and Tracey Gale. "Flyering Remains a Recruitment Tool for Hate Groups." *Southern Poverty Law Center*, February 1, 2021. https://www.splcenter.org/news/2021/02/01/flyering-remains-recruitment-tool-hate-groups.

Baum, Matthew A. et al. 2020. "*The State of the Nation: A 50-State Covid19 Survey Report #14: Misinformation and Vaccine Acceptance*." September. http://www.kateto.net/covid19/COVID19%20CONSORTIUM%20REPORT%2014%20MISINFO%20SEP%202020.pdf.

BBC Monitoring. 2021. "What Is the Great Reset - and How Did It Get Hijacked by Conspiracy Theories?" *BBC News*, June 24, 2021. https://www.bbc.co.uk/news/blogs-trending-57532368.

BBC News. 2020a. "Coronavirus: BCG Rumours and Other Stories Fact-Checked." *BBC News*, April 18, 2020. https://www.bbc.com/news/52310194.

———. 2020b. "Trump Deliberately Played Down Virus, Woodward Book Says." *BBC News*, September 10, 2020. https://www.bbc.com/news/world-us-canada-54094559.

———. 2021. "Covid Vaccine: Speech Comparing NHS Medics to Nazis Condemned." *BBC News*, July 25, 2021. https://www.bbc.com/news/uk-57962675.

Beauchamp, Zack. 2018. "Milo Yiannopoulos's Collapse Shows That No-Platforming Can Work." *Vox*, December 5, 2018. https://www.vox.com/policy-and-politics/2018/12/5/18125507/milo-yiannopoulos-debt-no-platform.

———. 2020. "Trump Says He's Taking Hydroxychoroquine to Ward Off Coronavirus." *Vox*, May 18, 2020. https://www.vox.com/policy-and-politics/2020/5/18/21262889/trump-taking-hydroxychloroquine-coronavirus.

Beaumont, Peter. 2021. "Leading Biologist Dampens His 'Smoking Gun' Covid Lab Leak Theory." *Guardian*, June 9, 2021. http://www.theguardian.com/world/2021/jun/09/leading-biologist-dampens-his-smoking-gun-covid-lab-leak-theory.

Beaumont, Peter, Julian Borger, and Daniel Boffey. 2020. "Malicious Forces Creating "perfect Storm" of Coronavirus Disinformation." *Guardian*, April 24, 2020, sec.

World news. https://www.theguardian.com/world/2020/apr/24/coronavirus-sparks
-perfect-storm-of-state-led-disinformation.

Beckman, Frida. 2022. *The Paranoid Chronotype*. Redwood City: Stanford University Press.

Bellemare, Andrea, Katie Nicholson, and Jason Ho Ho. 2020. "How a Debunked COVID-19 Video Kept Spreading after Facebook and YouTube Took It down | CBC News." *CBC*. May 21, 2020. https://www.cbc.ca/news/science/alt-tech-platforms
-resurface-plandemic-1.5577013.

Benkler, Yochai, Robert Faris, and Hal Roberts. 2018. *Network Propaganda: Manipulation, Disinformation, and Radicalization in American Politics*. Oxford: Oxford University Press.

Benkler, Yochai, Casey Tilton, Bruce Etling, Hal Roberts, Justin Clark, Robert Faris, Jonas Kaiser, and Carolyn Schmitt. 2020. "Mail-In Voter Fraud: Anatomy of a Disinformation Campaign." *SSRN Scholarly Paper ID 3703701*. Rochester, NY: Social Science Research Network. https://doi.org/10.2139/ssrn.3703701.

Bergmann, Eirikur. 2018. *Conspiracy and Populism: The Politics of Misinformation*. Cham, Switzerland: Springer.

———. 2021. "The Eurabia Conspiracy Theory." In *Europe: Continent of Conspiracies: Conspiracy Theories in and about Europe*, edited by Andreas Önnerfors and André Krouwel, 36–53. London: Routledge.

Bergmann, Eiríkur, and Michael Butter. 2020. "Conspiracy Theory and Populism." *The Routledge Handbook of Conspiracy Theory*, edited by Eiríkur Bergmann and Michael Butter, 330–343. London: Routledge.

Berinsky, Adam J. 2017. "Rumors and Health Care Reform: Experiments in Political Misinformation." *British Journal of Political Science* 47 (2): 241–62.

———. 2018. "Telling the Truth about Believing the Lies? Evidence for the Limited Prevalence of Expressive Survey Responding." *The Journal of Politics* 80 (1): 211–24. https://doi.org/10.1086/694258.

Bertin, Paul, Nero Kenzo, and Sylvain Delouvée. 2020. "Conspiracy Beliefs, Rejection of Vaccination, and Support for (Hydroxy)Chloroquine: A Conceptual Replication-Extension in the COVID-19 Pandemic Context." *Frontiers in Psychology* 11 (September): 1–9. https://doi.org/10.3389/fpsyg.2020.565128.

Birchall, Clare. 2006. *Knowledge Goes Pop: From Conspiracy Theory to Gossip*. Oxford: Berg.

Blackburn, J., R.W. Gehl, & U. Etudo. 2021. "Does 'Deplatforming' Work to Curb Hate Speech and Calls for Violence? 3 Experts in Online Communications Weigh In." *Conversation*, January 5, 2021. https://theconversation.com/does-deplatforming-work
-to-curb-hate-speech-and-calls-for-violence-3-experts-in-online-communications
-weigh-in-153177.

Blom, Tashina. 2020. "'My Body My Choice': Why the Anti-Lockdown Protesters Are Appropriating Memory." *Remembering Activism: The Cultural Memory of Protest in Europe* (blog), May 20, 2020. https://rememberingactivism.eu/2020/05/20/my
-body-my-choice-why-the-anti-lockdown-protesters-are-appropriating-memory/.

Bloom, Mia, and Sophia Moskalenko. 2021. *Pastels and Pedophiles: Inside the Mind of QAnon*. Stanford: Stanford University Press.

Bodner, John, Wendy Welch, and Ian Brodie. 2020. *COVID-19 Conspiracy Theories: QAnon, 5G, the New World Order and Other Viral Ideas*. Jefferson: McFarland.

Boltanski, Luc. 2014. *Mysteries and Conspiracies: Detective Stories, Spy Novels and the Making of Modern Societies*. Cambridge: Polity Press.

Bond, Shannon. 2020. "'The Perfect Storm': How Vaccine Misinformation Spread to the Mainstream." *NPR*, December 10, 2020. https://www.npr.org/2020/12/10

/944408988/the-perfect-storm-how-coronavirus-spread-vaccine-misinformation
-to-the-mainstrea?t=1610982846296.

———. 2021. "Just 12 People Are behind Most Vaccine Hoaxes on Social Media, Research Shows." *NPR*, May 14, 2021.

Borenstein, Eliot. 2019. *Plots against Russia: Conspiracy and Fantasy after Socialism*. Ithaca: Cornell University Press.

Bory, Paolo, Marta Tomasi, Stefano Crabu, Barbara Morsello, and Simone Tosoni. 2021. "Rethinking the Nexus between Science, Politics and Society in the Age of the SARS-CoV-2 Pandemic." *Tecnoscienza* 12 (2): 159–80.

Boston Women's Collective. 1973. *Our Bodies Ourselves*. New York: Simon, Schuster.

Boswell, Josh. 2021. "New Study Claims Chinese Scientists Created COVID 19 in a Lab." *Mail Online*, May 28, 2021. https://www.dailymail.co.uk/news/article-9629563/Chinese-scientists-created-COVID-19-lab-tried-cover-tracks-new-study-claims.html.

Bounegru, Liliana. *Digital Methods for News and Journalism Research*. London: Polity, forthcoming.

boyd, danah. 2018. "You Think You Want Media Literacy…Do You?" *Data and Society*, March 9, 2018. https://points.datasociety.net/you-think-you-want-media-literacy-do-you-7cad6af18ec2.

boyd, danah, and Michael Golebiewski. 2019. "Data Voids." *Data & Society*. https://datasociety.net/library/data-voids/.

Bracewell, Lorna. 2021. "Gender, Populism, and the QAnon Conspiracy Movement." *Frontiers in Sociology*, January 21, 2021. https://www.frontiersin.org/articles/10.3389/fsoc.2020.615727/full

Bragman, Walker, and Alex Kotch. 2021. "How The Koch Network Hijacked the War On COVID." *The Daily Poster*, December 22, 2021. https://www.dailyposter.com/how-the-koch-network-hijacked-the-war-on-covid/.

Brandes, Stuart. 1976. *American Welfare Capitalism, 1880–1940*. Chicago: University of Chicago Press.

Bratich, Jack Z. 2008. *Conspiracy Panics: Political Rationality and Popular Culture*. Albany: SUNY Press.

———. 2021. "Men, War, Capitalism and Conspiracy - with Jack Bratich." *Rival Radio Podcast*, August 23, 2021.

Breathnach, Cillian. 2020. "Stephen Carter Apologises for the 'Insensitive' Way He Stated His Flat Earth, Anti-Vaccination Views." *Guitar*, November 16, 2020. https://guitar.com/news/music-news/deftones-stephen-carpenter-flat-earth-response/

Brennan, J. Scott, Felix Simon, Phillip N. Howard, and Rasmus Kleis Nielsen. 2020. "Types, Sources and Claims of Covid-19 Misinformation." Reuters Institute for the Study of Journalism, University of Oxford, April 7, 2020. https://reutersinstitute.politics.ox.ac.uk/types-sources-and-claims-covid-19-misinformation.

Bridle, James. 2017. "Something Is Wrong on the Internet." *Medium*, November 6, 2017. medium.com/@jamesbridle/something-is-wrong-on-the-internet-c39c471271d2.

Broderick, Ryan. 2020a. "Bill Gates Conspiracy Theories Have Circulated for Years. It Took the Coronavirus Pandemic to Turn Him into a Fake Villain." *BuzzFeed News*, May 22, 2020. https://www.buzzfeednews.com/article/ryanhatesthis/coronavirus-bill-gates-conspiracy-theories.

———. 2020b. "5G Conspiracy Theorists Use Coronavirus Fears to Make Money." *BuzzFeed News*, April 7, 2020. https://www.buzzfeednews.com/article/ryanhatesthis/coronavirus-5g-conspiracy-profit.

Broniatowski, David A., Daniel Kerchner, Fouzia Farooq, Xiaolei Huang, Amelia M. Jamison, Mark Dredze, and Sandra Crouse Quinn. 2021. "Debunking the Misinfodemic: Coronavirus Social Media Contains More, Not Less, Credible Content." *ArXiv:2007.09682 [Physics]*, ver. 2. 6 January 2021. https://doi.org/10.48550/arXiv.2007.09682.

Broniatowski, David A., Jiayan Gu, Amelia M. Jamison, and Lorien C. Abroms. 2022a. "Evaluating the Efficacy of Facebook's Vaccine Misinformation Content Removal Policies." *ArXiv:2202.02172 [Cs, Eess]*, 4 February 2022. https://doi.org/10.48550/arXiv.2202.02172.

Broniatowski, David A., Daniel Kerchner, Fouzia Farooq, Xiaolei Huang, Amelia M. Jamison, Mark Dredze, Sandra Crouse Quinn, and John W. Ayers. 2022b. "Twitter and Facebook Posts about COVID-19 Are Less Likely to Spread Misinformation Compared to Other Health Topics." *PloS One* 17, 1 (January): e0261768. https://doi.org/10.1371/journal.pone.0261768.

Brotherton, Robert, Christopher C. French, and Alan D. Pickering. 2013. "Measuring Belief in Conspiracy Theories: The Generic Conspiracist Beliefs Scale." *Frontiers in Psychology* 4 (279): 1–15. https://doi.org/10.3389/fpsyg.2013.00279.

Brown, Wendy. 2019. *In the Ruins of Neoliberalism: The Rise of Antidemocratic Politics in the West*. New York: Columbia University Press.

Bruns, Axel, Stephen Harrington, and Edward Hurcombe. 2020. ""Corona? 5G? Or Both?": The Dynamics of COVID-19/5G Conspiracy Theories on Facebook." *Media International Australia* 177 (1, November): 12–29. https://doi.org/10.1177/1329878X20946113.

Burgess, Adam. 2003. *Cellular Phones, Public Fears, and a Culture of Precaution*. Cambridge: Cambridge University Press.

Burgess, Jean, and Nancy Baym. 2020. *Twitter: A Biography*. New York: New York University Press.

Butler, Kiera. 2020. "The Terrifying Story of How QAnon Infiltrated Mom's Groups." *Mother Jones*, September 23, 2020. https://www.motherjones.com/politics/2020/09/the-terrifying-story-of-how-qanon-infiltrated-moms-groups/.

Butter, Michael. 2014. *Plots, Designs, and Schemes: American Conspiracy Theories from the Puritans to the Present*. Berlin: Walter de Gruyter.

———. 2016. "The Continuing Attraction of Conspiracy Theory: From Dan Brown to Donald Trump." *CRASSH (event)*, March 3, 2016. https://www.crassh.cam.ac.uk/events/26672/.

———. 2020. *The Nature of Conspiracy Theories*. London: Polity.

Butter, Michael, and Peter Knight. 2016. "Bridging the Great Divide: Conspiracy Theory Research for the 21st Century." *Diogenes*, October. https://doi.org/10.1177/0392192116669289.

Butter, Michael, and Peter Knight. 2018. "The History of Conspiracy Theory Research: A Review and Commentary." In *Conspiracy Theories and the People Who Believe Them*, edited by Joseph E. Uscinski, 33–46. New York: Oxford University Press.

Calame, Byron. 2005. "The Miller Mess: Lingering Issues among the Answers." *New York Times*, October 23, 2005. https://www.nytimes.com/2005/10/23/opinion/the-miller-mess-lingering-issues-among-the-answers.html.

Calisher, Charles, Dennis Carroll, Rita Colwell, Ronald B. Corley, Peter Daszak, Christian Drosten, Luis Enjuanes, et al. 2020. "Statement in Support of the Scientists, Public Health Professionals, and Medical Professionals of China Combatting COVID-19." *Lancet* 395 (10226, March): e42–43. https://doi.org/10.1016/S0140-6736(20)30418-9.

Callison, William, and Quinn Slobodian. 2021. "Coronapolitics from the Reichstag to the Capitol." *Boston Review*, January 5, 2021. https://bostonreview.net/politics/william-callison-quinn-slobodian-coronapolitics-reichstag-capitol.

Campion-Vincent, Véronique. 2015. "Remarks on Conspiracy Entrepreneurs." *Diogenes* 249–250 (1, January): 99–106. https://doi.org/10.3917/dio.249.0099.

Carroll, Rory. 2020. "Madonna Leads Celebrity Vogue for Covid-19 Conspiracy Theories." *Guardian*, July 31, 2020. https://www.theguardian.com/music/2020/jul/31/madonna-takes-on-new-role-as-covid-19-conspiracy-theorist.

Cassese, Erin C., Christina E. Farhart, and Joanne M. Miller. 2020. "Gender Differences in COVID-19 Conspiracy Theory Beliefs." *Politics & Gender* 16 (4): 1009–1018. https://doi.org/10.1017/S1743923X20000409.

Cassidy, John. 2020. "The Great Coronavirus Divide: Wall Street Profits Surge as Poverty Rises." *New Yorker*, October 16, 2020. https://www.newyorker.com/news/our-columnists/the-great-coronavirus-divide-wall-street-profits-surge-as-poverty-rises.

Cendrovicz, Leo. 2022. "QAnon in Europe – How the Covid Pandemic Helped Spread the Cult Conspiracy Movement." *Independent*, January 15, 2022. https://inews.co.uk/news/world/qanon-europe-how-covid-pandemic-helped-spread-cult-conspiracy-movement-1401690.

CCDH (Center for Countering Digital Hate). 2020a. "DeplatformIcke: How Big Tech Powers and Profits from David Icke's Lies and Hate, and Why it Must Stop." Center for Countering Digital Hate. https://252f2edd-1c8b-49f5-9bb2-cb57bb47e4ba.filesusr.com/ugd/f4d9b9_db8ff469f6914534ac02309bb488f948.pdf.

———. 2020b. "Malgorithm: How Instagram's Algorithm Publishes Misinformation and Hate to Millions in a Pandemic." Center for Countering Digital Hate. https://252f2edd-1c8b-49f5-9bb2-cb57bb47e4ba.filesusr.com/ugd/f4d9b9_89ed644926aa4477a442b55afbeac00e.pdf.

———. 2020c. "The Anti-Vaxx Playbook." Center for Countering Digital Hate. https://www.counterhate.com/playbook.

———. 2021a. "Pandemic Profiteers: The Business of Anti-Vaxx." Center for Countering Digital Hate. 2021. https://www.counterhate.com/pandemicprofiteers.

———. 2021b. "The Disinformation Dozen." Center for Countering Digital Hate. https://252f2edd-1c8b-49f5-9bb2-cb57bb47e4ba.filesusr.com/ugd/f4d9b9_b7cedc0553604720b7137f8663366ee5.pdf.

Centre for Data Ethics and Innovation. 2021. "The Role of AI in Addressing Misinformation on Social Media Platforms." https://assets.publishing.service.gov.uk/government/uploads/system/uploads/attachment_data/file/1008700/Misinformation_forum_write_up__August_2021__-_web_accessible.pdf

Centre for the Future of Democracy. 2022. "The Great Reset: Public Opinion, Populism, and the Pandemic." Bennett Institute for Public Policy, University of Cambridge, January 14, 2022. https://www.bennettinstitute.cam.ac.uk/publications/great-reset/.

Chadwick, Andrew, Johannes Kaiser, Cristian Vaccari, Daniel Freeman, Sinéad Lambe, Bao S. Loe, Samantha Vanderslott, et al. 2021. "Online Social Endorsement and Covid-19 Vaccine Hesitancy in the United Kingdom." *Social Media + Society* 7 (2, April–June): 1–17. https://doi.org/10.1177/20563051211008817.

Chait, Jonathan. 2021. "How the Liberal Media Dismissed the Lab-Leak Theory and Smeared Its Supporters." *New York Magazine*, May 24, 2021. https://nymag.com/intelligencer/2021/05/lab-leak-liberal-media-theory-china-wuhan-lab-cotton-trump.html.

Cinelli, Matteo, Walter Quattrociocchi, Alessandro Galeazzi, Carlo Michele Valensise, Emanuele Brugnoli, Ana Lucia Schmidt, Paola Zola, Fabiana Zollo, and Antonio Scala. 2020. "The COVID-19 Social Media Infodemic." *Scientific Reports* 10: 16598. https://doi.org/10.1038/s41598-020-73510-5.

Citton, Yves. 2017. *The Ecology of Attention*. Cambridge: Polity.

Clarke, Laurie. 2021. "Covid-19: Who Fact Checks Health and Science on Facebook?" *BMJ* 373 (1170, May). https://doi.org/10.1136/bmj.n1170.

Clifford, Scott, Yongkwang Kim, and Brian W. Sullivan. 2019. "An Improved Question Format for Measuring Conspiracy Beliefs." *Public Opinion Quarterly* 83 (4, Winter): 690–722. https://doi.org/10.1093/poq/nfz049.

Coan, Travis G., Constantine Boussalis, John Cook, and Mirjam O. Nanko. 2021. "Computer-Assisted Classification of Contrarian Claims about Climate Change." *Scientific Reports* 11 (22320, November). https://doi.org/10.1038/s41598-021-01714-4.

Coleman, Alistair, and Shayan Sardarizadeh. 2022. "Anti-Vax Protests: 'Sovereign Citizens' Fight UK Covid Vaccine Rollout." *BBC News*, January 18, 2022. https://www.bbc.com/news/59870550.

Collins, Ben. 2019. "On Amazon, a QAnon Conspiracy Book Climbs the Charts - with an Algorithmic Push." *NBC News*, March 5, 2019. www.nbcnews.com/tech/tech-news/amazon-qanon-conspiracy-book-climbs-charts-algorithmic-push-n979181.

Collins, Ben, and Brandy Zadrozny. 2021. "Anti-Vaccine Groups Changing into 'Dance Parties' on Facebook to Avoid Detection." *NBC News*, July 22, 2021. https://www.nbcnews.com/tech/tech-news/anti-vaccine-groups-changing-dance-parties-facebook-avoid-detection-rcna1480.

Collins, Cory. 2021. "Reimagining Digital Literacy to Save Ourselves." *Learning for Justice 1 (Fall)*. https://www.learningforjustice.org/magazine/fall-2021/reimagining-digital-literacy-education-to-save-ourselves.

Collins-Dexter, Brandi. 2020. "Canaries in the Coal Mine: Covid-19 Misinformation and Black Communities." Harvard Kennedy School Shorenstein Center, Technology and Social Change Project. https://shorensteincenter.org/wp-content/uploads/2020/06/Canaries-in-the-Coal-Mine-Shorenstein-Center-June-2020.pdf.

Collinson, Patrick, and Jillian Ambrose. 2020. "Coronavirus Crisis Has Intensified UK's Wealth Divide, Data Reveals." *Guardian*, October 22, 2020. https://www.theguardian.com/world/2020/oct/22/coronavirus-crisis-uk-wealth-divide-bills-bame?CMP=Share_iOSApp_Other.

Colliver, Chloe. 2020. "Far-Right Exploitation of Covid-19." *Institute for Strategic Dialogue (ISD), Covid-19 Disinformation Briefing No.3*, May 12, 2020. https://www.isdglobal.org/isd-publications/covid-19-disinformation-briefing-no-3/.

Cook, John, Stephan Lewandowsky, and Ullrich K.H. Ecker. 2017. "Neutralizing Misinformation through Inoculation: Exposing Misleading Argumentation Techniques Reduces Their Influence." *PLoS ONE* 12 (5): e0175799. https://doi.org/10.1371/journal.pone.0175799.

Cooke, Jennifer. 2009. *Legacies of Plague in Literature, Theory and Film*. London: Palgrave Macmillan UK.

Cotton, Tom. 2020a. "1. Natural (Still the Most Likely, but Almost....". *Twitter Post (@SenTomCotton), Archive.Today*, February 16, 2020. http://archive.is/xm2zo.

———. 2020b. "We Still Don't Know Where Coronavirus Origina...." *Twitter Post (@SenTomCotton), Archive.Ph.*, January 30, 2020. http://archive.ph/sJdtm.

COVID-19 Income and Poverty Dashboard. n.d. http://povertymeasurement.org/covid-19-poverty-dashboard/.

Cox, Daniel A., and John Halpin. 2020. "Conspiracy Theories, Misinformation, COVID-19, and the 2020 Election." *Survey Center on American Life*. October 13, 2020. https://www.americansurveycenter.org/research/conspiracy-theories-misinformation-covid-19-and-the-2020-election/.

Crain, Matthew, and Anthony Nadler. 2019. "Political Manipulation and Internet Advertising Infrastructure." *Journal of Information Policy* 9 (December): 370–410. https://www.jstor.org/stable/10.5325/jinfopoli.9.2019.0370#metadata_info_tab_contents.

Crewe, Tom. 2016. "The Strange Death of Municipal England." *The London Review of Books* 38 (24, December). https://www.lrb.co.uk/the-paper/v38/n24/tom-crewe/the-strange-death-of-municipal-england.

Crocker, J., R. Luhtanen, S. Broadnax, and B.E. Blaine. 1999. "Belief in US Government Conspiracies against Blacks among Black and White College Students: Powerlessness or System Blame?" *Personality and Social Psychology Bulletin*, 25 (8, August): 941–953. https://doi.org/10.1177/01461672992511003.

Cuthbertson, Anthony. 2020. "Coronavirus Tracked: Hundreds of Deaths Linked to Conspiracy Theories and Other Misinformation, Study Finds." *MSN*, September 16, 2020. https://www.msn.com/en-gb/news/world/coronavirus-tracked-hundreds-of-deaths-linked-to-conspiracy-theories-and-other-misinformation-study-finds/ar-BB17WCdS.

Dacombe, Rod., Nicole Souter, and Lumi Westerlund. 2021. "Understanding Offline Covid-19 Conspiracy Theories: A Content Analysis of The Light 'Truthpaper'." *Harvard Kennedy School Misinformation Review*, Research note, September 17, 2021. https://doi.org/10.37016/mr-2020-80.

Dafaure, Maxime. 2020. *The "Great Meme War": The Alt-Right and Its Multifarious Enemies*. Angles: New Perspectives on the Anglophone World 10. https://journals.openedition.org/angles/369.

Darcy, Oliver. 2019. "How Twitter's Algorithm Is Amplifying Extreme Political Rhetoric." *CNN Business*, March 22, 2019. https://edition.cnn.com/2019/03/22/tech/twitter-algorithm-political-rhetoric/index.html.

Dastin, Jeffrey, Sheila Dang, and Anna Irrera. 2020. "Online Merchants Linked to QAnon Down, but Not Out, Following Platform Bans." *Reuters*, January 25, 2020. www.reuters.com/article/us-usa-trump-qanon-financing-idUSKBN29U193.

Davey, Melissa. 2020. "The Lancet Changes Editorial Policy after Hydroxychloroquine Covid Study Retraction." *Guardian*, September 22, 2020. http://www.theguardian.com/world/2020/sep/22/the-lancet-reforms-editorial-policy-after-hydroxychloroquine-covid-study-retraction.

———. 2021. "Huge Study Supporting Ivermectin as Covid Treatment Withdrawn over Ethical Concerns." *Guardian*, July 15, 2021. http://www.theguardian.com/science/2021/jul/16/huge-study-supporting-ivermectin-as-covid-treatment-withdrawn-over-ethical-concerns.

Davies, Will. 2019. *Nervous States: How Feeling Took Over the World*. London: Penguin.

Davis, David Brion, ed. 1971. *The Fear of Conspiracy: Images of Un-American Subversion from the Revolution to the Present*. Ithaca: Cornell University Press.

Davis, Erik. 2020. "Erik Davis on the Cosmic Right." *#ACFM Microdose (Podcast), Novara Media*, August 13, 2020. https://soundcloud.com/novaramedia/acfm-microdose-erik-davis-on-the-cosmic-right?utm_source=clipboard&utm_medium=text&utm_campaign=social_sharing.

Davis, Gregory. 2020. "Anti-5G Conspiracy Theories Are Dangerous - and Spreading Fast." *HOPE Not Hate Charitable Trust*, April 13, 2020. https://www.hopenothate.org.uk/2020/04/13/anti-5g-conspiracy-theories-are-dangerous-and-spreading-fast/.

de Keulenaar, Emillie, Antony Burton, and Ivan Kisjes. 2021. "Deplatforming, Demotion and Folk Theories of Persecution by Big Tech." *Evista Fronteiras – Estudos Midiáticos* 23 (2, May/August): 118–139. https://doi.org/10.4013/fem.2021.232.09.

de Zeeuw, Daniel, and Marc Tuters. 2020. "Teh [sic] Internet is Serious Business: On the Deep Vernacular Web and its Discontents." *Cultural Politics* 16 (2): 214–232.

Denvir, Daniel. 2020. "In the Ruins of Neoliberalism with Wendy Brown." *The Dig* (podcast), October 24, 2020. https://www.thedigradio.com/podcast/ruins-of -neoliberalism-with-wendy-brown/.

Deutch, Gabby. 2020. "How One Particular Coronavirus Myth Went Viral." *Wired*, March 19, 2020. https://www.wired.com/story/opinion-how-one-particular-coronavirus- myth-went-viral/.

DFRLab (Zarine Kharazian, and Tessa Knight). 2020. *"Why the Debunked COVID-19 Conspiracy Video 'Plandemic' Won't Go Away."* Research Report. Atlantic Council. https://medium.com/dfrlab/why-the-debunked-covid-19-conspiracy-video -plandemic-wont-go-away-c9dd36c2037c.

Dickson, E.J. 2020a. "QAnon YouTubers Are Telling People to Drink Bleach to Ward Off Coronavirus." *Rolling Stone* (blog), January 29, 2020. https://www.rollingstone .com/culture/culture-news/qanon-conspiracy-theorists-coronavirus-mms-bleach -youtube-twitter-944878/.

———. 2020b. "The Birth of QAmom." *Rolling Stone* (blog), September 2, 2020. https://www.rollingstone.com/culture/culture-features/qanon-mom-conspiracy -theory-parents-sex-trafficking-qamom-1048921/.

Disinfo.eu. 2020. "How Covid019 Conspiracists and Extremists Use Crowdfunding Platforms to Fund Their Activities." EU Disinfo Lab, Publications, October 19, 2020. https://www.disinfo.eu/publications/how-covid-19-conspiracists-and-extremists -use-crowdfunding-platforms-to-fund-their-activities/.

Doctorow, Cory. 2020. "Antitrust and Facebook's Paid Disinformation." *Pluralistic*, December 11, 2020. pluralistic.net/2020/12/11/number-eight/#curse-of-bigness.

Donovan, Joan, Brian Friedberg, Gabrielle Lim, Nicole Leaver, Jennifer Nilsen, and Emily Dreyfuss. 2021. "Mitigating Medical Misinformation: A Whole-of-Society Approach to Countering Spam, Scams, and Hoaxes." Technology and Social Change Research Project, March 24, 2021. https://doi.org/10.37016/TASC-2021-03.

Doughton, Sandi. 2020. "Covid-19 Meets Election 2020: The Perfect Storm for Misinformation." *Seattle Times*, July 5, 2020. https://www.seattletimes.com /seattle-news/health/covid-19-meets-election-2020-the-perfect-storm-for -misinformation/.

Douglas, Karen M., and Robbie M. Sutton. 2008. "The Hidden Impact of Conspiracy Theories: Perceived and Actual Influence of Theories Surrounding the Death of Princess Diana." *The Journal of Social Psychology* 148 (2): 210–22. https://doi.org/10 .3200/SOCP.148.2.210-222.

Douglas, Karen M., Joseph E. Uscinski, Robbie M. Sutton, Aleksandra Cichocka, Turkay Nefes, Chee Siang Ang, and Farzin Deravi. 2019. "Understanding Conspiracy Theories." *Political Psychology* 40 (S1): 3–35. https://doi.org/10.1111/ pops.12568.

"Dr. Deborah Birx on 'Face the Nation.'" 2021. *CBS News*, January 24, 2021. https:// www.cbsnews.com/news/transcript-deborah-birx-on-face-the-nation-january-24 -2021/.

Drochon, Hugo. 2021. "The Conspiracy Theory Bubble." *Persuasion*. October 20, 2021. Accessed March 16, 2022. https://www.persuasion.community/p/the-conspiracy- theory-bubble.

Durbach, Nadja. 2004. *Bodily Matters: The Anti-Vaccination Movement in England, 1853–1907*. Illustrated ed. Durham: Duke University Press.

Durkee, Alison. 2021. "Nearly 80% Of Vaccine-Hesitant Americans Won't Get The Shot, Poll Finds — But U.S. Can Still Hit Biden's 70% Goal." *Forbes*, June 7, 2021. https://www.forbes.com/sites/alisondurkee/2021/06/07/nearly-80-of-vaccine-hesitant-americans-wont-get-the-shot-poll-finds---but-us-can-still-hit-bidens-70-goal/.

Eatwell, Roger, and Matthew Goodwin. 2018. *National Populism: The Revolt against Liberal Democracy*. London: Penguin.

Eban, Katherine. 2021. "The Lab-Leak Theory: Inside the Fight to Uncover COVID-19's Origins." *Vanity Fair*, June 3, 2021. https://www.vanityfair.com/news/2021/06/the-lab-leak-theory-inside-the-fight-to-uncover-covid-19s-origins.

Ecker, Ullrich K.H., Stephan Lewandowsky, John Cook, Philipp Schmid, Lisa K. Fazio, Nadia Brashier, Panayiota Kendeou, Emily K. Vraga, and Michelle A. Amazeen. 2022. "The Psychological Drivers of Misinformation Belief and Its Resistance to Correction." *Nature Reviews Psychology* 1 (January): 13–29. https://doi.org/10.1038/s44159-021-00006-y.

Edelman. 2020. "*Twenty Years of Trust*." https://www.edelman.com/20yearsoftrust/.

Enders, Adam M., and Steven M. Smallpage. 2018. "Polls, Plots, and Party Politics: Conspiracy Theories in Contemporary America." In *Conspiracy Theories and the People Who Believe Them*, edited by Joseph E. Uscinski, 298–318. New York: Oxford University Press. https://doi.org/10.1093/oso/9780190844073.001.0001.

Enders, Adam M., Joseph E. Uscinski, Michelle I. Seelig, Casey A. Klofstad, Stefan Wuchty, John R. Funchion, Manohar N. Murthi, Kamal Premaratne, and Justin Stoler. 2021. "The Relationship Between Social Media Use and Beliefs in Conspiracy Theories and Misinformation." *Political Behavior*, July. https://doi.org/10.1007/s11109-021-09734-6.

Elliott, Philip. 2021. "How Distrust of Donald Trump Muddled the COVID-19 'Lab Leak' Debate." *Time*, May 26, 2021. https://time.com/6051414/donald-trump-wuhan-laboratory-leak/.

Engineering and Technology Staff. 2020. "Facebook Did Not Act on Own Evidence of Algorithm-Driven Extremism." *Engineering and Technology*, May 27, 2020. https://eandt.theiet.org/content/articles/2020/05/facebook-did-not-act-on-own-evidence-of-algorithm-driven-extremism/.

Essential. 2020. "Belief in Conspiracy Theories." Poll results. The Essential Report. https://essentialvision.com.au/belief-in-conspiracy-theories.

EUvsDisinfo. 2020a. "EEAS Special Report Update: Short Assessment of Narratives and Disinformation around the COVID-19 Pandemic." *EU vs DISINFORMATION*, April 1, 2020. https://euvsdisinfo.eu/eeas-special-report-update-short-assessment-of-narratives-and-disinformation-around-the-covid-19-pandemic/.

———. 2020b. "The Kremlin and Disinformation about Coronavirus." *EU vs DISINFORMATION*, March 16, 2020. https://euvsdisinfo.eu/the-kremlin-and-disinformation-about-coronavirus/.

Evanega, Sarah, Mark Lynas, Jordan Adams, and Karinne Smolenyak. 2020. "Coronavirus Misinformation: Quantifying Sources and Themes in the COVID-19 'Infodemic.'" https://int.nyt.com/data/documenttools/evanega-et-al-coronavirus-misinformation-submitted-07-23-20-1/080839ac0c22bca8/full.pdf.

Evans, Benedict. 2021. "Does Amazon Know What It Sells?" *Benedict's Newsletter*, May 5, 2021. https://www.ben-evans.com/benedictevans/2021/5/5/does-amazon-know-what-it-sells.

Evershed, Nick, Michael McGowan, and Andy Ball. 2021. "Anatomy of a Conspiracy Theory: How Misinformation Travels on Facebook." *Guardian*, March 10, 2021. http://www.theguardian.com/australia-news/ng-interactive/2021/mar/11/anatomy-of-a-conspiracy-theory-how-misinformation-travels-on-facebook.

Eysenbach, Gunther. 2009. "Infodemiology and Infoveillance: Framework for an Emerging Set of Public Health Informatics Methods to Analyze Search, Communication and Publication Behavior on the Internet." *Journal of Medical Internet Research* 11 (1): e1157. https://doi.org/10.2196/jmir.1157.

———. 2020. "How to Fight an Infodemic: The Four Pillars of Infodemic Management." *Journal of Medical Internet Research* 22 (6): e21820. https://doi.org/10.2196/21820.

Facebook. 2021. "Our Approach to Misinformation." Facebook Transparency Center, July 21, 2021. https://transparency.fb.com/en-gb/features/approach-to-misinformation/.

Faddoul, Marc, Guillaume Chaslot, and Hany Farid. 2020. "A Longitudinal Analysis of YouTube's Promotion of Conspiracy Videos." *arXiv:2003.03318 [cs.CY]*, March 6, 2020. https://arxiv.org/abs/2003.03318.

Fagan, Craig, and Clare Melford. 2019. "Cutting the Funding of Disinformation: The Ad-Tech Solution." *Global Index of Disinformation*. disinformationindex.org/wp-content/uploads/2019/05/GDI_Report_Screen_AW2.pdf.

Faraday Speaks (Caleb Cain). 2019. "My Descent into the Alt-Right Pipeline." *Faraday Speaks (YouTube channel)*, Published March 21, 2019. https://www.youtube.com/watch?v=sfLa64_zLrU.

Fazio, Lisa K., Nadia M. Brashier, B. Keith Payne, and Elizabeth J. Marsh. 2015. "Knowledge Does Not Protect against Illusory Truth." *Journal of Experimental Psychology: General* 144, (5): 993–1002. https://doi.org/10.1037/xge0000098.

Felski, Rita. 2015. *The Limits of Critique*. Chicago: University of Chicago Press.

Fenster, Mark. 2008. *Conspiracy Theories: Secrecy and Power in American Culture*. Minneapolis: University of Minnesota Press.

Ferrara, Emilio. 2020. "What Types of COVID-19 Conspiracies Are Populated by Twitter Bots?" *First Monday* 25 (6, May). https://doi.org/10.5210/fm.v25i6.10633.

Finlayson, Alan. 2020. "Six Key Takeaways! 1. People's Politics Derives from Their Interests 2 Interests are Multiple, Material & Ideal, & Often Contradictory 3. What We Think is in Our Interest Depends on the...." *Twitter Post (@ProfAFinlayson)*, November 4, 2020. https://twitter.com/ProfAFinlayson/status/1324011313182527491?s=20.

Finnegan, Conor, and Josh Margolin. 2020. "Pompeo Changes Tune on Chinese Lab's Role in Virus Outbreak, as Intel Officials Cast Doubt." *ABC News*, May 7, 2020. https://abcnews.go.com/Politics/pompeo-tune-chinese-labs-role-virus-outbreak-intel/story?id=70559769.

Fisher, Lucy and Chris Smyth. 2020. "GCHQ in Cyberwar on Anti-Vaccine Propaganda." *The Times*, November 9, 2020. https://www.thetimes.co.uk/article/gchq-in-cyberwar-on-anti-vaccine-propaganda-mcjgjhmb2.

Floridi, Luciano, and J.W. Sanders. 2004. "On the Morality of Artificial Agents." *Minds and Machines* 14 (3, August): 349–379. https://doi.org/10.1023/B:MIND.0000035461.63578.9d.

Foucault, Michel. 2008. *The Birth of Biopolitics: Lectures at the Collège de France, 1978–79*. Translated by Graham Burchell. New York: Palgrave Macmillan.

Frank, Thomas. 2020. *The People, No: A Brief History of Anti-Populism*. New York: Metropolitan Books.

Freeman, Daniel, Felicity Waite, Laina Rosebrock, Ariane Petit, Chiara Causier, Anna East, Lucy Jenner, et al. 2020a. "Coronavirus Conspiracy Beliefs, Mistrust, and

Compliance with Government Guidelines in England." *Psychological Medicine* 52 (May): 251–263. https://doi.org/10.1017/S0033291720001890.

———. 2020b. "We Should Beware of Ignoring Uncomfortable Possible Truths (a Reply to McManus et Al)." *Psychological Medicine* 52 (June): 559–559. https://doi.org/10.1017/S0033291720002196.

Frenkel, Sheera. 2021. "The Most Influential Spreader of Coronavirus Misinformation Online." *New York Times*, July 24, 2021. https://www.nytimes.com/2021/07/24/technology/joseph-mercola-coronavirus-misinformation-online.html.

Frenkel, Sheera, Ben Decker, and Davey Alba. 2020. "How the 'Plandemic' Movie and Its Falsehoods Spread Widely Online." *New York Times*, May 20, 2020. https://www.nytimes.com/2020/05/20/technology/plandemic-movie-youtube-facebook-coronavirus.html.

Frith, Jordan. 2020. "The Long History behind the 5G Coronavirus Conspiracy Theory." *Slate*, April 7, 2020. https://slate.com/technology/2020/04/coronavirus-covid19-5g-conspiracy-theory.html.

Fuchs, Christian, and Klaus Unterberger. 2021. *The Public Service Media and Public Service Internet Manifesto.* London: University of Westminster Press.

Full Fact. 2019a. "Hundreds of Birds Were Found Dead in the Netherlands but It Had Nothing to Do with 5G." *Full Fact*, August 21, 2019. https://fullfact.org/online/birds-5G-netherlands/.

———. 2019b. "These Trees Weren't Cut Down Because of 5G." *Full Fact*, May 30, 2019. https://fullfact.org/online/trees-not-chopped-down-for-5g/.

Gabielkov, Maksym, Arthi Ramachandran, Augustin Chaintreau, and Arnaud Legout. 2016. "Social Clicks: What and Who Gets Read on Twitter?" In Proceedings of the 2016 ACM SIGMETRICS International Conference on Measurement and Modeling of Computer Science, 179–92. Antibes Juan-les-Pins France: ACM. https://doi.org/10.1145/2896377.2901462.

Gallagher, Ryan. 2020. "5G Virus Conspiracy Theory Fueled by Coordinated Effort - Bloomberg." Bloomburg, April 9, 2020. https://www.bloomberg.com/news/articles/2020-04-09/covid-19-link-to-5g-technology-fueled-by-coordinated-effort.

Galloway, Alexander. 2020. "There Is No Rebellion (There's Only Me Earning a Paycheck)." July 6, 2020. http://cultureandcommunication.org/galloway/there-is-no-rebellion-theres-only-me-earning-a-paycheck.

Galloway, Anthony, and Eryk Bagshaw. 2021. "Coronavirus: How the Wuhan Lab COVID-19 Conspiracy Theory Was Sparked by a Book on Amazon." *Sydney Morning Herald*, May 13, 2021. https://www.smh.com.au/world/asia/going-viral-how-a-book-on-amazon-inspired-the-latest-covid-conspiracy-20210512-p57r6e.html.

Gambetti, Zeynep. 2018. "How 'Alternative' Is the Alt-Right?" *Critique and Praxis* 13/13, November 10. http://blogs.law.columbia.edu/praxis1313/zeynep-gambetti-how-alternative-is-the-alt-right/.

Garrett, Alexandra. 2021. "Election Misinformation Drops over 70 Percent after Social Media Platforms Suspend Trump." *Newsweek*, January 17, 2021. https://www.newsweek.com/election-misinformation-drops-over-70-percent-after-social-media-platforms-suspend-trump-study-1562206.

Garry, John, Rob Ford, and Rob Johns. 2020. "Coronavirus Conspiracy Beliefs, Mistrust, and Compliance: Taking Measurement Seriously." *Psychological Medicine* First View (December): 1–11. https://doi.org/10.1017/S0033291720005164.

Gatehouse, Gabriel. 2021. "The Coming Storm (Radio Show)." *BBC Radio 4*. https://www.bbc.co.uk/programmes/m001324r.

Gazendam, Aaron, Seper Ekhtiari, Erin Wong, Kim Madden, Leen Naji, Mark Phillips, Raman Mundi, and Mohit Bhandari. 2020. "The 'Infodemic' of Journal Publication Associated with the Novel Coronavirus Disease." *Journal of Bone and Joint Surgery* 102 (13): e64. https://doi.org/10.2106/JBJS.20.00610.

GDI (Global Disinformation Index). 2020. "Conspiracy Convergence: Coronavirus, QAnon and the Magical Miracle Solution." *Global Disinformation Index*, April 8, 2020. https://disinformationindex.org/2020/04/conspiracy-convergence-coronavirus-qanon-and-the-magical-miracle-solution/.

Gerbaudo, Paolo. 2016. "From Data Analytics to Data Hermeneutics. Online Political Discussions, Digital Methods and the Continuing Relevance of Interpretive Approaches." *Digital Culture & Society* 2 (2): 95–112. https://doi.org/10.14361/dcs-2016-0207.

Gertz, Bill. 2020. "Coronavirus Link to China Biowarfare Program Possible, Analyst Says." *Washington Times*, January 26, 2020. https://www.washingtontimes.com/news/2020/jan/26/coronavirus-link-to-china-biowarfare-program-possi/.

Gerts, Dax, Courtney D. Shelley, Nidhi Parikh, Travis Pitts, Chrysm Watson Ross, Geoffrey Fairchild, Nidia Yadria Vaquera Chavez, and Ashlynn R. Daughton. 2021. ""Thought I'd Share First" and Other Conspiracy Theory Tweets from the COVID-19 Infodemic: Exploratory Study." *JMIR Public Health and Surveillance* 7 (4 April): e26527. https://doi.org/10.2196/26527.

Ghebreyesus, Tedros Adhanom. 2020a. "Munich Security Conference: Speech by the WHO Director-General." World Health Organization, February 15, 2020. https://www.who.int/director-general/speeches/detail/munich-security-conference.

———. 2020b. "Speech at the Munich Security Conference." World Health Organization, February 15, 2020. https://www.who.int/director-general/speeches/detail/munich-security-conference.

Gilbert, Jeremy. 2020. "#ACFM Trip 12: The Cosmic Right." *Novara Media*, August 16, 2020. https://novaramedia.com/2020/08/16/trip-12-the-cosmic-right/.

Gillespie, Tarleton. 2018. *Custodians of the Internet: Platforms, Content Moderation, and the Hidden Decisions That Shape Social Media*. New Haven: Yale University Press.

Gilsinan, Kathy. 2020. "How China Deceived the WHO." *Atlantic*. April 12, 2020. https://www.theatlantic.com/politics/archive/2020/04/world-health-organization-blame-pandemic-coronavirus/609820/.

Ginzburg, Carlo. 2017. *Storia Notturna: Una Decifrazione del Sabba*. Milan: Adelphi.

Givens, Cameron. 2020. "Going Viral: COVID Conspiracies in Historical Perspective." *Origins: Current Events in Historical Perspective*. June. https://origins.osu.edu/connecting-history/covid-influenza-conspiracies-fake-news.

Goertzel, Ted. 1994. "Belief in Conspiracy Theories." *Political Psychology* 15 (4): 731–42. https://doi.org/10.2307/3791630.

Goldman, Adam. 2020. "Man Suspected of Planning Attack on Missouri Hospital Is Killed, Officials Say." *New York Times*, March 25, 2020. https://www.nytimes.com/2020/03/25/us/politics/coronavirus-fbi-shooting.html.

Goodman, Jack. "Covid-19 Leaflets: How Pandemic Disinformation Went Offline." *BBC News UK*, March 20, 2021. https://www.bbc.co.uk/news/56420379.

Gordon, Michael R., and Judith Miller. 2002. "Threats and Responses: The Iraqis." *New York Times*, September 8, 2002. https://www.nytimes.com/2002/09/08/world/threats-responses-iraqis-us-says-hussein-intensifies-quest-for-bomb-parts.html.

Gray, Jonathan. 2018. "Three Aspects of Data Worlds." *Krisis* 1: 4–17. archive.krisis.eu/three-aspects-of-data-worlds/.

Gray, Jonathan, Liliana Bounegru, and Tomasso Venturini. 2020. "'Fake News' as Infrastructural Uncanny." *New Media and Society* 22 (2 January): 317–341. https://doi .org/10.1177/1461444819856912.

Gray, Jonathan, Marc Tuters, Liliana Bounegru, and Thais Lobo. 2021. "Investigating Troubling Content on Amazon," *DataJournalism*, September 2, 2021. https:// datajournalism.com/read/longreads/investigating-troubling-content-on-amazon.

Gray, Matthew. 2010. *Conspiracy Theories in the Arab World: Sources and Politics.* London: Routledge.

GreatGameIndia. 2020. "Coronavirus Bioweapon: How China Stole Coronavirus From Canada and Weaponized It." *GreatGameIndia*, January 26, 2020. https:// web.archive.org/web/20210211220613/https:/greatgameindia.com/coronavirus -bioweapon/.

Greenspan, Rachel E., and Gabby Landsverk. 2020. "How QAnon Infiltrated the Yoga World." *Business Insider*, November 11, 2020. https://www.insider.com/qanon -conspiracy-theory-yoga-influencer-took-over-world-2020-11.

Gruzd, Anatoliy, and Philip Mai. 2020. "Going Viral: How a Single Tweet Spawned a COVID-19 Conspiracy Theory on Twitter." *Data & Society* 7 (2 July): 2053951720938405. https://doi.org/10.1177/2053951720938405.

Guardian. 2021. "Biden Calls on Facebook to Tackle Misinformation after Saying It's 'Killing People.'" *Guardian*, July 19, 2021. http://www.theguardian.com/us-news /2021/jul/19/joe-biden-facebook-covid-coronavirus-misinformation.

Guerin, Cécile. 2021. "The Yoga World Is Riddled with Anti-Vaxxers and QAnon Believers." *Wired UK*, January 28, 2021. https://www.wired.co.uk/article/yoga -disinformation-qanon-conspiracy-wellness.

Guillon, M., and P. Kergall. 2021. "Factors Associated with COVID-19 Vaccination Intentions and Attitudes in France." *Public Health* 198 (September): 200–207. https:// doi.org/10.1016/j.puhe.2021.07.035.

Guterres, António. 2020. "UN Secretary-General's Video Message on World Press Freedom Day 2020." May 3, 2020. https://www.un.org/sg/en/content/sg/statement /2020-05-03/secretary-generals-video-message-world-press-freedom-day-2020- %E2%80%9Cjournalism-without-fear-or-favour%E2%80%9D.

Hagan, Joe. 2009. "The Rising Power of Financial Blog Zero Hedge." *New York Magazine*, September 25, 2009. https://nymag.com/guides/money/2009/59457/.

Haiven, Max, A.T. Kingsmith, and Aris Komporozos-Athanasiou. 2021a. "Gaming the Conspiracy." *Arts of the Working Class* 19: 23.

———. 2021b. "Whither Harmony Square?: Conspiracy Games in Late Capitalism." *LA Review of Books*, Essays, November 13, 2021. https://lareviewofbooks.org/article /whither-harmony-square-conspiracy-games-in-late-capitalism.

———. n.d. Conspiracy Games and Countergames (webpage). https://conspiracy .games/#podcast

Han, Jeehoon, Bruce D. Meyer, and James X. Sullivan. 2020. "Income and Poverty in the COVID-19 Pandemic." *Brookings Papers on Economic Activity*, June 25, 2020. https://www.brookings.edu/wp-content/uploads/2020/06/Han-et-al-conference -draft.pdf.

Hanoki, Eric. 2020. "A QAnon Grifter Was Selling Colloidal Silver as a Supposed Coronavirus Treatment and Cure." *Media Matters*, April 8, 2020. https://www .mediamatters.org/coronavirus-covid-19/qanon-grifter-dustin-nemos-was-selling -colloidal-silver-supposed-coronavirus.

Harambam, Jaron. 2020. *Contemporary Conspiracy Culture: Truth and Knowledge in an Era of Epistemic Instability.* London: Routledge.

Harris Poll. 2020. "Covid-19 Wave 10." *Harris Poll*, May 4, 2020. http://theharrispoll
.com/wp-content/uploads/2020/05/Wave-2-10_tabs_Banner-11.pdf.

Hart, P. Sol, and Erik C. Nisbet. 2012. "Boomerang Effects in Science Communication: How Motivated Reasoning and Identity Cues Amplify Opinion Polarization about Climate Mitigation Policies." *Communication Research* 39 (6, August): 701–23. https://doi.org/10.1177/0093650211416646.

Hartman, Andrew. 2019. *A War for the Soul of America: A History of the Culture Wars.* 2nd ed. Chicago: University of Chicago Press.

Harvey, David. 2007. *A Short History of Neoliberalism.* Oxford: Oxford University Press.

Heilweil, Rebecca. 2020. "The Conspiracy Theory about 5G Causing Coronavirus, Explained." *Vox*, April 24, 2020.

Henley, Jon. 2021. "Pandemic Leaves Europeans More Likely to Believe Conspiracy Theories – Study." *Guardian*, February 22, 2021. https://www.theguardian.com/world/2021/feb/22/covid-pandemic-leaves-europeans-more-likely-to-believe-conspiracy-theories-study.

Henley, Jon, and Niamh McIntyre. 2020. "Survey Uncovers Widespread Belief in 'Dangerous' Covid Conspiracy Theories." *Guardian*, October 26, 2020, *sec. World news.* https://www.theguardian.com/world/2020/oct/26/survey-uncovers-widespread-belief-dangerous-covid-conspiracy-theories.

Hermansson, Patrik. 2020. 'Trust No One': Understanding the Drivers of Conspiracy Theory Belief." *HOPE Not Hate Charitable Trust*, April 27, 2020. https://hopenothate.org.uk/2020/04/27/trust-no-one/.

Hern, Alex. 2021. "Facebook Lifts Ban on Posts Claiming Covid-19 Was Man-Made." *Guardian*, May 27, 2021. https://www.theguardian.com/technology/2021/may/27/facebook-lifts-ban-on-posts-claiming-covid-19-was-man-made.

Hine, Christine. 2017. "From Virtual Ethnography to the Embedded, Embodied, and Everyday Internet." In *The Routledge Companion to Digital Ethnography*, edited by Larissa Hjorth, Heather Horst, Genevieve Bell and Anne Galloway, 21–28. London: Routledge.

Hofstadter, Richard. 1964. *The Paranoid Style in American Politics, and Other Essays.* Cambridge, MA: Harvard University Press.

Holden, Emily. 2020. "US Critics of Stay-at-Home Orders Tied to Fossil Fuel Funding." *Guardian*, May 21, 2020. https://www.theguardian.com/environment/2020/may/21/groups-fossil-fuel-funding-urge-states-reopen-amid-pandemic.

Holroyd, Matthew. 2021. "Most in North Macedonia Think COVID Was Made to Control Humans: Poll." *Euronews*, December 1, 2021. https://www.euronews.com/2021/12/01/two-thirds-in-north-macedonia-believe-covid-was-created-to-control-humans-study.

Hu, Zhiwen, Zhongliang Yang, Qi Li, and An Zhang. 2020. "The COVID-19 Infodemic: Infodemiology Study Analyzing Stigmatizing Search Terms." *Journal of Medical Internet Research* 22 (11): e22639. https://doi.org/10.2196/22639.

Huang, Binxuan, and Kathleen M. Carley. 2020. "Disinformation and Misinformation on Twitter during the Novel Coronavirus Outbreak." *ArXiv:2006.04278 [Cs]*, 7 June 2020. http://arxiv.org/abs/2006.04278.

Icke, David. 2003. *Tales from the Time Loop.* Ryde, UK: Bridge of Love Publications.

Imhoff, Roland, and Martin Bruder. 2014. "Speaking (Un–)Truth to Power: Conspiracy Mentality as a Generalised Political Attitude." *European Journal of Personality* 28 (1, January): 25–43. https://doi.org/10.1002/per.1930.

Imhoff, Roland, and Pia Lamberty. 2020. "A Bioweapon or a Hoax? The Link Between Distinct Conspiracy Beliefs About the Coronavirus Disease (COVID-19)

Outbreak and Pandemic Behavior." *Social Psychological and Personality Science*, July, 1948550620934692. https://doi.org/10.1177/1948550620934692.

Innes, H., and M. Innes. 2021. "De-Platforming Disinformation: Conspiracy Theories and Their Control." *Information, Communication and Society*, October. https://doi.org/10.1080/1369118X.2021.1994631.

ISD (Institute for Strategic Dialogue). 2020. "COVID-19 Briefing 2: Far-Right Mobilisation." April 9, 2020. https://www.isdglobal.org/wp-content/uploads/2020/06/COVID-19-Briefing-02-Institute-for-Strategic-Dialogue-9th-April-2020.pdf.

Islam, M.S., T. Sarkar, S.H. Khan, A.H. Mostofa Kamal, S. Hasan, A. Kabir, D. Yeasmin, M.A. Islam, K.I. Amin Chowdhury, K.S. Anwar, A.A. Chughtai, and H. Seale. 2020. "COVID-19-Related Infodemic and Its Impact on Public Health: A Global Social Media Analysis." *American Journal of Tropical Medicine and Hygiene*, 103 (4, October): 1621–1629. https://doi.org/10.4269/ajtmh.20-0812.

Ipsos. 2020. "Complottheorieën over Het Coronavirus." https://www.ipsos.com/sites/default/files/ct/news/documents/2020-05/ipsos_corona_complot_v1.0.pdf.

Ivory, Danielle, Lauren Leatherby, and Robert Gebeloff. 2021. "Least Vaccinated U.S. Counties Have Something in Common: Trump Voters." *New York Times*, April 17, 2021. https://www.nytimes.com/interactive/2021/04/17/us/vaccine-hesitancy-politics.html.

Jack, Andrew, and Darren Dodd. 2020. "FT Health: The Dangers of Data." *Financial Times*, November 4, 2020. https://www.ft.com/content/de36553c-deed-438c-bd76-f447e2750f18.

Jack, Caroline. 2017. "Lexicon of Lies: Terms of Problematic Information." *Data & Society*, August 9, 2017. https://datasociety.net/library/lexicon-of-lies/.

Jackson, Jasper, and Alexandra Heal. 2021. "Misinformation Market: The Money-Making Tools Facebook Hands to Covid Cranks." *The Bureau of Investigative Journalism*, January 31, 2021. https://www.thebureauinvestigates.com/stories/2021-01-31/misinformation-market-the-money-making-tools-facebook-hands-to-covid-cranks.

Jameson, Fredric. 1991. *Postmodernism or, The Cultural Logic of Late Capitalism*. London: Verso.

Jassa, Greta. 2020. "The Social Media Platform That Welcomes QAnon with Open Arms." *Open Democracy*, November 19, 2020. https://www.opendemocracy.net/en/countering-radical-right/social-media-platform-welcomes-qanon-open-arms/.

Jennings, Ralph. 2008. "Taiwan Suggests SARS Was China Warfare Plot." Reuters, October 7, 2008. https://www.reuters.com/article/us-taiwan-china-sars-idUSTRE49617120081007.

Jensen, K.B. 1994. "Reception as Flow: The 'New Television Viewer' Revisited." *Cultural Studies* 8 (2): 288–299. https://doi.org/10.1080/09502389400490461.

Jerolmack, Colin, and Shamus Khan. 2014. "Talk Is Cheap: Ethnography and the Attitudinal Fallacy." *Sociological Methods & Research* 43 (2, March): 178–209. https://doi.org/10.1177/0049124114523396.

Jolley, Daniel, and Jenny L. Paterson. 2020. "Pylons Ablaze: Examining the Role of 5G COVID-19 Conspiracy Beliefs and Support for Violence." *British Journal of Social Psychology* 59 (3, June): 1–13. https://doi.org/10.1111/bjso.12394.

Jones v Adams. 2008. Case No. 4:06CV00685 ERW (E.D. Mo. Nov. 14, 2008). https://casetext.com/case/icke-v-adams-3.

Jones-Jang, S. Mo, Tara Mortensen, and Jingjing Liu. 2021. "Does Media Literacy Help Identification of Fake News? Information Literacy Helps, but Other Literacies Don't." *American Behavioral Scientist* 65 (2, August): 371–88. https://doi.org/10.1177/0002764219869406.

Joyce, Kathryn. 2020. "The Long, Strange History of Bill Gates Population Control Conspiracy Theories." *Huffington Post*, May 12, 2020. https://www.huffpost.com/entry/bill-gates-coronavirus-vaccine-conspiracy_n_5eb9ab7ac5b69358ef8a9803.

Jurgenson, Nathan. 2012. "The IRL Fetish." *New Inquiry*, June 28, 2012. https://thenewinquiry.com/the-irl-fetish/.

Kang, Cecilia, and Sheera Frenkel. 2020. ""PizzaGate" Conspiracy Theory Thrives Anew in the TikTok Era." *New York Times*, June 27, 2020. https://www.nytimes.com/2020/06/27/technology/pizzagate-justin-bieber-qanon-tiktok.html.

Katz, Michael B. 2008. "The American Welfare State." *History in Focus* 14 (Winter). https://archives.history.ac.uk/history-in-focus/welfare/articles/katzm.html.

Kaufman, Frederick. 2020. "Pandemics Go Hand in Hand with Conspiracy Theories." *New Yorker*, May 13, 2020. https://www.newyorker.com/culture/cultural-comment/pandemics-go-hand-in-hand-with-conspiracy-theories.

Keeley, Brian L. 1999. "Of Conspiracy Theories." *Journal of Philosophy* 96 (3, March): 109–126. https://doi.org/10.2307/2564659.

Kearney, Matthew D., Shawn C. Chiang, and Philip M. Massey. 2020. "The Twitter Origins and Evolution of the COVID-19 'Plandemic' Conspiracy Theory." *Harvard Kennedy School Misinformation Review* 1 (3, October). https://doi.org/10.37016/mr-2020-42.

Kelly, Annie. 2020. "Mothers for QAnon." *New York Times*, September 10, 2020. https://www.nytimes.com/2020/09/10/opinion/qanon-women-conspiracy.html.

———. 2021. "Episode 122: Undercover at the London Anti-Lockdown Rally." May 2, 2020, *QAnon Anonymous Podcast, produced by Travis View, Julian Feeld, and Jake Rockatansky*, podcast, 49: 16. https://soundcloud.com/qanonanonymous/episode-110-mothers-for-qanon-w-annie-kelly?utm_source=clipboard&utm_medium=text&utm_campaign=social_sharing.

Kinetz, Erika. 2021. "Anatomy of a Conspiracy: With COVID, China Took Leading Role." *Associated Press News*, April 20, 2021. https://apnews.com/article/pandemics-beijing-only-on-ap-epidemics-media-122b73e134b780919cc1808f3f6f16e8.

Kitta, Andrea. 2012. *Vaccinations and Public Concern in History: Legend, Rumor, and Risk Perception*, 1st ed. New York: Routledge.

Klein, Naomi. 2007. *The Shock Doctrine: The Rise of Disaster Capitalism*. New York: Knopf.

———. 2020. "The Great Reset Conspiracy Smoothie." Intercept, December 8, 2020. https://theintercept.com/2020/12/08/great-reset-conspiracy/.

Klepper, David, Farnoush Amiri, and Beatrice Depuy. 2021. "The Superspreaders behind Top COVID-19 Conspiracy Theories." *ABC News*, February 15, 2021. https://abcnews.go.com/Health/wireStory/superspreaders-top-covid-19-conspiracy-theories-75898559.

Klofstad, Casey A., and Joseph E. Uscinski. 2020. "Conspiracy Survey." https://www.joeuscinski.com/uploads/7/1/9/5/71957435/codebook_pdf_version.pdf.

Knight, Peter. 2000. *Conspiracy Culture: From Kennedy to The X Files*. London: Routledge.

———. 2003. "Making Sense of Conspiracy Theories." In *Conspiracy Theories in American History: An Encyclopaedia*, edited by Peter Knight, 15–25. Santa Barbara: ABC-Clio.

———. 2007. *The Kennedy Assassination*. Edinburgh: Edinburgh University Press.

———. 2008. "Outrageous Conspiracy Theories: Popular and Official Responses to 9/11 in Germany and the US." *New German Critique* 103 (December): 165–93. https://doi.org/10.1215/0094033X-2007-024.

———. 2021. "Conspiracy, Complicity, Critique." *Symploke* 29 (1): 197–215. https://doi.org/10.1353/sym.2021.0011.

Kochhar, Rakesh, and Anthony Cilluffo. 2017. "How Wealth Inequality Has Changed in the US Since the Great Recession, by Race, Ethnicity and Income." *Pew Research*, November 1, 2017. https://www.pewresearch.org/fact-tank/2017/11/01/ how-wealth-inequality-has-changed-in-the-u-s-since-the-great-recession-by-race -ethnicity-and-income/.

Koontz, Dean. 2008. *The Eyes of Darkness*. New York: Berkley Books.

Kozinets, Robert. 2019. *Netnography: The Essential Guide to Qualitative Social Media Research*. Thousand Oaks: Sage.

Krishnan, Nandita, Jiayan Gu, Rebekah Tromble, and Lorien C. Abroms. 2021. "Research Note: Examining How Various Social Media Platforms Have Responded to COVID-19 Misinformation." *Harvard Kennedy School Misinformation Review* 2 (6, December). https://doi.org/10.37016/mr-2020-85.

Krouwel, Andre, Yodan Kutiyski, Jan-Willem van Prooijen, Johan Martinsson, and Elias Markstedt. 2017. "Does Extreme Political Ideology Predict Conspiracy Beliefs, Economic Evaluations and Political Trust?" *Journal of Social and Political Psychology*, 5 (2): 435–62.

Kuchler, Hannah. 2020. "Teva Charged in US Price-Fixing Investigation." *Financial Times*, August 26, 2020. https://www.ft.com/content/ee08593e-3ecc-40d5-b680 -bad87456b7a3.

Kuhn, Moritz, Moritz Schularick and Ulrike Steins. 2018. "How the Financial Crisis Drastically Increased Wealth Inequality in the U.S." *Harvard Business Review*, September 13, 2018. https://hbr.org/2018/09/research-how-the-financial-crisis -drastically-increased-wealth-inequality-in-the-u-s.

Kuhn, Sarah, Anne Kezia, Roselind Lieb, Daniel Freeman, Christina Andreou, and Thea Zander-Schellenberg. 2021. "Coronavirus Conspiracy Beliefs in the German-Speaking General Population: Endorsement Rates and Links to Reasoning Biases and Paranoia." *Psychological Medicine* First View (March): 1–15. https://doi.org/10.1017/ S0033291721001124.

Kunzru, Hari. 2020. "For the Lulz." *The New York Review*, March 26, 2020. https:// www.nybooks.com/articles/2020/03/26/trolls-4chan-gamergate-lulz/.

Kus, Basuk. 2006. "Neoliberalism, Institutional Change and the Welfare State: The Case of Britain and France." *International Journal of Comparative Sociology* 47 (6): 488–525.

Lancet. 2005. "Conspiracy Theories of HIV/AIDS." *Lancet* 365 (9458, February): 448. https://doi.org/10.1016/S0140-6736(05)17875-1.

Lantian, Anthony, Dominique Muller, Cécile Nurra, and Karen M. Douglas. 2016. "Measuring Belief in Conspiracy Theories: Validation of a French and English Single-Item Scale." *International Review of Social Psychology* 29 (1, February): 1–14. https://doi .org/10.5334/irsp.8.

Lapowsky, Issie. 2019. "YouTube Will Crack Down on Toxic Videos, But It Won't Be Easy." *Wired*, January 25, 2019. https://www.wired.com/story/youtube-recommendations -crackdown-borderline-content/.

Lasco, Gideon, and Nicole Curato. 2019. "Medical Populism." *Social Science and Medicine* 221: 1–8.

Lepore, Jill. 2020. *The Last Archive* (podcast). https://pushkin.fm/show/the-last-archive/.

Levin, Sam. 2017. "YouTube Alters Search Algorithm over Fake Las Vegas Conspiracy Videos." *Guardian*, October 6, 2017.

Lewandowsky, Stephan, Peter H. Jacobs, and Stuart Neil. 2022. "Leak or Leap? Evidence and Cognition Surrounding the Origins of the SARS-CoV-2 Virus." In *Covid-19 Conspiracy Theories in Global Perspective*, edited by Michael Butter and Peter Knight. London: Routledge.

Lewis, Becca. 2018. *Alternative Influence: Broadcasting the Reactionary Right on YouTube.* New York: Data & Society Research Institute. https://datasociety.net/wp-content/uploads/2018/09/DS_Alternative_Influence.pdf.

———. 2021. "Out of the Rabbit Hole: From Radicalization to Amplification of Far-Right Content Online." Stanford Cyber Policy Center (YouTube channel), Live streamed and published October 5, 2021. https://www.youtube.com/watch?v=00TfI_Fdp1Y.

Ligot, Dominic, Frances Claire Tayco, Mark Toledo, Carlos Nazareno, and Denise Brennan-Rieder. 2021. "Infodemiology: Computational Methodologies for Quantifying and Visualizing Key Characteristics of the COVID-19 Infodemic." *SSRN Electronic Journal* (January). https://doi.org/10.2139/ssrn.3771695.

Linden, Sander van der, Jon Roozenbeek, and Josh Compton. 2020. "Inoculating Against Fake News about COVID-19." *Frontiers in Psychology* 11 (October): 566790. https://doi.org/10.3389/fpsyg.2020.566790.

Linden, Sander van der, Graham Dixon, Chris Clarke, and John Cook. 2021. "Inoculating against COVID-19 Vaccine Misinformation." *EClinicalMedicine* 33 (February). https://doi.org/10.1016/j.eclinm.2021.100772.

Ling, Justin. 2022. "False Claims of U.S. Biowarfare Labs in Ukraine Grip QAnon." *Foreign Policy* (blog), March 2, 2022. https://foreignpolicy.com/2022/03/02/ukraine-biolabs-conspiracy-theory-qanon/.

Lopez, Jesse, and D. Sunshine Hillygus. 2018. "Why So Serious?: Survey Trolls and Misinformation." *SSRN Electronic Journal* (March). https://doi.org/10.2139/ssrn.3131087.

Los Angeles Times. 1903. "Medicos Meet." *Los Angeles Times*, June 3, 1903.

Lovelace, Berkeley. 2020a. "FDA Revokes Emergency Use of Hydroxychloroquine." *CNBC*, June 15, 2020. https://www.cnbc.com/2020/06/15/fda-revokes-emergency-use-of-hydroxychloroquine.html.

———. 2020b. "Trump Claims the Worsening U.S. Coronavirus Outbreak Is a 'Fake News Media Conspiracy' Even as Hospitalizations Rise." *CNBC*, October 26, 2020. https://www.cnbc.com/2020/10/26/coronavirus-trump-claims-the-worsening-us-outbreak-is-a-fake-news-media-conspiracy-even-as-hospitalizations-rise.html.

Lubove, Roy. 1986. *The Struggle for Social Security 1900–1935.* Pittsburgh: University of Pittsburgh Press.

MacFarquhar, Neil. 2021. "Far-Right Extremists Move from 'Stop the Steal' to Stop the Vaccine." *New York Times*, March 26, 2021. https://www.nytimes.com/2021/03/26/us/far-right-extremism-anti-vaccine.html.

Machete, Paul, and Marita Turpin. 2020. "The Use of Critical Thinking to Identify Fake News: A Systematic Literature Review." In *Responsible Design, Implementation and Use of Information and Communication Technology*, edited by Marié Hattingh, Machdel Matthee, Hanlie Smuts, Ilias Pappas, Yogesh K. Dwivedi, and Matti Mäntymäki, 235–46. Cham, Switzerland: Springer. https://doi.org/10.1007/978-3-030-45002-1_20.

Mahl, Daniela, Mike S. Schäfer, and Jing Zeng. 2022. "Conspiracy Theories in Online Environments: An Interdisciplinary Literature Review and Agenda for Future Research." *New Media & Society*, February, 14614448221075760. https://doi.org/10.1177/14614448221075759.

Makuch, Ben. 2020. "Man Who Planned to Bomb Hospital Amid Coronavirus Pandemic Dies in Incident with FBI." *Vice*, March 26, 2020. https://www.vice.com/en/article/g5xnem/man-who-planned-to-bomb-hospital-fighting-coronavirus-dies-in-in.

Mantyla, Kyle. 2020. "Liz Crokin Claims Celebrities Are Getting Coronavirus from Tainted 'Adrenochrome Supply'." *Right Wing Watch*, March 18, 2020. https://www.rightwingwatch.org/post/liz-crokin-claims-celebrities-are-getting-coronavirus-from-tainted-adrenochrome-supply/.

Maragkou, Eleni. 2021. *"From Snake Oil to Essential Oils: The Reactionary Epistemologies of Lifestyle and Alternative Wellness Instagram Influencers."* Unpublished dissertation, University of Amsterdam.

Marantz, Andrew. 2020. "Alex Jones's Bogus Coronavirus Cures." *New Yorker*, 30 March, 2020. www.newyorker.com/magazine/2020/04/06/alex-jones-bogus-coronavirus-cures.

Marcellino, William, Todd C. Helmus, Joshua Kerrigan, Hilary Reininger, Rouslan I. Karimov, and Rebecca Ann Lawrence. 2021. *Detecting Conspiracy Theories on Social Media: Improving Machine Learning to Detect and Understand Online Conspiracy Theories.* Santa Monica: RAND Corporation. https://doi.org/10.7249/RR-A676-1.

Marres, Noortje. 2018. "Why We Can't Have Our Facts Back." *Engaging Science, Technology, and Society* 4 (July): 423–443. https://doi.org/10.17351/ests2018.188.

Marshall, Matthew. 2021. *"You Will Own Nothing. You Will Be Happy: Defining Conspiracism Through a Receptive Study of the World Economic Forum's 'The Great Reset'."* Unpublished MA Thesis, MA Media Studies, University of Amsterdam, June 22, 2021.

Mason, Jessica. 2019a. "Making Fiction out of Fact: Attention and Belief in the Discourse of Conspiracy." *Narrative Inquiry* 29 (2, October): 293–312. https://doi.org/10.1075/ni.19023.mas.

Mason, Rowena. 2019b. "Nigel Farage Denies Being Conspiracy Theorist after Far-Right Talkshow Appearances." *Guardian*, May 7, 2019. https://www.theguardian.com/politics/2019/may/07/nigel-farage-denies-being-conspiracy-theorist-after-far-right-talkshow-appearances.

McGreal, Chris. 2020. ""It's a Hoax. There's No Pandemic": Trump's Base Stays Loyal as President Fights Covid." *Guardian*, October 3, 2020. http://www.theguardian.com/us-news/2020/oct/03/donald-trump-base-stays-loyal-president-fights-covid-19.

McHugh, Kevin J., Lihong Jing, Sean Y. Severt, Mache Cruz, Morteza Sarmadi, Hapuarachchige Surangi N. Jayawardena, Collin F. Perkinson et al. 2019. "Biocompatible Near-Infrared Quantum Dots Delivered to the Skin by Microneedle Patches Record Vaccination." *Science Translation Medicine* 11 (523, December). https://doi.org/10.1126/scitranslmed.aay7162.

McKenzie-McHarg, Andrew. 2019. "Experts versus Eyewitnesses. Or, How Did Conspiracy Theories Come to Rely on Images?" *Word and Image* 35 (2, June): 141–158. https://doi.org/10.1080/02666286.2018.1553388.

———. 2020. "On the Trail of the Paranoid Style." *Journal of the History of Ideas* blog, November 2, 2020. jhiblog.org/2020/11/02/on-the-trail-of-the-paranoid-style/.

McManus, Sally, Joanna D'Ardenne, and Simon Wessely. 2020. "Covid Conspiracies: Misleading Evidence Can Be More Damaging than No Evidence at All." *Psychological Medicine* 52 (3, June): 597–598. https://doi.org/10.1017/S0033291720002184.

McMunn, Anne, and Baowen Xue. 2021. "Gender Differences in Unpaid Care Work and Psychological Distress in the UK Covid-19 Lockdown." *PloS One*, 16 (3, March): e0247959. https://doi.org/10.1371/journal.pone.0247959.

Mede, Niels G., and Mike S. Schäfer. 2021. "Science-Related Populism Declining during the COVID-19 Pandemic: A Panel Survey of the Swiss Population before and after the Coronavirus Outbreak." *Public Understanding of Science* 31 (2, November). https://doi.org/10.1177/09636625211056871.

Medik, Velt. 2018. "Meet Donald Trump's Propagandist." *Der Speigel*, February 28, 2018. www.spiegel.de/international/worl d/a-visit-to-the-InfoWars-studios-of-alex -jones-a-1136654.html.

Melley, Tim. 2000. *Empire of Conspiracy: The Culture of Paranoia in Postwar America*. New York: Cornell University Press.

———. 2012. *The Covert Sphere: Secrecy, Fiction, and the National Security State*. Ithaca: Cornell University Press.

———. 2020. "Conspiracy in American Narrative." In *Routledge Handbook of Conspiracy Theories*, edited by Michael Butter and Peter Knight, 427–440. London: Routledge.

Menasce Horowitz, Juliana, Ruth Igielnik, and Rakesh Kochhar. 2020. "Most Americans Say There Is Too Much Economic Inequality in the U.S., But Fewer Than Half Call It a Top Priority." *Pew Research*, January 9, 2020. https://www.pewsocialtrends.org /2020/01/09/trends-in-income-and-wealth-inequality/.

Mencimer, Stephanie. 2019. "Welfare Reform Was a Disaster for the Poor. Trump Wants to Make It Even Worse." *Mother Jones*, August 24, 2019. https://www.motherjones .com/politics/2019/08/welfare-reform-was-a-disaster-for-the-poor-trump-would -make-it-even-worse/.

Mercier, Hugo. 2022. *Not Born Yesterday: The Science of Who We Trust and What We Believe*. Princeton: Princeton University Press.

Merlan, Anna. 2020. "The Conspiracy Singularity Has Arrived." *Vice News*, July 17, 2020. https://www.vice.com/en/article/v7gz53/the-conspiracy-singularity-has -arrived.

———. 2021. "Why Is the Intellectual Dark Web Suddenly Hyping an Unproven COVID Treatment?" *Vice*, June 24, 2021. https://www.vice.com/en/article/wx5z5y /why-is-the-intellectual-dark-web-suddenly-hyping-an-unproven-covid-treatment.

———. 2022. "COVID-19 Is Bringing Back One of the Oldest and Strangest Fake Cures." *Vice* (blog). January 6, 2022. https://www.vice.com/en/article/88g85x/ covid-19-is-bringing-back-one-of-the-oldest-and-strangest-fake-cures.

Miani, Alessandro, Thomas Hills, and Adrian Bangerter. 2021. "LOCO: The 88-Million-Word Language of Conspiracy Corpus." *Behavior Research Methods* (October). https:// doi.org/10.3758/s13428-021-01698-z.

Miller, Carl. 2020. "Coronavirus: Far-Right Spreads Covid-19 'Infodemic' on Facebook." *BBC News*, May 4, 2020. https://www.bbc.com/news/technology-52490430.

Milman, Oliver. 2020. "Seven of Donald Trump's Most Misleading Coronavirus Claims." *Guardian*, March 31, 2020. https://www.theguardian.com/us-news/2020/ mar/28/trump-coronavirus-misleading-claims.

Milner, Ryan M., and Whitney Phillips. 2021. *You Are Here: A Field Guide for Navigating Polarized Speech, Conspiracy Theories, and Our Polluted Media Landscape*. Cambridge, MA: MIT Press.

Moffitt, Benjamin. 2016. *The Global Rise of Populism: Performance, Political Style, and Representation*. Palo Alto: Stanford University Press.

Moffitt, J.D., Catherine King, and Kathleen Carley. 2021. "Hunting Conspiracy Theories During the COVID-19 Pandemic." *Social Media and Society* 7 (3), July. https://doi.org /10.1177/20563051211043212

Moonshot Team. 2021. "White Supremacy Search Trends in the US." *Moonshot*, June 16, 2021. https://moonshotteam.com/white-supremacy-search-trends/.

Moore, Alan, and Dave Gibbons. 1987. *Watchmen*. New York: DC Comics.

Moscow Times. 2021. "2 in 3 Russians Believe Coronavirus Is a Bioweapon – Poll." *Moscow Times*, March 1, 2021. https://www.themoscowtimes.com/2021/03/01/2-in -3-russians-believe-coronavirus-is-a-bioweapon-poll-a73101.

More in Common. 2020. "Britain's Choice: Common Ground and Division in 2020s Britain." October 2020. https://www.britainschoice.uk.

Muirhead, Russell, and Nancy L. Rosenblum. 2019. *A Lot of People Are Saying: The New Conspiracism and the Assault on Democracy.* Princeton: Princeton University Press.

Mulhall, Joe. 2019. "Deplatforming Works: Let's Get On With It." *Hope Not Hate*, October 4, 2019. www.hopenothate.org.uk/2019/10/04/deplatforming-works-lets-get-on-with-it/.

Müller, Jan-Werner. 2016. "Trump, Erdoğan, Farage: The Attractions of Populism for Politicians, the Dangers for Democracy." *Guardian*, September 2, 2016. https://www.theguardian.com/books/2016/sep/02/trump-erdogan-farage-the-attractions-of-populism-for-politicians-the-dangers-for-democracy.

———. 2017. "Donald Trump's Use of the Term 'The People' Is a Warning Sign." *Guardian*, January 24, 2017. https://www.theguardian.com/commentisfree/2017/jan/24/donald-trumps-warning-sign-populism-authoritarianism-inauguration.

Munn, Luke. 2020. "The Alt-Right Pipeline: Individual Journeys to Extremism Online." *Brewminate*, June 1, 2020. https://brewminate.com/the-alt-right-pipeline-individual-journeys-to-extremism-online/.

Nagle, Angela. 2017. *Kill All Normies: Online Culture Wars from 4Chan and Tumblr to Trump and the Alt-Right.* Winchester: Zero Books.

Nattrass, Nicoli. 2013. *The AIDS Conspiracy.* New York: Columbia University Press.

Nazar, Shahin, and Toine Pieters. 2021. "Plandemic Revisited: A Product of Planned Disinformation Amplifying the COVID-19 'Infodemic'." *Frontiers in Public Health.* https://doi.org/10.3389/fpubh.2021.649930.

NBC News. 2014. "Conspiracy Theories Abound as U.S. Military Closes HAARP." *NBC News*, May 23, 2014. https://www.nbcnews.com/science/weird-science/conspiracy-theories-abound-u-s-military-closes-haarp-n112576.

NCRI (Network Contagion Research Institute). 2021. "A Contagion of Institutional Distrust: Viral Disinformation of the COVID Vaccine and the Road to Reconciliation." *Network Contagion Research Institute.* https://networkcontagion.us/wp-content/uploads/NCRI-AntiVaccinationV6.pdf.

Nemos, Dustin. 2020. "Censored and Thriving." *WhiteHat Movement.* https://www.whitehatmovement.com/wp-content/uploads/2020/05/Case-Study-Dustin-Nemos.pdf.

———. 2021a. "RedPilled Profits." *WhiteHat Movement.* https://www.whitehatmovement.com/redpilled-profits/.

———. 2021b. "WhiteHat Movement." https://www.whitehatmovement.com/?utm_source=redpilliving&utm_medium=we-believ.

Newsnight. 2020. "Where Is the Anti-Lockdown Movement Heading?" *Newsnight, BBC*, July 5, 2020. https://www.bbc.co.uk/news/av/uk-57702177.

Nicas, Jack. 2018. "Alex Jones Said Bans Would Strengthen Him. He Was Wrong." *New York Times*, September 4, 2018. www.nytimes.com/2018/09/04/technology/alex-jones-InfoWars-bans-traffic.html.

Nielsen, Rasmus Kleis, Richard Fletcher, Antonis Kalogeropoulos, and Felix M Simon. 2020. "*Communications in the Coronavirus Crisis: Lessons for the Second Wave.*" The Institute for the Study of Journalism, University of Oxford, October 27, 2020. https://reutersinstitute.politics.ox.ac.uk/communications-coronavirus-crisis-lessons-second-wave.

Nielsen, Rasmus Kleis, Anne Schulz, and Richard Fletcher. 2021. "An Ongoing Infodemic: How People in Eight Countries Access News and Information about Coronavirus a Year into the Pandemic." Reuters Institute for the Study of Journalism.

https://reutersinstitute.politics.ox.ac.uk/ongoing-infodemic-how-people-eight
-countries-access-news-and-information-about-coronavirus-year.

Noble, Safiya Umoja. 2018. *Algorithms of Oppression: How Search Engines Reinforce Racism.* New York: New Year University Press.

Northrup, Christine. 1994. *Women's Bodies, Women's Wisdom.* London: Piatkus.

Nsubuga, Jimmy. 2020. "In Pictures: Thousands of Anti-Lockdown Protestors Gather in London." *Yahoo News,* August 29, 2020. https://www.yahoo.com/entertainment /anti-lockdown-protesters-151116254/photo-london-england-august-29-anti -000000853.html.

Nwachukwu, John Owen. 2020. "Covid-19: Fani-Kayode Makes Shocking Revelations about Illuminati, Killer Vaccine." *Daily Post,* March 22, 2020. https://dailypost.ng /2020/03/22/covid-19-fani-kayode-makes-shocking-revelations-about-illuminati -killer-vaccine/

Nyhan, Brendan, Jason Reifler, and Peter A. Ubel. 2013. "The Hazards of Correcting Myths about Health Care Reform." *Medical Care* 51 (2, February): 127–132. https:// doi.org/10.1097/MLR.0b013e318279486b.

Observatory on Social Media. n.d. "CoVaxxy." Accessed February 18, 2022. https:// osome.iu.edu/tools/covaxxy.

O'Connor, Ciaran. 2021. "The Conspiracy Consortium: Examining Discussions of COVID-19 among Right-Wing Extremist Telegram Channels." Institute for Strategic Dialogue, December 17, 2021. https://www.isdglobal.org/isd-publications/ the-conspiracy-consortium-examining-discussions-of-covid-19-among-right-wing -extremist-telegram-channel/.

O'Connor, Ciaran, and Moustafa Ayad. 2021. "MENA Monitor: Arabic COVID-19 Vaccine Misinformation Online." *ISD Global.* https://www.isdglobal.org/isd -publications/mena-monitor-arabic-covid-19-vaccine-misinformation-online/.

OECD. 2020. "*Income Inequality (Indicator).*" https://doi.org/10.1787/459aa7f1-en.

Office for National Statistics. 2021a. "Coronavirus and Vaccine Hesitancy, Great Britain." July 2, 2021. https://www.ons.gov.uk/peoplepopulationandcommunity/ healthandsocialcare/healthandwellbeing/bulletins/coronavirusandvaccinehesitancyg reatbritain/26mayto20june2021.

———. 2021b. "Coronavirus (Covid-19) Latest Insights." https://www.ons.gov.uk/ peoplepopulationandcommunity/healthandsocialcare/conditionsanddiseases/articles /coronaviruscovid19/latestinsights#ethnicity.

Oledan, Jan, Julia Ilhardt, Giorgio Musto, and Jacob N. Shapiro. 2020. "Fact-Checking Networks Fight Coronavirus Infodemic." *Bulletin of the Atomic Scientists,* June 25, 2020. https://thebulletin.org/2020/06/fact-checking-networks-fight-coronavirus -infodemic/.

Olivarius, Kathryn. 2021. "Necropolis: Disease, Power, and Immunity in Antebellum New Orleans." *UCLAmericas (YouTube Channel).* Published March 9, 2021. https:// www.youtube.com/watch?v=r2lyisIDELM.

Oliver, J. Eric, and Thomas Wood. 2014. "Medical Conspiracy Theories and Health Behaviors in the US." *JAMA Internal Medicine* 174 (5, May: 817–18. https://doi.org/10 .1001/jamainternmed.2014.190.

———. 2018. *Enchanted America: How Intuition and Reason Divide Our Politics.* Chicago: University of Chicago Press.

Olmsted, Kathryn. 2008. *Real Enemies: Conspiracy Theories and American Democracy, World War I to 9/11.* Oxford: Oxford University Press.

———. 2018. "A Conspiracy So Dense." *Baffler* 42, November 2018. thebaffler.com/ salvos/a-conspiracy-so-dense-olmsted.

Orr, Caroline. 2020. "Right-Wing Conspiracy Theories Go Mainstream amid Mounting COVID-19 Death Toll." *Canada's National Observer*. April 1, 2020. https://www.nationalobserver.com/2020/04/01/analysis/right-wing-conspiracy-theories-go-mainstream-amid-mounting-covid-19-death-toll.

Osmundsen, Mathias, Alexander Bor, Peter Bjerregaard Vahlstrup, Anja Bechmann, and Michael Bang Petersen. 2020. "Partisan Polarization Is the Primary Psychological Motivation behind Political Fake News Sharing on Twitter." *PsyArXiv*. https://doi.org/10.31234/osf.io/v45bk.

Pagán, Victoria E. 2008. "Toward a Model of Conspiracy Theory for Ancient Rome." *New German Critique* 103: 27–49.

———. 2013. *Conspiracy Narratives in Roman History*. Austin: University of Texas Press.

Pasquetto, Irene, Briony Swire-Thompson, and Michelle A. Amazeen. 2020. "Tackling Misinformation: What Researchers Could Do with Social Media Data." *Harvard Kennedy School Misinformation Review* 1 (8, December). https://doi.org/10.37016/mr-2020-49.

Partington, Richard. 2019. "Britain Risks Heading to US Levels of Inequality, Warns Top Economist." *Guardian*, May 14, 2019. https://www.theguardian.com/inequality/2019/may/14/britain-risks-heading-to-us-levels-of-inequality-warns-top-economist.

Patreon. n.d. "Pricing." https://www.patreon.com/en-GB/pricing-page-en.

Pauls, Karen, and Kimberly Ivany. 2021. "Mystery Around 2 Fired Scientists Points to Larger Issues at Canada's High-Security Lab, Former Colleagues Say." *CBC News*, July 8, 2021. https://www.cbc.ca/news/canada/manitoba/nml-scientists-speak-out-1.6090188.

Pauls, Karen, and Jeff Yates. 2020. "Online Claims That Chinese Scientists Stole Coronavirus from Winnipeg Lab Have 'No Factual Basis'." *CBC News*, January 27, 2020. https://www.cbc.ca/news/canada/manitoba/china-coronavirus-online-chatter-conspiracy-1.5442376.

Paynter, Jessica, Sarah Luskin-Saxby, Deb Keen, Kathryn Fordyce, Grace Frost, Christine Imms, Scott Miller, David Trembath, Madonna Tucker, and Ullrich Ecker. 2019. "Evaluation of a Template for Countering Misinformation: Real-World Autism Treatment Myth Debunking." *PloS One* 14 (1, January): e0210746. https://doi.org/10.1371/journal.pone.0210746.

Pennycook, Gordon, Ziv Epstein, Mohsen Mosleh, Antonio A. Arechar, Dean Eckles, and David G. Rand. 2021. "Shifting Attention to Accuracy Can Reduce Misinformation Online." *Nature* 592 (7855): 590–95. https://doi.org/10.1038/s41586-021-03344-2.

Pennycook, Gordon, Jonathon McPhetres, Yunhao Zhang, Jackson G. Lu, and David Gertler Rand. 2020. "Fighting COVID-19 Misinformation on Social Media: Experimental Evidence for a Scalable Accuracy Nudge Intervention." *Preprint*. *PsyArXiv*, March 17, 2020. https://doi.org/10.31234/osf.io/uhbk9.

Perrigo, Billy. 2020. "White Supremacist Groups Are Recruiting with Help From Coronavirus - and a Popular Messaging App." *Time*, April 8, 2020. https://time.com/5817665/coronavirus-conspiracy-theories-white-supremacist-groups/

Pesquetto, Irene V. et al. 2020. "Tackling Misinformation: What Researchers Could Do with Social Media Data." *Harvard Kennedy School Misinformation Review* 1 (8, December). https://misinforeview.hks.harvard.edu/article/tackling-misinformation-what-researchers-could-do-with-social-media-data/.

Petersen, Michael Bang, Mathias Osmundsen, and Kevin Arceneaux. 2018. "The 'Need for Chaos' and Motivations to Share Hostile Political Rumors." *PsyArXiv*, September 1, 2018. https://doi.org/10.31234/osf.io/6m4ts.

Pew Research. 2019. "Public Trust in Government: 1958–2019." *Pew Research Center*, April 11, 2019. https://www.pewresearch.org/politics/2019/04/11/public-trust-in -government-1958-2019/.

———. 2020. "A Look at the Americans Who Believe There Is Some Truth to the Conspiracy Theory that COVID-19 Was Planned." July 24, 2020. https://www .pewresearch.org/fact-tank/2020/07/24/a-look-at-the-americans-who-believe -there-is-some-truth-to-the-conspiracy-theory-that-covid-19-was-planned/.

Phillips, Whitney. 2018. "The Oxygen of Amplification." *Data and Society*, May 22, 2018. https://datasociety.net/library/oxygen-of-amplification/.

Phillips, Whitney, and Ryan M. Milner. 2021. *You Are Here: A Field Guide for Navigating Polarized Speech, Conspiracy Theories, and Our Polluted Media Landscape*. Cambridge, MA: MIT Press.

Pigden, Charles. 1995. "Popper Revisited, or What Is Wrong with Conspiracy Theories?" *Philosophy of the Social Sciences* 25 (1, March): 3–34. https://doi.org/10 .1177/004839319502500101.

PolitiFact. 2020. "In Context: What Donald Trump Said about Disinfectant, Sun and Coronavirus." *PolitiFact*, April 24, 2020. https://www.politifact.com/article/2020/ apr/24/context-what-donald-trump-said-about-disinfectant-/.

Pulido, Cristina M, Beatriz Villarejo-Carballido, Gisela Redondo-Sama, and Aitor Gómez. 2020. "COVID-19 Infodemic: More Retweets for Science-Based Information on Coronavirus Than for False Information." *International Sociology* 35 (4, April): 377– 92. https://doi.org/10.1177/0268580920914755.

Q. 2020. "Q Post 3896." *8kun/Qresearch*, March 24, 2020. https://qposts.online/post /3896.

QAnon Anonymous. 2020. "Episode 83: Coronavirus Conspiracy Theories." March 17, 2020, produced by Travis View, Julian Feeld, and Jake Rockatansky, podcast, 1:01:46. https://soundcloud.com/qanonanonymous/episode-83-coronavirus-conspiracy -theories?utm_source=clipboard&utm_medium=text&utm_campaign=social _sharing.

Qin, Amy, Vivian Wang, and Danny Hakim. 2020. "How Steve Bannon and a Chinese Billionaire Created a Right-Wing Coronavirus Media Sensation." *New York Times*, November 20, 2020. https://www.nytimes.com/2020/11/20/business/media/steve -bannon-china.html.

Qiu, Linda, Bill Marsh, and Jon Huang. 2020. "The President vs. the Experts: How Trump Played Down the Coronavirus." *New York Times*, March 18, 2020. https:// www.nytimes.com/interactive/2020/03/18/us/trump-coronavirus-statements -timeline.html.

Quinn, Eithne. 2002. "All Eyze on Me: The Paranoid Style of Tupak Shakur." In *Conspiracy Nation: The Politics of Paranoia in Post-war America*, edited by Peter Knight. New York: New York University Press.

Rahman, Grace. 2020. "Here's Where Those 5G and Coronavirus Conspiracy Theories Came From." *Full Fact*, April 9, 2020. https://fullfact.org/online/5g-and-coronavirus -conspiracy-theories-came/.

Rana, Manveen, and Sean O'Neil. 2020. "Russians Spread Fake News over Oxford Coronavirus Vaccine." *The Times*, October 16, 2020. https://www.thetimes.co.uk/ article/russians-spread-fake-news-over-oxford-coronavirus-vaccine-2nzpk8vrq.

Rauchfleisch, Adrian and Kaiser, Jonas and Kaiser, Jonas. 2021. "Deplatforming the Far-Right: An Analysis of YouTube and BitChute." *SSRN Electronic Journal (June)*. http:// dx.doi.org/10.2139/ssrn.3867818.

RedPillLiving. n.d. "We Believe." https://www.redpillliving.org/we-believe/.

Remnick, David. 2018. "Trump vs. The Times: Inside an Off-the-Record Meeting." *New Yorker*, July 30, 2018. https://www.newyorker.com/news/news-desk/trump-vs -the-times-inside-an-off-the-record-meeting.

Ren, Zhiying (Bella), Eugen Dimant, and Maurice E. Schweitzer. 2021. "Social Motives for Sharing Conspiracy Theories." *SSRN Electronic Journal* (September). https://doi .org/10.2139/ssrn.3919364.

Reuters. 2020a. "Financial Market Website Zero Hedge Knocked off Twitter over Coronavirus Story." Reuters, February 2, 2020. https://www.reuters.com/article/us -china-health-twitter-idUSKBN1ZW0PZ.

———. 2020b. "Twitter Restores Account of Financial Market Website Zero Hedge." Reuters, June 13, 2020. https://www.reuters.com/article/us-twitter-zerohedge -idUSKBN23K0H8.

———. 2022. "Meta Pauses New Users from Joining Analytics Tool Crowdtangle." Reuters, January 29, 2022. https://www.reuters.com/technology/meta-pauses-new -users-joining-analytics-tool-crowdtangle-2022-01-29/.

Rice, Jenny. 2020. *Awful Archives: Conspiracy Theory, Rhetoric, and Acts of Evidence.* Columbus: Ohio State University Press.

Richtel, Matt. 2020. "W.H.O. Fights a Pandemic Besides Coronavirus: An 'Infodemic.'" *New York Times*, February 6, 2020. https://www.nytimes.com/2020/02/06/health/ coronavirus-misinformation-social-media.html.

Ricoeur, Paul. 2008. *Freud and Philosophy: An Essay on Interpretation.* Translated by Denis Savage. New Haven: Yale University Press.

Right Wing Watch. 2020. "Mark Taylor: The Coronavirus Is 'a Cover' to Carry Out the Mass Arrests Long Promised by QAnon." https://vimeo.com/396698839.

Ritzer, George, and Nathan Jergenson. 2010. "Production, Consumption, Prosumption: The Nature of Capitalism in the Age of the Digital 'Prosumer'." *Journal of Consumer Culture* 10 (1): 13–36. https://doi.org/ 10.1177/1469540509354673.

Roberts, S.T. 2019. *Behind the Screen: Content Moderation in the Shadows of Social Media.* New Haven: Yale University Press.

Robertson, Katharine. 2020. "Vaccine Hysteria: The Role of Gender in the Anti-Vaccination Movement." *AMSA Journal of Global Health* 14 (1). http://ajgh.amsa.org .au/index.php/ajgh/article/view/83.

Robins-Early, Nick. 2020. "The Strange Origins of Trump's Hydroxychloroquine Obsession." *Huffington Post*, May 13, 2020. https://www.huffpost.com/entry/trump -hydroxychloroquine-coronavirus-fox-news_n_5ebaffdbc5b5fd63dac80.

Robinson, Gregory. 2020. "Eamonn Holmes Criticised for Giving Credence to Covid-19 5G Conspiracy Theory." *Guardian*, April 13, 2020. http://www.theguardian.com /technology/2020/apr/13/eamonn-holmes-says-5g-coronavirus-claims-may-not-be -false.

Rogers, Adam. 2020a. "Deplatforming: Following Extreme Internet Celebrities to Telegram and Alternative Social Media." *European Journal of Communication* 35 (3, May): 213–229. https://doi.org/10.1177/0267323120922066.

———. 2020b. "The Strange and Twisted Tale of Hydroxychloroquine." *Wired*, November 11, 2020. https://www.wired.com/story/hydroxychloroquine-covid-19 -strange-twisted-tale/.

Roisman, Joseph. 2006. *The Rhetoric of Conspiracy in Ancient Athens.* Berkeley: University of California Press.

Romano, Andrew. 2020. "Yahoo News/YouGov Poll Shows Coronavirus Conspiracy Theories Spreading on the Right May Hamper Vaccine Efforts." May 22, 2020. https:// news.yahoo.com/new-yahoo-news-you-gov-poll-shows-coronavirus-conspiracy

-theories-spreading-on-the-right-may-hamper-vaccine-efforts-152843610.html
?guccounter=2.

Romele, Alberto, Marta Severo, and Paolo Furia. 2020. "Digital Hermeneutics: From Interpreting with Machines to Interpretational Machines." *AI & Society* 35 (1, June): 73–86. https://doi.org/10.1007/s00146-018-0856-2.

Romer, Daniel, and Kathleen Hall Jamieson. 2020 "Conspiracy Theories as Barriers to Controlling the Spread of COVID-19 in the U.S." *Social Science & Medicine* 236 (October): 113356. https://doi.org/10.1016/j.socscimed.2020.113356.

Ronson, Jon. 2021. Things Fell Apart (radio show). *BBC Radio 4.* https://www.bb.co.uk /programmes/m0011cpr.

Roose, Kevin. 2019. "The Making of a YouTube Radical." *New York Times,* June 8, 2019. https://www.nytimes.com/interactive/2019/06/08/technology/youtube-radical .html.

———. 2020. "What if Facebook Is the Real 'Silent Majority'?" *New York Times,* August 22, 2020. https://www.nytimes.com/2020/08/27/technology/what-if-facebook-is -the-real-silent-majority.html.

Rosen, Guy. 2021. "How We're Tackling Misinformation across Our Apps." *Meta* (blog). March 22, 2021. https://about.fb.com/news/2021/03/how-were-tackling -misinformation-across-our-apps/.

Rosenfeld, Sophia. 2018. *Democracy and Truth: A Short History.* Philadelphia: University of Pennsylvania Press.

Ross, Alexander Reid, Malav Modi, Pamela Paresky, Lee Jussim, Alex Goldenberg, Paul Goldenberg, Danit Finkelstein, John Farmer, Kelli Holden, Denver Riggleman, Jacob Shapiro, and Joel Finkelstein. 2021. "A Contagion of Institutional Distrust: Viral Disinformation of the COVID Vaccine and the Road to Reconciliation." *Network Contagion Research Institute,* March 11, 2021. https://networkcontagion.us/reports/a -contagion-of-institutional-distrust/.

Rothkopf, David J. 2003. "When the Buzz Bites Back." *Washington Post,* May 11, 2003. https://www.washingtonpost.com/archive/opinions/2003/05/11/when-the-buzz -bites-back/bc8cd84f-cab6-4648-bf58-0277261af6cd/.

Rothschild, Mike. 2021. *The Storm Is upon Us: How QAnon Became a Movement, Cult, and Conspiracy Theory of Everything.* London: Monoray.

Royal Society. 2022. "The Online Information-Environment: Understanding How the Internet Shapes People's Engagement with Scientific Information." January 2022. https://royalsociety.org/-/media/policy/projects/online-information-environment/ the-online-information-environment.pdf.

Rupar, Aaron. 2020. "Trump Dismisses Hydroxychloroquine Study That Undermines Him as a 'Trump Enemy Statement.'" *Vox,* May 19, 2020. https://www.vox.com /2020/5/19/21263989/trump-hydroxychloroquine-study-enemy-statement-fda.

Rushkoff, Douglas. 2010. *Media Virus!: Hidden Agendas in Popular Culture.* New York: Random House.

Ryan, Jackson. 2021. "Inside Wikipedia's Endless War over the Coronavirus Lab Leak Theory." CNET, June 27, 2021. https://www.cnet.com/features/wikipedia-is-at -war-over-the-coronavirus-lab-leak-theory/.

Sallam, Malik. 2021. "COVID-19 Vaccine Hesitancy Worldwide: A Concise Systematic Review of Vaccine Acceptance Rates." *Vaccines* 9 (2, February): 160. https://doi.org /10.3390/vaccines9020160.

Samorodnitsky, Dan. 2020. "Don't Believe the Conspiracy Theories You Hear about Coronavirus and HIV." *Massive Science,* January 31, 2020. https://massivesci.com/ notes/wuhan-coronavirus-ncov-sars-mers-hiv-human-immunodeficiency-virus/.

Sandel, Michael. 2020. *The Tyranny of Merit*. London: Penguin.

Sardarizadeh, Shayan. 2021. "Speaking at Today's Anti-Vaccine, Anti-Lockdown Rally in London's Trafalgar Square, Former Nurse Kate Shemirani - Who Was Struck Off in June - Says Covid Vaccines Are 'Satanic'…." *Twitter Post (@Shayan86)*, July 24, 2021. https://twitter.com/shayan86/status/1418915810416934915?s=11.

Schaeffer, Katherine. 2020. *"A Look at the Americans Who Believe There Is Some Truth to the Conspiracy Theory That COVID-19 Was Planned."* *Pew Research Center* (blog). July 24, 2020. https://www.pewresearch.org/fact-tank/2020/07/24/a-look-at-the-americans-who-believe-there-is-some-truth-to-the-conspiracy-theory-that-covid-19-was-planned/.

Schwalbe, Nina, Susanna Lehtimaki, and Juan Pablo Gutierrez. 2020. "Non Communicable Diseases and Covid-19: A Perfect Storm." *The BMJ* (blog), June 10, 2020. https://blogs.bmj.com/bmj/2020/06/10/non-communicable-diseases-and-covid-19-a-perfect-storm.

Scott, Mark. 2020. "Conspiracy Theories Run Wild on Amazon." *Politico*, December 22, 2020. https://www.politico.eu/article/amazon-qanon-covid19-coronavirus-disinformation-conspiracy-theories/.

———. 2021. "Big Tech's Trying to Stop Coronavirus Misinformation. It's Not Enough." *Politico*, March 11, 2021. https://www.politico.eu/article/covid19-coronavirus-misinformation-fake-news-vaccine/.

Scott, Mark, and Sarah Wheaton. 2021. "Social Media's Coronavirus Challenge: Responsibility." *Politico*, July 21, 2021. https://www.politico.eu/article/coronavirus-pandemic-misinformation-facebook-google-twitter/?utm_medium=Social&utm_source=Twitter#Echobox=1639587427-1.

Sedgwick, Eve Kosofsky. 2003. *Touching Feeling: Affect, Pedagogy, Performativity*. Durham: Duke University Press.

Selvage, Douglas. 2019. "Operation 'Denver': The East German Ministry of State Security and the KGB's AIDS Disinformation Campaign, 1985–1986 (Part 1)." *Journal of Cold War Studies* 21 (4, Fall): 71–123. https://doi.org/10.1162/jcws_a_00907.

Selvage, Douglas, and Christopher Nehring. 2019. "Operation 'Denver': KGB and Stasi Disinformation Regarding AIDS." Wilson Center, July 19, 2019. https://www.wilsoncenter.org/blog-post/operation-denver-kgb-and-stasi-disinformation-regarding-aids.

Sessa, Maria Giovanna. 2021. "COVID-19 Vaccine Misinformation and Facebook: The Challenge of Moderating Anti-Vaxx and Vaccine Hesitant Stances." *EU DisinfoLab* (blog), April 1, 2021. https://www.disinfo.eu/publications/covid-19-vaccine-misinformation-and-facebook:-the-challenge-of-moderating-anti-vaxx-and-vaccine-hesitant-stances/.

Seymour, Richard. 2019. *The Twittering Machine*. London: Indigo.

Shahsavari, Shadi, Pavan Holur, Timothy Tangherlini, and Vwani Roychowdhury. 2020. "Conspiracy in the Time of Corona: Automatic Detection of Emerging COVID-19 Conspiracy Theories in Social Media and the News." *Journal of Computational Social Science* 3 (2, April): 1–39. https://doi.org/10.1007/s42001-020-00086-5.

Shane, Tommy, and Pedro Noel. 2020. "Data Deficits: Why We Need to Monitor the Demand and Supply of Information in Real Time." First Draft. September 28, 2020. https://firstdraftnews.org:443/long-form-article/data-deficits/.

Sharma, Ruhira. 2021. "Social Media Claims of Covid 'Miracle Drug' Ivermectin - and Why You Shouldn't Trust the Crowd." *i News*, February 24, 2021. https://inews.co.uk/news/health/invermectin-tablets-what-covid-miracle-drug-social-media-explained-882700.

Sheera, Frenkel, Ben Decker, and Davey Alba. 2020. "How the 'Plandemic' Movie and Its Falsehoods Spread Widely Online." *New York Times*, May 21, 2020. https://www.nytimes.com/2020/05/20/technology/plandemic-movie-youtube-facebook-coronavirus.html.

Sheppard-Dawson, Cornelia. 2021. "You'll NEVER GUESS How Conspiracy Theory is Being Used on YouTube: Conspiracy Theory Signalling." *Infodemic.* July 12. http://infodemic.eu/2021/07/12/conspiracy-signalling.html

Silverman, Craig, and Jane Lytvynenko. 2021. "Amazon Is Pushing Readers Down a 'Rabbit Hole' of Conspiracy Theories about the Coronavirus." *BuzzFeed News*, March 15, 2021. https://www.buzzfeednews.com/article/craigsilverman/amazon-covid-conspiracy-books.

Silverman, Craig, and Ryan Mac. 2020. "Facebook Gets Paid." *BuzzFeed News*, December 10, 2020. www.buzzfeednews.com/article/craigsilverman/facebook-ad-scams-revenue-china-tiktok-vietnam.

Simmons, W.P., and S. Parsons. 2005. "Beliefs in Conspiracy Theories among African Americans: A Comparison of Elites and Masses." *Social Science Quarterly* 86 (3): 582–598. https://doi.org/10.1111/j.0038-4941.2005.00319.x.

Simon, Felix M., and Chico Q. Camargo. 2021. "Autopsy of a Metaphor: The Origins, Use and Blind Spots of the 'Infodemic.'" *New Media & Society* (July). https://doi.org/10.1177/14614448211031908.

Simonsen, Kjetil Braut. 2020. "Antisemitism and Conspiracism." In *Routledge Handbook of Conspiracy Theories*, edited by Michael Butter and Peter Knight, 357–70. London: Routledge.

Singh, Maanvi, Helen Davidson, and Julian Borger. 2020. "Trump Claims to Have Evidence Coronavirus Started in Chinese Lab but Offers No Details." *Guardian*, May 1, 2020. https://www.theguardian.com/us-news/2020/apr/30/donald-trump-coronavirus-chinese-lab-claim.

Siwakoti, Samikshya, Kamya Yadav, Nicola Bariletto, Luca Zanotti, Ulas Erdogdu, and Jacob N. Shapiro. 2021. "How COVID Drove the Evolution of Fact-Checking." *Harvard Kennedy School Misinformation Review* 2 (3, May). https://doi.org/10.37016/mr-2020-69.

Skidelsky, Robert. 2018. "Ten Years On from the Financial Crash, We Need to Get Ready for Another One." *Guardian*, September 12, 2018. https://www.theguardian.com/commentisfree/2018/sep/12/crash-2008-financial-crisis-austerity-inequality.

Slobodian, Quinn. 2019. "The False Promise of Enlightenment." *Boston Review*, May 29, 2019. bostonreview.net/class-inequality/quinn-slobodian-false-promise-enlightenment.

Smallpage, Steven M, Hugo Drochon, Joseph E. Uscinski, and Casey Klofstad. 2020. "Who Are the Conspiracy Theorists?" *Routledge Handbook of Conspiracy Theories*, edited by Michael Butter and Peter Knight, 263–277. London: Routledge.

Smallpage, Steven M., Adam M. Enders, Hugo Drochon, and Joseph E. Uscinski. 2021. "The Impact of Social Desirability Bias on Conspiracy Belief Measurement across Cultures." *Political Science Research and Methods*, October 20, 2021. https://nottingham-repository.worktribe.com/output/7163463/the-impact-of-social-desirability-bias-on-conspiracy-belief-measurement-across-cultures.

Smith, Matthew. 2017. "Leave Voters Are Less Likely to Trust Any Experts: Even Weather Forecasters." *YouGov*, February 17, 2017. https://yougov.co.uk/topics/politics/articles-reports/2017/02/17/leave-voters-are-less-likely-trust-any-experts-eve.

———. 2018. "Which Conspiracy Theories Do Populists Believe?" *YouGov*. May 3, 2018.   https://yougov.co.uk/topics/politics/articles-reports/2019/05/03/which -conspiracy-theories-do-populists-believe.

Smith, Melanie, Erin McAweeny, and Lea Ronzaud. 2020. "The COVID-19 'Infodemic.'" *Graphika*. https://public-assets.graphika.com/reports/Graphika_Report_Covid19 _Infodemic.pdf.

Smith, Naomi, and Tim Graham. 2017. "Mapping the Anti-Vaccination Movement on Facebook." *Information, Communication & Society* 22 (9, December): 1310–1327. https://doi.org/10.1080/1369118X.2017.1418406.

Smith, Rory, Seb Cubbon, and Claire Wardle. 2020. "Under the Surface: Covid-19 Vaccine Narratives, Misinformation and Data Deficits on Social Media." First Draft, November 12, 2020. https://firstdraftnews.org:443/long-form-article/under-the- surface-covid-19-vaccine-narratives-misinformation-and-data-deficits-on-social- media/.

Sriskandarajah, Ike. 2021. "Where Did the Microchip Vaccine Conspiracy Theory Come from Anyway?" *Reveal News*, June 5, 2021. http://revealnews.org/article/where-did -the-microchip-vaccine-conspiracy-theory-come-from-anyway/.

Srnicek, Nick. 2017. *Platform Capitalism*. Cambridge: Polity.

Stang, Ivan. 1988. *High Weirdness by Mail: A Directory of the Fringe, Mad Prophets, Crackpots, Kooks and True Visionaries*. New York: Simon and Schuster.

Starbird, Kate. 2021. "Is Deplatforming Enough to Fight Disinformation and Extremism?" *NPR*, January 25, 2021. https://www.npr.org/2021/01/25/960466075 /is-deplatforming-enough-to-fight-disinformation-and-extremism.

Statt, Nick. 2021. "Facebook Usage Has Soared during the Pandemic, but the Company Warns of 'Significant Uncertainty' Ahead." *Verge*, January 27, 2021. https://www .theverge.com/2021/1/27/22253055/facebook-q4-2020-earnings-report-app-usage -record-user-numbers.

Stewart, Kathleen. 1999. "Conspiracy Theory's Worlds." In *Paranoia within Reason: A Casebook on Conspiracy as Explanation*, edited by G.E. Marcus, 13–20. Chicago: University of Chicago Press.

Stolberg, Sheryl Gay, and Noah Weiland. 2020. "A Study Found the 'Single Largest Driver' of Coronavirus Misinformation. It Was the President." *New York Times*, October 1, 2020. https://www.nytimes.com/2020/10/01/us/elections/a-study-found-the -single-largest-driver-of-coronavirus-misinformation-it-was-the-president.html.

Strong, Colin. 2020. "Tackling Conspiracy Theories." *Ipsos Mori*. https://www.ipsos .com/ipsos-mori/en-uk/tackling-conspiracy-theories.

Sujon, Zoetanya. 2021. *The Social Media Age*. London: Sage.

Surgo Ventures. 2021. "A Large-Scale Facebook Survey Of U.S. Adults: Leveraging Precision Health to Increase COVID-19 Vaccine Uptake." May 2021. https://static1 .squarespace.com/static/5f7671d12c27e40b67ce4400/t/60a3d7b3301db14adb211911 /1621350327260/FINAL+for+posting_Facebook+Survey+Summary+Document +for+Website.docx.pdf.

Sutton, Robbie M., and Karen M. Douglas. 2020. "Agreeing to Disagree: Reports of the Popularity of Covid-19 Conspiracy Theories Are Greatly Exaggerated." *Psychological Medicine* First View (July): 1–3. https://doi.org/10.1017/S0033291720002780.

Sweet, Jacob. 2021. "Can Disinformation be Stopped?" *Harvard Magazine*, July-August, 2021. https://www.harvardmagazine.com/2021/07/features-disinformation.

Taibbi, Matt. 2020. "Big Pharma's Covid-19 Profiteers." *Rolling Stone*, August 13, 2020. https://www.rollingstone.com/politics/politics-features/big-pharma-covid-19 -profits-1041185/.

Tangherlini, Timothy R., Shadi Shahsavari, Behnam Shahbazi, Ehsan Ebrahimzadeh, and Vwani Roychowdhury. 2020. "An Automated Pipeline for the Discovery of Conspiracy and Conspiracy Theory Narrative Frameworks: Bridgegate, Pizzagate and Storytelling on the Web." *PloS One* 15 (6, June): e0233879. https://doi.org/10.1371/journal.pone.0233879.

Taylor, Astrid. 2021. "In Defense of Liberal Conspiracies." *New Republic*, May 6, 2021. https://newrepublic.com/article/162318/astra-taylor-defense-liberal-conspirators.

Temperton, James. 2020. "How the 5G Coronavirus Conspiracy Theory Tore through the Internet." *Wired UK*, April 6, 2020. https://www.wired.co.uk/article/5g-coronavirus-conspiracy-theory.

Thalmann, Katharina. 2019. *The Stigmatization of Conspiracy Theory since the 1950s: "A Plot to Make Us Look Foolish."* London: Routledge.

"The Anti-Vax Files: How Anti-Vax Went Viral" (Audio broadcast). 2021. *BBC Trending*, March 20–22, 2021. https://www.bbc.co.uk/programmes/w3ct2dmb.

"The Economist/YouGov Poll." 2021. *YouGov*. https://docs.cdn.yougov.com/w2zmwpzsq0/econTabReport.pdf.

Thiem, Annika. 2020. "Conspiracy Theories and Gender and Sexuality." In *Routledge Handbook of Conspiracy Theories*, edited by Michael Butter and Peter Knight, 292–303. London: Routledge.

Thomas, Elise, and Albert Zhang. 2020. "ID2020, Bill Gates and the Mark of the Beast: How Covid-19 Catalyses Existing Online Conspiracy Movements." Australian Strategic Policy Institute. https://www.jstor.org/stable/resrep25082.

Tiffany, Kaitlyn. 2020a. "Something in the Air." *Atlantic*, May 14, 2020. https://www.theatlantic.com/technology/archive/2020/05/great-5g-conspiracy/611317/.

———. 2020b. "Reddit Squashed QAnon by Accident." *Atlantic*, September 23, 2020. https://www.theatlantic.com/technology/archive/2020/09/reddit-qanon-ban-evasion-policy-moderation-facebook/616442/.

———. 2020c. "The Women Making Conspiracy Theories Beautiful." *The Atlantic*, August 18, 2020. https://www.theatlantic.com/technology/archive/2020/08/how-instagram-aesthetics-repackage-qanon/615364/.

Timberg, Craig, and Isaac Stanley-Becker. 2020. "QAnon Learns to Survive—and Even Thrive—after Silicon Valley's Crackdown." *Washington Post*, October 28, 2020. www.washingtonpost.com/technology/2020/10/28/qanon-crackdown-election/.

Tinati, Ramine, Susan Halford, Leslie Carr, and Catherine Pope. 2014. "Big Data: Methodological Challenges and Approaches for Sociological Analysis." *Sociology* 48 (4, February). https://doi.org/10.1177/0038038513511561.

Tsioulcas, A. 2018. "Youtube, Apple and Facebook Ban Infowars, Which Decries 'Mega Purge'." *NPR*, August 6, 2018. https://www.npr.org/2018/08/06/636030043/youtube-apple-and-facebook-ban-infowars-which-decries-mega-purge.

Tufekci, Zeynap. 2014. "Big Questions for Social Media Big Data: Representativeness, Validity and Other Methodological Pitfalls." *ArXiv:1403.7400 [Physics]*, April. https://arxiv.org/abs/1403.7400.

———. 2017. "We're Building a Dystopia Just to Make People Click on Ads." *Ted, TedGlobal*, September 2017. https://www.ted.com/talks/zeynep_tufekci_we_re_building_a_dystopia_just_to_make_people_click_on_ads#t-163753.

Turner, Patricia A. 1993. *I Heard It through the Grapevine: Rumor in African-American Culture*. Berkeley: University of California Press.

Turvill, William. 2020. "Cash for Conspiracies: How David Icke, 'Alternative' Media and Tech Giants Make Money from Coronavirus Conspiracies." *Press Gazette*, June

3, 2020. www.pressgazette.co.uk/cash-for-conspiracies-how-david-icke-alternative -media-and-tech-giants-make-money-from-misinformation/.

Tuters, Marc, Emilija Jokubauskaitė, and Daniel Bach. 2018. "Post-Truth Protest: How 4chan Cooked Up the Pizzagate Bullshit." *M/C Journal* 21 (3). https://doi.org/10 .5204/mcj.1422

Tuters, Marc, and Tom Willaert. 2022. "Deep State Phobia: Narrative Convergence in Coronavirus Conspiracism on Instagram." *Convergence*, forthcoming.

UK Government. 2020. "Social Media Giants Agree Package of Measures with UK Government to Tackle Vaccine Disinformation." November 8, 2020. www.gov .uk/government/news/social-media-giants-agree-package-of-measures-with-uk -government-to-tackle-vaccine-disinformation.

University of Oxford. 2020. "Conspiracy Beliefs Reduce the Following of Government Coronavirus Guidelines." *News*, May 22, 2020. https://www.ox.ac.uk/news/2020 -05-22-conspiracy-beliefs-reduces-following-government-coronavirus-guidelines.

Urbinati, Nadia. 2019. "Political Theory of Populism." *Annual Review of Political Science* 22: 111–127. https://www.annualreviews.org/doi/pdf/10.1146/annurev-polisci -050317-070753.

Uscinski, Joseph E. 2020. *Conspiracy Theories: A Primer*. Lanham: Rowman & Littlefield.

Uscinski, Joseph E., and Joseph M. Parent. 2014. *American Conspiracy Theories*. New York: Oxford University Press.

Uscinski, Joseph E., Casey Klofstad, and Matthew D. Atkinson. 2016. "What Drives Conspiratorial Beliefs? The Role of Informational Cues and Predispositions." *Political Research Quarterly* 69 (1, January): 57–71. https://doi.org/10.1177/1065912915621621.

Uscinski, Joseph E., Darin Dewitt, and Matthew D. Atkinson. 2018. "A Web of Conspiracy? Internet and Conspiracy Theory." In *Handbook of Conspiracy Theory and Contemporary Religion*, edited by Asbjørn Dyrendal, David G. Robertson, and Egil Asprem, 106–130. Boston: Brill.

Uscinski, Joseph E., Adam M. Enders, Casey Klofstad, Michelle Seelig, John Funchion, Caleb Everett, Stephan Wuchty, Kamal Premaratne, and Manohar Murthi. 2020. "Why Do People Believe COVID-19 Conspiracy Theories?" *Harvard Kennedy School Misinformation Review* 1 (3), Special Issue: Covid 19 (April). https://doi.org/10.37016 /mr-2020-015.

Uscinski, Joseph E., Adam M. Enders, Casey A. Klofstad, Hugo Drochon, Michelle Seelig, Kamal Premaratne, and Manohar Murthi. 2022. "Have Beliefs in Conspiracy Theories Increased over Time?" https://interactive.miami.edu/connect/files/Con spiracyTheoriesOverTime.pdf.

Valensise, Carlo M., Matteo Cinelli, Matthieu Nadini, Alessandro Galeazzi, Antonio Peruzzi, Gabriele Etta, Fabiana Zollo, Andrea Baronchelli, and Walter Quattrociocchi. 2021. "The COVID-19 Infodemic Does Not Affect Vaccine Acceptance." *ArXiv:2107.07946 [Physics]*, July 16, 2021. http://arxiv.org/abs/2107.07946.

Valenti, Jessica. 2019. "The Measles Moms: Why Women are Leading the Anti-Vaxx Movement." *City Watch*, February 25, 2019. https://www.citywatchla.com/index .php/cw/los-angeles/17168-the-measles-moms-why-women-are-leading-the-anti -vaxx-movement.

Vallejo, Justin. 2020. "Coronavirus 'Patient Zero' Conspiracy Target Breaks Silence." *Independent*, April 27, 2020. https://www.independent.co.uk/news/world/americas /coronavirus-patient-zero-china-conspiracy-theory-maatje-benassi-a9487041.html.

van der Linden, Sander, Edward Maibach, John Cook, Anthony Leiserowitz, and Stephan Lewandowsky. 2017. "Inoculating against Misinformation." *Science* 358 (6367, December): 1141–1142. https://doi.org/10.1126/science.aar4533.

van der Linden, Sander, Graham Dixon, Chris Clarke, and John Cook. 2021. "Inoculating against COVID-19 Vaccine Misinformation." *EClinicalMedicine* 33 (100772, February). https://doi.org/10.1016/j.eclinm.2021.100772.

van Prooijen, Jan-Willem. 2020. "COVID-19, Conspiracy Theories, and 5G Networks." *Psychology Today*, April 10, 2020. https://www.psychologytoday.com /us/blog/morality-and-suspicion/202004/covid-19-conspiracy-theories-and-5g -networks.

van Prooijen, Jan-Willem, and Karen M Douglas. 2017. "Conspiracy Theories as Part of History: The Role of Societal Crisis Situations." *Memory Studies* 10 (3, July): 323–33. https://doi.org/10.1177/1750698017701615.

van Prooijen, Jan-Willem, and Michelle Acker. 2015. "The Influence of Control on Belief in Conspiracy Theories: Conceptual and Applied Extensions." *Applied Cognitive Psychology* 29 (5): 753–761.

van Prooijen, Jan-Willem, Andre P.M. Krouwel, and Thomas V. Pollet. 2015. "Political Extremism Predicts Belief in Conspiracy Theories." *Social Psychological and Personality Science* 6 (5, January): 570–578. https://doi.org/10.1177/1948550614567356.

van Prooijen, Jan-Willem, Tom W. Etienne, Yordan Kutiyski, and André P. M. Krouwel. 2021. "Conspiracy Beliefs Prospectively Predict Health Behavior and Well-Being during a Pandemic." *Psychological Medicine*, October, 1–25. https://doi.org/10.1017/ S0033291721004438.

Varol, Onur, Kai-Cheng Yang, Emilio Ferrara, Alessandro Flammini, Filippo Menczer. 2020. "IV. Data Sharing Protocols for Content Deletion and Identity Change Activities to Counter Online Manipulation," *Harvard Kennedy School Misinformation Review* 1 (8) in "Tackling Misinformation: What Researchers Could Do with Social Media Data" (December). https://misinforeview.hks.harvard.edu/article/tackling -misinformation-what-researchers-could-do-with-social-media-data/.

Velásquez, N. et al. 2020. "Hate Multiverse Spreads Malicious COVID-19 Content Online beyond Individual Platform Control." Preprint, April 21, 2020. https://arxiv .org/abs/2004.00673.

Vermeule, Cornelius A., and Cass R. Sunstein. 2009. "Conspiracy Theories: Causes and Cures." *Journal of Political Philosophy* 17 (2, April): 202–27. https://doi.org/10.1111/j .1467-9760.2008.00325.x.

Vivion, Maryline, Elhadji Anassour Laouan Sidi, Cornelia Betsch, Maude Dionne, Eve Dubé, S. Michelle Driedger, Dominique Gagnon, et al. 2022. "Prebunking Messaging to Inoculate against COVID-19 Vaccine Misinformation: An Effective Strategy for Public Health." *Journal of Communication in Healthcare* (March): 1–11. https://doi.org /10.1080/17538068.2022.2044606.

Volpicelli, Gian M. 2018. "As Fake News Flourishes, the UK's Fact-Checkers Are Turning to Automation to Compete." *Wired*, December 11, 2018. https://www.wired .co.uk/article/fake-news-full-fact-fact-checking-news.

Vorhaben, Ellie. 2022. "Technology Amplified Disinformation, Now It Must Demonetize It." *The Chicago Policy Review*, January 18, 2022. https://chicagopolicyreview.org /2022/01/18/technology-amplified-disinformation-now-it-must-demonetize-it/.

Vosoughi, Soroush, Deb Roy, and Sinan Aral. 2018. "The Spread of True and False News Online." *Science* 359 (6380, March): 1146–1151. https://doi.org/10.1126/science .aap9559.

Votta, Fabio. 2021. "The Infodemic on Instagram." https://favstats.github.io/corona _conspiracyland/#.

Wade, Nicholas. 2021. "The Origin of COVID: Did People or Nature Open Pandora's Box at Wuhan?" *Bulletin of the Atomic Scientists* (blog), May 5, 2021. https://thebulletin

.org/2021/05/the-origin-of-covid-did-people-or-nature-open-pandoras-box-at
-wuhan/.

Wakabayashi, Daisuke, Davey Alba, and Marc Tracy. 2020. "Bill Gates, at Odds with Trump on Virus, Becomes a Right-Wing Target." *New York Times*, April 17, 2020. https://www.nytimes.com/2020/04/17/technology/bill-gates-virus-conspiracy -theories.html.

Wang, Elise. 2019. "Why Some Conspiracy Theories Just Won't Die." *TedX Talks (YouTube channel)*. Filmed February 23, 2019 at TedxDuke at Duke University, Durham. Published May 16, 2019. https://www.youtube.com/watch?v=QjVNc AAf7pA.

Ward, Charlotte, and David Voas. 2011. "The Emergence of Conspirituality." *Journal of Contemporary Religion* 26 (1, January): 103–21. https://doi.org/10.1080/13537903 .2011.539846.

Washington, Harriet A. 2007. *Medical Apartheid: The Dark History of Medical Experimentation on Black Americans from Colonial Times to the Present*. New York: Doubleday.

Washington Post. 2020. "Twitter Sees Record Number of Users during Pandemic, but Advertising Sales Slow." April 30, 2020. https://www.washingtonpost.com/business /economy/twitter-sees-record-number-of-users-during-pandemic-but-advertising -sales-slow/2020/04/30/747ef0fe-8ad8-11ea-9dfd-990f9dcc71fc_story.html.

Waterson, Jim. 2020a. "Broadband Engineers Threatened Due to 5G Coronavirus Conspiracies." *Guardian*, April 3, 2020. http://www.theguardian.com/technology /2020/apr/03/broadband-engineers-threatened-due-to-5g-coronavirus -conspiracies.

———. 2020b. "How an Anti-Lockdown 'Truthpaper' Bypasses Online Factcheckers." *Guardian*, November 27, 2020. https://www.theguardian.com/world/2020/nov/27/ truthpaper-the-anti-lockdown-newspaper-bypassing-online-fact-checkers.

Weintraub, Karen. 2019. "Invisible Ink Could Reveal Whether Kids Have Been Vaccinated." *Scientific American*, December 18, 2019. https://www.scientificamerican .com/article/invisible-ink-could-reveal-whether-kids-have-been-vaccinated/.

Weissmann, Jordan. 2016. "The Failure of Welfare Reform." *Slate*, June 1, 2016. https:// slate.com/news-and-politics/2016/06/how-welfare-reform-failed.html.

Wendling, Mike, and Marianna Spring. 2020. "What Links Coronavirus Myths and QAnon?" *BBC News*, September 3, 2020. https://www.bbc.com/news/blogs -trending-53997203.

Whorton, James C. 2002. *Nature Cures: The History of Alternative Medicine in America*. Oxford: Oxford University Press.

Williams, Raymond. 1958. "Culture Is Ordinary." *Resources of Hope: Culture, Democracy, Socialism*. Edited by Robin Gable. London: Verso.

———. 1975. *Television: Technology and Cultural Form*. New York: Schocken Books.

Williamson, Elisabeth, and Emily Steel. 2018. "Conspiracy Theories Made Alex Jones Very Rich. They May Bring Him Down." *New York Times*, September 7, 2018. https://www.nytimes.com/2018/09/07/us/politics/alex-jones-business-infowars -conspiracy.html.

"Willingness to Get Vaccinated against COVID-19." 2022. *Our World in Data*, 2022. https://ourworldindata.org/grapher/covid-vaccine-willingness-and-people -vaccinated-by-month.

Wood, Matt. 2019. "The Political Dilemma of Expertise - More Than Just Public Trust in Experts." *LSE Blog*, June 17, 2019. https://blogs.lse.ac.uk/impactofsocialsciences /2019/06/17/the-political-dilemma-of-expertise-more-than-just-public-trust-in -experts/.

Wong, Edward. 2016. "Trump Has Called Climate Change a Chinese Hoax. Beijing Says It Is Anything But." *New York Times*, November 18, 2016. https://www.nytimes .com/2016/11/19/world/asia/china-trump-climate-change.html.

World Health Organization. 2020. "Novel Coronavirus (2019-NCoV). Situation Report—13." 13. https://www.who.int/docs/default-source/coronaviruse/situation -reports/20200202-sitrep-13-ncov-v3.pdf?sfvrsn=195f4010_6.

Wynne, Kelly. 2020. "YouTube Video Suggests 5G Internet Causes Coronavirus and People Are Falling for It." *Newsweek*, March 19, 2020. https://www.newsweek.com /youtube-video-suggests-5g-internet-causes-coronavirus-people-are-falling-it -1493321.

Yang, Kai-Cheng, Christopher Torres-Lugo, and Filippo Menczer. 2020. "Prevalence of Low-Credibility Information on Twitter during the COVID-19 Outbreak." ArXiv:2004.14484 [Cs], June. https://doi.org/10.36190/2020.16.

Yen, Hope. 2021. "AP Fact Check: Biden Distorts Trump's Words on Virus 'Hoax.'" *Associated Press News*, April 20, 2021. https://apnews.com/article/election-2020-virus -outbreak-ap-fact-check-politics-joe-biden-1eea443cca46df5f18e61b7c34549da2.

YouTube. 2019a. "Continuing Our Work to Improve Recommendations on YouTube." *YouTube Blog*, January 25, 2019. https://blog.youtube/news-and-events/ continuing-our-work-to-improve/.

———. 2019b. "The Four Rs of Responsibility, Part 2: Raising Authoritative Content and Reducing Borderline Content and Harmful Misinformation." *YouTube Blog*, December 3, 2019. https://blog.youtube/inside-youtube/the-four-rs-of-responsibility-raise-and-reduce/.

Zadrozny, Brandy, and Ben Collins. 2020. "Coronavirus Deniers Take Aim at Hospitals as Pandemic Grows." *NBC News*, March 30, 2020. https://www.nbcnews.com/tech /social-media/coronavirus-deniers-take-aim-hospitals-pandemic-grows-n1172336.

Zarocostas, John. 2020. "How to Fight an Infodemic." *Lancet* 395 (10225): 676. https:// doi.org/10.1016/S0140-6736(20)30461-X.

Zaveri, Mihir. 2020. "Engineer Crashes Train Near Hospital Ship in Los Angeles." *New York Times*, April 2, 2020. https://www.nytimes.com/2020/04/02/us/train-crash -los-angeles-coronavirus.html.

Zeng, Jing, and Mike S. Schäfer. 2021. "Conceptualizing 'Dark Platforms': Covid-19-Related Conspiracy Theories on 8kun and Gab." *Digital Journalism* 9 (9, June): 1321– 1343. https://doi.org/10.1080/21670811.2021.1938165.

Zimmer, Carl, and Benjamin Mueller. 2022. "New Research Points to Wuhan Market as Pandemic Origin." *New York Times*, February 26, 2022, sec. Science. https://www .nytimes.com/interactive/2022/02/26/science/covid-virus-wuhan-origins.html.

Žižek, Slavoj. 2019. *The Sublime Object of Ideology*. London: Verso.

———. 2020. *Pandemic!: COVID-19 Shakes the World*. Cambridge: Polity.

Zuboff, Shoshana. 2019. *The Age of Surveillance Capitalism: The Fight for a Human Future at the New Frontier of Power*. London: Profile.

Zwierlein, Cornel. 2013. "Security Politics and Conspiracy Theories in the Emerging European State System (15th/16th c.)." *Historical Social Research/Historische Sozialforschung* 38 (1): 65–95.

INDEX

For Product Safety Concerns and Information please contact our
EU representative GPSR@taylorandfrancis.com Taylor & Francis
Verlag GmbH, Kaufingerstraße 24, 80331 München, Germany